D1497858

BEHAVIOR MODIFICATION
IN
EDUCATION

ii

BEHAVIOR MODIFICATION IN EDUCATION

The Seventy-second Yearbook of the National Society for the Study of Education

PART I

By

THE YEARBOOK COMMITTEE
and
ASSOCIATED CONTRIBUTORS

Edited by

CARL E. THORESEN

Editor for the Society

HERMAN G. RICHEY

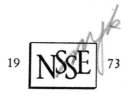

19 NSSE 73

Distributed by THE UNIVERSITY OF CHICAGO PRESS • CHICAGO, ILLINOIS

The responsibilities of the Board of Directors of the National Society for the Study of Education in the case of yearbooks prepared by the Society's committees are (1) to select the subjects to be investigated, (2) to appoint committees calculated in their personnel to insure consideration of all significant points of view, (3) to provide appropriate subsidies for necessary expenses, (4) to publish and distribute the committees' reports, and (5) to arrange for their discussion at the annual meeting.

The responsibility of the Society's editor is to prepare the submitted manuscripts for publication in accordance with the principles and regulations approved by the Board of Directors.

Neither the Board of Directors, nor the Society's editor, nor the Society is responsible for the conclusions reached or the opinions expressed by the Society's yearbook committees.

Library of Congress Catalog Card Number: 6-16938

Published 1972 by

THE NATIONAL SOCIETY FOR THE STUDY OF EDUCATION

5835 Kimbark Avenue, Chicago, Illinois 60637

Copyright, 1973, by KENNETH J. REHAGE, Secretary

The National Society for the Study of Education

First Printing, 10,000 copies

Printed in the United States of America

iv

The Society's Committee on
Behavior Modification in Education

ALBERT BANDURA

Professor of Psychology
Stanford University
Stanford, California

N. L. GAGE

Professor of Education and Psychology
Stanford University
Palo Alto, California

FREDERICK H. KANFER

Professor of Psychology
University of Cincinnati
Cincinnati, Ohio

FREDERICK J. MC DONALD

Director, Division of Educational Studies
Educational Testing Service
Princeton, New Jersey

B. F. SKINNER

Professor of Psychology
Harvard University
Cambridge, Massachusetts

CARL E. THORESEN

(Chairman)
Associate Professor of Education
Stanford University
Stanford, California

Associated Contributors

WESLEY C. BECKER

Professor of Special Education
University of Oregon
Eugene, Oregon

v

SIDNEY W. BIJOU

Professor of Psychology
University of Illinois
Urbana, Illinois

HAROLD L. COHEN

Executive Director of the Institute for Behavioral Research; and
President, Experimental College of the Institute for Behavioral Research
Silver Spring, Maryland

RAY E. HOSFORD

Associate Dean, Graduate School of Education
University of California at Santa Barbara
Santa Barbara, California

ROBERT L. KOEGEL

Assistant Research Psychologist
University of California at Santa Barbara
Santa Barbara, California

LEONARD KRASNER

Professor of Psychology
State University of New York
Stony Brook, New York

MIRIAM KRASNER

Elementary School Teacher
Three Village School District
Stony Brook, New York

O. IVAR LOVAAS

Professor
University of California at Los Angeles
Los Angeles, California

GERALD R. PATTERSON

Research Associate
Oregon Research Institute and University of Oregon
Eugene, Oregon

MICHAEL SCRIVEN

Professor of Philosophy
University of California
Berkeley, California

ARTHUR W. STAATS

*Professor of Psychology, and Professor of
Educational Psychology
University of Hawaii
Honolulu, Hawaii*

STEVEN M. ZIFFERBLATT

*Assistant Professor of Education
Stanford University
Stanford, California*

Editor's Preface

The Board of Directors in late 1969, after a survey of the publications of the Society, noted that although yearbooks had been published in the areas of learning, teaching, counseling, mental health, and classroom management, these publications, with a few exceptions, predated the upheaval in education generally referred to as the behavior modification movement. It was also noted that behavior modification, dealing specifically with methods of behavior change based on paradigms of operant conditioning, social modeling, and counterconditioning, was profoundly influencing many areas of education.

To help arrive at a conclusion concerning the feasibility of and need for a yearbook on the subject, the Board consulted with Professor Carl E. Thoresen. His report to the Board stated that the rapid growth of behavior modification had led to uneven development of theory, research, and practice, and that there was an urgent need to take stock of what had been taking place in this new force in the behavioral sciences.

Upon the invitation of the Board, Professor Thoresen presented a proposal for this yearbook in early 1970. He proposed that a yearbook should be prepared that would (a) provide a perspective on the historical and contemporary development of behavior modification, (b) analyze and synthesize the work on the subject as it relates to educational theory, (c) stimulate inquiry by professional educators as to the applicability of behavior modification in educational practice, (d) identify and deal with the issues of behavior modification as it relates to education, and (e) broaden professional perspectives of educational decision-makers concerning behavior modification.

The Board approved the proposal, appointed Professor Thoresen to the chairmanship of the yearbook committee, and approved his nominations for membership on that committee.

Professor Thoresen, a distinguished committee, and a group of recognized scholars in the field of behavior modification have ad-

mirably succeeded in producing a yearbook in which those engaged in teaching, counseling, and other fields of education will
find inspiration, perspective, and help, and from which many parents and other lay persons may achieve greater understanding of
and find solutions for some of the pressing problems with which
they are confronted.

HERMAN G. RICHEY
Editor for the Society

Table of Contents

SECTION I
Teaching in the Classroom

SECTION II
Specific Problem Areas

SECTION III
Behavioral Systems

SECTION IV

Problems and Prospects

TEACHING IN THE CLASSROOM

CHAPTER I

Behavior Modification—An Overview

FREDERICK H. KANFER

Although isolated instances of the application of learning principles have been reported much earlier, research and training in behavior modification is less than two decades old. Its development has been rapid and it is finding increased acceptance among professionals of various disciplines. Yet, continued extensions and refinements attest to the youth and incompleteness of behavior modification methods and their underlying theories. Behavior modification has attracted attention not because it offers a "comprehensive" theory about the complexities and nuances of the human mind. Neither has it set down in elegant prose an underlying philosophy about man's nature and destiny. Its appeal has been its apparent simplicity, emphasis on direct application, and encouragement of concrete action to change specific problem behaviors. Frequently, the choices of targets for behavior change have appeared superficial or trivial to dynamically oriented clinicians. This apparent neglect of the deep-seated origins of symptoms has resulted in strong criticism from many quarters. However, the selection of a specific behavior as a target response reflects the essentials of the behavioristic treatment strategy. It is assumed that even small changes in the patient's behavior or in the social environment bring about further changes in a desirable direction, culminating in a reorganization of the person's relationship with his environment and himself.

While the simplicity of the execution of behavior modification has been highlighted, an effective program encompasses much more than simple attachment of reward or punishment to a behavior.

This review was completed in conjunction with research supported in part by Research Grant No. MH 17902-03 from the National Institute of Mental Health, U.S. Public Health Service. The author wishes to express his appreciation to Dr. Paul Karoly for his critical reading of the manuscript.

What requires skill, patience, and a knowledge of underlying theoretical principles is the task of defining the problem situation and
deciding on an appropriate treatment strategy. Thus, knowing
when to do *what*, for *which* behavior, and with what *resources*, and
knowing how to *monitor* and *test* treatment effectiveness continuously is the challenging aspect of behavior modification. The most
difficult problem in designing a behavior modification program lies
in the fact that emphasis on behavior demands careful observation
rather than armchair speculation or interpretation. It requires training to formulate answerable questions, to pinpoint behavioral targets, and to decide on the particular behavior or environmental
feature whose change would eliminate the problem quickly and
economically, without creating a new one. The behavior modifier
in the schools, faced with a complaint about a child's misconduct,
lack of interest, underachievement, nervousness, or stubborness,
must examine the child's particular behaviors, the teacher's behavior and standards, the classroom setting, and often the home environment. He works with the teacher to help in specifying the
particular actions that cause difficulties, or the specific conditions
under which the problem behavior occurs. Finally, he makes a
record of his observations *prior* to behavioral intervention, *during*
the intervention, and *subsequent* to it in order to ascertain whether
the treatment program has been effective. Even casual observation
of everyday behavior suggests that these requirements contrast with
our habits of circumventing descriptions or giving pseudoexplanations by talking about a reticent child, an underachiever, a neurotic
child, or about a temper tantrum, an emotional outburst, a psychosis
(61, 62).

   In this chapter we will first note some historical trends. Then
we will present a brief overview of the main elements that must
be evaluated in preparation for formulation of a treatment program.
Then we will summarize the basic paradigms of behavior change
that form the foundation of the techniques described in subsequent
chapters. We will conclude with some comments on the problems
of extending methods from the laboratory to practice. The main
purpose of this chapter is to orient the reader to the approach, so
that he may retain an overall perspective as he reads in later chapters
the accounts of methods and research findings in specialized sub-
areas and with different populations.

Historical Overview

The earliest systematic application of conditioning principles to behavior problems is generally dated by the work of Pavlov and his co-workers in Russia at the turn of the twentieth century and of Watson in the United States at about the same time. Both groups began with classical conditioning as the basic model of learning and attempted to account for complex human interactions by elaboration of this paradigm. The Pavlovian approach is illustrated by the well-known experiment on training dogs to salivate (a conditional response) at the sound of a tuning fork (a conditioned stimulus) after the fork had repeatedly preceded the presentation of meat paste (the unconditioned stimulus). Pavlov's interest from the very first was in providing experimental procedures to test his comprehensive model of neurophysiology that would serve as a foundation for the understanding of neurotic disturbances. His model stated that formation of conditional reflexes is affected by the structural features of the organism as well as the environmental conditions. Cortical excitation, inhibition, and other changes in brain processes were seen as the central events underlying the observed behavioral disturbances under some conditions. For example, Pavlov found that he could establish "experimental neuroses" in his dogs by some form of conflict between or excessive activity of the two central processes of inhibition and excitation (22). Increasing the delay between presentation of a signal and food, use of intensive stimulation, inducing increasingly difficult tasks of conditional discrimination and continued alternation of positive and negative stimuli in a conditioning task were noted to result in maladaptive behavior in experimental animals. Since all the dogs did not respond similarly to the same conditions, Pavlov later theorized that the constitutional character of the nervous system determines the degree of response and tolerance for stress. As a result, he proposed different personality types to account for the individual differences among animals in reaction to conflicting stimuli. Consistent with his theoretical approach, several of his co-workers (9, 10, 27, 28) extended the basic classical conditioning paradigm to the realm of psychiatric disorders. In the United States, Watson, probably influenced by Pavlov (75), began with the simple conditioning paradigm and expanded it to encompass all human behavior. Watson viewed simple stimulus-response connections learned in early infancy as the basic building blocks for complex units of behavior acquired throughout life. He stressed the all-important role of environmental influences. In contrast to Pavlov's hope for providing a neurophysiological basis of behavior, Watson turned to a simplified mechanistic environmentalism that resulted in sharp criticism from his contemporaries.

Two classical experiments illustrate the establishment and removal of a conditioned fear response: the conditioning of a child (Albert) to fear a white rat by striking a steel bar behind the child's head (67) and the removal of the fear of rabbits in another child (Peter) by introducing a rabbit gradually closer into the room where the child was eating (29). These techniques are similar to reports by Krasnogorski (39) in an analysis of childrens' neuroses. Although the behavioristic approach to the treatment of psychological disorders failed to reach prominence in the United States in the following two decades, a number of investigations were carried out attempting to extend conditioning principles to a wide range of disorders.

In the United States the environmentalistic point of view was picked up by experimental psychologists and continued to exert strong influences in the study of the learning process. The learning theories of Guthrie, Hull, and Tolman, culminating in lively debates and extensive research by the late 1940s, provided fertile ground for the development of a learning psychology that eventually provided the base for behavior modification approaches. S-R theory was substantially furthered by the work of Hull and his students, who based their approach on an expanded version of classical conditioning theory, supplemented by a sophisticated conceptualization of the role of drives, conflicts, habit strength, and rewards in a formal hypothetico-deductive theory of learning. It is from the Hullian framework that Miller and Dollard (47), Dollard and Miller (16), Mowrer (49, 50), and many others developed a learning-based account of the development of neuroses and the psychotherapeutic process. In these approaches, conflict and anxiety were viewed as the central constructs, both in the development of neurotic symptoms as defenses against anxiety and in psychotherapeutic intervention as a reduction of anxiety and conflict.

In the early 1940s, Skinner's formulation emphasized the importance of operant conditioning methods in human behavior and provided the foundation for many of the behavior modification techniques used today. Skinner's work began with animals responding in a simple laboratory environment (60). It was gradually extended to more complex behaviors in animals and in humans. The major differentiation from other learning approaches was Skinner's early emphasis of the importance of response *consequences* rather than their antecedent stimuli. While Skinner accepted the classical conditioning paradigm for modification of autonomic behaviors and other reflexive biological stimulus response units (respondents), he proposed that, in the absence of knowledge of the controlling stimuli for most human behaviors, the operant paradigm be developed by primary emphasis on the nature of the relationship between a given response and its consequences.

Another line of the development of behavior modification can be traced to the influences of Eysenck in England who attempted to integrate a behavioristic view of abnormal behavior with a theory of personality based on experimental data of individual differences. Finally, as a result of his interest in abnormal behavior, Wolpe (73) proposed a therapeutic technique called *reciprocal inhibition* derived partially from Hull's learning theory and from some general neurophysiological considerations.

In the postwar years, the climate for acceptance of new approaches to the treatment of behavior deviations in the United States was favorable not only because of the increasing contributions of psychological research to the understanding of human behavior, but also because of the growing discontent with traditional psychotherapeutic models and the shortage of trained manpower to handle psychiatric disorders. The increasing evidence of the doubtful effectiveness of psychotherapy and of the questionable validity of projective techniques and dynamically oriented personality tests further heightened the receptivity of mental health workers to new approaches.

The first reported behavior modification projects were essentially experimental. Gradually, behavioral approaches were applied to populations for whom other approaches had been tried and found inadequate. Thus, early reports on behavior therapy with seriously disturbed psychotic patients (e.g., 36, 41, 42), with children (70), and with mental retardates (18, 19, 20, 48) reflected utilization of this approach in situations where environmental control could be most easily carried out. Increasingly, the approach spread to work with neurotic patients, to clients in counseling centers, and to other populations. At the same time, modern learning theory found increasing application in educational systems in revisions of traditional school curricula, in the introduction of a technology of teaching based on operant conditioning, and in the behavioral analysis of the process and content of academic programs and the entire school milieu (63).

Common Elements of Behavior Modification Methods

Behavior modification methods have been applied to a wider range of problems than have most methods of psychotherapy. This breadth rests mainly on the underlying assumption that most human actions, abnormal or normal, are learned behaviors. As such, they can be altered by application of learning principles, once the appropriate conditions for change are verified. Thus, the nature of the problem does not limit the applicability of the approach. It only influences the choice of the particular method of treatment. For example, study habits, disruptive classroom behaviors, assertive behaviors, or bizarre verbalization are all viewed as changeable behaviors. For each problem, however, the behavior modifier selects different procedures after ascertaining the conditions under which the behavior occurs, the effects which the behavior has on the patient's environment and on himself, and the resources at the clinician's disposal for altering the behavior (cf. 65, 66).

Since the initial application of conditioning techniques to clinical problems, numerous procedures have been added to the repertoire of the behavioral clinician. Some were derived from general psychology and others from clinical practices. Nevertheless, all the approaches share the assumption that behavior modification is essentially an *educational process*. Behavioral change may be brought about by reorganization of the person's environment, by deliberate training of new responses, by altering the person's repertoire of verbal controlling responses, or by changing motivational conditions. In all cases, the interventions aim to facilitate new learning.

Specific techniques are available for such different problems as the compliance with parental requests (e.g., 25), disruptive classroom behaviors (e.g., 64, 72), self-reactions (e.g., 15), aggressive or self-destructive activities (43, 52, 53), and reduction of anxiety (74).

Four basic learning models provide the foundations of behavior therapies: (a) the *classical* conditioning model, focusing on a substitution of stimuli that either elicit new behaviors to old stimuli or attach new stimuli to previously available responses; (b) the *operant* conditioning model, emphasizing the role of specific consequences (reinforcements) in altering the strength of a preceding response. Modification of behavior is accomplished either by direct change in the consequences of the behavior or by auxiliary techniques that bring behavior under the control of stimuli that have previously been experienced in conjunction with particular reinforcing consequences (discriminative stimuli); (c) the *observational* learning model, employing techniques in which learning is facilitated by rehearsals of new behaviors after observing their execution in other persons; (d) the *self-regulation* model, describing methods by which the individual can change his own behavior to conform to some standards that he had earlier set for himself, usually in situations in which strong conflicts exist. These different basic paradigms can be combined to suit the needs of a particular problem or used serially to attack a number of target behaviors that constitute the individual's problems. This common feature is noteworthy because it also reflects the rejection by behavior modifiers of some assumptions, commonly encountered in nonbehavioral models. For example, behavior theory implies that behavior change is not to be expected simply on the basis of increased insight or after emotional catharsis. It rejects the assumption that positive changes toward adaptive behavior will result from an innate growth tendency of the human organism to actualize dormant potentials or to guide a person toward "healthy behavior," once inhibitions or emotional conflicts are removed.

The learning-based models focus on *behavior*. Their content is the activity of a person in relation to his environment. They emphasize the importance of describing empirical events in a language that carefully separates behaviors from theoretical constructs and from inferences about the significance or meaning that these events may have for the behaving individual. Thus, the purpose of the clinical intervention is *always* the change of a set of behavioral events. Treatment is not aimed at removing defenses, unconscious conflicts, or altering personality traits since it is assumed that these concepts are not subject to direct attack. Their introduction into a therapeutic formulation adds no new knowledge about the person beyond the actual observations from which they are inferred. These constructs do not aid in evaluation of treatment, since the ultimate criterion must be a comparison of the pre- and post-treatment status of the particular behavior to which the constructs are tied. This feature has a sweeping impact on the behavioral clinician's exploration of the problem situation and on his formulation of treatment plans. Because of the emphasis on behavior, questions are constantly raised about available means for effecting particular responses. Since society tends to phrase behavioral problems in terms of inferred causes rather than in terms of the particular bothersome behavior, inquiry and observation is often required to discover what specific behaviors are involved in the typically vague complaint. For example, the teacher's avowal that the child is unmanageable, the student's presentation of his difficulty as a state of depression, or a mother's request for help with an aggressive or inhibited child requires careful specifications of the particular behaviors to which these complainants refer and of the conditions under which such behaviors occur.

Behavior modifiers place a premium on quantification of data. Prior to onset of a treatment procedure, base-line observations are made in order to establish the initial frequency or intensity of a target response. Quantification of these data provides the opportunity to establish a criterion for success in treatment and to offer evidence concerning treatment progress and approximation to the outcome criterion. In addition to its function as a check on treatment progress, record-keeping also aids the clinician in ascertaining whether his original problem definition was adequate and whether his treatment strategy is effective. In many cases the records are used to provide the client with feedback and to motivate him by using his record of improvement to reinforce his current behaviors and to serve as encouragement for further efforts. The most important function of the quantification of behavioral changes is as

a constant reminder to the clinician that his therapeutic enterprise
is behavior-oriented and pragmatic. Personal feelings or anecdotal
testimony concerning the patient's progress are not admissible evidence of the efficacy of treatment.

The learning model views all behaviors as operating under uniform psychological principles. Most dynamic theories distinguish
between laws of learning, applicable to the acquisition of knowledge, and laws of personality integration, relevant to the development of social, emotional and interpersonal patterns of behavior.
This distinction yields a concept of layers of personality, each subject to different laws of organization. For example, psychoanalytic
writers have often distinguished *ego psychology* as dealing with
conscious and cognitive aspects of behavior, while *depth psychology* deals with unconscious, emotional and motivational behaviors.
Such a distinction is not made by learning approaches.

Behavior modification demands no special theory-related skills
of observers, but it does require ability to make appropriate observations and measurements. Dynamically oriented clinicians accept
inferences about behavior as equivalent to observations of the behavior itself. Therefore, the observer must have thorough familiarity with the underlying theory. Although training is necessary to
enable any observer to recognize and reliably report the incidence
of a specified behavior, no greater theoretical knowledge is pre-
supposed for execution of a behavior modification program than
for many other activities that lie in the domain of social interactions.
Precise definition of the behavior to be observed or treated and the
requirement for dealing only with publicly observable responses
permits the use of observers and technicians, who have only limited
knowledge of psychological theory. In fact, the following chapters
illustrate the use of parents, teachers, nurses, child care workers,
and in some cases persons who themselves had previously been
clients, in the shaping of the behavior of other clients. A most convincing illustration of the utilization of nonprofessional personnel
is found in recent reports of *pyramid therapy* (69) in which mental
retardates served as assistants in the execution of behavior modification programs. However, the use of nonprofessionals does not extend to the level of decision-making and case management, involving
the formulation of the person's problems, the selection of an appro-

priate therapy strategy, and the constant monitoring of the progress of treatment. For these purposes, persons with training and familiarity in general psychological principles and in dealing with problem behaviors are required.

Another feature shared by most behavior modification techniques is the interest in *current* behavior rather than in the history of its development. Although the knowledge of the conditions under which a problem developed may be useful in some cases, it is assumed that only those past influences which are manifested in the current interpersonal interactions need to be considered. This does not suggest that behavioral clinicians fail to take into account important historical events, such as past learning experiences, or biological conditions which limit a person's potential for behavioral change. However, it does imply that such information is gathered only insofar as it affects the current behavior problem and not for the purpose of reconstructing the etiology of the problem. Supporting this approach has been the frequent demonstration that behavior modification techniques can successfully alter problematic behavior without thorough investigation of the history of the problem.

A frequent accusation against behavior modification techniques has been that they are mechanistic and disregard the importance of the relationship between the treatment agent and the client. It is understandable that such a stereotype has developed since the earlier techniques for behavior change focused mainly on manipulation of environmental consequences, mostly in institutional settings. As the utilization of behavioral techniques expanded to encompass attacks on complex problems in one-to-one therapeutic relationships, the therapist's behavior toward the client (his potentialities to encourage, guide, and reinforce his client's behaviors) became more prominent in determining treatment progress. In such programs as the token economy, for example, treatment techniques remain relatively impersonal with correspondingly lesser contact between therapist and client and lesser importance of the relationship (cf. 1). Even in those situations in which the contact between therapist and client is rather intimate and personal, analysis of "relationship factors" can be carried out within the framework of the behavioral approach (71), and some of these variables may themselves become instruments for bringing about therapeutic changes. The mechanistic stereotype caricatures behavior modification as if it were applied to the client as a passive organism. In fact, any good treatment program takes into account the importance of the client's response to the treatment agent, the treatment goal, and the techniques as essential ingredients of the change process. Behavior modification techniques are not *imposed* on clients who are capable of sharing in the decision process about the treatment program. With these clients behavior therapists generally discuss the relevant techniques and desirable goals and attempt to reach consent and joint decisions about methods and goals in advance.

The emphasis on learning provides a natural continuation between educational processes, counseling, and conditioning techniques. In educational activities the preparation of material, organization of the classroom for optimal learning conditions, attention to objective criteria to establish learning, and provision of reinforcers for the acquisition of new knowledge have their parallel in the therapeutic endeavor. Beyond that, many of the current innovations in educational techniques, including curriculum establishment, the use of teaching machines, and the emphasis on immediate reinforcement of appropriate responses, as well as the detailed establishment of specific criteria for what is to be learned, closely resemble many of the procedures in which the behavioral therapist engages (cf. 7).

The Analysis of a Problem Situation

Human behavior is characterized by continuity and change. The kaleidoscopic pattern of behavior, its constant blending of actions and environments, taxes any observer who attempts to abstract critical elements of the pattern for formulation of a problem. Be it in the classroom, in playground activity, or in interpersonal relationships, reinforcements, sources of stimulation, and the biological and emotional state of a child change from moment to moment in a delicate pattern. For convenience of analysis in abstraction, the full behavior must be partitioned into segments that can be studied without losing the key elements of the behavior or of the supporting environmental conditions. No behavioral analysis can describe all aspects of a given event; it can only focus on a description of features and interrelationships that are relevant to resolution of the presented problem. Thus, observation of a child's interaction in the classroom requires a prior statement of the purpose of observation in terms of some behavioral effects or results. For example, an observer might wish to record all activities of a child that constitute productive contributions to the classroom proceedings. The next step would be to define the limits of observation to those features of the environment and the child's behavior that relate to this end. Similarly, observation may be aimed at clarifying the conditions and actions that constitute a complaint about the child's restless or disruptive behaviors. Thus, the behavioral analysis is not an attempt to describe faithfully *everything* that goes on at a given time, but only that which is relevant to a stated problem.

The choice of a unit for behavioral analysis unfortunately implies a description that is adequate only for a given moment in time. Actually, the conceptualization often includes a series of repeated units of analysis which are then tied together at a higher level of abstraction into a more comprehensive description over longer time periods. An analysis of a situation into its essential components, traditionally defined as stimuli and responses, may give the impression of a *static* analysis. In fact, however, efforts are made to relate in time the antecedent conditions and behavioral consequences to the action at a level of generality that best suits the task at hand. The choice of a temporal unit usually involves some decision about the functional equivalence of various behavior patterns with regard to their outcome. For instance, a fine-grain analysis of a child's disruptive behavior in a classroom may reveal innumerable motor acts beginning with initial restlessness and shifting in his seat to raising his hand, jumping out of his seat, and walking over to the window. However, the specific motor components of such behavior may be relatively unimportant at a level of analysis that is concerned with the child's impact on the classroom and the teacher. In other situations—for example, in modifying speech behavior, in enuresis, or in acquisition of writing skill—microanalysis of the entire sequence may be called for. Once the particular target responses are established, the question arises concerning the variables that initiate or maintain these behaviors. For purpose of analysis the various components can be separated into those elements that affect the learning or maintenance of a behavior. These components constitute a behavioral formula which summarizes the conditions, *acting at the time of the response*, that may have relevance to the probability of response occurrence. The behavioral formula includes an analysis of five components and the relationships among them. These components are:

S — prior stimulation
O — biological state of the organism
R — response repertoire
K — contingency relationship
C — consequence

To indicate the relative temporal relationships and the centrality of the response, the formula may be written:

Antecedent   Effects
$$S \rightarrow O \rightarrow R \rightarrow K \rightarrow C$$

In most instances, the behavioral consequences (the last element) serve again as stimuli. They provide feedback to the person and activate the next set of behaviors. The formula suggests that all behavior is considered a function of specific determinants and that these determinants can be fully represented by the elements in the formula. The traditional classical conditioning paradigm emphasizes the relationship of events prior to the occurrence of the response, whereas the operant conditioning paradigm stresses the aftereffects of the response. In situations where observational learning is a central element of treatment, both antecedent and consequent conditions must be taken into account. Similarly, in situations in which the client is encouraged toward self-directed change, the person is helped to monitor antecedent and consequent conditions and to note their effects on his behavior.

A full behavioral analysis includes some statement about each of these components. In many cases, information may not be available or it may be irrelevant. A relatively simple case of the functional analysis of a child's temper tantrums (response) may reveal that the behavior occurs only in the presence of the mother (stimulus), when the child is fatigued (biological state), with the effect that mother withdraws a demand or hugs the child and consoles him (consequence), and she does this on each occurrence of a temper tantrum within ten minutes of its onset (contingency relationship).

ANTECEDENT EVENTS

This category includes a description of all the stimulus components and specifies the environmental conditions related to the target behavior. On what occasion does the behavior occur; what triggers it? Is it a stimulus for autonomic reflex responses or for a learned behavior? Care must be taken to define the stimulus components from the viewpoint of the behaving person rather than from that of the observer. The stimulus elements include not only external stimulation, but also the person's internal environment. An important feature of the stimulating condition is the role of the social environment that has established a history for appropriate behaviors in a variety of conditions. Thus, for a child with an adequate social learning history a school bell serves as a signal for going to a classroom; the mother's frown or the teacher's reprimand specifies that aversive consequences can be anticipated unless the child alters his behavior; an infinite variety of verbal stimuli indicate to the listener the conditions for reinforcement of specific responses by means of the verbal statement.

BIOLOGICAL STATE

The assessment of *biological* variables in the behavioral formula is especially useful to ascertain whether the expected response is within the biological limits of the individual. Such organismic states as a long delay since the last meal, a full bladder, or the soporific effect of a sedative may be powerful determinants of the target response. In most cases, the critical biological variables can be ascertained rather quickly by eliminating unusual, deviant, or temporarily acute conditions that would alter a person's response or his motivation.

RESPONSES

Learning theorists have differentiated responses into two classes. The responses that are elicited by a particular stimulus without

training have been characterized as *respondents*. Establishment of new connections between a stimulus and the original response follows the principle of classical conditioning or sign learning. The second class of responses, called *operants*, are conditioned by the consequences, that is, by reinforcement or punishment. Although there are some theoretical disagreements concerning this distinction (e.g., 8), the behavior modifier, from a pragmatic view, is aided by this distinction because respondents are affected by antecedent effects while operants are affected by their consequences. However, even operant responses are usually embedded in a sequence of events that include some discriminative stimuli preceding the response. Therefore, both stimulus and reinforcement control can be applied to discriminated operants. Presumably, respondents cannot be affected directly by their consequences. But recent work in changing autonomic responses suggests that control of respondent behavior by reinforcement is feasible.

Responses can be classified either on the basis of topographic similarity or on the basis of their similarity in leading to the same consequences. The latter classification is generally preferred in the analysis of complex behaviors. It permits a more comprehensive description of the behavioral units relevant to the problem under consideration. But decisions on which basis of classification to use depend on whether the topography *or* the consequence of the target behavior is defined as objectionable or inadequate. When the behavioral consequences are identical, but the style or manner in which the behavior is executed is objectionable, classification by topography would be undertaken. On the other hand, discrimination of different consequences for topologically similar responses may be the therapeutic target. For example, in treatment of exhibitionists, the behavior of undressing is topologically identical, regardless of whether it is carried out in the bedroom or in the park. It is the functional consequence that differs for the two behaviors.

The definition of a response includes the full range of motor and verbal behaviors as legitimate objects of study. It is not limited to a physicalistic definition of body movements. However, two important methodological limitations are observed. First, social and verbal responses are considered responses in their own right, not as substitutes for mental events or internal states. A verbal response

may be under control of the event to which it refers *or* of the
audience to whom it is addressed. It can be observed and modified
as a response in its own right, rather than as an indicant of an
internal state or mental event. A second limitation concerns the
treatment of behaviors that are normally covert, including thinking,
perceiving, or deciding. When these responses form a target class,
their occurrence must be made accessible to observation.

BEHAVIOR EFFECTS

The consequences of a response which serve to maintain or increase its future occurrence are called *reinforcers*. Before using consequences to alter behavior, some proof should be available of the
two properties assigned to reinforcing stimuli: (a) their power to
alter the probability of the preceding response, and (b) their direc-
tive function on behavior. Most commonly, the observation that a
response does not occur in the *absence* of the specified consequences
or in the *absence* of signals indicating the availability of specific reinforcers and that the response does occur in their *presence* is sufficient for a practical description of events in this category. The
second criterion is met when a consequence can be shown to influence the learning of a novel response. It should be noted that
reinforcers are not discrete and specific material events only. While
it is convenient to conceptualize a pellet of food for a hungry animal as a reinforcing stimulus, the social behavior of people, verbal
statements, gestures, reduction in aversive consequences, and numerous other events may serve as reinforcing stimuli. In behavior
modification, reinforcing events that are clearly discernible and
often tangible may have an initial advantage in maintaining or
altering behavior because of their clear contingency on a given
response. Ultimately, reinforcing stimuli may subtly merge into
the total environment or may be attached to self-generated verbal
statements. In the analysis of this category it is often helpful to
establish a reinforcement hierarchy, a list of situations, activities
and events that are especially desirable or influential in guiding and
maintaining the behavior of an individual.

CONTINGENCY RELATIONSHIP

The last category, K, refers to the parametric relationship of the
response-reinforcement arrangement. Learning research has clearly

indicated that the ratio of responses per reinforcement and the temporal schedule of reinforcing events for operant responses affect both acquisition and maintenance of the behavior (21). A complete analysis, therefore, must include some statement about the schedule that controls response-consequence arrangements, any changes in such schedules from earlier situations, or the simultaneous control of a behavior by different schedules. For example, different K values in the interaction of a child with his mother and father would describe the fact that the mother tends to reinforce each occurrence of an approach behavior while the father reinforces it only infrequently. Since different schedules have predictably different performance characteristics, this category should not be neglected.

The behavioral analysis as described above essentially replaces the traditional diagnostic formulation that labeled individual personality characteristics on the basis of particular syndromes. Analysis of a client's problem is a continuous process and requires reevaluation throughout the progress of treatment. The process of selecting an appropriate behavioral unit for analysis and the decision concerning the target responses may require considerable inquiry and observation prior to the behavioral analysis itself. Discussion of techniques for collecting information and observation necessary for behavioral analysis can be found elsewhere (34). A brief sketch of the directions which a behavioral analysis might take in investigating the poor school performance of a youngster illustrates the clinical application of the approach.

By observation and interview with parents, teachers, and the child, the following items would be among those explored in a tentative formulation of the problem:

S variables. Attitudes and modeling of parents and siblings toward school; the child's expectations of success; teacher demands and attitudes; nature and specificity of requirements for school performance. Conditions for study and class performance; attitudes in the sociocultural milieu toward school success; characterization of the child by others as bright, dull.

O variables. General physical health, including vision, hearing, etc.; basic intellectual capacity; relevant medical and physical history; drug use; and so forth.

Response repertoire. Skills acquired by prior school experiences;

study habits; reading skills; emotional responses to academic tasks; responses related to school performance that control the behavior of teachers, peers, parents and others; responses that are incompatible with attending in class, studying at home, or displaying knowledge.

K relationships. Consistency and schedules of rewards for studying and for using knowledge or skills; patterns of administration of positive and negative consequences by teachers, parents, or peers for behaviors that conflict with studying or learning.

Consequences. Common obtainable reinforcements for learning and for not learning, such as approval or punishment by parents, ridicule, contingent privileges; consequences particularly associated with achievement or nonachievement of success in school (e.g., mother tutoring in failing subjects, display of report cards to family and strangers, etc.); reinforcement for incompatible responses, such as doing chores instead of studying; requiring more of a child who does well in school; use of punishment for failure only; peer encouragement for not doing well, and so forth.

In each case additional inquiry and observation should yield some formulation about the most critical factors that either interfere with good school performance or maintain poor performance. This formulation then becomes the basis for a treatment strategy.

The Basic Paradigms

CLASSICAL CONDITIONING

The classical conditioning paradigm has been used most frequently in treatment when the client makes an autonomic or affective response to stimuli that elicit different behaviors in most members of the culture. For example, in the sexual perversions, in alcoholism, and in phobias, classical conditioning is employed to alter the response made to a conditioned stimulus by introducing a competing unconditioned reflex. The sight or thought of feminine underclothing may serve as a CS (conditioned stimulus) for sexual arousal in some individuals. When paired with electric shock or another aversive UCS (unconditioned stimulus) the CS acquires a new "meaning" in the context of repeated aversive events. Similarly, real or imagined presence in a crowded space to a phobic patient serves as a CS for a fear response. When the patient is re-laxed and comfortably resting, pairing of the relaxed state with the previously fear-arousing CS eventually reduces the patient's earlier anxiety.

The classical conditioning paradigm has been most widely ap-plied under two conditions: (a) when autonomic components make up a significant part of the complaint, and (b) when counter-conditioning is attempted to reduce the affective value of the CS by introduction of a strong and invariant reflex with aversive connotations. A group of treatment procedures known as *aversion therapy* relies heavily on the classical conditioning paradigm to create a conditioned aversion to undesirable habits. The use of classical conditioning in behavior modification is limited, however, by the fact that the classical conditioning paradigm requires care-ful attention to the timing of the interval between the CS and UCS, most frequently involves administration of a noxious UCS, and serves mainly to eliminate or reduce a person's reaction to a CS rather than to build up a more effective way of dealing with a problematic situation. In fact, these limitations have led most authors to advocate the use of classical conditioning in combination with operant techniques. Perhaps the most significant utilization of this paradigm is embedded in the complex procedure of reciprocal inhibition or systematic desensitization, mainly applied to phobias or interpersonal anxiety (73, 74).

OPERANT CONDITIONING

Essential in operant conditioning is the programming of par-ticular consequences following the occurrence of a given response. Operant conditioning has been applied in a wide range of situa-tions and to an endless variety of responses. Underlying this tech-nique is the reinforcement principle, which states that the prob-ability of occurrence of a given response is altered by its consequences. The operant paradigm can be used to increase or decrease the frequency of a target behavior by appropriate re-sponse reinforcement contingency arrangements. In most clinical cases, the identified problem behavior often leaves the clinician with the choice of increasing some deficient but desirable behavior or decreasing an undesirable response by attaching aversive consequences to it. For example, disruptive behavior of a child in a classroom can be affected by positive reinforcement for various working behaviors, such as attending to his assignment, executing a constructive task, *or* by introducing a reward for nonoccurrence of the undesirable behavior. At the same time, the disruptive behavior might be attacked by attaching such aversive consequences as loss of a reward or time out from pleasurable activities. The basic operations involving response reinforcement contingencies are summarized in table 1. It should be noted that three basic

TABLE 1

BASIC OPERATIONS INVOLVING RESPONSE REINFORCEMENT CONTINGENCIES

Operation	Positive Consequence: $C+$	Aversive Consequence: $C-$
Contingent Delivery	Positive reinforcement $R \rightarrow C+$ Child obeys request → adult's friendly approval	Punishment $R \rightarrow C-$ Child refuses request → adult scolds
Contingent removal	Response cost $R \rightarrow \downarrow C+$ Child disobeys request → adult removes attention	Negative reinforcement (escape or aversion-relief) $R \rightarrow \downarrow C-$ Child apologizes → adult stops scolding
Withheld after series of presentations	Extinction $R \rightarrow 0$ Child yells demand → adult ignores	Avoidance $R \rightarrow 0$ Child obeys when first requested → adult withholds scolding

From Kanfer and Phillips (33)

operations—contingent delivery, contingent removal, or cessation of a particular consequence—permit a variety of combinations in the utilization of the paradigm. In addition to the manipulation of the response rate by reinforcement contingencies, numerous techniques are available that combine sequences of the operant procedures for diverse effects. For example, deliberate variations in the schedule of reinforcement, or carefully engineered programs of successive acquisition and extinction of responses that more and more closely approximate the desired behavior (shaping), building up of differential behaviors by stimulus control, increasing response strength by gradual reduction of discriminative or supportive cues (fading), and many other technical procedures are available for application in particular situations (cf. 26).

Since the operant conditioning paradigm requires that the behavior modifier have control of some effective reinforcing events, techniques have been developed that increase this control in treatment. The utilization of generalized conditioned reinforcers is the best-known technique for dealing with individual differences in preference for reinforcers, and with the temporal fluctuations that make some reinforcers such as food more or less attractive at a given time. These reinforcers are illustrated by the use of social approval, tokens, points, gold stars, or trading stamps for appropriate responding. The common feature of all generalized reinforcers is their exchangeability for many different goods or services. Just like money, a common form of generalized reinforcer, tokens are relatively independent of the momentary mood and need of the person. In work with children, for example, earned points or chips might be exchanged for candy, toys, time on the playground, television time, or other attractive items. Thus, the basic operant conditioning paradigm has been expanded to provide a rich variety of specific techniques that follow the general reinforcement principle and that lend themselves for application to many different situations.

MODELING AND VICARIOUS LEARNING

Behavior modification methods are not limited to the direct application of conditioning procedures. The human organism is capable of learning by observation of the behavior of others (5, 47). It would also be foolhardy to disregard man's capacity to use language in learning from the observed or reported experiences of others. Recent research on observational learning has demonstrated that under proper conditions individuals can undergo considerable behavior changes by systematic exposure to models. The basic vicarious learning paradigm is one in which a person is given the opportunity to observe a model and is then required to perform the same task as the model. Numerous variations of this paradigm have been studied (2, 33). For example, observation can be combined with rehearsal and guidance during and after observation; observation of the behavior and its execution can be alternated; and observation of emotional behavior can induce a conditioned emotional response in the observer (14). Although the specific mechanisms in vicarious learning are still not clear, numerous illustrations of the technique have shown that behavior change can be brought about in such diverse situations as the alteration of responses to phobic stimuli (12), the acquisition of social and cognitive behaviors (2,), and the establishment of criteria for one's own performance (3). Not only deviant behaviors, but also the interpersonal behaviors that are required in the conduct of interview therapy (e.g., self-disclosure) can be changed by model exposure (45). The modeling experience can be transmitted by observation of live models but, more economically, by the use of films (4) or by videotape observations (40).

A somewhat broader application of modeling techniques is inherent in the use of deliberate reconstructions of situations in which a person has difficulty. For example, role-playing and behavior rehearsal in therapeutic groups represent opportunities for individuals to observe the behavior of others and to make inferences from such observations about their own behavior. These techniques have also been used in therapies that are not based on the behavioral model. In many sensitivity training and encounter groups, modeling, feedback, and selective reinforcement for particular behaviors are emphasized (17). Psychodrama, family and group therapies employ observational learning and other methods compatible with behavioral principles of treatment. Even when observational learning does not represent a therapeutic technique, behavior modification in group settings is often affected by modeling, working in consonance with or against the treatment strategy that may have been devised for an individual. For example, the behavior of a sibling in a family or of a child in a classroom may not only be altered by utilization of modeling techniques, but it must also be considered that the child's behavior provides a model for other members of the group. Consistent reinforcement of the younger child's demanding behaviors can provide an excellent modeling opportunity for an observing older child.

SELF-REGULATION

In working with older persons the behavior modifier frequently finds that he cannot establish or monitor reinforcing contingencies, nor can he utilize classical conditioning or modeling for practical or ethical reasons. When the client is highly motivated to alter his own behavior, he can be taught a number of techniques that can assist him to direct his own behavior change, following established learning principles. These techniques of self-directed change (and occasionally of self-control) are based on the assumption that individuals are able to regulate their own behavior in the absence of external supports after such behavior change has been initiated and motivated in the therapeutic situation (33). The conceptual model suggests that a person can be taught to monitor his own behavior in order to make a more accurate assessment of his actions, to compare these behaviors to standards which are established jointly with a therapist, and to provide positive or negative self-reinforcement to maintain a newly acquired response. The experimental foundation for these techniques has been more difficult to build than has the foundation for easily observable responses, because their inaccessibility makes it difficult to attach consequences to them, or even to evaluate them thoroughly. For example, the acts of observing oneself, imagining past or future events, or evaluating and rewarding one's behavior are generally covert and private. The therapeutic methods of self-control have been used most frequently in attempts to reduce excessive eating, smoking, aggressive outbursts or similar "impulsive" behaviors. However, application of self-reinforcement techniques for study habits, reduction of hyperactive behavior in children, increased social effectiveness, and reduction of masturbation and other sexual excesses have also been reported. Essentially, these methods assume that it is possible to train individuals to establish target responses, to alter the probability of the execution of undesirable behaviors, and to provide self-reinforcement in ways that parallel the classical and operant conditioning techniques, except that the procedures are ultimately administered not by another person but by the client himself (31).

Recent reports have indicated the possibility of using biofeedback mechanisms for self-directed behavior change. These studies have shown that persons who are exposed to a continuing visual or auditory record of their physiological responses, such as the alpha rhythm or heart rate, can be taught to alter their own autonomic activity (e.g., 30, 46, 59). These studies (cf. 6) have important implications for possible treatment of patients with psychosomatic disorders. For example, hypertensive patients might be trained to lower their blood pressure by this procedure. Current reports suggest some limitations to this approach despite the rather spectacular findings. A second implication of these studies, however, lies in the demonstration that autonomic responses can be operantly conditioned. As we have noted earlier, most theorists have based their justification for a dual learning model (classical *and* operant conditioning) on the assumption that autonomic responses cannot be modified by reinforcement. Even though these reports and others raise serious questions about the separability of operant and classical conditioning (e.g., 35), it is pragmatically useful to deal separately with the operational procedures for classical and operant conditioning, providing convenient paradigms for clinical application, even if the underlying learning mechanisms may overlap much more than previously suspected.

INTERVIEWS IN BEHAVIOR THERAPY

Although the thrust of behavior modification is on alteration of environmental contingencies, the interview continues to be useful in an integrated behavioral approach. In contrast to its role as the main vehicle for traditional therapy, the interview in behavior modification may occupy a position that varies from peripheral to central in the total program. As an assessment device, the interview can be used to obtain specific information about the client's behavior patterns, environmental circumstances, and covert behaviors. It can also be used to observe the client's behavior in two-person interactions and to assess his self-attitudes. Frequently the interview paves the way for therapy by establishing a positive relationship, exploring and offering social reinforcements that may later serve as an incentive to enhance client cooperation. This approach resembles the establishment of "rapport." It is employed most frequently in cases in which other sources of reinforcement are weak, and only for a time span sufficiently long to encourage the patient to undertake the treatment program.

The interview is an especially useful vehicle in programs involving self-regulation. In the dyadic relationship the patient can be trained to monitor his own behavior, to establish criteria for self-reinforcement, and to participate in the establishment of reinforcing stimuli that either the client himself or other therapeutic agents then utilize. Problems requiring the client's self-exploration, the establishment of life goals, or the alteration of private behaviors (such as thinking or decision-making) are most likely to benefit from the interview technique.

The interview is widely used with clients as well as with mediating therapeutic agents (mothers, teachers, and so on). Ample demonstration has been given of the importance of the interviewer as a reinforcing agent in modifying verbal content of the interview as well as the client's self-attitudes (cf. 32, 38). On the whole, however, there are no guides available for particular interview procedures to accomplish a given purpose that approach the detailed descriptions of applications of other behavior modification techniques. Nevertheless, the importance of the intimate contact in interviews that permits increased self-disclosure, selective reinforcement for particular behaviors or accomplishments, and the general social reinforcement provided by the attention and helpful attitude of the interviewer cannot be underestimated with clients for whom environmental reinforcement contingencies cannot be worked out easily.

From Theory to Practice

Although behavior modification techniques have been derived from tightly controlled laboratory studies and use relationships that were obtained in studies with animals as well as humans, the clinical setting makes demands on the clinician which are quite different from those made on the researcher. Above all, practical application requires that primary consideration be given to weighing the probable benefits and risks of a treatment program for the client. The client's problems demand immediate action, even though scientifically validated explanations or methods may not be available. The clinician's decisions, therefore, usually rest not only on objective data, but also on his "educated guesses" and are guided by consideration of the social forces which have brought the client into treatment. The clinician's task is to observe and treat a single individual in the most economical way. But the behavior of a person is subject to numerous influences and uncontrolled variables. At best, only a small segment of behavior can be studied, yielding a limited and biased base for treatment. Therefore, relevant scientific knowledge has to be used side by side, or in mixture, with personal experiences and other information that does not originate in the scientific discipline of psychology.

Although the clinician may be able to design a treatment plan that would affect a problematic behavior, he must also consider any impact of the client's behavior change on other persons in the client's environment. Thus, he must evaluate his goals and methods in terms of their effectiveness and their social consequences. These practical considerations often override technical decisions or conclusions derived from careful study of a client. For example, the ideal solution for changing maladaptive behavior of a child may be to remove him from his parental home. The ideal solution for a neurotic adult may lie in gaining freedom from anxiety over poverty, in separation from a marital partner, or in practice with skillful heterosexual partners. Obviously, these ideal solutions are often unavailable or unacceptable to the client or to society. Thus, the translation of procedures derived from experimental work requires that they be tempered by the clinician's judgment of the welfare and interests of the affected individuals. The best treatment program is usually one that is achieved by compromise between the rationally most desirable and practically most feasible alternatives.

The most important contributions that psychologists can offer to educators and counselors are represented by a point of view of human behavior. Bijou has expressed these as "(a) a set of concepts and principles derived entirely from the experimental analysis of behavior, (b) a methodology for the practical application of these concepts and principles, (c) a research method that deals with changes in individual behavior, and (d) a philosophy of science that says, 'Look carefully to the relationships between observable and environmental and behavioral events and their changes' " (11). It is quite likely that the multiplicity of variables that combine to produce a problem situation in any one individual is rarely duplicated exactly in any other. Therefore, ultimately a catalogue of cookbook procedures for remedying such behaviors as hyperactivity, underachievement, depression, or confusion about vocational goals is not only difficult to achieve, but not even desirable. In fact, the very essence of the behavioral approach is to deny the utility of such summarizing index terms as proper targets for attack by behavior modification. Only a careful analysis of the individual case can reveal what responses, cues, and reinforcers contribute to the social label of a child as an underachiever, as hyperactive, or as alienated.

Scientific methodology, however, remains the basic tool for the clinician in the sense that the execution of a change program should be conducted as rigorously as conditions permit and as closely resembling a laboratory experiment as can be done. Collection of information in quantitative form prior, during, and after treatment should be carried out to permit assessment of the change and attribution of behavioral changes to particular therapeutic operations. The therapist's behavior should remain as faithful to the outlined procedure as is feasible. Considerations of social responsibility, treatment goals, and ethical standards should enter most heavily in the deliberations that result in outlining a treatment program. Once the program is established, these considerations usually need not be given much further attention, except in cases where the program runs into difficulties or unexpected obstacles. The continuing monitoring of treatment progress serves as a further check to alert the clinician that changes in the procedure may be necessary, or that it is ineffective and that reevaluation of the case is required.

The ultimate goal of behavior modification techniques is to alleviate a problem situation. In this sense it differs both from laboratory research and traditional clinical approaches. The behavioral clinician is not aiming to prove a hypothesis, to alter personality structures, or to remove some hypothetical disease complex. If changes in situational context can remove some of the problems that increase effectiveness, further intervention may not be required. If a small behavioral change relieves the client's discomforts, removes a mother's or complainant's concern, or restores an acceptable level of functioning, then further intervention may not be required. This *principle of least intervention* suggests that behavior modification programs are best designed by establishing minimal goals at first, expanding these only when their accomplishment is insufficient to remedy a difficult situation.

The most far-reaching effective changes would be those which better equip the person to overcome his developmental (psychological and biological) handicaps, thus enabling him to handle increasingly difficult situations in the future. There is currently insufficient evidence of the genetic and early developmental processes that may predispose individuals toward maladaptive behaviors in a wide range of situations. If such invariant personality characteristics or basic psychological processes were known, modification of the underlying behavioral or biological processes that result in secondary adjustment problems might be feasible. For example, in extreme cases our knowledge of such factors as the genetic abnormalities in Huntington's chorea, or phenylketonuria lead us to attack the faulty biological mechanisms (etiological factors) that account for a large share of the causal determinants of the behavior deviations. But in psychotic disturbances (e.g., schizophrenia or autism) the causal determinants—and even the basis for diagnosis—are hotly debated and quite unclear. In milder disturbances there is little evidence for attributing the difficulty to particular developmental or situational causes.

Current work in several areas (e.g., 23, 24, 57, 58) is holding out the hope that some early learning experiences might account for individual behavior deviations from the social norm, and point to target behaviors that transcend the specific problem situations. For example, if early exposure to unavoidable pain does indeed result in later nonlearning of avoidance responses, or if early social isolation results in later nonresponse to social reinforcers, treatment programs might be designed to rectify these broader deficits or deviations rather than attack situation-specific targets. Many behavior therapists are already following such a procedure. For instance, when a child has multiple problems, including temper tantrums, poor school performance, and nonresponsiveness to parents, a behavior therapist might find an extremely low rate of reinforcement by the family for the child's constructive behaviors. The clinician may then decide to give priority to altering the mother's rate of contingent reinforcement for positive behaviors in various settings, rather than to attack the tantrums or academic work first, if he considers the specific problems to be related to a common factor that is subject to change.

Consistent with a behavioral framework, it can barely be expected that changed behaviors would persist over a wide range of changes in situations. Ultimately, some point may be reached where a treated person finds himself again in a situation for which he is ill prepared, or in which previous reinforcing events are no longer available, or in which some life event has altered his repertoire. It is for these reasons that many writers have stressed the importance of shifting the control over the client's behavior, as much as possible, away from the environment and to the client. To train a person to select appropriate environments, to respond differentially to his environment, and to maintain behavior by self-reinforcement should extend the beneficial effects of a behavior modification program. In token reinforcement programs in the classroom, O'Leary and Drabman (51) have suggested that involvement of the child in the program by training him to evaluate his own behavior and gradually withdrawing these artificial environmental reinforcers would enhance the residual effects of treatment. With notoriously treatment-resistant autistic children, Lovaas, Koegel, Simmons, and Stevens (44) have suggested that two-year follow-ups after treatment showed considerable residual improvement in children whose parents had been trained to carry out the behavior therapy, thus extending the therapeutic program to new situations. The behavior therapist, therefore, should view his treatment program as a *starting point* for altering a client's life pattern, a family's interactional pattern, or a classroom's social system. He should attempt to secure some future resource for maintenance of positive behaviors and withdraw as soon as changes have given the individual the opportunity to develop adequate adjustmental patterns on his own.

This chapter has attempted to prepare the groundwork for the following presentation of the most useful behavioral approaches relevant to education. For the reader with limited familiarity in learning psychology or behavior modification, a brief appendix may serve as an incentive to consult other books for more detailed treatment or background in particular areas. The novice in behavior modification will also find some excellent texts that describe simple projects for the beginning behavior modifier. However, students of behavior modification usually find that textbook prescriptions are insufficient substitutes for apprenticeship, in which clinical judgment can be integrated with technical skills for the successful and ethically justifiable application of behavior modification methods.

As befalls any successful therapeutic approach, behavior therapy has become the target of a number of critical evaluations and attacks (13, 37, 54, 55, 56, 68). While there is insufficient space to deal here with these criticisms, many are taken up in later chapters. Some of the criticisms emphasize that the attitude of behavior modifiers must be an open one if the framework is to continue its scientific basis. Any scientific theory is temporary, an approximation to the complexities of natural events. Self-criticism, skepticism about universal truths, constant reevaluation of the underlying framework, and a flow of research data and new investigations are the hallmark of a scientific approach. Therefore, behavior modification should not be regarded as a complete and unalterable approach, either to a theory of human behavior or to the solution of human problems. Growth, change, and continuing revision are the most critical reinforcers for survival and refinement of this approach toward the development of a comprehensive scientific theory and a framework for social application.

APPENDIX

The following selection is intended to guide the reader in his further exploration of behavior modification. The books have been chosen from a rapidly growing list of titles to provide a short introduction to different subspecialties. Many excellent books, both scholarly and practical, have been omitted and some of the suggested titles may fall short of the reader's expectations. The only intentional bias in collecting the list has been the author's familiarity with available titles and his attempt to balance quality and coverage in the shortest possible list.

1. Background in learning principles. These books stress theories and research in the field of learning that have special relevance to application.

Ferster, C. B., and Perrott, Mary Carol. *Behavior Principles*. New York: Appleton-Century-Crofts, 1968.

Millenson, J. R. *Principles of Behavioral Analysis*. New York: Macmillan Co., 1967.
Reynolds, G. S. *A Primer of Operant Conditioning*. Glenview, Ill.: Scott, Foresman & Co., 1968.
Salzinger, K. *Psychology: The Science of Behavior*. New York: Springer Publishing Co., 1969.
Skinner, B. F. *Science and Human Behavior*. New York: Macmillan Co., 1953.

2. Comprehensive surveys of the theory and practice of behavior modification. These volumes are written at an advanced level appropriate for those already familiar with the fundamentals of behavior modification.

Bandura, A. *Principles of Behavior Modification*. New York: Holt, Rinehart & Winston, 1969.
Franks, Cyril M., ed. *Behavior Therapy: Appraisal and Status*. New York: McGraw-Hill Book Co., 1969.
Kanfer, F. H., and Phillips, J. S. *Learning Foundations of Behavior Therapy*. New York: John Wiley & Sons, 1970.

3. Behavioral views in abnormal psychology and behavior pathology. These books cover the traditional contents of abnormal psychology from a learning-based point of view. The first and last books are more advanced, assuming some familiarity with traditional material; the second book builds a sociobehavioral outlook, beginning at a less advanced level.

Costello, C. G., ed. *Symptoms of Psychopathology: A Handbook*. New York: John Wiley & Sons, 1970.
Ullmann, L. P., and Krasner, L. *A Psychological Approach to Abnormal Behavior*. Englewood Cliffs, N.J.: Prentice-Hall, 1969.
Yates, Aubrey J. *Behavior Therapy*. New York: John Wiley & Sons, 1970.

4. Description of specific treatment techniques. These books are written mainly for the practicing clinician and incorporate reviews of necessary background materials.

Meyer, V., and Chesser, Edward S. *Behaviour Therapy in Clinical Psychiatry*. Harmondsworth, England: Penguin Books, 1970.
Rachman, S., and Teasdale, J. *Aversion Therapy and Behavior Disorders*. Coral Gables, Fla.: University of Miami Press, 1969.
Wolpe, Joseph. *The Practice of Behavior Therapy*. New York: Pergamon Press, 1969.

5. Application of behavior modification methods by parents and teachers. These books describe simple methods of altering children's behaviors, mostly in programmed form. They are especially appropriate for use by individuals with minimal background in psychology.

Becker, Wesley C. *Parents are Teachers*. Champaign, Ill.: Research Press, 1971.

Buckley, N. K., and Walker, H. M. *Modifying Classroom Behavior: A Manual of Procedure for Classroom Teachers*. Champaign, Ill.: Research Press, 1970.

Deibert, A. N., and Harmon, A. J. *New Tools for Changing Behavior*. Champaign, Ill.: Research Press, 1970.

Homme, L. *How to Use Contingency Contracting in the Classroom*. Champaign, Ill.: Research Press, 1969.

Patterson, G. R., and Gullion, M. E. *Living with Children: New Methods for Parents and Children*. Champaign, Ill.: Research Press, 1968.

Becker, Wesley C.: Engelmann, S.; and Thomas, D. R. *Teaching: A Course in Applied Psychology*. Chicago: Science Research Associates, 1971.

6. Application in institutional settings. These books are designed primarily for professional consultants and individuals with some familiarity with psychological principles. They should be helpful in establishing programs in institutions or other social systems.

Ayllon, T., and Azrin, N. *The Token Economy*. New York: Appleton-Century-Crofts, 1970.

Gardner, William I. *Behavior Modification in Mental Retardation*. Chicago: Aldine Publishing Co., 1971.

Tharp, R. G., and Wetzel, R. J. *Behavior Modification in the Natural Environment*. New York: Academic Press, 1969.

7. Application of behavioral principles in working with individuals. These books deal primarily with techniques that use the traditional one-to-one setting of the dyadic relationship as a basic treatment vehicle.

Krumboltz, John D., and Thoresen, Carl E., eds. *Behavioral Counseling: Cases and Techniques*. New York: McGraw-Hill Book Co., 1969.

Lazarus, Arnold A. *Behavior Therapy and Beyond*. New York: McGraw-Hill Book Co., 1971.

Osipow, Samuel H., and Walsh, W. Bruce. *Behavior Change in Counseling: Readings and Cases*. New York: Appleton-Century-Crofts, 1970.

Sloane, Howard N. Jr., and MacAulay, Barbara D., eds. *Operant Procedures in Remedial Speech and Language Training*. Boston: Houghton Mifflin Co., 1968.

8. Selected books of readings with case presentations and discussion of issues. These books are most useful for readers with some background in learning psychology and the fundamentals of behavior modification.

Ullmann, L. P., and Krasner, L. *Case Studies in Behavior Modification*. New York: Holt, Rinehart & Winston, 1965.
Ulrich, R.; Stachnik, T.; and Mabry, J. *Control of Human Behavior*, vol. I. Glenview, Ill.: Scott, Foresman & Co., 1966.
———. *Control of Human Behavior—From Cure to Prevention*, vol. 2. Glenview, Ill.: Scott, Foresman & Co., 1970.

9. Periodical Journals. Among the many journals that carry articles on behavior modification, these offer clinical materials almost exclusively from a behavioral point of view.

Behaviour Research and Therapy, Pergamon Press.
Behavior Therapy, Academic Press.
Journal of Behaviour Therapy and Experimental Psychiatry, Pergamon Press.
Journal of Applied Behavior Analysis, Society for the Experimental Analysis of Behavior, Ann Arbor, Michigan.

Another journal, not exclusively devoted to behavior modification but often including articles on it, is:

Journal of Experimental Analysis of Behavior, Society for the Experimental Analysis of Behavior, Ann Arbor, Michigan.

REFERENCES

1. Ayllon, T., and Azrin, N. *The Token Economy*. New York: Appleton-Century Co., 1968.
2. Bandura, A. *Principles of Behavior Modification*. New York: Holt, Rinehart & Winston, 1969.
3. Bandura, A., and Kupers, C. J. "Transmission of Patterns of Self-Reinforcement through Modeling." *Journal of Abnormal and Social Psychology* 69 (1964): 1-9.
4. Bandura, A., Ross, D., and Ross, S. A. "Imitation of Film-mediated Aggressive Models." *Journal of Abnormal and Social Psychology* 66 (1963): 3-11.

5. Bandura, A., and Walters, R. H. *Social Learning and Personality Development*. New York: Holt, Rinehart & Winston, 1963.
6. Barber, T.; DiCara, L. V.; Kamiya, J.; Miller, N. E.; Shapiro, D.; Stoyva, J., eds. *Biofeedback and Self-Control*. Chicago: Aldine Publishing Co., 1971.
7. Becker, W. C.; Engelmann, S.; and Thomas, D. R. *Teaching: A Course in Applied Psychology*. Chicago: Science Research Associates, 1971.
8. Beecroft, R. S. *Classical Conditioning*. Goleta, Calif.: Psychonomic Press, 1966.
9. Bekhterev, V. M. "Die Anwendung der Methode der motorischen Assoziations-reflexe zur Aufdeckung der Simulation." *Zeit. ges. Neurol. Psychiat.* 13 (1912): 183-91.
10. ———. "Die Krankenheiten der Persönlichkeit vom Standpunkt der Reflexologie." *Zeit. ges. Neurol. Psychiat.* 80 (1923): 265-309.
11. Bijou, S. W. "What Psychology Has to Offer Education—Now." *Journal of Applied Behavior Analysis* 3 (1970): 65-71.
12. Blanchard, E. B. "Relative Contributions of Modeling, Informational Influences and Physical Contact in Extinction of Phobic Behavior." *Journal of Abnormal Psychology* 76 (1970): 55-61.
13. Breger, Louis, ed. *Clinical-Cognitive Psychology*. Englewood Cliffs, N.J.: Prentice-Hall, 1969.
14. Craig, K. D. "Physiological Arousal as a Function of Imagined, Vicarious, and Direct Stress Experiences." *Journal of Abnormal Psychology* 73 (1968): 513-20.
15. Davison, G. C. "Self-Control through Imaginal Aversive Contingency and 'One-Downsmanship.'" In *Behavioral Counseling: Cases and Techniques*, edited by J. D. Krumboltz and C. E. Thoresen. New York: Holt, Rinehart & Winston, 1969.
16. Dollard, J., and Miller, N. E. *Personality and Psychotherapy: An Analysis in Terms of Learning, Thinking and Culture*. New York: McGraw-Hill Book Co., 1950.
17. Egan, G. *Encounter: Group Processes for Interpersonal Growth*. Belmont, Calif.: Brooks/Cole, 1970.
18. Ellis, N. R., ed. *Handbook of Mental Deficiency*. New York: McGraw-Hill Book Co., 1963.
19. ———. "Toilet Training and Severely Defective Patient: An S-R Reinforcement Analysis." *American Journal of Mental Deficiency* 68 (1963): 98-103.
20. Ellis, N. R.; Barnett, C. D.; and Pryer, M. W. "Operant Behavior in Mental Defectives: Exploratory Studies." *Journal of Experimental Analysis of Behavior* 3 (1960): 63-69.
21. Ferster, C. B., and Skinner, B. F. *Schedules of Reinforcement*. New York: Appleton-Century-Crofts, 1957.

22. Franks, C., ed. *Behavior Therapy: Appraisal and Status.* New York: McGraw-Hill Book Co., 1969.
23. Harlow, H. F., and Harlow, M. K. "The Affectional Systems." In *Behavior of Nonhuman Primates,* vol. 2, edited by A. M. Schrier, H. F. Harlow, and F. Stollnitz. New York: Academic Press, 1965.
24. Harlow, H. F., and Suomi, S. J. "Nature of Love—Simplified." *American Psychologist* 25 (1970): 161-68.
25. Hawkins, R. P.; Peterson, R. F.; Schweid, E.; and Bijou, S. W. "Behavior Therapy in the Home: Amelioration of Problem Parent-Child Relation with the Parent in a Therapeutic Role." *Journal of Experimental Child Psychology* 4 (1966): 99-107.
26. Honig, W. K., ed. *Operant Behavior: Areas of Research and Application.* New York: Appleton-Century-Crofts, 1966.
27. Ivanov-Smolensky, A. G. "Neurotic Behavior and the Teaching of Conditioned Reflexes." *American Journal of Psychiatry* 84 (1927): 483-88.
28. ———. "Uber die bedingten Reflexe in der depressiven Phase der manisch-depressiven Irreseins." *Mschr. Psychiat. Neurol.* 58 (1925): 376-88.
29. Jones, M. C. "A Laboratory Study of Fear: The Case of Peter." *Pedagogical Seminary* 31 (1924): 308-15.
30. Kamiya, J. "Conscious Control of Brain Waves." *Psychology Today* 1 (1968): 56-60.
31. Kanfer, F. H. "Self-Regulation: Research, Issues and Speculations." In *Behavior Modification in Clinical Psychology,* edited by C. Neuringer and J. L. Michael. New York: Appleton-Century-Crofts, 1970.
32. ———. "Verbal Conditioning: A Review of Its Current Status." In *Verbal Behavior and Its Relation to General S-R Theory,* edited by T. R. Dixon and D. L. Horton. Englewood Cliffs, N.J.: Prentice-Hall, 1968.
33. Kanfer, F. H., and Phillips, J. S. *Learning Foundations of Behavior Therapy.* New York: John Wiley & Sons, 1970.
34. Kanfer, F. H., and Saslow, G. "Behavioral Diagnosis." In *Behavior Therapy: Appraisal and Status,* edited by C. Franks. New York: McGraw-Hill Book Co., 1969.
35. Katkin, E. S., and Murray, E. N. "Instrumental Conditioning of Autonomically Mediated Behavior: Theoretical and Methodological Issues." *Psychological Bulletin* 70 (1968): 52-68.
36. King, G. F.; Armitage, S. G.; and Tilton, J. R. "A Therapeutic Approach to Schizophrenics of Extreme Pathology: An Operant-Interpersonal Method." *Journal of Abnormal and Social Psychology* 61 (1960): 276-86.
37. Klein, M. H.; Dittmann, A. T.; Parloff, M. B.; and Gill, M. M.

"Behavior Therapy: Observations and Reflections." *Journal of Consulting and Clinical Psychology* 33 (1969): 259-68.

38. Krasner, L. "Studies of the Conditioning of Verbal Behavior." *Psychological Bulletin* 15 (1958): 148-71.

39. Krasnogorski, N. I. "The Conditioned Reflexes and the Children's Neuroses." *American Journal of Diseases of Children* 30 (1925): 753-68.

40. Krumboltz, J. D.; Varenhorst, B. B.; and Thoresen, C. E. "Non-Verbal Factors in the Effectiveness of Models in Counseling." *Journal of Counseling Psychology* 14 (1967): 412-18.

41. Lindsley, O. R. "Operant Conditioning Methods Applied to Research in Chronic Schizophrenia." *Psychiatric Research Reports* 5 (1956): 118-39.

42. Lindsley, O. R., and Skinner, B. F. "A Method for the Experimental Analysis of the Behavior of Psychotic Patients." *American Psychologist* 9 (1954): 419-20.

43. Lovaas, O. I. "A Behavior Therapy Approach to the Treatment of Childhood Schizophrenia." In *Minnesota Symposium on Child Psychology*, edited by J. Hill. Minneapolis: University of Minnesota Press, 1967.

44. Lovaas, O. I.; Koegel, R.; Simmons, J. Q.; and Stevens, J. "Some Generalization and Follow-up Measures on Autistic Children in Behavior Therapy." Mimeographed, 1971.

45. Marlatt, G. A.; Jacobson, E. A.; Johnson, D. L.; and Morrice, D. J. "Effect of Exposure to a Model Receiving Evaluative Feedback upon Subsequent Behavior in an Interview." *Journal of Consulting and Clinical Psychology* 34 (1970): 104-12.

46. Miller, N. E. "Learning of Visceral and Glandular Responses." *Science* 163 (1969): 434-45.

47. Miller, N. E., and Dollard J. *Social Learning and Imitation.* New Haven: Yale University Press, 1941.

48. Minge, M. R., and Ball, T. S. "Teaching of Self-Help Skills to Profoundly Retarded Patients." *American Journal of Mental Deficiency* 71 (1967): 864-68.

49. Mowrer, O. H. *Learning Theory and Personality Dynamics.* New York: Ronald Press, 1950.

50. ———. "A Stimulus-Response Analysis of Anxiety and Its Role as a Reinforcing Agent." *Psychological Review* 46 (1939): 553-65.

51. O'Leary, K. Daniel, and Drabman, Ronald. "Token Reinforcement Programs in the Classroom: A Review." *Psychological Bulletin* 75 (1971): 379-98.

52. Patterson, G. R. "An Application of Conditioning Techniques to the Control of a Hyperactive Child." In *Case Studies in Behavior Modification*, edited by L. P. Ullmann and L. Krasner. New York: Holt, Rinehart & Winston, 1965.

53. ———. "Social Learning: An Additional Base for Developing Behavior Modification Technologies." In *Behavior Therapy: Appraisal and Status,* edited by C. Franks. New York: McGraw-Hill Book Co., 1969.

54. Portes, Alejandro. "Behavior Therapy and Critical Speculation." *Journal of Consulting and Clinical Psychology* 36 (1971): 320-24.

55. ———. "On the Emergence of Behavior Therapy in Modern Society." *Journal of Consulting and Clinical Psychology* 36 (1971): 303-13.

56. Ryan, V. L., and Gizynski, M. N. "Behavior Therapy in Retrospect: Patients' Feelings about Their Behavior Therapies." *Journal of Consulting and Clinical Psychology* 37 (1971): 1-9.

57. Seligman, M. E. P., and Groves, D. P. "Nontransient Learned Helplessness." *Psychonomic Science* 19 (1970): 191-92.

58. Seligman, M.; Maier, S.; and Solomon, R. "Unpredictable and Uncontrollable Aversive Events." In *Aversive Conditioning and Learning,* edited by F. R. Brush. New York: Academic Press, 1971.

59. Shapiro, D.; Tursky, B.; Gershon, E.; and Stern, M. "Effects of Feedback and Reinforcement on the Control of Human Systolic Blood Pressure." *Science* 163 (1969): 588-90.

60. Skinner, B. F. *The Behavior of Organisms: An Experimental Analysis.* New York: Appleton-Century Co., 1938.

61. ———. *Beyond Freedom and Dignity.* New York: A. A. Knopf, 1971.

62. ———. *Science and Human Behavior.* New York: Macmillan Co., 1953.

63. ———. *The Technology of Teaching.* New York: Appleton-Century-Crofts, 1968.

64. Thomas, D. R.; Becker, W. C.; and Armstrong, M. "Production and Elimination of Disruptive Classroom Behavior by Systematically Varying Teachers' Behavior." *Journal of Applied Behavior Analysis* 1 (1968): 35-46.

65. Ullmann, L. P., and Krasner, L. *Case Studies in Behavior Modification.* New York: Holt, Rinehart & Winston, 1965.

66. ———. *A Psychological Approach to Abnormal Behavior.* Englewood Cliffs, N.J.: Prentice-Hall, 1969.

67. Watson, J. B., and Rayner, R. "Conditioned Emotional Reactions." *Journal of Experimental Psychology* 3 (1920): 1-14.

68. Weitzman, B. "Behavior Therapy and Psychotherapy." *Psychological Review* 74 (1967): 300-17.

69. Whalen, C. K., and Henker, B. A. "Creating Therapeutic Pyramids Using Mentally Retarded Patients." *American Journal of Mental Deficiency* 74 (1969): 331-37.

70. Williams, C. D. "The Elimination of Tantrum Behaviors by Extinction Procedures." *Journal of Abnormal and Social Psychology* 59 (1959): 269.

71. Wilson, G. T.; Hannon, A. E.; and Evans, W. I. M. "Behavior Therapy and the Therapist-Patient Relationship." *Journal of Consulting and Clinical Psychology* 32 (1968): 103-9.
72. Wolf, M. M.; Giles, D. K.; and Hall, R. V. "Experiments with Token Reinforcement in a Remedial Classroom." *Behaviour Research and Therapy* 6 (1968): 51-64.
73. Wolpe, J. *Psychotherapy by Reciprocal Inhibition.* Stanford: Stanford University Press, 1958.
74. ———. *The Practice of Behavior Therapy.* New York: Pergamon Press, 1969.
75. Yates, A. J. *Behavior Therapy.* New York: John Wiley & Sons, 1970.

CHAPTER II

Behavior Modification in Teacher Education

FREDERICK J. MCDONALD

Introduction

The content of this chapter is the modification of teaching behavior treated as a general class of behaviors. Teacher education programs may be conceptualized as behavior modification systems designed to modify complex behavioral repertoires which are adaptable to a variety of learning problems. Developing a teacher education program which applies behavior modification concepts would be simpler if we knew how to use these principles to control student learning. At the present time, however, only a relatively small number of student behaviors can be brought under behavioral control by applying these principles. Some of these are behaviors which the student must have available to participate in learning experiences; for example, bringing student attending behavior under behavioral control prepares students to acquire the behaviors which are the goals of the learning system (30, 26). Behavior modification systems, however, have not been developed for teaching complex behaviors such as problem-solving. Other teacher behaviors, such as planning and evaluating, may be taught in systems which apply behavior modification principles, but such systems are not yet available (37).

Thus, there are three problems to be solved in designing behavior modification systems for teacher education. First, systems must be designed which facilitate the acquisition of diverse classes of teaching behavior, such as developing goal descriptions, planning learning strategies, evaluating, establishing mutually self-enhancing relations with students, using teaching methods, and acquiring professional attitudes. The second problem is to train teachers to use applications of behavior modification principles by applying the same principles to the acquisition of the use of the method. The third problem is to develop behavior modification systems for students to learn such complex behaviors as reasoning, problem-solving, and aesthetic evaluation.

It seems obvious that as the third problem is solved it will be easier to solve the first problem. But, in the meantime, behavior modification principles should be used to train for the acquisition of the best teaching methods that we presently accept. Although this latter strategy seems wasteful, two reasons support its adoption: (a) applying behavior modification principles will stimulate a reorganization of teacher education programs so that their primary goals are behavior change and the acquisition of teaching skill; and (b) designing a system to modify teaching behavior will stimulate an analysis of the student behavior to be acquired and the conditions likely to facilitate its acquisition.

Discussion

CURRENT STATUS OF BEHAVIOR MODIFICATION IN TEACHER EDUCATION

Teacher education programs are designed to modify classes of behavior of unique significance—significant because teaching behaviors are among the necessary conditions for producing student learning. The intriguing characteristic of teaching behavior is that it is behavior acquired by one person used to modify another person's behavior. Teaching behavior is sets of responses emitted by one human being which will elicit and strengthen desired responses in another. To arrive at specific instances of teaching behavior we ask what student behaviors do we wish to modify; and then we work back to the behaviors to be emitted by a teacher which will elicit or strengthen the desired student behaviors or weaken those which are undesirable.

This definition is marginally useful but at the present time it is about the best that can be offered. Our suspicion is that it excludes nothing; however, two delimitations can be made in the scope of behaviors included in the concept. First, teaching behavior does not include stimuli emitted by nonhuman instructional devices such as computers and books. Second, teaching behavior includes those behaviors which mediate the acquisition of the behaviors usually associated with formal schooling.

A comment should be made on the first limitation. It is only in the last decade that the invention of a number of nonhuman instructional devices has forced us to consider a distinction between teaching and instruction. The ability to create a simulation of human work in teaching has raised the question of what is unique about the actions of humans in educating other humans. No quick and easy answer can be given to that question; nor is it useful to pursue an answer solely by philosophical analyses. The answer or answers will emerge as more sophisticated simulations of teaching are developed. It is useful for the present to consider instruction as the broader concept under which teaching, as a specific human activity, may be subsumed. Teacher education should, therefore, be concerned primarily with the training of those behaviors which cannot at present be simulated by machines. For a decade or so, however, it will have to be concerned about training for those functions which will eventually be mediated by machines.

The second limitation is, of course, problematic, particularly in affluent societies where schooling embraces a large part of a child's life and where the range of what may be learned in school is also large. Current discussions about the arbitrariness of distinctions between "life" and school further complicate delimiting what is meant by teaching. In industrialized urban societies the trend is more and more for school to become life, to extend formal schooling into adult years, and to turn over to other agencies the educative functions of the family, the church, and the community.

This expansion of the scope of schooling would seem to make a definition of teaching behavior meaningless. Actually, this development may help to relieve a confused situation. Teaching will become many different kinds of functions and individual teachers will mediate only a few of them. The education of teachers will become more amenable to the application of the principles of behavior modification because the nature of the training tasks will be clearer.

BEHAVIORAL ANALYSIS IN TEACHER EDUCATION

The words devoted above in explicating a very general definition of teaching behavior may seem wasted. But they may be instructive for those who are interested in applying the principles of behavior modification to the training of teachers for what they imply about the problems of changing teacher education to a behavior modification base. The continuing expansion of the goals of education complicates the problem of deciding what is to be learned because this revisionism stirs discussion about the priorities of what is to be learned. The application of behavior modification principles to teacher education may be submerged in the pervasive analysis of the goals of education.

The behavior modifier, however, typically takes as a given the desirability of changing a response. For example, many of the applications in therapy have been developed where there is general agreement on the desirability of the change. In teacher education there is some agreement on undesirable teaching behaviors, little agreement on desirable behaviors, and practically none on the significance of what is to be learned in order to teach. Therefore, the first task in designing a behavior modification training system, behavioral analysis, is difficult to perform. Some will think quite correctly that a logical beginning is to locate those teaching behaviors which have been shown to have a significant effect on student learning. But previous research is of little help in this respect (27, 28).

One strategy is to select either undesirable behaviors or a behavior which is likely to be useful in a variety of teaching situations (24). Another is to become involved in the task of developing taxonomies of teaching behavior (22). In any case the behavior modifier will find unrewarding his traditional stance: "Tell me what you want to teach, and I will design a system to teach it."

There are many reasons why behavior modification theory and practice have had relatively little impact on teacher education programs. One of the most important is the lack of agreement on training objectives. This situation frustrates those who wish to change the training systems and frequently exposes them to charges of trivializing teacher education when they attempt applications of behavior modification principles. The confusion surrounding training objectives is likely to persist for some time. The wisest course for the behavior modifier to pursue is to seek to make whatever applications he can devise, knowing that his work will help to ameliorate this problem.

TRAINING PARADIGMS IN TEACHER EDUCATION

It will be useful to consider briefly the kinds of training paradigms that undergird most teacher training programs. This analysis will suggest what possibilities may exist for applying behavior modification principles to teacher education, what kinds of problems will have to be solved, and what kinds of theories will compete with behavior modification concepts.

Most teacher education programs contain components which assume an acceptance, perhaps unwittingly, of behavior modification principles. Observation of teaching, for example, assumes that one can learn about teaching by watching another person teach. So do variations on the apprenticeship arrangement, such as placing prospective teachers as teachers' aides. Similarly, practice teaching usually provides some form of feedback in which desired teaching behaviors are rewarded. These training procedures do not represent a systematic application of behavior modification principles. Rather, they reflect an understanding of the most primitive forms of the concepts of modeling and reinforcement.

Such procedures do not represent an application of the principles of behavior modification for three reasons. First, no attempt has been made to sort out what is to be learned by observing and what is to be learned by practice. Presumably, one is to practice what one has observed, but provision is not made for the possibility that most of what is to be learned may have been acquired by observation.

Second, the conditions that make observing and practicing effective are not carefully controlled. Frequently the observer is given only general directions about what is to be observed; rarely is attention directed to specific teaching behaviors, the conditions under which they occur, and their effects.[1] Similarly, the feedback schedule provided with teaching practice is opportunistic rather

1. Flanders's *Interaction Analysis* system has been used as an observing system to measure the dependent variable. It is also used extensively in training. The instrument is useful, and positive effects have been found when teachers have been trained to modify their behavior as described in the system's categories. But the categories in the system combine many kinds of specific behaviors into categories with one very general class property—for example, asking questions. See Flanders (13). For a critique of observation systems relevant to the point being made here, see Rosenshine (27:284-86).

than planned, is rarely given on any schedule known to be effective, and typically covers many specific behaviors.

Third, the order in which these two components occur in training depends on the vagaries of university schedules and the availability of sites for observation and practice. The consequence is that there is no systematic provision of different kinds of models nor of different conditions of practice.

One could enumerate the many deficiencies of these components as effective training instrumentalities; they are fairly obvious. But it is more important for the behavior modifier to recognize that the first two components do provide a means for applying behavior modification principles. This insight may prove useful in developing a strategy for applying behavior modification principles to teacher education.

The third major component of teacher education programs, however, presents the greatest practical difficulties for the behavior modifier. The teacher trainee spends most of his time listening to what teaching ought to be. Some of this information is specific to teaching behavior; much of it is explanation of general principles or philosophic disquisitions on the nature of education. If it is reasonable to assume that a person's behavior reflects his beliefs, one must conclude that teacher educators believe that *knowing about* is a necessary condition for *learning to do*.

The basic paradigm of teacher training appears to be, in its best form,

Learning a   Observing a   Practicing Apply-
Principle ⟶ Principle Applied ⟶ ing a Principle

The implementation of this paradigm leaves much to be desired. Some of the problems in this respect were noted above. Other problems include isolating these three components into courses which are unrelated to each other; lack of feedback that includes an analysis of how the trainee thought he or she was applying the principle; and lack of specific training methods to insure that the application of the principle can be observed.

These and other defects in the implementation of the paradigm might be attributed to poor engineering. But it is useful to consider whether they may be attributed to a conviction about how teaching behavior is learned. Factually, we do not know how many teacher educators have formalized their conceptions of appropriate training methods in terms of this paradigm, nor how many have explored the assumptions underlying it. But such facts make little difference when most teacher educators hold so rigidly to the paradigm.

What assumptions about behavior change might underlie such conviction? Many teacher educators prefer a gestaltist conception of learning; therefore, they think that change in perceptions is the necessary condition for changes in behavior. Although the connection between receiving information about something and behaving differently towards it is tenuous, many instructors assume that an important characteristic of information is its potential for changing perceptions. Thus, knowing about students is important information because it changes our perceptions of them, helps us understand them and, therefore, enables us to teach them more effectively. Similarly, information about teaching methods and goals will change our perceptions of what is effective teaching.

Further, the gestaltist view of learning is deeply entrenched in educational thinking (23). Many educators assume that it is the view most consistent with philosophic conceptions of problem-solving and inquiry, which are among the major goals of educational processes. Behaviorism is seen as concerned with molecular and insignificant responses. For those who hold this view, a change to behavior modification conceptions may be impossible, though one may be hopeful that evidence of effective behavior modification procedures in training effective teachers may be persuasive.

Other educators see teaching as requiring decision-making and problem-solving. They can make a strong argument that knowledge is necessary for effective problem-solving. Increasing a teacher's repertoire of information when organized in concepts and principles is likely to improve his problem-solving ability. Though this rationale has much to recommend it, the disjunction in education between theory and practice is great. Thus, one finds few attempts to analyze the decision-making required in teaching and fewer attempts to train for it. There has been no systematic research on training in decision-making processes.

This point of view, however, lends itself to behavior modification applications. To the degree that decision-making behaviors can be explicit and demonstrated in modeling sessions, they can be imitated (35). Analyses of decision-making strategies used provide an opportunity for giving feedback on appropriate strategies. Similarly, the effects of using a decision-making strategy are the contingencies that can be used to modify decision-making behavior.

The conclusion from the foregoing analysis is that the training paradigm underlying most teacher education programs has little to recommend it. The basic format of these programs must be revised extensively if behavior modification principles are to be applied. Initial efforts at change may be mediated by tinkering with components, by introducing modules that tie knowledge and practice together more tightly, or by introducing segments of training for specific purposes.

CRITIQUE OF TEACHER EDUCATION PROGRAMS

The discussion above describes many of the defects of current training programs if behavior modification concepts are used to analyze them. These and others criticisms may be generalized into the following points:

1. Behavioral analysis of teaching tasks has not preceded the design of these programs. Descriptions of desired teaching behaviors are frequently too general. Many diverse training objectives are accepted as desirable but no systematic ordering of these has been developed.
2. Most programs mix general principles of learning, philosophic concepts of learning, and principles of methodology derived from many sources into a set of unrelated training experiences.
3. The sequence of experiences through which the trainee passes is not correlated with a set of tasks to be mastered or behaviors to be acquired.
4. The conditions under which teaching behaviors are elicited are opportunistic, require production of many diverse behaviors, and are under the control of unplanned and uncontrolled contingencies.
5. Mediated contingency control of teaching behavior acquisition is sporadic, infrequent, and unrelated to the systematic acquisition of behavioral skills; further, the power of the reinforcers used is limited and confined to verbal reinforcers administered by a supervisor.
6. Modeling techniques are primitive and are unrelated to other training procedures.

Lest these criticisms seem harsh and sweeping, it is necessary to point out that other professional training programs show little evidence of the influence of behavior modification principles. An exception is the Stanford Behavioral Training program in counseling. There is reason to be optimistic, however, that behavior modification concepts will be used more extensively in the future. The models designed for the revision of elementary education programs embody many of the concepts of behavior modification (33). In the following sections we will cite some attempts to apply behavior modification concepts to teacher training programs. These efforts have had considerable influence in developing models for the application of behavioral analysis and behavior modification principles to teacher training.

APPLICATION OF BEHAVIOR MODIFICATION PRINCIPLES IN TEACHER TRAINING

Three questions should be answered in assessing the extent of the application of behavioral modification principles to teacher education: (a) What progress has been made in the response analysis of teaching acts? (b) How have reinforcement principles been applied? (c) How have modeling procedures been used?

RESPONSE ANALYSIS IN TEACHER EDUCATION

Teaching behavior is not an unstudied phenomenon. There are over fifteen hundred articles in the literature which identify, describe, or define about five hundred teaching behaviors. One would assume that such an abundant literature would describe a response system rather completely. It does not, for several reasons. The first reason we may pass over quickly because it is a common defect in such analyses—the behaviors are frequently described as traits, such as "enthusiasm," "warmth," "interest in students"; others describe characteristics of teaching methods, such as "inductive teaching behavior," or characteristics of lessons, such as "pacing" or "organization of ideas." Such descriptions, of course, need to be refined in terms of observable behaviors.

But there are other difficulties with these descriptions. Many teaching behaviors are contingent on the responses of students. Hence, a description must include a listing of the cues to which the teaching behavior is to be paired. For example, such traits as "enthusiasm" might be described in terms of the kinds of words a teacher should use, his tone of voice, and the animation of his gestures. But when are these behaviors to occur?

A third problem in the analysis of teaching behavior is that very little, if anything, is known about the connections among behaviors. Some behaviors are defined so that an increase in one should be linked to a decrease in another since they are conceptual opposites, such as *indirect* and *direct influence*. But empirically the kind of reversals expected if one of the behaviors is learned does not always occur. Positive and negative reinforcement by the teacher of pupils' participation in discussions remain positively correlated even after training to increase the number of positive reinforcements is administered (24:56). This correlation suggests that specific training to increase one kind of behavior and specific training to decrease another kind are both needed.

Finding relations of this kind is important because they highlight the difference between a conceptual relation between behaviors and an empirical one. The reason such relations occur is that each kind of teaching behavior may be linked to a different kind of student behavior. For example, a teacher may learn to reward students' attempts to participate in a discussion, but he must unlearn the response of making negative comments when the students' statements contain inaccurate information, ill-conceived ideas, or poor reasoning. Further, it is important to help the teacher to learn *when* each kind of response may be appropriate.

A fourth problem is that many teaching behaviors represent classes of behaviors which have a very large number of specific behavioral representations. Teachers' questions are an example. Evaluative questions, for instance, have a common characteristic— they include any question which asks a student to compare something, such as a conclusion, a chain of reasoning, or an item of information, against a criterion for assessing its truth value. The difficulty that these classes of behavior present for analysis is that of describing the many different verbal forms such questions may take.

This problem is not insoluble, but its resolution will require tedious analysis. This analytic work may be expedited, however, by doing the analysis within domains of teaching tasks rather than across all kinds of such tasks.[2] For example, the type of evaluative question to be asked in teaching mathematics is fairly easy to specify because the nature of the content being taught delimits the scope of the evaluation response expected of the student. Similarly, when teaching literature it is easier to be specific about the type of aesthetic evaluative responses expected of the student; hence, the type of question to elicit this response is easier to describe.

A fifth problem in the analysis of teaching responses is that one kind of student behavior may be linked to more than one kind of teaching behavior. Teachers' responses, for example, which follow a student response may take many different forms—a rewarding comment, a revision of the student's remarks, another question of the same student, a question of another student, or combinations of these. Teachers must learn these multiple combinations and the discriminative cues which signal when a particular pair is required.

Knowledge is not available that describes the various combinations of teacher-student response pairs and the appropriate conditions for eliciting them. The development of this kind of knowledge requires an analysis of response pair chains and their effects. This empirical analysis can be conducted in two ways. First, analyses can be made of protocols of teacher-student interactions. This type of analysis is tedious and likely to consume several years of research work. One way to accelerate this kind of inductive analysis is to obtain protocols of different teachers teaching identical content to comparable students.[3] Another method of analysis is to program the teacher to make certain kinds of responses in one instance and another kind in the second instance and compare the effects of each type of teacher response.[4]

2. There is a difference of views about whether teaching skills are general across teaching tasks or specific to types of content or students being taught. Until empirical data are available, there is no compelling reason to come down on either side of this issue. Note that either a general or specific skill can be defined in terms of concrete, observable behaviors.

3. This type of methodology is being used by the Teacher Behavior Research Group at Educational Testing Service. It is proving to be extremely useful for developing a coding system to be applied to analyses of teaching behavior.

4. It is technologically feasible to use this strategy. An audio receiver plug (bug in the ear) is worn by the teacher. An observer makes suggestions

An analysis of teaching tasks, as the list of problems outlined above suggests, will require considerable empirical work. Available descriptions of teaching behavior are more or less useful for this purpose, but the kind of information needed about response pairs is not available in the research on systems for observing and classifying teacher behavior.

Flanders's Interaction Analysis. Theories of teaching or learning seem to be implicit in many descriptions of teaching behavior; in some cases the theory or the basic assumptions are made explicit. The best known, and perhaps the most widely used system, Flanders's Interaction Analysis (3, 13), is an example.

Flanders's basic principle is that the character of the interpersonal relations between teacher and student is the primary determinant of student learning, intended and unintended. Flanders hypothesizes that indirect influence is more likely than direct influence to have positive effects on student learning. His category system sorts teacher behavior into instances of indirect influence, such as "praising and encouraging," "asking questions," and "using students' ideas," and instances of direct influence, such as "lecturing," "giving directions," and "criticizing."(3:12) The amount of student talk, particularly if initiated by the students, is also used as a measure of the amount of direct influence by the teacher.

This system has the advantage of being grounded in a set of concepts that can be related in formal hypotheses which are testable (4, 14). As in most other systems, the behavior of the teacher is assumed to be linked to that of the students; for example, if teacher talk decreases, student talk will increase. While the evidence is consistent with this proposition, research on the system has not shown the causal links among the behaviors recorded.

This lack of knowledge presents a problem for the behavior modifier; he does not know what responses to strengthen. For example, will strengthening "accepting feeling" or "praising and encouraging" produce more student-initiated talk?

The categories present a special problem. Four of them are contingent on students' responses. This relation complicates the

---

to the teacher into this audio hookup, sometimes by means of telemetric equipment. Obviously, the "naturalness" of the teaching situation is changed, but that is always so in experiments.

training process since the teacher's behavior cannot occur until the students' behavior occurs. Other categories, such as "asking questions," are behaviors which should elicit certain kinds of student behavior. It is relatively easy to shape this behavior using behavior modification techniques (10), but it will not be maintained if appropriate student responses fail to occur.

Two kinds of teaching responses may be identified in all such systems: (a) those that elicit specified pupil responses; (b) those that reinforce desired student responses. One can conceive of a third kind, a response that both elicits a new response and rewards one previously made; for example, "Susan, I think your question is excellent; what's your best answer to it?" Obviously, eliciting and rewarding responses can be linked around a student response.

This brief analysis of Flanders's categories should make clear the difference between his system and one produced by behavioral analysis. Flanders's system describes teaching behavior phenotypically; a behavioral analysis yields a genotypic system. Hence, the application of behavioral analysis to such systems reduces them, when that is possible, to categories which describe the functional or cause-and-effect characteristics of teaching responses. The behavior modifier, however, should not overlook the educational significance of phenotypical descriptions.

Three conclusions are appropriate. First, a response classification system grounded in theory does not necessarily resolve the problems of behavioral analysis which have been discussed here. Second, using such a system or parts of it in behavior modification training designs is treacherous because the connections between the behaviors are unknown, or reflected, at best, in correlations. Hence, even though a behavior may be modified, it may have insignificant effects on pupil behavior. Third, until the connection between teacher behavior and student behavior is specified, one is not likely to develop effective behavioral engineering techniques. Fourth, unless the contingencies of student behavior are also managed, either by direct intervention or through the teacher's behavior, the acquired teaching behavior is not likely to be maintained.

Process-descriptive systems. Some investigators have developed response descriptions of the processes of teacher-student talk but have not grounded their system in a theory. Rather, they have observed many instances of teaching and have inducted a system which seems to describe what they have observed.

The best known of these systems is Medley's OSCAR system (25). Medley's system comes closest to a behavioral analysis device. For example, the system classifies utterances into *entry* and *exit* statements and questions; the former is defined as an initiating statement or question, the latter as a response to someone else's utterance. Entry utterances appear to be eliciting responses; exit utterances subsume various kinds of verbal reinforcers.

Other categories are variations on the kinds of *entries* and *exits;* for example, one such category is *considering-supporting,* a teacher's utterance expressing positive affect; *rebuking-criticizing* is expressing negative affect. The categories also require a distinction between questions and statements related to the topic of a lesson or an interchange and those that are not.

Behaviorally, these distinctions may not be important, except those made among kinds of reinforcers. If, however, large amounts of nonsubstantive comments were symptomatic of disinterest, or incipient disorder, or lack of understanding, then counting such behaviors is useful. An analysis of the teacher's responses which preceded them might help us to identify causal links. But the system does not record utterances to which the teacher does not attend, thus probably ignoring some remarks that might be indicators of undesirable pupil behavior or pupil behavior that might have been used constructively by the teacher.

Medley's system requires careful attention to each response made by the teacher and students and their relations to each other (25:29-38). This characteristic and others, with the qualifications noted above, make Medley's system a potentially useful tool for behavioral analysis.

A comparison of Medley's and Flanders's systems suggests that the behavioral analysis of teaching behavior is not simply a problem of specifying teaching behavior in terms of observables. (Both systems are sufficiently specific for reliable coding.) A behavioral analysis should specify linkages between teacher behavior and student behavior. The operational definition of teacher behavior requires a description of the response expected of the student or of the effect that the teacher's response is to have on the student responding. Neither Medley's nor Flanders's systems meets this requirement.

Technical skills of teaching. An early experiment in behavior modification of teacher behavior illustrates how behavioral analysis may be applied to meet these criteria (24:27-58). In this experiment the teacher behavior to be acquired was a reinforcing behavior to be linked to students' responses in a discussion-type lesson. Each time a student made a comment or asked or answered a question the teacher was to reward this participatory response. The rewarding behavior was to be positive verbal or nonverbal approval, given as soon as possible after a student's utterance and, when feasible, during it. Rewarding behavior was offered irrespective of the formal correctness of the student's comment.

The test of the success of the behavior modification procedure, which consisted in reinforcing the desired teacher behavior, was the increase in teacher and student responses. The two most effective procedures showed marked increases in both teacher-rewarding behavior and student participatory behavior (24:40-56).

Related behavior modification experiments used similar linkages as the behaviors to be acquired by both teachers and students. The dependent variables in these experiments came to be called the *technical skills of teaching* because they were general skills that could be used independently of the content being taught (8). Technical skills were of two kinds: reinforcers, and eliciting responses, such as *probing* (a teacher's response which followed a student's response to a previous question and which was to elicit further elaboration by the student). Unfortunately, students' responses were not always analyzed in all of these experiments; while the data indicate substantial changes in teacher behavior, similar data are not available for changes in student behavior.[5]

Unfortunately, the concept of the technical skills of teaching

5. There were several reasons for this omission. The primary concern in the research was the modification of teaching behavior. It was thought that student behavior could be brought to maximum strength. Also, there were only very general ideas about what kinds of student behavior would be modified by the specific teaching behavior. These reasons are not necessarily compelling. But they were reassuring to the investigators who had a complex research program to manage and to those students who performed some of this research to meet the requirements of a doctoral dissertation.

has been overly promoted and inaccurately described.[6] They are not basic or essential because there are no data to show that a teacher who uses them produces more effective learning. They may have important effects on learning but that remains to be shown.

These skills are behavioral dyads which are easily acquired when behavioral modification techniques are used. The concept of a technical skill does embody the definitional requirements spelled out above. Each skill was an observable and easily countable teacher response linked (with some exceptions) to a specified and also easily countable student behavior. These response pairs were thus defined functionally and independently of the substantive character of verbal utterances on the topic of interchange between teacher and student.

This set of teaching skills does not represent a theory of teaching nor were they inducted from observations of teachers in classrooms. Relatively few instances of them occur in everyday teaching. Rather, the experimental work in which these skills were the dependent variables illustrates both the concept of teaching responses as behavioral dyads and the ease with which such dyads may be acquired when their learning is engineered by using behavioral modification techniques.

Some problems became apparent when more complex behaviors, such as asking "higher-order" questions, were chosen as dependent variables. Higher-order questions require evaluating, analyzing, synthesizing, and generalizing behaviors from students. Asking an evaluative question, for example, is a necessary but not a sufficient condition for eliciting an evaluative response. We may speculate that either of two kinds of responses must be inserted after the teacher's question: a second response by the teacher which models the desired response and is followed by another question; or, a series of subquestions which shape the desired response. (We assume that when the appropriate student response occurs or is approximated that it is reinforced.)

These studies generally showed significant changes in teacher behavior, but when student behavior was examined, changes were

---

6. See Cooper and Allen (11) for an example of the trivia out of which a case is made for the technical skills–microteaching approach.

not as marked.[7] Obviously, the teacher behavior was controlled more by the experimenter than by the students, but we would expect the change to disappear when the experimenter's control was removed.

These analyses suggested that the conception of the behavioral response complex was too simple. The appropriate stimulus to elicit, at least initially, a complex student behavior such as an evaluative response is probably a set of teacher responses. A behavioral analysis of teaching will, therefore, yield complexes of responses functionally related to each other. Some will be dyads, some triads, and others, chains. Combinations of eliciting, modeling, and reinforcing responses will be involved.

Such an analysis should begin with a description of the desired student response. Then, combinations of teachers' responses should be attached to them. Some of these functional complexes may be discovered in actual teaching; others will have to be generated heuristically and tested empirically.

RESEARCH ON THE MODIFICATION
OF TEACHING BEHAVIOR

The use of the videotape camera and recorder and the development of microteaching have prepared the way for the application of behavior modification techniques to teacher training. However, there are relatively few instances of the use of these devices in behavior modification paradigms. Instead, they have been used in the practice-feedback paradigm. Their power for behavioral control has not been exploited because the behavioral analysis needed to create such power has been neglected.[8]

A typical example is the study by Young (38). Young's experiment had the following components: (a) a behavior or set of behaviors to be changed was selected, serving as the dependent variable in the experiment; (b) teacher trainees were assigned to

7. For example, the author had the data in the Claus study (10) analyzed to see if the students imitated the teachers' behavior by asking more higher-order questions. The changes in student behavior were inconsequential.

8. Carl E. Thoresen and his associates at Stanford are studying the personal competencies of classroom teachers, using a behavior modification model that stresses behavior analysis and assessments, among other things.

experimental and control groups and taught four brief sessions to a small group of students (microteaching); (c) feedback was provided using videotapes of the immediately preceding teaching session—in this study the feedback was mediated either by a colleague or an experienced supervisor. The frequency of the behaviors chosen as the dependent variable is counted, and a statistical test is performed to compare the experimental and control groups.

The dependent variable in Young's experiment was two sets of teaching behaviors, *orienting students to the learning task*, and *reinforcing student behavior*. Each of these categories was defined by a list of easily observable and countable behaviors. Using the count of "total specific behaviors" for *orienting students to the learning task*, a significant difference was found favoring the experimental group. The reinforcing behaviors were separated into two kinds, verbal and nonverbal. Out of eight verbal behaviors, three produced significant differences, two favoring the control group; of ten nonverbal behaviors, three were significant, all favoring the control group.[9] The results were meager and equivocal.

Another experiment by Roush (29) is also illustrative of the experimental paradigms in which videotape recorders have been used as part of the feedback system. Roush assigned a teacher trainee to each of five groups: (a) videotape feedback only; (b) video-audio feedback; (c) audio feedback only; (d) video-audio critiques and typescript; (e) no feedback. The criterion variable was the I/D ratio, an index derived from using the categories in Flanders's system (the ratio of indirect influence behaviors to the total of direct and indirect influence behaviors). Roush found no differences among the treatment groups.

The reader may wonder why two studies which produced so little are described here. There are several reasons. First, these experiments have the aura of behavior modification about them but do not fit the behavior modification paradigm. Second, they have features which, if modified, would make them "true" behavior modification experiments. Third, they are aspects of these studies which make demonstrating behavior modification very difficult.

9. The control group is not properly labeled in this experiment. It is another treatment which differs from the experimental treatment only in the source of the feedback.

This type of experiment appears to be a behavior modification experiment for two reasons, one quite superficial. Experiments such as these purport to "change behavior." In both cases, however, even though the behavior to be changed is defined concretely enough to be observed, a behavioral analysis has *not* been made of the dependent variables. One proof of this assertion is that some of the behaviors in Young's two categories do not even occur. Hence, the experimental treatment is reinforcing only those behaviors which do occur.

This comment may not seem like a justifiable criticism unless one considers that in modifying teaching behavior one must be concerned about both operants and responses which must be elicited. One could wait, of course, until the latter type occurs. Many of these behaviors, however, are already under the control of contingencies *other* than those mediated by the experimenter. *Smiling*, chosen to be reinforced because it is assumed to be a reinforcer for students, is under stimulus control over which the experimenter has little influence.

The experimental treatment must be designed in one way for strengthening operants and another way for eliciting and strengthening responses for which the base rate is zero. A behavioral analysis of each teacher's response repertoire must *precede* the choice of a treatment to be applied to modify his behavior. Many, if not all, of the experiments performed with the videotape recorder, as well as the procedures which are used in practice, ignore this rule.

The second defect of this type of study from the viewpoint of behavior modification principles is that the reinforcement contingencies are not precisely defined. In Young's experiment, the supervisory sessions involved self-analysis and discussion. The contingency technique is not related to specific behaviors except in a very general way. Roush's experiment illustrates that the camera is essentially a display device and no more. Watching one's recorded performance may be a mechanism through which reinforcements may be mediated vicariously. But this process is not likely to occur in the early stages of learning.

Experiments cast in this paradigm are not likely to produce significant behavior changes because the treatment is not under tight experimental control for the reasons cited above. The procedures used might be effective if carried out over longer periods of time. But in this form they are at best rather remote approximations to behavior modification procedures.

Unfortunately, the widespread usage of the videotape recorder has led to the belief that it is a touchstone to instant success in training. The nostrums prescribed for its use are simplistic. For example, the "best" techniques for using the videotape recorder have been described by Cyphert and Andrews (12). The methods suggested include immediate feedback to the trainee as well as demonstration and feedback on specific teaching behaviors. Although these suggestions are reasonable, and even though they use the language of behavior modification, their application in research and practice shows little sophistication in behavior modification techniques.

An example of the appropriate use of a behavior modification paradigm is provided in an experiment by McDonald and Allen (24). In this study, the dependent variable was a teacher response, rewarding students' participatory responses. Four experimental treatments were used: (a) self-viewing of one's videotaped performance, rating it on very general characteristics; (b) self-viewing, rating the performance on frequency of rewarding behaviors; (c) viewing one's performance with an experimenter who emitted positive reinforcers every time the desired behavior appeared on the videotaped projection; and (d) self-viewing with an experimenter who both reinforced the desired responses and noted instances where the responses should have been emitted.

Four learning trials were used. The teaching took place in the teacher's regular classes. Twenty-minute video recordings were made of the main portion of the lessons in which teachers conducted a class discussion.

The third and fourth treatments produced significantly more behavior changes, the fourth yielding more than the third. Data were also collected on the frequency of student response. The same treatments produced significantly more student responses in the same pattern as was observed for the changes in the teachers' behavior.

A limited kind of behavioral analysis preceded this experiment.

It was known that teachers varied considerably in the frequency with which they emitted the reinforcing response to be learned. The data from the first learning trial confirmed this experience; each teacher manifested the desired behavior in some form.

An assumption about the nature of the independent variable was made that should be noted. Subcategories of verbal and nonverbal reinforcers were treated as psychologically equivalent. Thus, a smile or a head nod were both classified as positive nonverbal reinforcers. Various kinds of verbal statements were treated as positive verbal reinforcers.

There are advantages in this procedure. One advantage is that the reinforcement contingencies administered by the experimenter are applied to a class of behaviors so that the response class makes educational sense. Another advantage is that the procedure also increases the number of reinforcers that the experimenter will emit, thus increasing the probability that the treatment will be effective. A third advantage is that analyzing each discrete behavior in a category may be avoided, a procedure likely to lead to inclusive results for purely statistical reasons.

The disadvantage is that the validity of the assumption of comparable reinforcing effects of subcategories is unknown. It is also untestable in experiments of this kind where the teachers are conducting lessons with different content and where, if the teaching occurs in regular classrooms, the students have not been assigned randomly to treatments.

Variations in feedback processes. Now that the point has been made that studies using the video recorder at best approximate an application of a behavior modification paradigm to a training problem, credit should be given to those investigators, like Young and Roush, for experimenting with feedback variables. Their studies accomplish two purposes. They test popular conceptions of what constitutes appropriate feedback procedures. They also help us understand the kinds of contingencies that are likely to be effective in modifying teaching behavior.

Investigators, for example, have studied "openness to feedback" (7, 15), combinations of live supervision and supervision from video recordings (31), the relation of correction feedback to opportunity to practice after feedback (5), critical self-appraisal (9), and direct and indirect supervisory feedback (1). With the exception of Aubertine's study, these studies yielded no significant differences favoring any treatment. This lack of differences is not interpretable.

The consistent lack of differences across these different variations on feedback is striking. One explanation is that the lack of differences is due to poor experimental design and methodology. Another explanation is one we have repeatedly alluded to—the dependent variable is so grossly defined that it is simply a very poor metric for detecting treatment differences. The most persuasive explanation is that the treatments provide very weak contingency management.

This lack of results provides a cautionary note about assuming that video recordings have some inherent magic for modifying behavior. It also alerts us that our commonsense notions about effective characteristics of supervisory feedback are simplistic.

Unstudied variables in the feedback process. There are several kinds of variables that may be associated with the feedback process, most of which have not appeared in the research literature. One category of such variables is that describing the source of the feedback. Feedback may be self-administered (rarely an effective treatment), or administered by another person who may be a peer or a superior, such as a supervisor, or one's students. Feedback may be provided by persons who are more or less prestigious, of the same or different sex, age, race, or personality characteristics.

The feedback may occur in a face-to-face interchange or may be mediated through recordings, transcripts, ratings, or frequency counts. The feedback may be immediate or delayed. (The meanings of these terms change when a video recording is used. In that context, "immediate" means as soon after the teaching session as possible.)

A third category includes the different kinds of substantive and affective content exchanged between trainer and trainee. The substance may be no more than positive or negative comments on a teaching performance, or descriptive commentary, or suggestions for altering behavior. The interchange style may be a set of indirect influence attempts, heuristic strategies, or didactic instructions. The affective tone may be personal or impersonal.

Few comparisons have been made among these potential modalities of the feedback system. The relatively few comparisons that have been tried do not seem to enhance the effectiveness of the feedback. The exception is a feedback system based on contingency reinforcement management techniques.

Whether it is worth making the large number of comparisons derivable from this list is moot, particularly when the proposed comparison has little to recommend other than current beliefs about effective strategies. A theoretical model of the feedback process ought to be the stimulus for research on characteristics of the feedback process likely to be effective in modifying teaching behavior.

Variations on feedback as contingency management. The simplest and most promising approach from a behavior modification point of view is to analyze modes of feedback as variations in contingency management. A relatively complex example will illustrate the point.

Tuckman et al. (36) manipulated the feedback process in relation to the discrepancy between a teacher's self-perception of his teaching behavior and his observed behavior. Three conditions were feedback treatments; in one treatment trainees were given information (verbal feedback) on their behavior by an observer in the form of frequency counts; in a second condition the trainees listened to their own performance; in the third condition trainees coded each other's teaching performances and exchanged the information. The fourth treatment was a no-feedback control group.

Behavior change occurred in all feedback groups, but the giving of feedback by an independent observer produced the most, and only, statistically significant change. Self-perceptions also changed in the direction of greater consistency with actual performance.

Reduction in discrepancy may be regarded as a reinforcing event.[10] Thus, the lack of an interaction between feedback and initial discrepancy scores may be regarded as the consequence of the introducing of a reinforcing event after each trial. The design does not permit deriving empirical support for this interpretation; some support for it is found in the fact that teachers with the highest discrepancy scores changed their perceptions the most.

10. For a discussion of cognitive representations of reinforcing events see Bandura (6:35-37).

The most effective treatment, *verbal feedback*, was the most informative. Obtaining information to reduce a perceptual discrepancy may also be regarded as a reinforcing event. Thus, two kinds of reinforcing events might be present in these treatments.

Although some investigators may prefer a dissonance theory interpretation of these results (though it is debatable whether the design permits such an interpretation), a contingency management analysis of the study is suggestive of ways in which complex feedback systems may be analyzed in terms of the contingency management paradigm.[11] If studies which yielded no differences among feedback treatments were analyzed to identify reinforcing events and then redesigned, more consistent and significant results might be obtained.

OBSERVATIONAL LEARNING AND

THE MODIFICATION OF TEACHING BEHAVIOR

It was pointed out earlier in this chapter that teacher educators advocate that teacher trainees observe experienced teachers and other forms of demonstrations of effective teaching. Despite what appears to be an almost universal acceptance of the importance of such observational learning, training processes have remained untouched by recent developments in social learning theory (6). There is a paucity of research in teacher education on observational learning. Although there is an extensive literature on the observation of teacher performance, a miniscule number of studies exist on how to *learn from observing*. (This lack is also true of other professional training programs, such as counselor training.)

A few comments on the observational paradigm are appropriate. To learn by observing another's performance, three conditions seem necessary: (a) the learner must be able to watch the actions of the person from whom he or she is learning; (b) the learner must be cued on what is to be watched and later performed; (c) the learner must have the capacity for making the responses to be acquired. The watching process may be either direct observation of another's behavior or viewing of his performance on film and videotape, reading a description of his performance, or listening to an audio-

11. For an experimental analysis of the relation of beliefs about reinforcing events to behavior change see Kaufman, Baron, and Kopp (17).

tape of the other person's verbal performance (6:6-7). Other conditions include: (a) the learner must be motivated to want to adopt the behavior of the person whom he is observing; (b) the learner must be reinforced for adopting the behavior, either vicariously or by an external agent or event (6:20-35). While all of these conditions do not apply to all kinds of observable learning, they seem warranted in maximizing learning through observation.

To use these principles in teacher training requires only that training sessions be organized so that the principles are used. Essentially this means that there must be an opportunity to observe a teaching behavior and reinforcing events associated with emitting the behavior.

A typical training paradigm includes a session for observing a model who emits a behavior to be learned by the trainee, followed by a session in which the trainee attempts the same behavior, followed by another session in which he is reinforced for those instances of the desired behavior which he has emitted. Video recording and microteaching are very useful for organizing a tight and economical set of training sessions.

The trainee in the first session views a model performing a teaching behavior such as reinforcing students for participating in the classroom discussion. After watching the model, the trainee teaches a brief session in which he or she attempts the same behavior. This practice session is followed by another in which the trainee is reinforced for imitating the observed behaviors.

The addition of this last session may or may not be necessary because the event in which the teaching behavior is emitted may or may not provide reinforcing events. A teacher asking higher-order questions, for example, may receive few, if any, answers desired. The teacher is not being reinforced for asking these questions and is likely to stop asking them. A session in which the teacher views his teaching with an experimenter provides an opportunity for reinforcing this behavior.

The research that has undergirded Bandura's social learning theory attacked the problem of the relation of reinforcing contingencies to the acquisition of behavior by observing another's behavior. The problem is quite complex (6). In general, some kind of reinforcing event must be present even though it may be attached only to the model's behavior. The principle generally accepted is that observation by the learner is sufficient for acquiring a behavior even if this behavior is not reinforced during the acquisition. The necessary condition, however, is that the model's behavior must be reinforced by its consequences. It is also generally accepted that the behavior which has been acquired will be maintained in strength only if it is reinforced when performed.

The training paradigm described above assumes that the model's behavior is not being reinforced. If, however, it were being reinforced, the addition of the reinforcement session may not be necessary. Extrapolation of the results of studies in other contexts suggests that this reinforcement session would be unnecessary during the acquisition phase.

A study by Claus supports this prediction (10). Claus assigned trainees randomly to one of four conditions. The training paradigm involved two viewing sessions—one of a model, the other, of one's own performance. An experimenter was present during both, neither, or one or the other of the two sessions, thus yielding four experimental treatments. The function of the experimenter was to point out instances of the desired behavior in the model's or trainee's teaching.

If we assume that cueing during the feedback sessions was a reinforcing event, then this experiment provides a comparison of modeling and reinforcement sessions during the acquisition phase of learning a teaching behavior. The assumption is plausible since the trainees knew what behavior they were to acquire. The cueing during feedback had no significant effect. Even observing a model without cueing from an experimenter was more effective than cueing during a feedback session.

This study also supports another principle derived from other research relevant to social learning theory: that controlling the observer's attention is necessary. In Claus's study, a cued modeling session was more effective than a noncued session. This result is particularly important for developing training paradigms using modeling because it supports the necessity of using cueing procedures. The learner must actually observe the behavior to be acquired, which seems rather obvious. But observing teaching is complicated by the large number of behaviors that may be observed.

A cueing procedure is necessary to focus the trainee's attention on the behavior to be acquired.

Imitating a teacher's behavior. The idea of imitating another teacher's behavior arouses several different reactions. Slavish imitation is generally regarded as undesirable and certainly as beneath an adult. Another view is that teaching requires creativity, so observing another teacher may be helpful as a way of storing problem-solving alternatives. A third view is that imitating some classes of responses may be helpful but each teacher has his or her own style. These views are somewhat removed from reality. Teachers do inquire of other teachers to learn effective teaching practices. (Giving information in this way is an attenuated form of symbolic modeling.) Teachers will imitate another teacher slavishly, and observations of teachers do not reveal great variations in teaching style.

Behind these views, however, is a significant point. Students vary from class to class, particularly in their responsivity to teachers. The content taught also differs. In real life it is rarely practicable to imitate highly specific teaching responses. But, some responses are quite imitable; for example, a question that initiates a discussion: "Why do you think that Napoleon chose to campaign in Russia?" Similar substantive questions occur again and again.

The issues posed by these various views do not seem to have much substance, but they do point to a practical difficulty. Unless the conditions of teaching are highly similar, transfer to one's own teaching of what has been learned by observing may be difficult.

There is also another problem. Even if the teaching conditions in the observed and practice sessions are highly similar, as they are when microteaching is used, the learner may have to generate other instances of a class of behaviors.

After we had performed a series of experiments (the first of which is reported in McDonald and Allen), I became concerned about the inconsequential and insignificant results we were obtaining. There were a number of explanations that seemed plausible, such as too many experimental groups for too few subjects, differences between sex of the model and the observers, inadequate cueing procedures, and others. However, I noted that in the early studies of modeling the responses imitated were highly specific and represented only a class of responses in the mind of the researcher. It seemed that we might be having problems because the learners had to generate their own instances of classes of responses. Therefore, we designed a study in which some trainees had to teach the same lesson as the model while others taught a lesson of their own choosing (8:8-24). The trainees all taught a lesson of their own choosing in the last of the training trials, thus providing a test of the transferability of the skills which were observed and to be learned.

Those trainees who practiced the same lesson as the model taught produced significantly more instances of the behavior which was to be observed. But the differences washed out on the transfer task. Our concern about the problem of generating new instances in a class of responses seemed justified.

A study by Lange (20) illustrates another facet of this problem. Lange exposed trainees to a "high I/D" model. Trainees in this treatment produced significantly more I/D behavior than other trainees exposed to a nonhigh model. You will recall that Flanders's Interaction Analysis produces counts of more gross kinds of teaching behavior. The system also uses categories that describe processes such as asking questions and which, with the exception of categories describing affect, does not use the content of an interchange to classify it. In contrast, to ask higher-order questions, which was the dependent variable in the study described above, the teacher must do considerable cognitive work. It seems reasonable, therefore, to hypothesize that modeling will be more or less effective depending on the cognitive complexity of the behavior being observed. It is my opinion, however, that the modeling techniques themselves created some difficulties for the observer.

Cueing. To sort out those characteristics of the modeling procedures which will make them uniformly effective is not easy. In the study described above we used two other experimental conditions to work on this problem. Some trainees saw a "pure" model, that is, one where only instances of the desired behavior occurred. Others saw a mixed model. These differences in modeling conditions did not produce significant differences. We had always used a minimal form of cueing. Trainees were given some information about the behavior to be learned, but obviously this technique was not very powerful. The Claus study, discussed above, was designed to test a more powerful cueing, which turned out to be highly effective. These results were particularly significant because the same class of behaviors were studied as had been in the earlier experiment, using pure and mixed models.

Symbolic vs. perceptual modeling. Considerable amounts of printed training materials are distributed to teachers. Some of these are descriptions of methods to be used; others are protocols of classroom interactions. They describe responses to be made or responses that were made. Presumably, a trainee can learn how to reproduce these responses from reading descriptions of them. (The conditions under which such learning occurs simply has not been studied.)

This type of presentation has been called *symbolic* modeling because the responses to be acquired are described in symbols—words. It contrasts with *perceptual* modeling, which is a display of an actual performance, live or mediated. Although it may seem that perceptual modeling will be more effective than symbolic modeling, the difficulties involved in controlling an observer's attention when he is viewing a performance considerably attenuate whatever advantages such displays may have, as we have seen.

We conducted several studies comparing these two kinds of modeling. One kind is included in the study using pure and mixed models and two kinds of practice sessions described above. The models were presented in both symbolic and perceptual forms. These treatments failed to yield significant differences.

The first study comparing these modes was done by Orme and is reported in McDonald and Allen (24:83-144). Orme varied the two modes to give them different degrees of assumed strength. For example, during feedback sessions an experimenter provided instructions on instances where the behavior being learned might occur. In other conditions, an experimenter cued the observer while the latter watched the model. There were no significant differences among the groups although the means were in the predicted order of differences in effectiveness.

These results were particularly disappointing since the treatments had the necessary conditions in them, such as cueing, and the behavior to be learned was a simple, process-type response. An experiment by John J. Koran (18) which contrasted modeling to a problem-solving training technique and used symbolic and perceptual models also produced no differences between the modeling modes. Again, however, his results were suggestive since his group differences, although not statistically significant, were arrayed according to his predictions.

We were encouraged by the consistency of the results, though we were aware that they had limited meaning because of the lack of statistical significance. The only explanation that we could generate for these results was a statistical one: there were too many experimental conditions for the number of trainees in each treatment. Latter experiments, such as the one done by Claus, reduced the number of treatments and found modeling conditions to be differentially effective.

One line of attack on this problem was to study the effects of differences in aptitude for processing the different kinds of information represented in symbolic and perceptual models. Perceptual models require aptitudes for processing visual information; symbolic models, aptitudes for processing semantic information. Perhaps the lack of differences that we were finding resulted from using measures of the performances of learners with different aptitudes who had been exposed to the same type of model. Mary L. Koran et al. used symbolic and perceptual models with trainees whose aptitudes for processing different kinds of information had been measured (19). She found statistically significant differences favoring the perceptual modeling treatment and complex interactions between aptitude and treatment. These interactions, however, did little to improve our understanding of the function of aptitude in this kind of training.

This summary of research and experience should make clear that the problems of using modeling procedures for facilitating the acquisition of teaching behavior are complex. The results are consistent with previous research but not as conclusive. When results were not significant, they were at least seemingly ordered in line with theoretical expectations. In retrospect, the experimental designs may have been so complicated that they were leading us into a Type II error of inference.

In my opinion there is little question that this line of research should be continued. There is every reason to believe that the easy availability of the video recorder will stimulate the use of demonstrations in training. We should learn how to make effective use of modeling concepts and principles. Economy and efficiency will be achieved if we can develop more effective modeling procedures to teach effective teaching behavior.

The reader probably has generated a number of variables characterizing the modeling process whose influence should be studied. Two major lines of inquiry should not be overlooked. First, the optimum relation of modeling to reinforcement techniques has not been found. Second, the optimum differential use of modeling and reinforcement procedures for learning different kinds of teaching behavior has not been studied.

MICROTEACHING AS A BEHAVIOR MODIFICATION TECHNIQUE

Much of what has been written about microteaching is promotional and even misleading. The claims made for its effectiveness have little substance in fact. More disappointing is the fact that the original conception and rationale for microteaching has been lost sight of, a point significant in the context of a discussion of behavior modification in teacher education. Originally, microteaching was devised as a procedure for facilitating behavioral control.[12] Further, it was used as a way of creating a more effective experimental paradigm which for the first time made it possible to use sophisticated experimental designs in learning studies. The purpose of these learning studies was to assess the relative effectiveness of modeling and reinforcement variables in facilitating the acquisition of teaching behaviors.

Microteaching, as almost everyone knows, is a brief teaching episode. The length of the teaching session is typically in the range of five to twenty minutes. The size of the class is variable, usually four to seven students. In the course of the early experimental research which studied the application of behavior modification techniques, the length of the teaching session was limited to five minutes. The reason for this choice was a practical one. A series of five-minute sessions interspersed with short feedback or demonstra-

12. The first experiment using microteaching was performed by Aubertine (5). I suggested that he use brief teaching sessions and small groups. I got the idea from reading Horowitz's research reported in Tagiuri and Petrullo (32:191-208).

tion sessions yielded a practicable number of learning trials for behavior modification experiments. Also, limiting the number of students in the teaching session made it practical to run a large number of teaching sessions. The reader can make the point of these changes dramatic by calculating the number of students needed to perform an experiment involving four successive teaching sessions for each of fifty trainees if different students are used each session. Similar calculations will illustrate the practical advantages of using sessions of five minutes' length.

It quickly becomes apparent that microteaching had considerable utility for training. But many of the people who began to use it apparently saw it as a controlled type of practice. Many users of microteaching apparently did not see the relevance of behavior modification principles used in the experimentation which was being done.[13] These experiments amply demonstrated how to apply behavior modification principles and supplied useful guidelines for using them in microteaching.

Microteaching remains an unstudied technique. The literature that purports to be research on it is deplorable. A recent review makes the usual mistake of confusing behavior modification studies with research on microteaching (21). There is only one study listed in that review that is a study of the technique itself. That study shows no demonstrable effect of microteaching (16).

The basic question of the relation of microteaching training to subsequent real-life performance has never been established. Studies cited to support the claim of a positive correlation between performances in the two settings have been badly designed. These studies have used the *Stanford Appraisal Guide*, a questionable measurement device to measure teaching effectiveness. Little connection exists between the training that occurred in the microteaching clinic at Stanford and what that instrument measured. Unfortunately, this research was never published. Because of this, the excessive claims made for microteaching have not been tempered by the data of empirical studies.

---

13. For example, the Microteaching Clinic at Stanford under Dwight W. Allen's direction made only the most casual application of behavior modification techniques. Moreover, the clinic was regularly staffed by substantial numbers of assistants who had antibehaviorist views.

The most undesirable consequence of the promotion of micro-teaching was that the role of behavior modification in training was obscured. When a trainee acquired a skill, it was because he or she had been reinforced for attempting the skill or had observed a model performing the skill. Microteaching made it possible to apply these techniques with great efficiency. Aspects of microteaching are worth investigating for very practical reasons. The optimum length of the session should be studied, as it bears on the learning of different skills. The sheer practice aspects of the technique should also be studied. Systems of microteaching modules ought to be studied to assess the effect of consistent and integrated training on subsequent performance and as a way of analyzing the acquisition and development of complex skills.

Beyond research of this kind there is very little else about microteaching as a methodological device that is worth studying. What is worth investigating is the applications of behavioral modification principles that can be made when microteaching is used.

Conclusion

Hopefully, this chapter has said to the reader that the training of teachers is a rich field to mine for applications of behavior modification technology. The research discussed here has shown what can be done and what problems need to be solved. The technology of microteaching and the video recorder increase the scope of application tremendously.

One of the interesting features of the research on these applications and pseudoapplications is their experimental character. In some cases the research designs leave much to be desired. But, again, the available technology will improve the work being done. More importantly, teacher educators and psychologists have begun to realize that we can experiment with training processes.

Most reassuring is the fact that when behavior modification principles have been used, they have worked. Many more applications, however, must be made before teacher educators will be convinced of the viability of this approach. Hopefully, this chapter will have illustrated the wisdom and utility of pursuing these applications.

REFERENCES

1. Acheson, Keith A. "The Effects of Feedback from Television Recordings and Three Types of Supervisory Treatments." Ph.D. dissertation, Stanford University, 1964.
2. Allen, Dwight W., and Ryan, Kevin A. *Microteaching.* Reading, Mass.: Addison-Wesley Publishing Co., 1969.
3. Amidon, Edmund J., and Flanders, Ned A. *The Role of the Teacher in the Classroom: A Manual for Understanding and Improving Teachers' Classroom Behavior.* Minneapolis, Minn.: Paul S. Amidon Associates, 1963.
4. Amidon, Edmund J., and Simon, Anita. "Teacher-Pupil Interaction." *Review of Educational Research* 25 (1965): 130-40.
5. Aubertine, Horace E. "The Set Induction Process and Its Application in Teaching." *Journal of Educational Research* 61 (1968): 363-67.
6. Bandura, Albert. *Social Learning Theory.* New York: General Learning Press, 1971.
7. Baron, Bennie G. "An Investigation of the Effect of Videotape and Microteaching Technique on Openness." Ph.D. dissertation, University of Southern Mississippi, 1967.
8. Berliner, David C. *Microteaching and the Technical Skills of Teaching Approach to Teacher Training.* Technical Report no. 8, Stanford Center for Research and Development in Teaching, Stanford, Calif., 1969.)
9. Brooks, Albert D. "Effect of Alternate Techniques for Modifying Teacher Behavior." Ph.D. dissertation, Stanford University, 1967.
10. Claus, Karen. *Effects of Modeling and Feedback Treatments on the Development of Teachers' Questioning Skills.* Technical Report no. 7, Stanford Center for Research and Development in Teaching, Stanford, Calif., 1969 (ED 033 081).
11. Cooper, James M., and Allen, Dwight W. *Microteaching: History and Present Status.* Final Report, Research Project, no. OEC 0-8-080490-2706(010), U.S. Office of Education, Washington, 1970. (ED 036 471)
12. Cyphert, Frederick R., and Andrews, L. L. "Using the Videotaper in Teacher Education." *Audiovisual Instruction* 12 (1967): 1067-69.
13. Flanders, Ned A. *Analyzing Teaching Behavior.* Reading, Mass.: Addison-Wesley Publishing Co., 1970.
14. Flanders, Ned A. *Teacher Influence, Pupil Attitudes, and Achievement.* Cooperative Research Monograph, no. 12, OE-25040. Washington: U.S. Government Printing Office, 1965.
15. Fuller, Frances F., et al. *Effects of Personalized Feedback during Teacher Preparation on Teacher Personality and Teacher Behavior.*

Report Series, no. 4. University of Texas Research and Development Center on Teacher Education.

16. Kallenbach, W. W., and Gall, M. D. "Microteaching versus Conventional Methods in Training Elementary Intern Teachers." *Journal of Educational Research* 63 (1969): 136-41.

17. Kaufman, Arnold; Baron, Alan; and Kopp, Rosemarie E. "Some Effects of Instructions on Human Operant Behavior." *Psychonomic Monograph Supplements* 1 (1966): 243-50.

18. Koran, John J. *The Relative Effects of Imitation versus Problem Solving on the Acquisition of Inquiry Behavior by Intern Teachers.* Technical Report, no. 11, Stanford Center for Research and Development in Teaching, Stanford, Calif., 1970.

19. Koran, Mary L.; Snow, Richard E.; and McDonald, Frederick J. "Teacher Aptitude and Observational Learning of a Teaching Skill." *Journal of Educational Psychology* 62 (1971): 219-28.

20. Lange, Donald N. "An application of Social Learning Theory in Effecting Change in a Group of Student Teachers Using Video Modeling Techniques." *Journal of Educational Research* 65 (1971): 151-54.

21. McAleese, W. R., and Univin, Derick. "A Selective Survey of Microteaching." *Programmed Learning and Educational Technology* 8 (1971): 10-21.

22. McDonald, Frederick J. "The Evaluation of Teaching Behavior." In *Competency-based Teacher Education: Progress, Problems, and Prospects*, edited by R. B. Howsam and W. R. Houston. Chicago: Science Research Associates, forthcoming.

23. McDonald, Frederick J. "The Influence of Learning Theories on Education (1900-1950)." In *Theories of Learning and Instruction*, Sixty-third yearbook of the National Society for the Study of Education, Part I, edited by E. R. Hilgard, pp. 1-16. Chicago: Distributed by the University of Chicago Press, 1964.

24. McDonald, Frederick J., and Allen, Dwight W. *Training Effects of Feedback and Modeling Procedures on Teaching Performance.* Final Report, Research Project, no. OE-6-10-078, U.S. Office of Education. Stanford, Calif.: Stanford University, 1967.

25. Medley, Donald M.; Schluck, Carolyn G.; and Ames, Nancy P. *Assessing the Learning Environment in the Classroom: A Manual for Users of OSCAR SV.* Research Memorandum 68-9. Princeton, N.J.: Educational Testing Service, 1968.

26. Ramp, Eugene; Ulrich, Roger; and Dulaney, Sylvia. "Delayed Timeout As a Procedure for Reducing Disruptive Classroom Behavior: A Case Study." *Journal of Applied Behavior Analysis* 4 (1971): 235-40.

27. Rosenshine, Barak. "Evaluation of Classroom Instruction." *Review of Educational Research* 40 (1970): 279-300.

28. Rosenshine, Barak. "The Stability of Teacher Effects upon Student Achievement." *Review of Educational Research* 40 (1970): 647-62.
29. Roush, Robert E. *A Study of Change in Selected Teacher Education Interns' Behavior Using Videotape Recordings.* Final Report, Research Project, no. 8-G-944, U.S. Office of Education, Washington, n.d.
30. Salzburg, Bernard H., et al. "The Effect of Intermittent Contingent Access to Play on Printing of Kindergarten Children." *Journal of Applied Behavior Analysis* 4 (1971): 163-72.
31. Schueler, Herbert, and Gold, Milton J. "Video Recordings of Student Teachers—A Report of the Hunter College Research Project Evaluating the Use of Kinescopes in Preparing Student Teachers." *Journal of Teacher Education* 15 (1964): 358-64.
32. Tagiuri, R., and Petrullo, L., eds. *Person Perception and Interpersonal Behavior.* Stanford, Calif.: Stanford University Press, 1958.
33. "Teacher Education Models." *Journal of Research and Development in Education* 2 (1969): 3-136.
34. Thoresen, C. E. Paper on file.
35. Thoresen, C. E., and Krumboltz, J. D. "Relationship of Counselor Reinforcement of Selected Responses to External Behavior." *Journal of Counseling Psychology* 14 (1967): 140-44.
36. Tuckman, Bruce W.; McCall, Kendrick M.; and Hyman, Ronald T. "The Modification of Teacher Behavior: Effects of Dissonance and Coded Feedback." *American Educational Research Journal* 6 (1969): 607-18.
37. Waimon, Morton D.; Bell, Dennis D.; and Ramseyer, Gary C. "The Effects of Microplanning on the Performance and Attitudes of Prospective Teachers." Paper presented at the American Educational Research Association Conference, New York, February 1971.
38. Young, D. "A Preliminary Report on the Effectiveness of Colleague Supervision on the Acquisition of Selected Teaching Behavior in a Microteaching Series." Paper presented at the meeting of the American Educational Research Association, 1970.

CHAPTER III

Applications of Behavior Principles in Typical Classrooms

WESLEY C. BECKER

Some False Beliefs

Most of the "innovative" ideas from behavioral psychology which are being finally accepted today in educational settings have been known and used by many psychologists and educators for forty years or more. However, widespread applications of this knowledge have been hindered by two factors: (a) conflicting false beliefs and (b) the failure of earlier psychologists to produce research data powerful enough to counter the false beliefs. Only in the past decade have the methods of experimental analysis, originated by B. F. Skinner in laboratory work with animals, been extended to classroom studies in ways which have produced effective demonstrations of the relevance of learning principles to every teaching activity.

TREAT CAUSES NOT SYMPTOMS

In the Thirty-fourth Yearbook of the National Society for the Study of Education, published in 1935, Willard Olson pinpointed the first false belief of concern to us in this discussion.

In general the formulation, 'Treat causes, not symptoms,' is sound, in that it tends to force a study of the factors behind the symptoms. There has appeared, however, from time to time, an uncritical condemnation of the treatment of symptoms in behavior problems—a condemnation based on mere analogy with organic disease or on a wholesale acceptance of theories of behavior causation that reject the formulations of the academic psychology of learning. If the symptom is the result of the repetition of some phase of behavior that has satisfying consequences, there is a clear analogy to the laws of learning as formulated in the acquisition of skill and information or through the experimentation with conditioned reflexes. If such is the case, the removal of the symptom through direct work on a learning basis is synonymous with cure. This view is, of course, heretical to many persons dominated by other systematic approaches.

Nursery schools and other schools are constantly demonstrating that behavior problems in normal children can be modified through the same direct attacks characteristic of learning in other fields (37:374).

The equation of behavior problems with symptoms of disease represents a belief that hindered acceptance of ideas and evidence presented by people like Olson in the 1920s and 1930s and is still a common misconception among professional educators today. Fortunately, classroom teachers have been willing to open their doors to psychologists of different persuasions and allow them to collect evidence to show such beliefs to be false.

SOME CAUSES CAN'T BE HELPED—THIS CHILD CAN'T LEARN

As long as the educational climate was such that teaching failures could be blamed on the children, there was no pressure on the teacher to learn more effective means of dealing with children. Over the years, psychologists, mental health workers, and special educators have trained teachers to ship their failures to someone else or at least to blame the child's home background, his low IQ, his poor motivation, his emotional disturbance, his lack of readiness, or his physical disability for the teaching failure. With the recent advent of the label *learning disability* (for children with normal IQ who fail to learn) there is no teaching failure which cannot be blamed on the child. Very often the belief that a given child cannot learn leads to a self-fulfilling prophecy. If teachers do not try, children do not learn.

Fortunately, this attitude toward failure is changing. The idea that the teacher is responsible for the learning of her students is gaining momentum as persons applying behavior principles in education show that retarded children can learn to read, disadvantaged children can learn language concepts and reading if they are taught, and learning disabilities disappear when more effective beginning reading programs are used. In some of our own work to be reported later, we have provided clear demonstrations that appropriate student behavior is a function of the teacher's behavior.

The teacher is responsible. Furthermore, a variety of demonstrations have shown that teachers can be taught to use effectively the developing technology of education (11, 39).

LEARNING IS THE CHILD'S RESPONSIBILITY

Some teachers may have learned to treat behavior at face value and not to blame children for teaching failures. These teachers may still be hobbled, however, by clichés of the past three decades, namely, "Self-directed learning is the only meaningful learning," "The child must learn at his own rate," "Active participation of the learner is essential," "I can't teach him if he doesn't want to learn." The belief that the child must responsibly participate in the learning process has a valid observational basis for some teachers. Teachers often present lessons which only some children have been prepared for under conditions where only some children are motivated by the teacher's procedures. Under such conditions, only those children who appear to be responsible participants appear to learn. But the premises are false. The problem lies not with the children but with the teaching method. Children can all be made to be active participants in the learning process by a responsible teacher who has learned how to use reinforcing events to motivate active participation in learning and how to select or program instructional sequences appropriate to the individual child's entry behaviors.

As Olson observed in 1934, knowledge of how the principles of learning can be applied in the classroom leads to a straightforward understanding of the teaching process as one of arranging the antecedent and consequent stimulus events which determine what a child learns. With such assured knowledge, the myths about behavior and learning which have held us back can be discarded.

Use of Commonly Available Consequences

The behavioral technologist entering the typical classroom can be at once both overwhelmed by the range and variety of potential reinforcers available to teachers and dismayed by the infrequency with which potential reinforcers are used. In the author's experience with all kinds of classroom behavior problems, it seems that 80 to 90 percent of such problems can be handled by little more than a change in the teacher's verbal behavior, e.g., when she says what to whom. There are three classes of consequences typically available to teachers (without introducing food, prizes, or token systems) which will be investigated in detail in this section. Our objective is to make clear to the reader the research basis underlying the conclusions to be drawn.

The research strategies used in the majority of studies covered by this report share the following three features: First, individuals are studied under specified experimental conditions, with the same individuals going through the various phases of the experiment. This approach leads more directly to knowledge of procedures which will work with individual children. Second, the experimental procedure is often withdrawn after being introduced to show its effect more clearly. For example, when teacher praises *more*, task behavior *increases;* when teacher praises *less*, task behavior *decreases*. Third, the behaviors to be changed are defined in terms of observables—events which the teacher can see and do something about. Reliability of observations is established before the experiment starts by checking the agreement between several observers. A review of field experimental research procedures may be found in Bijou, Peterson, and Ault (8).

SOCIAL REINFORCERS

Stimulus events which are based on the behavior of people are called social stimuli. Such events include physical nearness, contact, verbal behavior, and physical movements such as smiles. Social stimuli which function to strengthen behaviors which they follow are called *social reinforcers*. The following studies illustrate the range of behaviors found to be controlled by social reinforcers in a variety of settings.

Preschool studies. Work in the experimental preschools at the University of Washington, University of Kansas, and University of Illinois by Wolf, Baer, Bijou, and their students laid the groundwork for extensions of operant procedures to public schools.

1. An aggressive girl.—Hart, Reynolds, Baer, Brawley, and Harris (24) carefully studied the consequences that were controlling the obnoxious behavior of a five-year-old girl who was "balky, verbally insulting, occasionally foul-mouthed and prone

to tell disjointed stories about violent accidents." The general results of the study are graphed in figure 1.

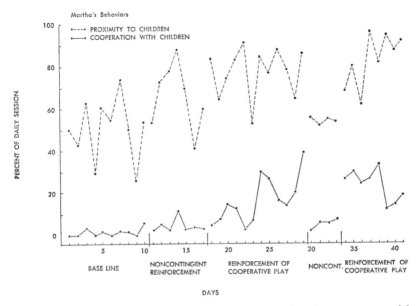

Fɪɢ. 1. Daily percentages of proximity and cooperative play over sequential
experimental conditions. From Hart, Reynolds, Baer, Brawley, and Harris (24).

During the first ten days Martha's teachers maintained their
ongoing pattern of responding to her. This initial *base-line* period
served as a basis for comparing experimental effects. During base
line Martha was found to be near other children about 50 percent
of the preschool time but played cooperatively less than 5 percent
of such time. The teachers interacted with Martha about 10 percent of the available time.

For the next seven days, the teachers showered Martha with
social reinforcement and desirable material goods. They attended
closely to her—laughing, conversing, and showing admiration. Such
attention was given about 80 percent of the available time. Some
psychologists might have predicted that this "unconditional love"
would have led Martha to be more cooperative. Cooperative play,
however, remained below five percent. This period is labeled *noncontingent reinforcement* in figure 1 since events which usually

function as reinforcers were presented on a random basis rather than being contingent upon a class of behaviors.

In the third phase of the experiment, Martha's cooperative behavior was directly followed by attention, praise, and presentation of play equipment or materials. Her behavior was ignored when she showed her obnoxious behaviors; *ignored* in this case simply means withdrawal of attention of all sorts from Martha and giving attention to another child. Cooperative play rose to 40 percent.

When noncontingent reinforcement was again introduced, cooperative behavior decreased. Finally, reinstatement of reinforcement for cooperative play increased such play.

One must conclude from this study that social reinforcers from adults can serve to strengthen behaviors followed by such reinforcers. Just being nice is not enough. It is very likely that Martha's obnoxious behaviors were being maintained by the attention they received although the present study did not address itself to that question.

2. Regressive girl.—Harris, Johnston, Kelley, and Wolf (23) studied a three-year-old who spent 80 percent of the time crawling on the floor. When the teachers gave attention only for standing and walking, a normal walking pattern was established within a week. Switching attention back to crawling and not attending to standing reinstated "regressive" crawling for 80 percent of the time periods. Again switching back to attention for standing reinstated a normal pattern of upright behavior.

3. Withdrawn girl.—Buell, Stoddard, Harris, and Baer (10) examined the effects of reinforcing play on outdoor equipment on the development of social skills. Polly was physically inactive and showed little social interaction with her peers. When physically active play was strengthened by using social reinforcement, it was found that other desirable behaviors appeared. There were more social contacts with peers in the form of talking and cooperative play, and there was less baby behavior.

4. Peer social reinforcement.—Social reinforcement can also be used by peers. Wahler (45) has demonstrated profound effects of attention to or ignoring of behaviors by preschool peers. For example, Sally's doll play greatly diminished when peers were instructed to ignore such behavior. Play with other toys increased

in the meantime. When the peers again reinforced doll play, its rate returned to the base-line level. Dick's aggressive behaviors were similarly controlled by the presence or absence of peer attention.

In his review of preschool studies, Baer (3) concluded that a large number of studies have produced very similar outcomes to those just reported. These studies involved a variety of behavior problems such as hyperactivity, dependence, inattentiveness, extreme aggression, and inarticulate langauge. There is strong reason to believe that social reinforcers dispensed by adults are a very critical factor in the generation and elimination of behavior problems of children.

Elementary classroom studies. Studies by Becker and by Hall and their students have been conducted to assess the possibility of extending the findings on preschool children to the elementary school setting.

1. Combined effects of rules, ignoring, and praise.—Becker, Madsen, Arnold, and Thomas (6) chose two problem children from each of five elementary school classes. Categories of child behaviors were defined which disrupted learning or violated the teacher's rules. For example, gross motor behavior was defined as getting out of seat, standing, running, skipping, jumping, and the like. Other disruptive behaviors included making noise with objects, aggression, orienting away from work, blurting out, talking to peers, and other off-task behavior. Observers were trained to rate reliably the frequency of occurrence of these behaviors. Deviant behavior was defined as any twenty-second interval in which one or more disruptive behaviors occurred. The children were rated for three twenty-minute sessions each week. Observations of teacher behaviors were made to determine if the experimental program was being carried out effectively.

After a five-week base line, the teachers began the experimental program which had three components. The teacher's *rules* for classroom behavior were made explicit and repeated frequently. Teachers were also to *show approval* for appropriate behaviors (conducive to learning) and to *ignore* disruptive behaviors. If a child was hurting someone, the teacher could intervene as she saw fit. This rarely happened. The teachers were instructed to give praise for achievement, prosocial behavior, and following the rules of the group. They were to praise students for such behaviors as concentrating on individual work, raising hand when appropriate, responding to questions, paying attention to directions, following directions, sitting at desk, studying, and sitting quietly. They were instructed to use variety and expression in their comments and to smile when delivering praise. Teachers were to walk around the room during study time and give a pat on the back to children doing a good job. The teachers were given daily feedback regarding their effectiveness in showing approval contingent on appropriate behavior and in ignoring inappropriate behavior.

The percentage of intervals of deviant behavior for the ten children dropped from 62.1 percent of the time during base line to 29.2 percent of the time during the experimental program when approval, ignoring deviant behavior, and rules were introduced. Detailed results for only two of the five classes are presented here. The data for Don and Dan are found in figure 2. Don is a boy of average IQ who earlier as a fourth-grader had been recommended for placement as an educable retarded. He had a high frequency of moving about the room and talking during study time. He responded well to approval and his level of deviant behavior fell from 40 percent to 20 percent. Dan, who was more than two years behind

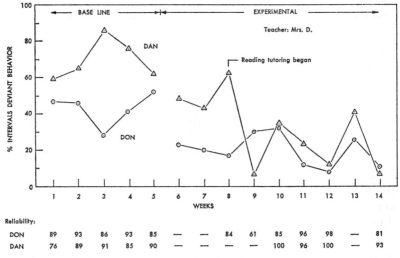

FIG. 2. Percentages of deviant behavior for two children in Class D. From Becker, Madsen, Arnold, and Thomas (6).

in reading, responded well to teacher attention only after tutoring in reading was begun. It was not enough to reinforce him for staying in his seat if he could get no measure of success from his academic work. Dan was considered by the school psychologist to be a severely disturbed boy who required psychotherapy if he was going to be able to function in school.

Teacher E (figure 3) had relied mainly on shouting to maintain order in an "unruly" class. The children engaged in much whistling, running about the room, yelling at other children, loud incessant talk, hitting, pushing, and shoving. The average level of deviant

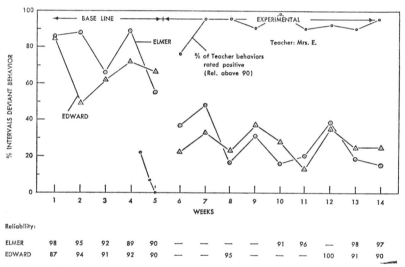

FIG. 3. Percentages of deviant behavior for two children in Class E, and change in teacher E's behavior. From Becker, Madsen, Arnold, and Thomas (6).

behavior for the two boys fell from about 70 percent to about 25 percent, a drastic reduction. The teacher also reported many changes in other members of her class.

Hall, Lund, and Jackson (21) reported a series of experiments further demonstrating the effects of teacher social reinforcement for study behavior and withdrawal of attention (ignoring) for disruptive behaviors. For example, Robbie (see figure 4) was a very disruptive boy who spent much of his time snapping rubber bands, talking and laughing with peers, and playing with toys from his

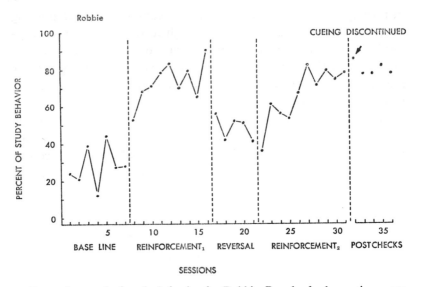

FIG. 4. A record of study behavior for Robbie. Postcheck observations were made during the fourth, sixth, seventh, twelfth, and fourteenth weeks after the completion of Reinforcement₂ conditions. From Hall, Lund, and Jackson (21).

pocket. He spent less than 25 percent of work time actually working. During the base-line period, 55 percent of the attention Robbie received followed nonstudy behavior. When off-task behavior was ignored and good work behavior praised, Robbie improved dramatically. In this classroom the teacher was signaled by the experimenter when to praise or otherwise give attention to study behavior. This was done to help her learn to manage her own behavior more effectively. The reversal condition demonstrated the critical importance of the teacher's behavior in maintaining Robbie's on-task behavior. Reinstatement of the reinforcement condition once again established good study behavior. Follow-up checks made during the fourteen weeks following the experimental conditions showed that the teacher was able to maintain good study behavior without continued assistance. Similar positive findings were reported with other children and with other teachers.

In a subsequent report, Hall et al. showed again (with a variety of problem children) the continuing importance of teacher attention in changing problem behaviors. Furthermore, he showed that teachers can reliably take data themselves on the children they are helping (20). By using a second person to check the reliability of observations, Hall found the percent of agreements ranging from 84 to 100 percent. The implication is that teachers can be trained to monitor their own plans for helping children with behavior problems. Other studies (22, 25, 39, 48) on the training of teachers are also to be noted.

2. Separate effects of rules, ignoring disruptive behavior, and praise.—Madsen, Becker and Thomas (32) attempted to determine the relative effectiveness of the three components of the experimental program used in their first study. After base line, each of the three components of the experimental program (rules, ignoring, and praise) were introduced separately. The general experimental design can be discerned from figure 5.

The *rules* phase of the experiment consisted of the teacher forming four or five rules (or instructions) for classroom behavior and repeating them four to six times a day, e.g., "Sit quietly while working," "Walk," "Raise hand," and so forth.

The *ignore* phase of the experiment consisted of the teacher attempting not to respond to disruptive behaviors with scolding or reprimands. She was to act as if such behavior had not happened. This part of the program was very difficult for the teacher to follow.

Finally, *praise* was added to rules and ignoring inappropriate behavior. Appropriate behaviors incompatible with deviant inappropriate behaviors were to be given social approval. The teacher was to show approval of as many good behaviors as possible during the first few days. A prime rule was "Catch the children being good." Moreover, she was to give approval to improvements in behavior in order to shape the child's behavior. For example, a problem child who frequently wandered around the room would be given approval when found in his seat even if he was not working on a task. As the time spent in his seat increased, the teacher would begin to praise him only when he was both seated and working on a task. In each case, the teacher would explicitly state the behaviors she approved, e.g., "Tommy is sitting nicely and working hard on his assignment."

The results indicate that the introduction of rules alone was

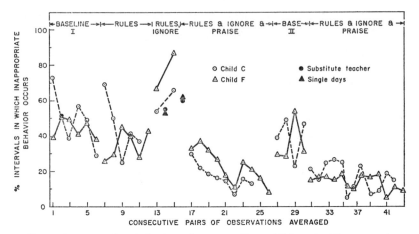

FIG. 5. Inappropriate behavior of two problem children in Classroom A as a function of experimental conditions. From Madsen, Becker, and Thomas (32).

not effective in modifying behavior (figure 5). The procedure of ignoring inappropriate behavior was difficult for the teacher to maintain. She would ignore for a while and then scold as the children got out of hand. When praise for appropriate behavior was added in conjunction with the ignoring of inappropriate behavior, the latter behavior fell from about a 70 percent level (during base line) to 30 percent. Inappropriate behavior returned to the base-line level when the teacher approximated her behavior of the base-line period. Finally, when the experimental procedures were reinstated, the level of inappropriate behavior again fell. This correspondence between the experimental changes in teacher's behavior and the level of inappropriate child behavior points to the marked influence a teacher can have over classroom behavior.

These findings indicate that simply instructing children what to do is not enough. Reinforcement for following instructions is also necessary. A study by Schutte and Hopkins (42) with five kindergarten children helps to show more clearly the contribution of instructions to classroom management. A list of ten instructions related to classroom routines was formed, such as "Pick up the toys," "Sit down," "Write your name on the paper," "Get out your mat," "Be quiet." These instructions were repeated daily for twenty days. The data recorded were the number of instructions followed each day. When instructions only were given (without praise for following the instructions), 60 percent of the instructions were followed by the five children. When praise was added, following instructions increased to 78 percent. A return to the instructions without praise led to a drop in following instructions to 69 percent and the addition of praise led to an increase to 84 percent.

These findings are in keeping with laboratory-based findings on the discriminative control of behavior. Signals or instructions as discriminative stimuli become important because certain behavior has been followed by reinforcers in their presence, but not in their absence. Such signals cannot stand alone and remain effective. They must at least periodically be supported by reinforcing consequences.

3. The reinforcing effects of critical comments.—Often our attempts to correct children by telling them what not to do fail. Madsen, Becker, Thomas, Koser, and Plager (33) obtained clear evidence to show that the more frequently first-grade teachers asked their children to "sit down," the more frequently the children stood up. This finding was true even though the children usually followed the instruction to "sit down." Only when the children were given praise for sitting and working did the frequency of standing decline. It appears that the teacher attention which went along with saying "sit down, Johnny" served to reinforce standing (a preceding response) and to cue sitting (a following response). Under these circumstances the teacher was trapped into thinking that saying "sit down" worked (because the children did sit down), but the long-term effect was to make the situation worse.

The study summarized in figure 6 shows two important effects of teacher behavior (44). First, that with well-behaved children it is possible for a teacher to produce a poorly behaved classroom. Second, that teacher disapproval can serve to reinforce the very behavior she is trying to eliminate. The data in figure 6 are based on observations of ten children for two minutes each every day. The children were bright second-graders who were being observed doing seat work during a morning reading time when some children were in a reading group with the teacher. Disruptive behavior was measured in a way similar to that reported earlier by Becker et al. (6).

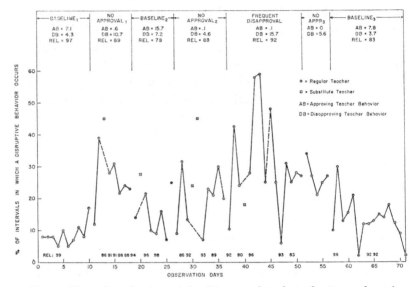

FIG. 6. Disruptive classroom behaviors as a function of nature of teacher behavior. Data points represent 2-minute samples on 10 children each day. Dotted lines cross observations where the regular teacher was absent due to a recurrent illness, including a 10-day hospitalization between days 39 and 41. The dotted line connecting days 44 and 45 represents the Easter vacation break. The data for day 25 was taken with the teacher out of the room. From Thomas, Becker, and Armstrong (44).

The first four experimental phases compared base-line conditions (1 and 3) with conditions when all praise was withdrawn (2 and 4). The effect of withdrawal of teacher's praise for appropriate behavior was to increase disruptive behavior from under 10 percent to approximately 28 percent. Teacher's praise for appropriate behavior is important in maintaining a well-functioning classroom.

During phase 5 of the experiment (frequent disapproval), the teacher's critical comments were tripled so that they were occurring almost once a minute. Disruptive behaviors hit a new high. *Teacher disapproval appears to be reinforcing disruptive behavior.*

Phase 6 of the experiment simply returned to the no-approval condition again with a lower level of criticism. Little change resulted.

Finally, in phase 7, the reinstatement of approval reactions by teacher reduced disruptive behaviors to the original low level.

4. The contingency is important.—It is not sufficient that the

teacher just increase the amount of praise she uses and decrease her criticism. Earlier in discussing an aggressive nursery school girl it was noted that "unconditional love" alone did nothing to change her aggressive behavior. The positive consequences had to be contingent on cooperative behaviors. Two other studies show further that praising some children in a classroom for appropriate behaviors does little to help other children behave better unless they also receive some praise (9, 7). In each of these studies, praise given to one child (or group) improved the behavior of that child but had little effect on the second child (or group). When the conditions were reversed so that the child (or group) not given praise at first received praise, improvement was shown.

So what's new? It was asserted at the beginning of this review that the main thing new about the current popularity of behavior modification ideas in education is the quantity and quality of the experimental data to support these ideas. The basic ideas have been known by many psychologists for forty years or more. It is therefore fitting that this section on social reinforcement be closed with the "proof of the pudding." Once again we quote from Olson's contribution to the thirty-fourth NSSE yearbook.

> The universality of the use of language in human relations makes it a tool of large actual and potential importance in the control and modification of child behavior. Scattered studies on the use of praise and reproof, or on the effect of the simple formula, "Right" and "Wrong," indicate the importance of a more conscious use of the tool.
>
> Some of the finer nuances in language control are now being studied by Wilker in the child development laboratories at the University of Michigan. She has experimented with the effect of variation in the language formula on the behavior elicited in a large number of situations. Experimental and control groups have been employed with various criteria on the efficacy of control. In general, she finds that effective response is secured in so far as the words used are directive and point to the desired goal. Words that block action rather than direct attention along the desired line are clearly to be avoided. "Do" is more effective than "Don't." Words should be encouraging rather than discouraging and point to success rather than failure. Words must be selected that have some relation to the child's stage of learning, and they are more effective when accom-

panied by the postural, gestural, emotional, or material influences necessary to help the child respond to them.

A study in progress by Olson and Wilkinson at the University of Michigan suggests that the effective teaching personality as a whole is indicated, at least in part, by the nature of the language used by the teacher in the control of behavior. Sheer quantity of verbalism seems to be relatively unimportant. The extent, however, to which the teacher is positive and constructive in her words used for behavior control is an item of some importance. The teachers with the most favorable general ratings avoid negative statements. Similarly, the effective teacher directs her statements to the person she wishes to reach and does not, from irritability, indulge in blanket responses to the class of children as a whole (37:376-77).

ACTIVITY REINFORCERS

The Premack principle. The basic procedures established by research with social reinforcers can be readily extended to a host of activity reinforcers available to teachers. The basis for this extension is the elegantly simple Premack principle which has a strong foundation in laboratory research (40). Simply stated, the principle is this: "For any pair of responses, the more probable one will reinforce the less probable one." Homme (28) has noted that grandma knew all about the Premack principle which was expressed in such sayings as "First you work and then you play." The principle is extremely important to the teacher in trying to find reinforcers for children. All she need do is watch and see what children do frequently when given a choice. Activities such as running, playing games, drawing pictures, singing, going to recess, going home, helping teacher, going on a trip, and playing teacher are readily available in most classrooms and function as reinforcers for most children.

Examples of classroom research. Homme described an early application of the Premack principle in his training of three active three-year-olds (29). The psychologists noted that the children did a lot of running and screaming when brought into an experimental classroom. A contract was made. "Sit quietly and watch what I do at the blackboard; then you may run and scream until the timer goes 'ding'." Slowly the contract was changed until the children were earning tokens for learning which could be exchanged later for fun things to do. The authors noted that the control was so good that a new observer would likely conclude that a threat of punishment was being used. Homme (27, 28) has reported a number of other applications of this principle in working with a variety of educationally handicapped children where access to a play area was used to reinforce academic learning.

Osborne (38) studied a teacher of the deaf who had trouble keeping her eleven- to thirteen-year-old charges in their seats. He used the fact that they liked to get out of their seats and do other things in the room to teach them to remain in their seats when requested to do so. The teacher simply set the rule, "You will get five minutes free time in fifteen minutes (later changed to twenty-five minutes) if you do not get out of your seat during this next work period." In-seat behavior during work periods became nearly perfect.

Lovitt, Guppy, and Blattner (31) were also able to show that free time functioned as a reinforcer. They reinforced spelling accuracy in a group of fourth-graders. Hopkins, Schutte, and Garton (30) used access to a playroom to increase work rate and accuracy in the printing of first-grade children and writing of second-grade children. Prior to introduction of the playroom consequence the children were required to wait while the teacher checked the papers of other children. This consequence lead to inefficient work habits compared to that of being able to go to the playroom. It should be noted that increases in accuracy of printing and writing occurred even though the children were reinforced by access to the playroom only for speed. The teacher's approval and disapproval probably operated as a contingency for improvement in quality of work.

Schmidt and Ulrich (41) used the Premack principle to help a teacher reduce the noise level in her classroom. A sound-level meter was used to measure noise level. These contingencies were applied: (a) for each ten minutes of quiet time (noise below forty-two decibels) the whole class would earn two minutes of extra time for gym plus two minutes free time at the end of each ten minutes of quiet; (b) if the noise exceeded the critical level, a timer was reset to a new ten-minute interval in which the criterion had to be met. The procedure quickly reduced classroom noise level. A similar reduction in noise was produced in a second classroom where out-of-seat behavior was also reduced by making loss of five minutes of gym time the punishment for being caught out of seat.

It should be apparent that with a little thought the Premack principle opens unlimited vistas for the teacher in using activities to strengthen desired classroom behaviors. Most teachers currently give away their reinforcers rather than use them to aid the learning of their pupils. The basic question is, "How can I use what is coming up next to help reinforce what I want the children to learn now?"

PUNISHMENT

The third class of consequences normally available to teachers are punishing stimuli. There is probably no other area of behavior theory about which there is more confusion, misunderstanding, and emotion than the use of punishing stimuli. Many believe they should not punish because it does not work or because it only produces a temporary suppression of behavior. Some believe that any use of punishment is immoral. The facts are that many stimulus events can be found which will weaken (punish) behaviors they follow, just as many stimulus events can be found which will strengthen (reinforce) behaviors they follow (1). Whether their use is moral or not depends on judgments of the total benefits for the person and society which follow from their use or nonuse. Few parents have trouble deciding that punishment is desirable and ethical when the safety of their child is at issue.

How not to punish. Punishers can be stimulus events which are *presented* after a response (e.g., a spanking, a threat of a spanking) or they can be stimulus events which are *terminated* or taken away after a response (e.g., loss of free time). In general, the use of punishment involving the presentation of strong stimulus events (called *aversive stimuli*) should be avoided by teachers. In those few cases where presentation of strong aversive stimuli may be needed because of the frequency or intensity of the problem behavior, the problem should probably be handled by a specially trained professional.

The main reason teachers should not use presentation of aversive stimuli as a control method is that people learn to escape from and avoid sources of punishment unless they are restrained from doing so. School should not be a place to be avoided by children. Kurt

Lewin once described this phenomenon as "leaving the field." When the child "leaves the field," the adult loses some control over the future development of the child. Punishing adults teach children a variety of avoidance and escape behaviors which they then blame on the children, e.g., lying, hiding, cheating, sneaking, and being truant. In addition, the use of aversive stimuli has the potential of conditioning children's anger and fear reactions to people, places, and activities associated with them. Finally, as Bandura and Walters (4) and others have shown, the use of physical punishment provides the child with a model of aggression which may be imitated in controlling others.

Research on punishment. Most knowledge of punishment procedures arises from laboratory research and clinical applications (see reviews by Solomon [43] and Azrin and Holz [1]). This body of research shows punishment procedures to be generally effective when intelligently used. For the reasons already given, this discussion will consider only applications not involving presentation of strong aversive stimuli. There are three basic procedures: use of conditioned aversive stimuli ("don't signals"), time-out from positive reinforcement, and response cost.

1. "Don't signals."—In general, basic research has shown that "don't signals" or reprimands will work only if they are now and then backed up by effective punishers (19). Most classroom research has shown that "don'ts" are not very effective as punishers, probably because they are not backed up properly. In fact, as shown earlier in this review, punishers often function as reinforcers to increase inappropriate behavior. O'Leary's studies with grade-school children confirm the ineffectiveness of loud reprimands. However, he has found that quiet reprimands can be effective in reducing undesired behavior for some children (35, 36).

2. Time-out.—Time-out from reinforcement has been shown to be an effective punishment procedure in the laboratory, clinic, home, and school as long as there is a way the child can learn to avoid the time-out through alternative responding (2, 18, 26, 34, 47). The essential ingredients of an effective time-out procedure in the classroom are (a) an ongoing reinforcing situation which the child does not want to miss, (b) a clear statement of the consequence of the behavior to be punished by removal from the rein-

forcing situation, (c) a warning, and (d) actual execution of the removal if the warning is not followed. Time-out might consist of placement in a quiet room for five minutes. It might consist of removal from the group to a corner of the room until the child is ready to work. It might consist of removal of a *Sullivan Programmed Reader* for failure to follow the self-instruction rules and of being required to sit quietly for the remainder of the reading period. Because time-out involving a quiet room is often associated with isolation and "prison-like" conditions, it would be wise for the teacher not to use it without the informed consent of supervisors and parents.

3. Response cost.—Response cost involves the taking away of a reinforcer, usually a conditioned reinforcer like points, tokens, credits for future reinforcers, contingent upon an undesired response. In the world of money, this is equivalent to a fine by the traffic court. Weiner (46) has shown this to be an effective procedure, even more effective than time-out. In the study by Schmidt and Ulrich (41) which was discussed earlier, the procedure of subtracting five minutes of individual gym time from earned credits each time a person was caught out-of-seat was a response cost procedure. Similarly, in their other classroom, the procedure of resetting the timer to zero if the noise got too loud involved a response cost procedure. The children lost the time credit they had earned toward their next reinforcer. It is not difficult for teachers to misuse a response cost procedure. It is only necessary to set up a situation where the fines outweigh the credits to create a fiasco. For example, one teacher we know started the morning with Ronald, using this rule: "Each time I notice you hitting one of the girls, an X goes in this box on the blackboard; if you get four X's, no recess." Ronald had four X's by 9:30 A.M. and the teacher had lost control of him. When she was taught to have Ronald earn each minute of recess through each ten minutes of no fighting, his behavior quickly improved.

Rules for the effective use of punishment. The basic problem in a situation where one might want to use punishment is that the behavior of the person to be punished has been (is being) reinforced. Once this is realized, it should be clear that punishment would have to be used forever if our goal is to get rid of the undesired behavior, unless some way is found to provide reinforcement for an incompatible behavior or to eliminate all reinforcement for the undesired behavior. Thus, the first two rules of effective punishment are to: (a) *give reinforcement for behavior incompatible with the punished response,* and (b) *be sure the undesired behavior is no longer reinforced.*

The third rule follows from the undesired side effects of presenting aversive stimuli and the fact that termination of a punishing state can be used as a reinforcer: *effective punishment relies on taking away reinforcers and provides a clear-cut method for earning them back.* In order to reduce the future need for strong punishers, rule four states that *effective punishment is preceded by a warning signal.* The warning signal can then later be used as a conditioned punisher. The last rule simply recognizes the empirical fact that immediate consequences are usually more effective than delayed consequences, e.g., punish immediately where possible (5:157).

Classroom Applications Involving Antecedent Stimulus Events

Consequences make learning happen while antecedent stimulus events determine what is learned. This section briefly identifies three areas in which the basic knowledge of procedures for using antecedent stimulus events is relevant for the teachers. When behavior is under the control of antecedent stimuli, the child knows when to do what. To establish stimulus control over a response, the basic procedure is to reinforce one kind of response in the presence of one class of stimuli and not reinforce that kind of response in the presence of another class of stimuli. Once children have learned to follow most instructions, however, the antecedent stimulus control of a response can often be quickly established with a few instructions and appropriate social reinforcement for following the instructions. The teacher of the future will need to be intimately acquainted with procedures for establishing stimulus control.

STIMULUS CONTROL IN CLASSROOM MANAGEMENT

There is an endless number of ways of engineering the space and time of a classroom day and year to facilitate the management of the learning process. The following example illustrates many of the ways in which both classroom structure and program structure can be engineered to facilitate management of a large group of young children.

A kindergarten teacher wanted to prepare her class for small-group and individualized instruction in reading and math. She divided the children into four groups with color names. The classroom was divided into four group-study areas, a music area with a rug on which all could sit, and a teaching area for a small group. Materials and supplies for a fun activity (painting, modeling clay, records, etc.) were placed next to each group-study area.

The teacher started the year by assigning everyone a simple task she knew all could do (coloring). When the routines of getting things out, working, and putting things away were learned, she added a second task to the assignment. "When you finish your work sheets, you may start a second activity on your own, using the materials next to your group table." By using colored name tags corresponding to group names she could rotate the group locations easily each day without confusion, so that all children had turns with all activities.

The next step was to introduce a reading or arithmetic work activity prior to the fun activity. Because the children could manage themselves for two activities on their own, the teacher could begin small-group instruction in reading and math. The teacher devised a very interesting way of helping the children finish their second tasks (fun tasks) and clean up without a lot of fuss. At 10:45 she would put a record on at the music area. The first child who was ready sat in the leader's chair in the music area and was the first "teacher" for imitation games played to the music. The rest of the children had five minutes to finish before the music period actually started. To an observer, the whole process seemed like magic, since no verbal instructions were given to the children. The teacher seemed to have an easy job. She put her effort into planning for good management, not trying to overcome poor planning.

The final step was to individualize the work-period tasks by making a folder for each child and placing his materials for the work period in the folder before class. The children were able to pick up their own folders from a rack designed for them and return them when they were finished. When the children needed help from the teacher, they did not sit around waving an arm in the air; rather, they set up a little red paper tent (kept in the folders) and went on to the next task. The tent signaled the teacher to come when she could (5:175-76).

Many of the ideas used in this example can be used in any classroom. Planning provided for the fact that not all children finished at the same time. Systematic cues were provided to let the children know where they should be and what they should be doing. The daily routine helped to make the completion of one activity the cue to get ready for the next. Activities were sequenced so that activities to come served to reinforce completion of the activity before it. Good engineering made for a happy teacher and happy children.

STIMULUS CONTROL IN TEACHING TASKS 181809

While the teacher aims to teach general concepts, operations, and problem-solving skills (which combine concepts and operations), she is always faced with the paradox that the general case can be taught only through the teaching of specific tasks. Analysis shows that teaching any task involves the use of a variety of antecedent stimuli. First, it is necessary to provide signals to get the children's attention ("Listen, everybody watch me"). Next, the task must be presented in such a way that the children are cued as to what stimulus to attend to and what response is required by the task. For example, "Look at this picture of an animal." (Point to the picture of an elephant.) "See, it has a long trunk. What do we call this animal?" In this example, the basic task is to name the animal in the picture. Appropriate directions to control attending and responding are given. On completion of the presentation the teacher tests to see what was learned and presents corrective tasks as needed. The systematic use of attention signals, prompts, directions, and "respond now" signals offer much promise for improving the effectiveness of small-group instruction in basic skills. The Engelmann-developed Distar [tm] programs (12, 13, 14, 15, 16, 17) currently incorporate many of these ideas. Well-developed self-instructional programs and teaching machines also incorporate good stimulus control procedures to insure that the student's attention is directed to the critical stimulus events important in the lesson.

STIMULUS CONTROL IN PROGRAMMING

A classical issue is the generality versus specificity of what is taught. The issue is often stated vaguely with words about rote learning versus meaningful learning or habits versus concepts and operations. While a solution of these issues cannot be fully developed here (see Becker, Engelmann, and Thomas [5], chapters 18-21), it should be made clear that the logical analysis and experimental study of stimulus control procedures provide important answers to these issues. Consider this example. A first-grade teacher is teaching the sounds for *m*, *a*, and *s* to a group of children. The sounds are written on the chalkboard and the children take turns saying the sounds until each child "knows" them. The next day the teacher brings the group back and writes these letters on the board: *s*, *m*, *a*. Many mistakes are made and the teacher assumes the children have "forgotten." Further analysis shows that the children attended to the location of the letters the day before and not the letters themselves—*s* was on the right, *a* in the middle, and *m* on the left. The teacher's presentation allowed stimuli other than those she wanted to control correct responses. When the order of letters was changed, the children still responded according to location and the errors appeared.

In developing a sequence of teaching tasks (a program), it is necessary to vary two kinds of stimulus events if a more general case is to be taught. By its very nature each instance of a concept is also an instance of many other concepts. In the above example, the letter *s* was also an instance of "the one on the right," "letter," "chalk mark," and so forth. The teaching program must include many concept instances in which the irrelevant stimulus characteristics are varied, while essential characteristics remain. It is also necessary to present a range of not-instances to help define the essential concept characteristics. For example, if in teaching *m* the not-instances included only *s*, *a*, and *b*, it is very likely that on presentation of *n* the child would say "mmm." The teaching program did not yet require that he discriminate the number of downward characteristics to correctly respond to *m*.

Another aspect of the specificity-generality issue involves the way in which a programmer chooses his teaching objectives. Often instruction is programmed to teach specific tasks (read the "word" *sam*, add 4 + 5). Alternative programming strategies could make each task an example of more general concepts or operations which are being taught at the same time. For example, teaching reading by the sight method is an example of task programming. There is very little if any carry-over from learning to read one word to learning the next, unless the child accidentally teaches himself some phonics in the process. On the other hand, if the program teaches about forty sounds and blending skills, the student has a basis for attacking all of the regular-sound words in the English language. The gain in efficiency is tremendous.

Summary

This chapter has examined three classes of consequences of potential importance to all teachers and provided examples and suggestions pointing to the developing importance of knowledge of stimulus control procedures for teachers.

Social reinforcers can be used very effectively in changing a variety of problem behaviors of nursery school and elementary school children. The basic procedure is to follow the behaviors to be strengthened with attention and praise and withdraw attention from behaviors to be weakened. Rules alone do little to influence behavior. They must be made important by providing reinforcement for behaving according to the rules. Many kinds of verbal commands may appear to be effective in eliminating undesired behavior. However, appearances may be deceiving. While commands and critical comments may cue the child to stop the unwanted behavior (standing, talking, etc.), the attention given to that behavior by the persons making the command or critical comment may actually increase its future occurrence. Learning not to respond to disruptive behaviors is important for effective teaching.

The teacher, through the use of her verbal behavior, can create "good" or "bad" classroom behaviors. Since the controlling variables can be isolated and modified, there is little reason why all teachers cannot be *taught* to be effective teachers. The blame can no longer be put on the unchangeable *personality* of the teacher or the pupils.

Educational psychologists have often indicated that the good teacher is the one who is warm and positive with her children. The work reported here is consistent with such findings but it leads to a more specific recommendation. The frequency of use of positive social reinforcers (smiles, praise, etc.) per se is not related to improvement in behavior. *It matters when the teacher praises whom and for what behavior.*

The basic procedures involving the use of social reinforcers can be extended for use with *activity reinforcers*. Because any higher frequency behavior can be used to strengthen a lower frequency behavior, powerful reinforcers are available for use by every teacher without adding any unusual reinforcers such as M & Ms or ice cream. Classroom research using activity reinforcers clearly demonstrates their value in improving classroom management, student motivation, and academic progress.

Teachers can punish children physically (although this is seldom allowed) or by taking away reinforcers. They can also use threats as punishers. Punishment which involves presenting aversive stimuli can only be effective if the person punished cannot escape from the punisher. This is not usually the case in schools. Furthermore, punishment by presenting aversive stimuli can generate fear and anger and it provides an aggressive model for the child. For these reasons, this kind of punishment should be avoided.

Various conditioned punishers such as threats, reprimands, and "dont's" may be effective if they are now and then backed up with an effective punisher. In classrooms, however, these procedures are generally found not to work because the teacher has difficulty providing the backup punishments when required.

The two varieties of punishers likely to be of value to teachers are time-out and response cost procedures. Both involve loss of reinforcers. If these procedures are accompanied by good positive reinforcement systems and the children have clear ways to avoid getting punished, the occasional use of these procedures can be useful in managing a variety of problem behaviors. In general, the effective use of positive reinforcers usually makes it unnecessary to use punishment procedures.

The closing section of this chapter touched only on a few key points showing the importance of knowledge of stimulus control technology in everyday classroom instruction. Classroom management, basic teaching methods, and curriculum design procedures all require careful attention to stimulus control principles if they are to be effective. It is in this area that the next decade will produce dramatic changes in educational process and programs. The basic principles are known. What is needed are more innovative applications for field testing.

REFERENCES

1. Azrin, N. H., and Holz, W. C. "Punishment." In *Operant Behavior: Areas of Research and Application*, edited by W. K. Honig, pp. 380-447. New York: Appleton-Century-Crofts, 1966.
2. Baer, D. M. "Laboratory Control of Thumbsucking by Withdrawal and Representation of Reinforcement." *Journal of the Experimental Analysis of Behavior* 5 (1962): 525-28.
3. ———. "Remedial Use of the Reinforcement Contingency." Paper presented at the Annual Convention of the American Psychological Association, Chicago, Illinois, 1966.
4. Bandura, A., and Walters, R. H. *Social Learning and Personality Development*. New York: Holt, Rinehart & Winston, 1963.
5. Becker, W. C.; Engelmann, S.; and Thomas, D. R. *Teaching: A Course in Applied Psychology*. Palo Alto: Science Research Associates, 1971.
6. Becker, W. C.; Madsen, C. H., Jr.; Arnold, Carole R.; and Thomas, D. R. "The Contingent Use of Teacher Attention and Praise in Reducing Classroom Behavior Problems." *Journal of Special Education* 1 (1967) 287-307.
7. Becker, W. C.; Thomas, D. R.; and Carnine, D. *Reducing Behavior Problems: An Operant Conditioning Guide for Teachers*. ERIC. Urbana, Ill.: Clearinghouse in Early Childhood, 1969.
8. Bijou, S. W.; Peterson, R.; and Ault, Marion H. "A Method to Integrate Descriptive and Experimental Field Studies at the Level of Data and Empirical Concepts." *Journal of Applied Behavior Analysis* 1 (1968): 175-91.
9. Broden, Marcia; Bruce, C.; Mitchell, Mary Ann; Carter, Virginia; and Hall, R. V. "Effects of Teacher Attention on Attending Behavior of Two Boys at Adjacent Desks." *Journal of Applied Behavior Analysis* 3 (1970): 199-203.
10. Buell, Joan; Stoddard, Patricia; Harris, Florence R.; and Baer, D. M. "Collateral Social Development Accompanying Reinforcement of Outdoor Play in a Preschool Child." *Journal of Applied Behavior Analysis* 1 (1968): 167-73.
11. Cooper, Margaret L.; Thomson, Carolyn L.; and Baer, D. M. "The Experimental Modification of Teacher Attending Behavior." *Journal of Applied Behavior Analysis* 3 (1970): 153-57.

12. Engelmann, S., and Bruner, Elaine C. *Distar Reading I.* Chicago: Science Research Associates, 1969.
13. ———. *Distar Reading II.* Chicago: Science Research Associates, 1969.
14. Engelmann, S., and Carnine, D. *Distar Arithmetic I.* Chicago: Science Research Associates, 1969.
15. ———. *Distar Arithmetic II.* Chicago: Science Research Associates, 1970.
16. Engelmann, S., and Osborn, Jean. *Distar Language II.* Chicago: Science Research Associates, 1970.
17. Engelmann, S.; Osborn, Jean; and Engelmann, Terese. *Distar Language I.* Chicago: Science Research Associates, 1969.
18. Ferster, C. B. "Control of Behavior in Chimpanzees and Pigeons by Timeout from Positive Reinforcement." *Psychological Monographs* 72 (1958): whole no. 461.
19. Hake, D. F., and Azrin, N. H. "Conditioned Punishment." *Journal of the Experimental Analysis of Behavior* 8 (1965): 279-93.
20. Hall, R. V.; Fox, R.; Willard, D.; Goldsmith, L.; Emerson, M.; Owen, M.; Davis, F.; and Porcia, E. "The Teacher As Observer and Experimenter in the Modification of Disputing and Talking-out Behaviors." *Journal of Applied Behavior Analysis* 4 (1971): 141-49.
21. Hall, R. V.; Lund, Diane; and Jackson, Deloris. "Effects of Teacher Attention on Study Behavior." *Journal of Applied Behavior Analysis* 1 (1968): 1-12.
22. Hall, R. V.; Panyan, Marion; Rabon, Deloris; and Broden, Marcia. "Instructing Beginning Teachers in Reinforcement Procedures Which Improve Classroom Control." *Journal of Applied Behavior Analysis* 1 (1968): 315-22.
23. Harris, Florence R.; Johnston, Margaret K.; Kelley, C. Susan; and Wolf, M. M. "Effects of Positive Social Reinforcement on Regressed Crawling of a Nursery School Child." *Journal of Educational Psychology* 55 (1964): 35-41.
24. Hart, Betty M.; Reynolds, Nancy J.; Baer, D. M.; Brawley, Eleanor R.; and Harris, Florence R. "Effect of Contingent and Noncontingent Social Reinforcement on the Cooperative Play of a Preschool Child." *Journal of Applied Behavior Analysis* 1 (1968): 73-76.
25. Hawkins, R. P., ed. *School Applications of Learning Theory.* Kalamazoo, Mich.: Kalamazoo Valley Intermediate School District, 1968.
26. Holz, W. C.: Azrin, N. H.; and Ayllon, T. "Elimination of Behavior of Mental Patients by Response-produced Extinction." *Journal of the Experimental Analysis of Behavior* 6 (1963): 407-12.
27. Homme, L. E. "Contingency Management." *Educational Technology Monographs* 2 (1968): no. 2.

28. ———. "Human Motivation and Environment." *Kansas Studies in Education* 16 (1968): 30-39.

29. Homme, L. E.; de Baca, P. C.; Devine, J. V.; Steinhorst, R.; and Rickert, E. J. "Use of the Premack Principle in Controlling the Behavior of Nursery School Children." *Journal of the Experimental Analysis of Behavior* 6 (1963): 544.

30. Hopkins, B. L.; Schutte, R. C.; and Garton, Kathleen L. "The Effects of Access to a Playroom on the Rate and Quality of Printing and Writing of First- and Second-Grade Students." *Journal of Applied Behavior Analysis* 4 (1971): 77-87.

31. Lovitt, T. C.; Guppy, T. E.; and Blattner, J. E. "The Use of Free-time Contingency with Fourth Graders to Increase Spelling Accuracy." *Behaviour Research and Therapy* (7 (1969): 155-56.

32. Madsen, C. H. Jr.; Becker, W. C.; and Thomas, D. R. "Rules, Praise, and Ignoring: Elements of Elementary Classroom Control." *Journal of Applied Behavior Analysis* 1 (1968): 139-50.

33. Madsen, C. H. Jr.; Becker, W. C.; Thomas, D. R.; Koser, Linda; and Plager, Elaine. "An Analysis of the Reinforcing Function of 'Sit Down' Commands." In *Reading in Educational Psychology*, edited by R. K. Barker. Boston: Allyn & Bacon, 1968.

34. McReynolds, Leija V. "Application of Timeout from Positive Reinforcement for Increasing the Efficiency of Speech Training." *Journal of Applied Behavior Analysis* 2 (1969): 199-205.

35. O'Leary, K. D., and Becker, W. C. "The Effects of a Teacher's Reprimands on Children's Behavior." *Journal of School Psychology* 7 (1969): 8-11.

36. O'Leary, K. D.; Kaufman, K. F.; Kass, Ruth E.; and Drabman, R. S. "The Vicious Cycle of Loud Reprimands." *Exceptional Children*, in press.

37. Olson, W. C. "The Diagnosis and Treatment of Behavior Disorders of Children." *Educational Diagnosis*, Thirty-fourth Yearbook of the National Society for Study of Education, Part 2. Bloomington, Ill.: Public School Publishing Co., 1935.

38. Osborne, J. G. "Free-Time As a Reinforcer in the Management of Classroom Behavior." *Journal of Applied Behavior Analysis* 2 (1960): 113-18.

39. Phillips, D. "Application of Behavior Principles to Classroom Settings." In *An Empirical Basis for Change in Education*, edited by W. C. Becker. Palo Alto: Science Research Associates, 1971.

40. Premack, D. "Reinforcement Theory." *Nebraska Symposium on Motivation 1965*, edited by D. Levine, pp. 123-28. Lincoln: University of Nebraska Press, 1965.

41. Schmidt, G. W., and Ulrich, R. E. "Effects of Group Contingent Events upon Classroom Noise." *Journal of Applied Behavior Analysis* 2 (1969): 171-79.

42. Schutte, R. C., and Hopkins, B. L. "The Effects of Teacher Attention on Following Instructions in a Kindergarten Class." *Journal of Applied Behavior Analysis* 3 (1970): 117-22.
43. Solomon, R. L. "Punishment." *American Psychologist* 19 (1964): 239-53.
44. Thomas, D. R.; Becker, W. C.; and Armstrong, M. "Production and Elimination of Disruptive Classroom Behavior by Systematically Varying Teacher's Behavior." *Journal of Applied Behavior Analysis* 1 (1968): 35-45.
45. Wahler, R. G. "Child-Child Relationships in Free Field Settings: Some Experimental Analyses." *Journal of Experimental Child Psychology* 5 (1967): 278-93.
46. Weiner, H. "Some Effects of Response Cost upon Human Operant Behavior." *Journal of the Experimental Analysis of Behavior* 5 (1962): 201-8.
47. Wolf, M. M.; Risley, T.; and Mees, H. "Application of Operant Conditioning Procedures to the Behavior Problems of an Autistic Child." *Behaviour Research and Therapy* 1 (1964): 305-12.
48. Wood, S. W. "The Lincoln Elementary School Projects: Some Results of an In-service Training Course in Behavioral Psychology." *Educational Technology Monographs* 1(1968): No. 2.

CHAPTER IV

Behavioral Approaches to Counseling

CARL E. THORESEN
and
RAY E. HOSFORD

In this chapter some selected observations on behaviorally oriented approaches to counseling are presented.[1] A discussion of historical developments and current definitions of behavioral counseling is followed by an examination of current techniques. The relevance of behavioral techniques to contemporary social problems is discussed.[2]

A Look Back

Colby (19) observed that "chaos prevails" after reviewing theory and research in counseling and psychotherapy. Colby's observation a decade ago reflected the disintegration of rigid theoretical rationales and techniques that had once dominated the field. Rogers (102) came to a similar conclusion in observing that the field was "in a mess" in terms of theoretical rationales and empirical findings. Indeed,

Preparation of this chapter by the first author was supported in part by the Stanford Center for Research and Development in Teaching. The authors gratefully acknowledge the helpful suggestions of Beverley Potter, Michael McHargue, and Michael Menefee.

1. In this chapter the term *counseling* is used as synonymous with therapy. *Counseling* and *psychotherapy* as terms typically connote different processes and different client problems. For example, counseling is often limited to problems of "relatively intact" children and adolescents (57), while therapy refers to more complex problems of children and adults. This distinction, however, is not used in this chapter.

2. The reader is referred to Kanfer's introductory chapter for an overview of behavioral concepts and developments. Several texts on behavioral approaches to counseling are available for a more comprehensive discussion (52, 65, 136). A comprehensive review of research in behavioral approaches to counseling by Krasner is available (57).

in the early 1960s much of counseling could be aptly described as a "happening," i.e., as a cluster of unconnected events (117). One of the problems was that many counselors did not perceive counseling as amenable to rigorous scientific investigation. They argued that such inquiry would destroy the delicate fabric of this mysterious process. To them counseling was inherently good, obviously valid, and thus not to be tinkered with in any scientific fashion. The essence of this a priori position was captured in a critique by Astin (2), who quoted one traditional defender as saying: "It is not the point to discuss the efficacy or lack of efficacy of psychotherapy . . . psychotherapy is a method for studying the human psyche . . . whether it is a good or bad method is not at issue."

COUNSELING AS INDIVIDUALIZED LEARNING

Despite these views a quiet revolution started during the decade of the 1950s, a revolution that has challenged the validity of counseling theory and practice in all major respects. The challenge came from behaviorally oriented psychologists who suggested that counseling could be understood in terms of social behavior rather than as a unique human relationship. Counseling was presented more as a *teaching-learning* situation and as an *educational process*. The major emphasis was placed on the *outcomes* of counseling, stated as specific changes in the observable actions of clients.[3]

Some had acknowledged counseling as a learning process (e.g., 25, 105), although few had accepted the full implications of this position: if counseling is a teaching-learning process, then counseling techniques should be derived from theory and research in learning. Techniques should reflect the hypotheses and findings of experimental and social psychology and other empirical fields investigating learning processes. Viewing counseling as an educational process rather than as a treatment for a sickness suggested that the major task was to create corrective learning situations for the client.

3. The historical development of behavioral approaches in counseling can be traced to many sources such as the early work of Thorndike and other educational psychologists, the influence of Russian psychology, especially Pavlov, the development of behavior therapy in England and South Africa during the 1950s with the work of Eysenck, Shapiro, Wolpe, and Lazarus, and the operant conditioning studies of Skinner and his colleagues, especially Lindsley. See Kanfer's introductory chapter as well as Kanfer and Phillips (52) and Yates (136) for a complete discussion of historical developments.

In this way new behaviors could be learned to replace the ineffective ways of handling problem situations.

The interview was not seen as the most effective method for all clients and all problems. Obviously everyone does not require the same kind of learning since each situation involves a particular pattern of behavior. Hence, counseling could not remain as a one-to-one kind of verbal interaction to the exclusion of other learning situations. Instead, the form and type of counseling should *follow* from the specific concerns of individual clients; that is, clients should not be fitted to one type of counseling. As such, counseling could no longer remain a predetermined, prescribed, and stylized activity (117). Rather, the counselor should tailor a sequence of procedures to assist a particular client to behave in certain ways. The counselor became an applied scientist using techniques on a tentative yet systematic basis, gathering data through careful observation as he proceeded and making evaluations along the way.

Ford and Urban (34) reflected this change with the following comment:

> The picture of psychotherapy as a condition in which two people sit privately in an office and talk about the thoughts and feelings of one of them with the expectation that changes in these will automatically produce changes in overt behavior outside the office has been shattered. . . .
> Simple understanding is not considered enough. The primary emphasis seems to be on *behavior* as it presently occurs, present behavior defined to include feelings, thoughts, and images; physiological responses; interpersonal relationships; and motor behavior. That is, to include all facets of human behavior (pp. 366-67).

Behaviorally oriented psychologists were advocating counseling as an applied behavioral science—experimental, data-oriented, observational, technical, specific, and tentative. Counseling was no longer a philosophy of life proselytizing an all-purpose general procedure for all kinds of clients and problems. Instead, counseling was being conceptualized as a technology for behavior change, incorporating a variety of empirically based techniques suggested by theory and research in psychology.

BANDURA AND KRUMBOLTZ

Although many influenced the introduction of behavioral approaches in counseling, Albert Bandura played a major role in setting the stage for the employment of the broad spectrum of techniques currently in use. Bandura (6) authored an important review article, "Psychotherapy as a Learning Process," suggesting that many different learning theories and techniques, such as positive reinforcement, counterconditioning, and imitation, were relevant to counseling. He emphasized that behavioral approaches were *not* limited to a particular treatment technique such as systematic desensitization. This broad-spectrum "social learning" orientation of Bandura's provided a valuable experimentally based foundation for contemporary approaches and proved particularly important because it rejected the more limited perspective of some "conventional" behaviorists concerned only with external behavior that could be readily observed and measured by others (see 116).

The selection of goals in counseling is a key issue in behavioral approaches on both ethical and technical grounds. Counselors have often imposed, unwittingly, their values or desired goals on clients because such goals have remained very vague. Sometimes, for example, the counselor's views of self-actualization or self-realization are in effect imposed on the client. Concerned about who decides on goals, John Krumboltz (59, 60) pioneered the concept that the goals of counseling should be stated differently for each and every individual client, in contrast to the idea of conventional "standardized" goals for all clients. Krumboltz stated that goals should be tailored to each client and stated in observable behaviors. A major task of the counselor, therefore, is to work with each individual to clarify his concerns into specific action terms. In effect, the client is asked "What actions would you like to change?" Krumboltz emphasized that goals should not be decided exclusively by the counselor but by mutual agreement of client and counselor. The counselor is limited, of course, by questions of ethics and competence in agreeing to work with clients on particular goals.[4]

4. Perhaps the most difficult task of the behavioral counselor is to help clients examine their concerns in such a way that a behaviorally stated objective(s) can be developed, i.e., a goal that states what actions will take place, under what conditions or circumstances, and to what extent. This objective becomes the "target of treatment." See Krumboltz and Thoresen (65) for examples of how behavioral objectives are established with clients.

Behavioral Counseling?

A definition of behavioral counseling is difficult since the notion of a global theoretical rationale and a major all-purpose process has been rejected. Instead, a heterogeneous combination of theories and techniques exist. Krasner (57), for example, has suggested that the unifying factor in all behavioral approaches is that procedures are derived from *experimentally* established procedures and principles. Kanfer and Phillips (52) suggest that behavioral approaches represent a scientific point of view where an experimental orientation is used in establishing a "unique combination of procedures to fit individual cases" (p. 13). Frequently, mention is made of "modern learning theory" or the "principles of conditioning" (31, 35). Although "modern learning theory" does characterize behavioral approaches, a *variety* of learning theories exist, sometimes in conflict (5). At present, behavioral approaches employ a variety of techniques based *in part* on operant, counterconditioning, and social-modeling rationales.

The core of behavioral approaches is the scientific method with its emphasis on systematic observation, careful control, quantification of data, and replication of results. Counseling is not limited to certain techniques nor to particular types of client problems. This is important to stress because some persons have erroneously viewed behavioral approaches as the use of "standardized" techniques such as contingent positive reinforcement or systematic desensitization (see 71).

The following definition seems appropriate for behavioral counseling: *the use of the experimental approach in the treatment of the individual client.* The place of learning theory is central along with general experimental psychology in behavioral approaches. We concur, however, with Yates (136) and others (13, 52) who argue that the distinguishing feature of the behavioral approach to counseling is its stress on the experimental investigation of the single case:

Behavior therapy is the attempt to utilize systematically that body of empirical and theoretical knowledge which has resulted from the application of the experimental method in psychology and its closely related disciplines (physiology and neurophysiology) in order to explain the genesis and maintenance of abnormal patterns of behavior; and to apply that knowledge to the treatment or prevention of those abnormalities by means of controlled experimental studies of the single case, both descriptive and remedial (136:18).

The "best" counseling is that which works for the individual (71); however, the data-oriented, experimental study of the individual client will best insure use of techniques that are effective and efficient. The task of the counselor is tailoring a treatment program to the circumstances of the particular case. Hence, behavioral counseling is not *the* standard application of learning-based techniques to clients, but rather the experimental application to the individual client of techniques derived from the behavioral sciences.

ENVIRONMENTAL FOCUS

A problem in clarifying what constitutes behavioral counseling is distinguishing counseling from other methods of learning and instruction. Traditionally, counseling was neatly conceptualized as a unique kind of relationship wherein the individual called a client or patient sought the assistance of a professionally trained counselor or therapist. The counseling took place almost entirely in an office setting, often over many sessions of one hour or more in length. The change process involved primarily verbal interaction between two persons or within a small group.

In contrast, behavioral approaches often "treat" the person in his everyday environment rather than in the counselor's office. The person's current environment is identified as a basic determinant (and maintainer) of the problem behavior. Hence, treatment that directly changes that environment, such as the actions of other persons, will more likely bring about the desired change in the client's actions. Counseling, therefore, is not confined to the relative isolation of the counseling office because this is not the target environment in which the problem behavior occurs. In this way, counseling is not restricted to those activities where the client comes to the counselor's office and talks once or twice a week.

Behavioral counseling represents a more complex conception of the meaning of counseling. For example, a counselor may spend relatively little time talking with the client; instead, he may work with the significant others in the client's everyday life, such as parents, teachers, siblings, or mate to change the client's environment. Much of this work is teaching or educative in that the counselor, for example, may be training parents or teachers in new ways of acting, much like a teacher helps students learn certain academic skills.

The clear-cut traditional distinctions between counseling, teaching, social work, and other helping services, based on logical definitions, are far less distinct in a behavioral framework. For instance, teaching a mother the basic principles of social reinforcement along with providing guided practice for use with her children is counseling; instructing a group of classroom teachers in methods of behavioral observation can also be counseling. Counseling in a behavioral view is not restricted to the exchange of words in an office setting.

THE ENVIRONMENT AS CLIENT

A related problem involves clarifying who is the client. Traditionally, the question was clear-cut: the person requesting help and accepted for treatment was the client. The client was viewed as self-contained in the sense that the counselor could work exclusively with the client. Problems were typically seen as *within* the person. The behavioral perspective, however, rejects this narrow view. The behavior of people (internal as well as external) is a function of environmental events, hence *the environment in many ways is often the client*. That is, the focus of treatment is not exclusively with the person experiencing problems but with what is taking place in the person's environment. Institutional arrangements, for example, such as certain school rules, methods of organizing the curriculum, or classroom examinations, may be maintaining the problem behaviors of students. Counseling is directed at modifying these institutional arrangements as a way of modifying their consequences on student behavior. This environmental or ecological perspective of behavioral approaches expands the concept of *client*. The person no longer is *always* treated as if he must adjust to the circumstances being experienced.[5]

5. Unfortunately, many reported studies in the behavior modification literature suggest that environmental arrangements have been uncritically accepted as valid. Therefore, the focus of behavioral studies in educational settings has

Current Techniques

Behavioral approaches employ a variety of specific techniques within the context of viewing counseling as a social influence situation. As suggested earlier, behavioral approaches are best viewed as the application of the experimental method to individual treatment. Most behavioral procedures currently being used can be grouped under four main categories: operant, desensitization, social modeling, and aversive techniques. Sometimes a procedure, e.g., desensitization, may be used exclusively with a particular client, while at other times a combination of techniques might be most effective (e.g., 78).

OPERANT PROCEDURES

The use of positive reinforcement to promote behavioral change is perhaps the most widely used technique in behavioral counseling. In operant conditioning the individual must first emit a response, and the consequences which follow the response, i.e., type and timing of the reinforcement, influence his subsequent behavior. It is Skinner's (106, 107) view that all behavior is a function of the contingencies of reinforcement, i.e., of preceding events that prompt the behavior (discriminative stimuli or S^D) *and* subsequent reinforcing events (reinforcing stimuli or S^R). The antecedents or discriminative stimuli of a behavior can be rearranged to alter behavior; *stimulus control* techniques are based on changing these antecedent cues. The positive events or reinforcing stimuli that immediately follow a behavior can also be rearranged to change the behavior; *reinforcement* has usually referred to changing the consequences of a behavior.

Studies demonstrating the efficacy of operant conditioning procedures with human subjects are numerous, and evidence is accumulating to support its use in a variety of settings with many problem behaviors. In the past few years the extent to which systematic reinforcement procedures have been employed in modifying

---

been on altering the individual's response to such environments, even when the environment is the problem. Winett and Winkler (132) have characterized classroom studies using behavioral approaches with the phrase "be still, be quiet, be docile" to describe their emphasis.

individual and group behavior in school and nonschool settings has greatly increased. Innovative applications of reinforcement techniques will be discussed in the next section. Comprehensive surveys showing the marked increase in usage as well as in breadth of application of operant principles (e.g., 5, 37, 57) are available and will not be covered here.

Self-control as a treatment strategy. Self-control involves those situations in which the person is the agent of his own behavior change. In this treatment strategy the counselor arranges the contingencies in such a way that the client progresses from external to internal control of his own behavior. Thoresen and Mahoney (122) discuss self-control as a choice situation, where the person has two or more response options and there is an absence of immediate constraints. In demonstrating self-control the person engages in a behavior which has a prior probability less than another behavior. For example, a shy girl in initiating a conversation rather than avoiding the situation is demonstrating self-control. Self-control can be accomplished by engaging in self-observation, environmental planning, and behavioral programming (122). It is important to note that internal behaviors such as thoughts, images, and physiological responses as well as external behaviors are involved in self-control methods.

Self-control requires knowledge of the contingencies as well as skill in manipulation of these contingencies to modify and control one's behavior. Cautela (15) points out that in reality all behavioral techniques may be conceptualized as training in self-control in that the desired outcome is for the individual to regulate his own behavior by arranging the appropriate contingencies. The procedure generally consists of the counselor teaching the client to initiate some self-control responses with external reinforcement in those situations in which the undesired behavior normally occurs.

Mahoney (79) provides an interesting example of the use of self-control techniques in the modification of covert behavior. His goal was to increase positive self-thoughts (PST) and decrease self-depreciatory obsessions on the part of a twenty-two-year-old male who experienced "pervasive and uncontrollable thoughts about being brain-damaged, persecuted and odd." In the first treatment period a self-punishment technique, i.e., snapping a heavy-gauge rubber band worn around the wrist, was used immediately after each negative thought. This procedure eliminated these obsessional thoughts. Eight weeks after counseling began, Mahoney implemented a "priming" technique. Four index cards were attached to the client's cigarette package. The client was asked to cite some positive things about himself. These positive comments were written on three of the cards, e.g., "I'm proud of being in good physical trim"; the fourth card was blank. Before taking a cigarette he read (subvocalized) the top card attached to the cigarette package, placed it on the bottom, and then reinforced himself with a cigarette. When the top card was blank, the client had to generate a new positive self-thought and write it on the card. The procedure greatly increased the client's frequency of positive self-thoughts in a period of seven weeks. Mahoney reported that "the client stated that spontaneous PSTs were occasionally self-reinforced with cigarettes, but that most of them constituted their own reward because of their pleasantness." Gains in self-confidence and general behavioral adjustment followed treatment.

It is interesting that in the first part of the study Mahoney used a self-punishment technique (the client's snapping of wrist with a heavy-gauge rubber band) to reduce negative thoughts. This procedure was effective in reducing the frequency of negative thoughts; however, it was still necessary to use a separate intervention procedure to increase positive self-thoughts. More recently Hannum (43) has demonstrated that a teacher's self-esteem can be increased by using high-probability behaviors (e.g., looking at the wall clock) to increase positive self-thought.

Kolb, Winter, and Berlew (55) investigated self-directed change strategies as a method of helping a group of graduate students specify goals for themselves and attain changes in behavior, thoughts, and feelings commensurate with these goals. The individuals were taught (a) to reflect on their own behavior and to select a limited but well-defined goal, (b) to self-observe and graph their own goal-related behavior, and (c) to decide for themselves how long they wanted to continue and when their goals were achieved. Participation in T groups provided means by which feedback and reinforcement could be given each person for progress. Two kinds of feedback were utilized: that gained from self-observation and feedback received from others in the group. Persons in the group with both kinds of feedback were more successful than those who did not receive the feedback from others in the group. Those who indicated they were highly committed to their goals demonstrated more observable changes in behavior than did low-committed persons. The findings of this study also indicated that feedback in the later stages of the group sessions carried out over a semester was more highly correlated with degree of change than was feedback provided during the first sessions. The authors did not acknowledge that feedback from others actually represented social reinforcement. The study suggests that self-control is facilitated when the person receives contingent external reinforcement for efforts to change his own behavior.

The value of self-instructional procedures in modifying behavior lies not only in their effectiveness in bringing about specific behavioral change, since clients also learn a method of problem-solving which can be generalized to other problems. Further, the person learns to perceive counseling as well as his problems from a teaching-learning perspective, where the person can serve as his own teacher. Indeed, Lang (67) points out that "absence of programs for shaping cognitive sets and attitudes may contribute to the not infrequent failure of transfer of treatment effects" (p. 94).

Studies conducted by Meichenbaum (83) and his associates indicate that training in the self-monitoring of cognitive responses not only is effective in itself in bringing about a desired behavioral change but that such training greatly enhances the efficacy of the behavior modification technique per se, e.g., social modeling and desensitization (cf: 50, 83, 84). Meichenbaum (83) and his associates have also studied ways in which impulsive children use their private speech. These children exhibit less verbal control over their motor behaviors and use private speech less effectively than do nonimpulsive children in regulating their actions. Meichenbaum and Goodman (85) used a self-guidance technique to train impulsive children to control their nonverbal behavior. The use of modeling and rehearsal to develop self-instructions and self-reinforcement resulted in a significant improvement on the *Porteus Maze*, in performance IQ on the *WISC*, and in a test of cognitive reflectivity. A second study indicated that modeling alone was not as effective as modeling combined with self-instructional training. Meichenbaum (83) and his associates have subsequently used similar cognitive modification procedures to improve hospitalized schizophrenics' performance on attention and cognitive tasks, to reduce college students' test anxiety, to modify smoking behavior, to reduce speech anxiety, and to reduce avoidance behavior, e.g., fear of snakes.

Teachers and parents as reinforcing agents. Skinner (108) defines teaching as an "arrangement of the contingencies of reinforcement under which students learn" (p. 64). A child learns not because he is shown or told, but because certain consequences follow, i.e., "interesting things should happen *after* a student has read a page or looked with care. . . ." In many instances it may be far more effective and efficient for a counselor, concerned with helping children modify their behavior, to train teachers and/or parents in the use of operant principles than to employ the same technique himself in dyadic or group counseling situations.

Programs for training teachers and others to utilize behavioral techniques are numerous. (See, for example, 12, 47, 63, 89, 92.) Patterson (89) presents an excellent overview of the procedures which have been developed in the last decade for modifying the behavior of those significant "others," e.g., parents and teachers, who interact with the child whose behavior is the target for change. These include studies concerned with teaching parents and others (a) to attend more effectively to the child's as well as their own behavior, (b) to observe and pinpoint target behaviors, (c) to alter reinforcement contingencies, and (d) apply the principles effectively.

Lindsley (75) in working with a three-year-old child who had been constipated most of his life and who defecated only on administration of a medicated suppository taught the parents to use social and other positive consequences *contingent* upon any bowel movement. The child acquired elimination response immediately following the first behavior modification session. After eight months Lindsley indicated that the child was still free from constipation. Bernal (11) and her associates (12) used a combination of reinforcement and videotape feedback to teach parents in modifying children's behavior. The procedures included (a) home observations to determine the reinforcement contingencies maintaining the inappropriate behavior; (b) instructions to the parents in a systematic procedure, e.g., positive reinforcement, punishment, and extinction techniques when the child behaves in specific ways; (c) guided practice and videotape feedback for the parent in utilizing these procedures with the child. Bernal et al. (12) presented several cases which demonstrate the effectiveness of these training procedures for modifying deviant behaviors.

An interesting by-product of teaching parents and teachers the use of reinforcement principles for modifying a child's behavior is that often the parents' or teacher's behavior changes as well. Kanfer and Phillips's (52) conclusions of their review of training others as change agents suggest that:

> Therapeutic agents who are a natural part of the patient's environment can enhance immediate effects, assure the maintenance of change, and provide generalization of newly acquired behaviors. Since the therapeutic agent is often part and parcel of the problem behavior or problematic system of behavior interaction, as when family members reinforce each other's undesirable behavior, intervention by people who are actually on the spot involves Reissman's "helper" principle in a very direct way. By its very nature, behavior therapy should continue to expand in the use of nonprofessional intervention agents . . . (p. 560).

Indeed, Hosford (48) found that teaching teachers to reinforce shy students for participating orally in class discussion not only increased the frequency of oral participation by the students, but that it encouraged change in the teachers' behavior as well. The teachers not only used positive reinforcement to increase class participation, but also quickly generalized the technique to other problems. Similarly, Bernal et al. (12) indicated that teaching parents in the use of these procedures brought about a sharp decline in parents' ineffective responses with their children.

There are numerous field studies utilizing operant procedures in dyadic and group counseling settings. Krumboltz and Thoresen (66) were instrumental in implementing a series of investigations in which counselor verbal reinforcement was given contingent upon the client's reference to planning to carry out the desired behavior. Many other studies have followed to support the efficacy of counselor verbal reinforcement as a treatment modality (e.g., 64, 65, 86, 103, 121).

Reinforcement techniques applied in groups. Counselor reinforcement has also been shown to be effective for developing counselor-client rapport and bringing about other affective outcomes in group relationships. Liberman (74) demonstrated that the therapist's use of selective prompts and reinforcement caused more group cohesiveness and affective behaviors than did conventional intuitive, group-centered procedures. In addition, he found that the counselor's reinforcing for affective responses was initiated by group members, i.e., they began reinforcing each other for affective behavior. Some other interesting innovations in the use of operant techniques include reinforcement menus (e.g., 21, 49), contingency management with delinquents (e.g., 98), and self-determined reinforcement (e.g., 38).

The results of studies by Warner and Hansen (127) and Warner (126) conducted in regular school settings suggest that verbal reinforcement and model-reinforcement group counseling procedures are effective not only in reducing student feelings of alienation, but also in producing overt changes in behavior when measured six months after termination of counseling. Students who scored one standard deviation above the mean on a scale of alienation (23) were randomly assigned to four treatments. Each experimental group met for six forty-minute sessions. In the reinforcement groups, the counselor attempted to keep the discussion "focused on the students' feelings of alienation and to give positive verbal reinforcement to statements made by students which suggested positive attitudes toward their positions in the social structure." More specifically, the counselor was attempting to encourage statements of specific actions the students could take to eliminate their feelings of alienation. The model-reinforcement procedures were identical to those employed in the verbal reinforcement groups except that two student models, one male and one female, selected by teachers and peers because of their overall adjustment to society, were added to each group. (Both the students and the models were unaware of the special selection of the models.) In the placebo discussion treatment the counselors made no attempt to direct the discussion or to reinforce specific kinds of statements. Both the reinforcement and model-reinforcement procedures were significantly more effective than the other procedures in reducing feelings of alienation.

After six months, teacher ratings of student overt behaviors were collected. The *Teachers Behavior Rating Scale* (20) was used to measure fifteen categories of behavior on a daily basis. Ratings of students who had been in the reinforcement groups were significantly more positive than those in the placebo or inactive control groups.

Kramer (56) evaluated the effects of two kinds of group counseling procedures—reinforcement counseling and traditional counseling—with sixty freshmen students enrolled in a study-skills course. The objective was to increase the amount of questioning, responsibility, and positive verbal statements. Counselors in the reinforcement groups actively recognized and approved students when they expressed comments in these three categories. Other statements were either rephrased or passively accepted. In the "traditional counseling" group the counselors reflected, clarified, or interpreted students' comments during the group sessions. During the first and fourth sessions, both groups were exposed to one of two social model tapes designed to facilitate group discussions. After the sixth session an analysis was made of the above responses in relation to total responses made in each group. Students in the reinforcement group demonstrated a significantly higher proportion of questioning, responsibility, and positive responses to total responses than did those in the traditional group. Further analysis indicated counselors actively reinforced individuals in both groups, the main difference being the reinforcement situation: in the reinforcement groups counselor reinforcements were systematic and contingent on specific student responses whereas in the traditional counseling group the counselor's reinforcements were not systematic and not contingent on one response type.

DESENSITIZATION

Counterconditioning techniques are frequently used to modify anxiety reactions, behavioral inhibitions, phobic responses, and various types of hypochondriases. The most widely used approach for anxiety-related problems has evolved from Wolpe's (134) systematic desensitization based on the principle of reciprocal inhibition.

Although many clinicians employed counterconditioning methods prior to the development of systematic desensitization, it was Wolpe's formulation of systematic desensitization "which eventually stimulated the outburst of research and clinical application that has characterized this decade" (57:500). The principle of reciprocal inhibition hypothesizes that a person cannot be simultaneously relaxed and anxious. This suggested that teaching a person the incompatible response of relaxation in the presence of an anxiety-provoking stimulus would reduce or even eliminate the anxiety. While the neurophysiological principle of reciprocal inhibition has not been experimentally verified (130, 131), research has demonstrated that systematic desensitization does produce a reduction in anxiety reactions. The efficacy of these procedures has been attributed to a number of factors, e.g., operant conditioning (73), interpersonal factors (129), and counterconditioning (22).

After reviewing some seventy-five studies and case reports in which systematic desensitization was the primary counseling intervention, Paul (95) concluded:

> The findings were overwhelmingly positive, and for the first time in the history of psychological treatments, a specific therapeutic package reliably produced measurable benefits for clients across a broad range of distressing problems in which anxiety was of fundamental importance. "Relapse" and "symptom substitution" were notably lacking, although the majority of authors were attuned to these problems. Investigations of equal quality and scope have not been carried out with other treatment techniques . . . (pp. 158-59).

The technique of systematic desensitization involves several steps. First, the counselor and client together identify what specific situations are associated with the client's emotional reactions. Second, these situations are arranged in a hierarchy from least to most aversive in terms of physical proximity, frequency, time, or other gradients. Training in deep muscle relaxation usually follows next. Although muscular relaxation is most often used to counteract the anxiety responses, other stimuli such as foods, assertive and sexual behaviors, medications, or strong affective relationships can be used effectively. During subsequent counseling sessions the counselor relaxes the client and asks him to imagine as vividly as possible the least anxiety-provoking item on the hierarchy. As the client learns to relax in the presence of imagining or experiencing *in vivo* scenes higher on the hierarchy, he gradually becomes able to be exposed to the most aversive situation without experiencing the accompanying anxiety.

Desensitization procedures have been used in dyadic and group situations with a great variety of problem behaviors. Reviews and discussions such as those of Krasner (57), Paul (94, 95), Krumboltz and Thoresen (65), and Bandura (8) indicate that these procedures are highly effective and are not limited to any particular type of emotion-arousing situation. Indeed, Bandura (8:464) suggests that desensitization procedures could even "be employed to neutralize the negative valence of Oedipal fantasies in clients for whom this might constitute a problem." Desensitization procedures or their modifications have been used successfully to modify public-speaking anxiety (48, 97), school phobia (36), anxiety toward disasters (1), sexual problems (112), diarrhea (18), and test anxiety (29).

Desensitization procedures have been utilized in a variety of innovative ways. Programmed automated desensitization has been employed successfully with and without the therapist present (26, 68). Lang et al. (68) used a magnetic tape device which instructed the client in the relaxation procedures and presented in sequence the prerecorded stimuli from the hierarchy. Hekmat (44) has suggested *semantic* desensitization as an alternative to systematic desensitization. In this treatment the client practices using positive words as images in response to certain problem stimulus words such as *spider* or *snake*. The objective is to eliminate the conditioned negative words or images that have become associated with the target stimulus. (See Staats [109] for a further discussion.) Other examples include the use of role-playing sequences rather than visualized scenes (48), standardized and individualized hierarchies (29), and the use of slide projections rather than emotive imagery (39).

Group desensitization. Paul and Shannon (97) demonstrated that group desensitization procedures combined with discussions of feelings were not only efficient and effective means for reducing interpersonal performance anxiety of male undergraduates, but were as effective as individual desensitization and significantly better than insight-oriented therapy or attention-placebo treatments. Ten men who served the preceding semester as "wait-list" controls for a study conducted by the first author (93) and who showed no reduction in anxiety scores during this wait period were given nine weekly one-hour desensitization sessions conducted in groups of five subjects each. The systematic desensitization procedures were similar to those utilized in dyadic situations explained above. Each group constructed an anxiety hierarchy of situational elements common to all subjects in that group. For example, one group's hierarchy began with "You are discussing your approaching speech with friends two weeks before it is due" and ended with "You are standing in the center of Assembly Hall presenting a speech to a packed house." Anxiety scales, grade-point averages, and comparisons of pre-post personality and anxiety scale changes of subjects receiving treatment in groups with those having had the individual sessions the semester earlier were used to evaluate the effectiveness of the group procedures. The data indicate that subjects assigned to the group desensitization treatment (a) reported a significant decrease in interpersonal performance anxiety and (b) demonstrated a significant gain in grade-point averages when compared with untreated controls. No significant differences were found between individual and group desensitization. Further, a two-year follow-up of group desensitization subjects (96) indicated that significant gains were maintained over the two-year period.

Dua (27) tested the effectiveness of three group desensitization massing procedures, twelve-hour, five-day, and fifteen-day, for reducing fear of physical contact with the opposite sex. Standard desensitization procedures of relaxation and visualization practice followed by systematic and graduated exposure to a standard ten-item anxiety hierarchy were used. Pre- and post-assessments of the subjects' approach-avoidance responses to the opposite sex as well as subject self-reports were used to assess the effectiveness of the three treatment conditions. Although all three treatments yielded significant improvements in the subjects' performance of the behavioral task, subjects exposed to the five-day massing procedure improved the most. The fifteen-day treatment group on the other hand showed greatest reductions in self-ratings of fears as measured by two fear survey scales. Thus, the more intensive massing of treatment produced the greatest overt behavioral changes, while self-ratings were changed more if spaced over a longer period of time.

SOCIAL MODELING

The use of social modeling in counseling has increased in recent years (123). Modeling is based on "vicarious" learning in which the client can learn new behaviors or reduce problem behaviors with no practice or direct reinforcement. Basically, this technique involves the presentation under controlled conditions of "live" (physically present) or symbolic models (audiotapes or videotapes, written descriptions) which demonstrate specific desired behaviors. Usually, the modeling demonstration is used in conjunction with systematic counselor reinforcement and guided client rehearsal of the modeled behavior.

The modeling process is not new; vicarious or imitative learning is probably the most common process involved in the early learning of children. However, the systematic application of planned modeling in counseling is new. There are several advantages in using modeling. It is an efficient method of demonstrating complex behaviors. Indeed, many complex *human* behaviors may be learnable only by means of observational experiences. Another advantage is the fact that social modeling seems to work equally well in group and dyadic situations (e.g., 66). Furthermore, as Bandura (8) points out, almost any learning which can be gained by direct experience can also be learned from observational or vicarious situations. It is true that operant conditioning is highly effective in strengthening existing behavior; however, helping a client acquire a completely new or a particularly complex behavior through reinforcing successive approximations of that behavior (shaping) can often be complex and time-consuming. Experiments by Bandura (7, 8) and others have demonstrated that the presentation of appropriate modeling experiences can be an effective counseling procedure in three major areas: (a) changing new client behaviors, (b) increasing or decreasing well-established behaviors, and (c) facilitating the performance of behaviors that seldom occur.

Using models in counseling. Krumboltz and Thoresen (65) and their associates have been instrumental in generating a large number of studies which have utilized social modeling procedures in actual counseling situations. Although the specific modeling procedures vary from study to study, they generally consist of the counselor providing, often in sequential steps, real or symbolic models who demonstrate the specific behaviors which the client needs to gain in order to solve his problem. The counselor employs guided practice and systematic counselor reinforcement in addition to counselor follow-up and reinforcement when the client applies these behaviors outside the counseling situation.

One of the first investigations to study these procedures in field counseling settings was that of Krumboltz and Thoresen (66). They demonstrated that social modeling procedures combined with specific operant techniques can be used in dyadic and group counseling settings to promote specific decision-making behaviors on the part of male and female high school students. Their procedures, termed *model-reinforcement counseling*, included having the counselors present audiotape recordings of a counselor-client interview in which the model client was verbally reinforced by the model counselor as he discussed various decision-making behaviors he had used or would use in making his educational and career decisions. After listening to the audiotape, the subject(s) was reinforced verbally by the counselor for verbal responses that indicated imitation of or similar responses to those demonstrated by the model. In general, modeling plus reinforcement was found to be more effective for male subjects whereas females were responsive to either social reinforcement or modeling with reinforcement. Group treatment was just as effective as individual counseling; male subjects, however, demonstrated more information-seeking behavior when counseled in groups.

Meyer, Strowig, and Hosford (86) replicated these findings with high school students attending small rural high schools. Other studies have replicated and expanded this use of social modeling in counseling (3, 28, 65, 88, 100, 113).

A number of variables affecting the social modeling process in counseling have been studied. The type and source of reinforcement as well as the characteristics and stimulus situation of the model, client, and counselor have been subjected to empirical tests. Among the many variables studied have been sex of the model and the sex of the client (119); prestige of the model and/or counselor (62, 118); ethnic background of model, counselor and/or client (50, 113); and the athletic, social, and academic success of the model and observer (65, 118). Reviews (8, 48, 87, 123) provide discussions of numerous variables affecting the efficacy of the social model learning process.

In addition to employing modeling procedures to help clients acquire new behaviors or to strengthen behaviors already in their repertoires, these techniques can be used to help clients extinguish existing or develop new emotional responses. Modeling procedures in these categories are usually referred to as vicarious extinction, vicarious arousal, and replication techniques. In vicarious extinction the counselor exposes the client to a series of modeled events in which the model's approach to the feared stimulus or performance of the anxiety-provoking behavior leads to positive rather than aversive consequences. Theoretically, exposure to these modeling procedures allows the client to experience emotional reactions vicariously but at a lower level of arousal than that which normally would cause the client to avoid the problem situation. Bandura (5) reports several studies in which individuals have been able to lower a variety of fear arousal responses by being exposed to graduated sequences of symbolic, i.e., film or videotape, and actual model procedures. Most of the investigations have utilized modeling techniques alone; however, some have used combinations of modeling and other approaches, e.g., guided practice. Still others have been comparisons between modeling and alternative behavioral and non-behavioral techniques.

An excellent example of this group of studies is that reported by Bandura, Blanchard, and Ritter (8). Working with adolescent and adult subjects whose lives were restricted in some way (e.g., job performance, recreation, etc.) by their extreme anxieties of snakes, the authors compared four treatments: (a) self-administered symbolic modeling (film) and relaxation procedures, (b) graduated live modeling with immediate guided practice by the observer, (c) systematic desensitization, and (d) an assessment control group procedure. All three experimental treatments significantly reduced avoidance responses in comparison to the control procedure; 92 percent of the subjects in the live-modeling-with-guided-practice treatment were successful in completely extinguishing the fear of snakes as measured by a behavioral test compared to 33 percent and 25 percent for symbolic modeling and systematic desensitization respectively.

Shaw (104) in working with extreme dental phobics also compared video-presented modeling with systematic desensitization. He found that the modeling with covert (imaginary) practice was completely successful with 77 percent of the subjects, compared with 44 percent for desensitization. Shaw used multiple models to demonstrate a variety of feared behaviors (e.g., having novacaine injection) associated with having dental work done. Subjects were considered completely successful when they voluntarily went to the dentist and had at least one cavity filled.

Vicarious arousal procedures are used particularly with clients who fail to respond emotionally or respond with inappropriate emotion in certain situations. After exploring with the client and, when possible, observing the extent of his arousal in the situations in which he responds inappropriately, the counselor arranges for the client to be exposed to specific real and/or symbolic models who display in the stimulus setting the appropriate arousal responses which the individual needs to acquire. Theoretically, the transmission of the model's emotional reactions to the observer occurs by contiguous association (42). According to Bandura (5), the extent to which the transmission of arousal occurs depends on the similarity between distinctive cues of the modeled situation and those which the observer himself has experienced. A clinical example of this technique is provided by Hosford and Rifkin (51) in which they worked with a client who, because of an aversive and anxiety-provoking sexual experience early in his life, had been unable to experience sexual arousal with females. Although he was a practicing homosexual, he desired to become at least partly heterosexual. In addition to desensitization and relaxation training, the authors exposed the client to filmed models of graduated intensity of sexual arousal in a variety of female-related sexual situations. Although used only a few times, the technique did result in sexual arousal and penile erection response to female stimuli.

The principles of replication therapy are closely related to those of social modeling in that such counseling involves the counselor utilizing simulations, i.e., modeling situations which replicate various aspects of the client's environment. The procedure allows the client to practice with the counselor in low-stress situations those behaviors in which he is deficient, thus facilitating both the reduction of avoidance responses and the production of approach responses. The simulated low-stress situations bring about a reduction of anxiety, so that guided practice (135), role-playing or modifications of psychodrama (133), or play therapy can be used (see 52:232-36). Patterson's study (90) provides an excellent example of the use of this technique with a school-phobic child. By using dolls in play therapy in a graduated simulation of going to school, staying at school, playing and working with others, the child learned vicariously to cope with the environmental stress situations and was able to generalize these behaviors to the real-life situation.

AVERSIVE TECHNIQUES

Another behavioral approach to counseling is the use of aversive techniques. Some behavioral (and nonbehavioral) counselors reject the use of aversive procedures on principle alone; however, few can deny their effectiveness in modifying many deviant behaviors for which other therapies have failed. Aversive techniques, e.g., use of electric shock, aversive imagery, or applying a variety of other stimuli commonly thought of as punishment, are most often employed to modify behaviors that are physically or socially damaging to the individual and for which other techniques have not been effective. In addition, aversive techniques can inhibit a self-defeating behavior long enough to teach the person a positive behavior that is incompatible with the problem behavior.

Self-injurious behavior, in particular, has been shown to be amenable to aversive techniques. Such behaviors occur when potentially harmful or socially deviant stimuli acquire potent immediate reinforcement value for the individual. In many cases the client has to be kept under continuous restraint and, in severe instances, the self-destructive behavior leads to death. Few therapeutic techniques have been shown effective with such problems, although aversive procedures, such as the use of electric shock contingent upon the manifestation of the self-injurious behavior, have resulted in immediate suppression and often complete elimination of that behavior (41, 76, 99, 115). Usually, averse techniques are employed as a last resort; when they are used, they are applied only for a limited period of time until the client can gain control over his deviant responses by learning more appropriate ways of responding (5).

Techniques utilized in this area follow classical conditioning (the punishing stimuli is paired with the problem, i.e., *stimulus contingent*), instrumental conditioning (the punishing stimuli immediately follows the problem behavior, i.e., *response contingent*), or combinations of both procedures. Stimulus-contingent models are usually referred to as *aversion therapy* while response-contingent procedures are termed *punishment paradigms*. Whether a procedure is considered aversion therapy or punishment, however, depends more on the theoretical affinity of the experimenter than on the analysis of the techniques employed (52).

Punishment. When aversive stimuli are employed contingent upon the demonstration of a particular behavior, the procedure is usually referred to as "punishment." Punishment generally follows the operant conditioning model but several theoretical formulations have been advanced to explain punishment per se and its subsequent effects (e.g., 17, 24, 107).

Precise definitions of what constitutes a punishing stimulus are difficult to formulate when dealing with real clients in a clinical setting. One definition which has the advantage of avoiding the subjectivism frequently encountered is that of Azrin and Holz (4). They define punishment as "*a reduction of the future probability of a specific response as a result of the immediate delivery of a stimulus for that response.* The stimulus is designated as a *punishing stimulus*; the entire process is designated as punishment" (p. 381). In this case a punishing stimulus differs from a reinforcing stimulus in that it reduces rather than increases the frequency of a behavior.

A variety of punishing stimuli employed in response-contingent models have been shown effective in modifying behavior. In many cases, particularly in those involving self-destructive behaviors, a punishment approach to therapy has been effective in reducing the deviant behavior after other approaches have failed. The aversive events include such diversive stimuli as electric shock (4, 99), noise (10), delayed auditory feedback (40), and contingent removal of positive reinforcement, such as time-out (33) and response-cost (128) procedures. Of these, electric shock appears to be the punishing stimulus used most extensively and the most effective in reducing and/or eliminating deviant responses (4).

An excellent example of the effect of electric shock in modifying a self-destructive behavior is provided by Lang and Melamed (69). The client was a nine-month-old boy who suffered from ruminative vomiting. No organic basis could be found for the vomiting, and medication as well as other kinds of therapy proved to be ineffective in stopping the behavior. It was necessary for Lang and Melamed to employ aversive techniques in order to save the child's life. Base rates of the vomiting were established by observation and electromyograph (EMG) recordings. Although he did not vomit during eating, the child vomited within ten minutes after eating and continued to do so periodically thereafter. The treatment consisted of a one-second electrical shock to the leg administered at one-second intervals from the start of vomiting until it ended. A reduction in the frequency of vomitings occurred immediately. Because the child began the avoidance response of curling his foot to avoid receiving the shock, it was then given to the child's calf. The frequency of vomiting decreased again. After only six sessions the vomiting stopped completely. Two days later the child was still free from vomiting and his frequency of other positive responses, e.g., smiling, had increased.

Time-out and response-cost procedures. In some cases the administration of unconditioned aversive stimuli may be accompanied by undesired side effects which can eliminate or greatly attenuate the success of any counseling. Indeed, it may result in the client's complete withdrawal from counseling. Time-out and response-cost procedures utilize the withdrawal of positive reinforcement in contrast to the administration of aversive stimuli and appear to be free from negative side effects. The time-out procedure is defined by Ferster (33) as a technique in which the removal of a positive stimulus serves as the aversive stimulus. Removing a disruptive child from the classroom and withholding of dessert from a child eating too fast are examples of such procedures.

Thoresen and Mahoney (122) have termed the use of time-out and response-cost procedures as "positive punishment," since the person can learn to administer these procedures himself without directly being administered an aversive stimulus by someone else. Leitenberg (73) concluded from a review of the experimental evidence that time-out from positive reinforcement does appear to have aversive properties for most individuals. Thus, avoidance of the aversiveness of time out is gained by displaying positive behavior. Some question remains, however, as to whether the procedure reduces the probability of the deviant response or whether it encourages avoidance responses (4). Furthermore, while time out is an effective procedure which produces effects different from those produced by electric shock, the latter appears to be more effective in suppressing a behavior (4, 72).

Response-cost procedures involve the contingent removal of positive reinforcers; money, points, or tokens are subtracted *contingent* upon the demonstration of the deviant behavior. This procedure is frequently employed in token economies and has been used effectively in several contexts of behavioral control (4, 52).

Aversion therapy. Aversion therapy follows the classical conditioning model and usually involves the systematic pairing of a positively valenced stimulus, e.g., alcohol, with an aversive stimulus, e.g., nausea, so that the formerly positive stimulus begins to evoke aversive responses. Whether this process causes automatic or self-induced aversive reactions to the target stimulus is not clear. Bandura (5), for example, suggests that, as in punishment, the effects of aversive counterconditioning may manifest themselves in causing the individual to activate a self-stimulation that causes him to experience vicariously the aversive stimuli encountered during the counterconditioning process. What is important to counselors is that the acquired association between the conditioned and unconditioned stimulus develops, followed by a cessation or marked reduction in the deviant behavior.

Three methods of aversive counterconditioning account for most of the research utilizing aversion therapy: (a) electrical stimulation, (b) nauseous pharmacological intervention, and (c) symbolically induced aversion. Because of the ease with which electric shock can be administered and controlled, it is the most extensively used procedure. Typically, electric shocks are administered to the arms, legs, or feet of the client contiguous with the presentation of the conditioned stimulus. Electric shock has been employed successfully with transvestites, fetishists, homosexuals, exhibitionists, and a variety of masochistic types who demonstrate self-destructive behaviors (cf: 5, 35, 52, 91).

One of the first instances of using electric shock in a clinical setting to modify homosexual behavior was its use by Feldman and MacCulloch (32). The client was asked to rank a variety of slides of males in various stages of undress in terms of their attractiveness to him. Next, the hierarchy of slides was presented to the client in ascending order of attractiveness. Each slide was presented with an electric shock which the client could discontinue whenever he wished; however, the slide was removed from the screen at the same moment the shock was terminated. Although the client was told to leave the slide on the screen as long as it was sexually attractive to him, he was not shocked if the slide was removed within eight seconds. The strength of the shock, however, was increased until the slide was removed. After a slide no longer elicited sexual arousal, the next one on the hierarchy was presented. This sequence was followed by a second hierarchy in which slides of females of descending order of attractiveness were presented to the client so that the reduction of anxiety became associated with the female stimulus. About one-half of the clients who used this procedure were still heterosexual at the end of a one-year follow-up period.

Chemical aversion therapy has also been used to modify a variety of self-destructive and socially deviant behaviors. This procedure is used most frequently and successfully in cases of alcoholism. However, nauseous pharmacological agents have also had moderate success in the treatment of sexual disorders, with the possible exception of homosexuality (5, 52, 91). In actual treatment the client is usually administered a nausea-producing medication such as emetine. Just prior to the onset of the nausea, he is exposed to the conditioned stimulus. In the case of alcoholism, for example, the client is asked to smell, taste, and sip liquor as the nausea heightens. The pairing of the nausea with the conditioned stimulus (alcohol) is repeated over several sessions until the client can become nauseous just thinking about or hearing comments concerning alcohol, the conditioned stimulus.

One of the classic cases using chemical aversion therapy with cases other than alcoholism is Raymond's (101) successful treatment of a fetishistic client by apomorphine aversion therapy. The subject, a thirty-three-year-old married man, had a history of becoming sexually aroused by prams and handbags and physically attacking them to release his tension. Several arrests, confinement to mental hospitals, and psychoanalysis did not reduce his problem. Finally, aversion therapy was employed. The procedure consisted of injections of apomorphine followed by exposure to handbags and prams just before the nausea occurred. Repeated pairings were carried out day and night for one week with the patient being kept awake by amphetamines. After eight days a second treatment was administered for nine days with the individual showing strong aversion to the prams and handbags. An additional follow-up treatment was administered six months later. After two years the client was still free of his fetishistic behavior and reported that his sexual relations with his wife had greatly improved.

Several other case studies in which chemical aversion therapy has been the principle mode of treatment in alcoholism and sexual deviancy cases exist to support its effectiveness as a counseling procedure. Although pharmacological agents have been used quite extensively, they have many disadvantages. For example, individuals may react differently to the same drug or to the same quantity of the drug at different times. In addition, the effects are often gradual and, therefore, not amenable to control by the therapist. Side effects such as physiological changes are also possible (35).

Symbolically induced aversion is the third principal method of aversion therapy. Because this procedure does not involve physically aversive stimulation, it is less likely to be resisted by clients than are electrical and chemical techniques, and possible side effects are minimized. The procedure employs symbolically induced aversion in which the client imagines an experience of repulsion during the presentation of the problem. The conditioned stimulus, e.g., a small child in the case of a pedophile, may also be symbolically reproduced. As in other forms of aversion therapy, the repeated pairings condition the negative association.

The treatment may proceed with the unconditioned stimulus (UCS) being imagined, e.g., nausea associated with a hangover, while the conditioned stimulus (CS) is real, e.g., a variety of alcoholic beverages with the smell of alcohol emanting in the room. In other cases both the CS and USC may be imaginal as in the procedure of covert sensitization (15a). In this approach the objective is to extinguish the conditioned inappropriate behavior, e.g., excessive drinking, by imaging noxious stimuli before and after imagining or experiencing the inappropriate behavior. As in desensitization, the client is taught to relax and his problem and the procedure are explained in terms of learning principles. He is then asked to visualize step-by-step the behaviors associated with the problem behavior. When the client can visualize the target scene, he is told to imagine an experience that is very noxious to him, e.g., vomiting uncontrollably. The pairing of visualizing the target behavior with that of some noxious situation is repeated until the subject feels nauseous or experiences similar aversive feelings while imaging only the problem behavior. The pairing of positive scenes with those in which the client refrains from or otherwise discontinues the inappropriate behavior is also effective. Behavioral problems for which covert sensitization procedures have been applied include smoking (15a, 124), sexual deviation (9), obesity (54, 16, 70), and alcoholism (16).

Another type of therapy which uses symbolically induced aversion but within a stimulus-response paradigm is implosive therapy (111). This procedure immediately exposes the client to the most intense level of an imagined fear-arousing situation. Hogan (45) provides a vivid description of the process.

> . . . an acrophobic would be requested to imagine himself falling off a high building or cliff, or perhaps be instructed to picture himself falling through space and in complete darkness. Ideally, the person should be made aware of his feeling and sensations while falling. Then he should feel the impact of his body with the ground and view his crushed, broken body. It is important that the therapist emphasize how the person looks and feels throughout the scenes. If the client should recall an actual traumatic experience, the clinician should center succeeding imagery around that experience (p. 26).

This model is based on Pavlov's classical extinction principle that when a conditioned response (fear or anxiety) is repeatedly paired with a conditioned stimulus without periodic pairings with the unconditioned stimulus (actual pain), the conditioned response gradually extinguishes. Stampfl and Levis (111) view such extinction as taking place most rapidly when similarity between the stimulus extinction conditions and the original anxiety-eliciting situation is maximized.

Controlled studies supporting the efficacy of implosive therapy are few at present but are increasing in number. Hogan and Kirchner's work (46) with rat-phobic college subjects provides an example. The investigators devised two one-session treatment strategies in which the experimental subjects received, on the average, thirty-nine minutes each of individually tailored intense exposure to fear-arousing situations with rats, e.g., imagining the rats eating their internal organs, etc., and the controls received only neutral imagery and some relaxation training. At the end of only one session, fourteen of the twenty-one implosive subjects were able to pick up a white rat while only two of the twenty-two control subjects did so.

Some issues. Many issues can be raised about using aversive techniques in counseling. Some counselors reject them on principle alone. Blanket rejection, however, of the responsible use of punishment and aversion procedures is hardly warranted in view of their demonstrated effectiveness in modifying a variety of deviant responses. Further, such techniques have demonstrated a decided superiority over other techniques in reducing self-destructive behaviors. As Bandura (5) points out, surgical and dental patients must and often desire to undergo brief aversive experiences in order to reduce or eliminate more serious and long-lasting suffering.

It is true that in some cases, especially those involving electric shock or chemical aversion procedures, clients may demonstrate certain side effects such as pain, rejection of counseling, and a variety of avoidance behaviors. Azrin and Holz (4) point out that the possible termination or disruption of social relationships represents a critical side effect when one person administers an aversive stimulus to another. As is often the case, clients who demonstrate deviant behaviors already have defects in social relationships.

Reviews of aversive techniques research (e.g., 4, 5, 52, 99), however, indicate that such side effects are often more expected than observed and can be made inconsequential with appropriate controls. Symbolic aversive techniques may offer a more attractive alternative for those cases in which side effects or ethics are involved. Ethical considerations are best resolved by informing the client of the alternative forms of therapy available and having the client participate in the decision. Indeed, the client's volunteering for counseling, with awareness of the aversive procedures to be used, may serve to enhance the effect of the treatment.

CONCLUDING COMMENT ON TECHNIQUES

In the final analysis, counselors must be ready to use any and all techniques that help clients change their behavior. Behavioral approaches are in a state of "healthy infancy" (52), relying on an amalgam of intuitive artistry and scientific methodology. An open "technical eclecticism" rather than a closed theoretical allegiance is very much needed with respect to techniques (71). The counselor's focus must be problem-oriented rather than technique- or method-oriented. Existing limitations in our understanding of complex human behavior make it imperative that the counselor be committed to being experimental and tentative, always ready to be guided by the data being gathered on the client's progress and always ready to try another procedure.

Some of the techniques already discussed work effectively and others not discussed here hold great promise. For example, the recently developing area of "covert behavior modification" (52, 80, 82, 122) suggests that procedures based on operant, modeling, desensitization, and aversive rationales can be carried out *within* the person, often under the person's own direction. Self-reinforcement, self-punishment, self-modeling, and self-desensitization are all possible techniques. In addition, stimulus control methods are being developed and used. For instance, behavioral architecture (137) represents a strategy based in part on redesigning physical and social environments to cue or prompt desired behaviors and discourage others. Recently, weight-loss programs with obese clients have successfully employed stimulus control methods, among others, to help persons alter their eating behavior and reduce weight (114, 81).

Clearly, no one technique is always effective with all clients, even if they are experiencing the same type of problem. The overriding need, therefore, is to approach each client as an experimental situation, carefully gathering data *before* a treatment procedure is decided upon and continuously gathering data *during* counseling to facilitate ongoing evaluation of progress and provide the basis for changing techniques if necessary.

Contemporary Problems

Behavioral approaches to counseling can be helpful in understanding and resolving some current problems. The conceptualization of problems from a behavioral perspective and prevention strategies represent two important areas. Teaching the client to be "his own counselor" offers an approach of considerable relevance to the problems experienced by many persons.

CONCEPTUALIZATION OF PROBLEMS

In behavioral approaches the counselor attempts to modify the problem behavior itself. The emphasis is on the here-and-now environment, not on internal, hypothetical constructs and labels; "alienation," "sexual problems," "poor self-concept," and other labels are not viewed as typologies or personality traits. The conceptualization of the individual is not in terms of *who* the person is, but what the person *does* (87). A recent poem of Skinner (41) well reflects this point: "Truth's to be sought in *does* or *doesn't*, not *is* or *isn't* or *was* or *wasn't*." (Italics added.)

Behavioral approaches do not conceptualize problems as sickness in a medical sense. Rather than administer a myriad of psychological tests that provide a mental sickness label (e.g., paranoid) based on assumptions of etiology or symptoms, the behavioral counselor seeks to assess the *response capability* of the person. Indeed, the psychological labeling and grouping of persons based primarily on philosophical rather than scientific data has done much to *create* human problems. Clients are often labeled "schizophrenic" or "emotionally disturbed"; this labeling inadvertently does much to produce the behaviors associated with these stereotypes. The psychological labeling process in effect often manufactures the "madness" we earnestly seek to alleviate. Too often these labels as descriptions of behavior quickly become rigid pseudoexplanations of behavior (110, 117). For example, we first describe the person as "neurotic" and then slip into the tautology of explaining his actions by the very same label "because he is neurotic!" Once labeled and "explained," the person is typically left to confirm the validity of the label.

The question that should be asked concerns what does the client *do* under what conditions and to what extent. Kanfer and Saslow (53) have pioneered efforts to develop a behavioral-analytic or functional approach to assessment. The major objective is to coordinate in a very direct fashion "diagnosis" with "treatment," i.e., the assessment should tell the counselor what the client is *doing* to the extent that a direction for treatment is emphasized. In this model the major categories of assessment include: (a) analysis of problem situation including behavioral excesses, behavioral deficits, and behavioral assets; (b) clarification of the problem situation including what are the consequences of the behavior in question and under what conditions (biological, symbolic, social, vocational, etc.) do the problematic behaviors occur. Motivational analysis, developmental analysis, self-control skills, and an analysis of the social-cultural-physical environment is also involved. A behavioral analysis assesses the various current environments that influence the client's action as well as the client's capability to engage in certain actions. Such an analysis leads directly to understanding more thoroughly what is currently going on and what modifications might bring about meaningful change in the client's behavior.

Behavioral approaches are not divorced from real life. To attempt to change the individual without modification of his environment or to help him adjust to a bad environment are equally self-defeating. In the case of school counseling it is not enough (nor always desirable) for the counselor to work with a student to adjust him to an aversive classroom situation; it is more important to help the teacher who is responsible for that aversive classroom to modify his own behavior. An important aspect of behavioral approaches is that the counselor *must* work with those individuals and organizations which have a direct effect on the individual's behavior. This criterion contributes to the relevance of behavioral approaches to contemporary problems. The problem is not always seen as something within the person nor is the solution always considered the sole responsibility of the individual making the change.

On a broader scale this conceptualization of counseling is equally applicable to bringing about changes in society as a whole. Problems of excessive amounts of aggression and alienation, for example, may be solved when we have developed a more scientific analysis of behavior. Conceptualizing problems in terms of specific behaviors and their relationship to current environments can provide the needed data to (a) better understand the problems, and (b) apply interventions to change the behavior in question. Reliance on global concepts and abstract generalizations without detailed behavior analysis will continue to provide vague and abstract understandings and ineffectual solutions.

Commitment to prevention is another way in which behavioral approaches are relevant to finding solutions for contemporary individual and societal problems (65). Dealing with behavior after it is well established is much more difficult and much less efficient than modifying those environmental arrangements that produce such behavior in the first place. It is, as Skinner (108) points out, rather sad that the most reinforcing thing that many students have in a school day is the three o'clock bell. Too often schools and other institutions operate on negative contingencies: escaping from an aversive environment encourages avoidance of school. Counselors are better able to identify and anticipate which school, societal, parental, and/or personal contingencies foster which aversive outcomes if a scientific analysis of behavior is developed and used. There are, for example, many institutional and individual practices which increase the very behavior for which individuals seek counseling: anxiety, withdrawal, and aggression, to name only a few. Bandura's (5) work in social modeling provides evidence that when persons are exposed to aggressive behavior, they act more aggressively than do persons exposed for the same amount of time to nonaggressive models. Yet we fail to recognize the significance of the relationship between television, movies, games, and other means by which children are constantly exposed to aggressive and other maladaptive behaviors.

If counselors operated more from a scientific analysis of behavior, they would use data such as that gathered by Bandura and would not group emotionally disturbed children together or place slow learners only with other slow learners; nor would counselors place persons with learning deficits in mental hospitals with the expectation that they will be "cured" when the data suggests that such environments consistently model and reinforce maladaptive behavior. Few seem to realize, however, that the so-called treatment environment is maintaining the problem behaviors. Clearly, it is society (in terms of a social institution such as schools, families, mental hospitals, and housing projects) who is the client. The "institution as client" notion is highly consistent with behavioral strategies since the problem is not always seen as something within the client. In this sense counseling can be seen as a "subversive activity" seeking to modify institutional arrangements that produce human problems. It is imperative that such subversion be based on empirical rather than ideological grounds.

One solution is the systematic planning of physical and social situations, such as classrooms and home settings, as programmed learning environments. The use of comprehensive token reinforcement systems in classrooms, mental institutions, and group homes for predelinquents represents one type of planned environment (58). Such systems require a detailed behavioral analysis of the antecedents and consequences of specific behaviors in finding out what events are cueing and maintaining behavior.

Establishing behavioral training programs for parents on a community basis can prevent human problems. Most parents typically use aversive or coercive control techniques in managing children— as do schools, hospitals, and penal institutions. Parent use of aversive techniques inadvertently models aversive behavior to children. In this way parents, in effect, are teaching their children to use aversive techniques—and a vicious cycle is maintained wherein aversive techniques often produce behavior that the techniques are used to control. In effect, the cure is causing the problem.

Behavioral training programs in basic behavior principles and techniques can be established for young parents. They offer exciting possibilities in preventing the aversive home environments that "teach" maladaptive behavior to children. Patterson (91) and others (80, 98) have advocated such training programs based on experimental field research with children and their parents. Effective "parenting skills" can be learned *if* we create learning environments for parents which help them acquire and maintain such skills.

Finally, behavioral approaches can contribute to the prevention of human problems through social engineering and physical technology. Etzioni and Remp (30) recently commented on the extremely limited use to date of physical technology in preventing and solving human problems. These authors argued that we must combine our traditional methods of providing human services, such as counseling, with technological devices that prevent problems.

Several examples, such as instructional television, breath analyzers in highway safety, and the intrauterine devices (IUD), were reviewed as promising technological methods. The use of physical or "hardware" technologies in counseling remains very underdeveloped. Too often the issue is posed as "man versus machines" rather than as how can we integrate technological devices with existing ways of helping. Several promising examples of how machines can be effective in counseling are available, such as films and audiotapes to reduce fears (8, 104), a "jukebox" to disperse educational and occupational information (77), career kits that simulate the working conditions of many occupations, and life-career games that anticipate a host of everyday life problems (125). The recently popular biofeedback programs designed to foster self-control of internal processes such as heart rate, EEG alpha wave patterns, and blood pressure have utilized physical technologies in the feedback process. Krasner and Krasner (58) review efforts at engineering classroom environments designed to prevent problems and foster educational progress of each student.

If we are seriously concerned about *preventing* human problems, then we must create physical technologies and engineer changes in social environments that now produce human problems. We need to create and use social and physical inventions as well as fully examine existing technologies such as computers, films, television, and game simulations.

THE CLIENT AS HIS OWN COUNSELOR

Behavioral approaches have until recently been focused primarily on external control, that is, the counselor has used techniques to help either institutionalized persons or clients who have presented themselves for counseling. Recently, however, some have suggested that the main task of counseling is to *teach* the client the skills of behavior change. For example, Carkhuff (14) states that "the business of counseling is one of transforming helpees into helpers . . . most efficiently transformed into helpers by training them directly in helper's skills (p. viii)." The teaching-learning rationale of behavioral approaches is particularly well suited for teaching clients how to function as their own counselors. Behavioral concepts have recently been extended in the area of self-control (52, 122). The question has been asked: How can we give the person more power to control his or her own actions? Is it possible to teach the person how to self-regulate internal as well as external responses in such a way that the person can produce and maintain desirable behavior in his natural environment? Thoresen and Mahoney (122) have suggested one strategy based on three self-controlling methods: (a) self-observation, (b) environmental planning, and (c) behavioral programming. These authors argue that it is quite possible to teach persons self-control skills such as self-observation, self-reinforcement, self-punishment, and stimulus control. Often the client's problem is a situation in which the immediate consequences of an action are extremely positive yet detrimental in the long run, such as drinking, smoking, aggressive behavior, social withdrawal, using drugs, or avoiding school work. Behavioral self-control techniques can provide the person with the *response capability* of engaging in alternative actions, sometimes by rearranging the social environment and sometimes by changing the person's own internal environment through selective imagery or covert verbalizations. A person, for example, can learn how to use physical relaxation and positive imagery responses to prevent or reduce stress and tension behavior in anxiety-producing situations. He can use systematic self-observation skills to become more aware of certain behaviors, often to the extent that desired actions are increased and negative behavior is reduced.

When the focus in counseling is on the client becoming his own counselor, the person can gain much greater freedom to determine his own actions. This is true because the client is learning how his behavior is influenced and how to alter the various environments, including his own internal environment, to promote meaningful change for himself.

Concluding Comment

Counseling must change if it is to help a greater number of persons deal successfully with the variety of human problems they experience. In the past two decades behavioral approaches have developed methods that promise more effective and efficient ways of helping.

Conceptualizing counseling as a teaching-learning process within the context of the experimental investigation of the individual case offers an open, empirically based strategy for creating and using techniques to assist persons to change. Little is currently known about the multiple causes and consequences of many complex human problems. No rigid predetermined counseling approach can successfully handle the myriad of client problems. A flexible experimental stance to theory and technique seems most appropriate, with the view of the counselor as an applied behavioral scientist. Strict theoretical orthodoxies that have often dominated theory, research, and practice in counseling are anachronistic in a time that seeks to expand and broaden the conception of counseling and the role of the counselor. Counselor training programs and counseling research methods must be critically examined to determine if training and research are providing the variety of skills and the kind of data most needed to help counselors function as flexible, data-oriented, effective helpers. The concept of client must be expanded to include persons and institutional arrangements that contribute to and perhaps cause human problems. Problems can be prevented if careful behavioral analyses and the systematic modifications of environments are made. The notion of clients as their own counselors offers a very promising way of reaching a larger number of persons in trouble. The decade of the seventies hopefully will see a careful expansion of behavioral theory and techniques in counseling for the benefit of the client. The day of the one-method, one-theory counselor is past.

REFERENCES

1. Ashem, B. "The Treatment of a Disaster Phobia by Systematic Desensitization." *Behaviour Research and Therapy* 1 (1963): 81-84.
2. Astin, A. "The Functional Autonomy of Psychotherapy." *American Psychologist* 16 (1961): 75-78.
3. Atkinson, D. R. "Effect of Selected Behavior Modification Techniques on Student-initiated Action." *Journal of Counseling Psychology* 18 (1971): 395-400.
4. Azrin, N. H., and Holz, W. C. "Punishment." In *Operant Behavior: Areas of Research and Application*, edited by W. K. Honig. New York: Appleton-Century-Crofts, 1966.
5. Bandura, A. *Principles of Behavior Modification*. New York: Holt, Rinehart & Winston, 1969.
6. ———. "Psychotherapy As a Learning Process." *Psychological Bulletin* 58 (1961): 143-59.

7. ———. "Psychotherapy Based upon Modeling." In *Handbook of Psychotherapy and Behavior Change*, edited by A. Bergin and S. Garfield, pp. 653-708. New York: John Wiley & Sons, 1971.

8. Bandura, A.; Blanchard, E. B.; and Ritter, B. "Relative Efficacy of Desensitization and Modeling Approaches for Inducing Behavioral, Affective and Attitudinal Changes." *Journal of Personality and Social Psychology* 13 (1969): 173-99.

9. Barlow, D. H.; Leitenberg, H.; and Agras, W. S. "The Experimental Control of Sexual Deviation through Manipulation of the Noxious Scene in Covert Sensitization." *Journal of Abnormal Psychology* 74 (1969): 596-601.

10. Barrett, B. "Reduction in Rate of Multiple Tics by Free Operant Conditioning Methods." *Journal of Nervous and Mental Diseases* 135 (1962): 187-95.

11. Bernal, M. E. "Behavioral Feedback in the Modification of Brat Behavior." *Journal of Nervous Mental Disorders* 148 (1969): 375-86.

12. Bernal, M. E., et al. "The Use of Videotape Feedback and Operant Learning Principles in Training Parents in Management of Deviant Children." *Advances in Behavior Therapy*, VIII, edited by R. D. Rubin. New York: Academic Press, 1971.

13. Brady, J. P. "Behavior Therapy: Fad or Psychotherapy of the Future." Presidential address, Fifth Annual Meeting of Association for the Advancement of Behavior Therapy. Washington, D.C. September, 1971.

14. Carkhuff, R. Foreword in A. E. Ivey, *Microcounseling*. Springfield, Mass.: C. C Thomas, 1971.

15. Cautela, J. R. "Behavior Therapy and Self Control: Technique and Implication." *Behavior Therapy: Appraisal and Status*, edited by D. H. Franks. New York: McGraw-Hill Book Co., 1969.

15a. ———. "Covert Conditioning." In *The Psychology of Private Events*, edited by A. Jacobs and L. B. Sachs. New York: Academic Press, 1971.

16. ———. "Treatment of Compulsive Behavior by Covert Sensitization." *Psychological Record* 16 (1966): 33.

17. Church, R. M. "The Varied Effects of Punishment on Behavior." *Psychological Review* 70 (1963): 369-402.

18. Cohen, S. E., and Reed, J. L. "The Treatment of 'Nervous Diarrhea' and Other Conditioned Autonomic Disorders by Desensitization." *British Journal of Psychiatry* 117 (1968): 1275-80.

19. Colby, K. M. "Psychotherapeutic Processes." In *Annual Review of Psychology*, Vol. 15, edited by P. Farnsworth, O. McNemar, and Q. McNemar, pp. 347-70. Palo Alto, Calif.: Annual Reviews, 1964.

20. Cowen, E. L., et al. *Adjustment to Visual Disability in Adolescence*. New York: American Foundation for the Blind, 1961.

21. Daley, M. F. "The 'Reinforcement Menu': Finding Effective Reinforcers." In *Behavioral Counseling: Cases and Techniques*, edited by J. D. Krumboltz and C. E. Thoresen. New York: Holt, Rinehart & Winston, 1969.

22. Davison, G. C. "Systematic Desensitization As a Counterconditioning Process." *Journal of Abnormal Psychology* 73 (1968): 91-99.

23. Dean, D. G. "Alienation: Its Meaning and Measurement," *American Sociological Review* 26 (1961): 753-58.

24. Dinsmoor, J. A. "Punishment: I. The Avoidance Hypothesis." *Psychological Review* 61 (1954): 34-46.

25. Dollard, J., and Miller, N. E. *Personality and Psychotherapy*. New York: McGraw-Hill Book Co., 1950.

26. Donner, L. "Effectiveness of Pre-Programmed Group Desensitization Treatment for Test Anxiety with and without a Therapist Present." Ph.D. dissertation, Rutgers University, 1967.

27. Dua, P. S. "Group Desensitization of a Phobia with Three Massing Procedures." *Journal of Counseling Psychology* 19 (1972): 125-29.

28. Eisenberg, S., and Delaney, L. "Using Video Simulation of Counseling for Training Counselors." *Journal of Counseling Psychology* 17 (1970): 15-19.

29. Emery, J. R., and Krumboltz, J. D. "Standard versus Individualized Hierarchies in Desensitization to Reduce Test Anxiety." *Journal of Counseling Psychology* 14 (1967): 204-9.

30. Etzoni, A., and Remp R. "Technological 'Shortcuts' to Social Change." *Science* 175 (1972): 31-38.

31. Eysenck, H. "Behavior Therapy as a Scientific Discipline." *Journal of Consulting and Clinical Psychology* 36 (1971): 7.

32. Feldman, M. P., and MacCulloch, M. J. "The Application of Anticipatory Avoidance Learning to the Treatment of Homosexuality. 1. Theory, Technique and Preliminary Results." *Behaviour Research and Therapy* 2 (1965): 165-83.

33. Ferster, C. B., and Skinner, B. F. *Schedules of Reinforcement*. New York: Appleton-Century-Crofts, 1957.

34. Ford, D., and Urban, H. "Psychotherapy." In *Annual Review of Psychology*, Vol. 18, edited by P. Farnsworth, O. McNemar, and Q. McNemar, pp. 333-72. Palo Alto, Calif.: *Annual Reviews*, 1967.

35. Franks, C. M., ed. *Behavior Therapy: Appraisal and Status*. New York: McGraw-Hill Book Co., 1969.

36. Garvey, W. P., and Hegrenes, J. R. "Desensitization Techniques in the Treatment of School Phobia." *American Journal of Orthopsychiatry* (1966): 147-52.

37. Gelfand, D. M., and Hartman, D. P. "Behavior Therapy with Children." *Psychological Bulletin* 69 (1968): 204-15.

38. Glynn, E. L. "Classroom Applications of Self-determined Rein-

forcement." *Journal of Applied Behavioral Analysis* 3 (1970): 123-32.

39. Goldberg, J., and D'Zurilla, T. J. "Demonstration of Slide Projection as an Alternative to Imaginal Stimulus Presentation in Systematic Desensitization Therapy." *Psychological Reports* 23 (1968): 527-33.

40. Goldiamond, I. "Fluent and Nonfluent Speech (Stuttering): Analysis and Operant Techniques for Control." *Research in Behavior Modification*, edited by L. Krasner and L. Ullmann. New York: Holt, Rinehart & Winston, 1965.

41. Gross, A. "Interview with B. F. Skinner." *Mademoiselle*, January 1972.

42. Guthrie, E. R. *The Psychology of Learning*. New York: Harper & Bros., 1935.

43. Hannum, J. W. "The Modification of Evaluative Self-Thoughts and Their Effect on Overt Behavior." Ph.D. dissertation, Stanford University, 1972.

44. Hekmat, H. "The Role of Imagination in Semantic Desensitization." *Behavior Therapy* 3 (1972): 223-31.

45. Hogan, R. A. "Implosive Therapy in the Short-Term Treatment of Psychotics." *Psychotherapy: Theory, Research and Practice* 3 (1966): 25-32.

46. Hogan, R. A., and Kirchner, J. H. "Preliminary Report of the Extinction of Learned Fears via Short-Term Implosive Therapy." *Journal of Abnormal Psychology* 72 (1967): 106-9.

47. Homme, Lloyd, et al. *How to Use Contingency Contracting in the Classroom*. Champaign, Ill.: Research Press, 1969.

48. Hosford, R. E. "Behavioral Counseling: A Contemporary Overview." *Counseling Psychologist* 1 (1969): 1-33.

49. Hosford, R. E., and Bowles, S. A. "Reinforcement Counseling Techniques with Mexican-American Children." A paper presented at the 20th Annual Convention, American Personnel and Guidance Association, Atlantic City, New Jersey, April 1971.

50. Hosford, R. E., and deVisser, L. "Ethnic Variable in Social Modeling." Unpublished manuscript, University of California, Santa Barbara, 1972.

51. Hosford, R. E., and Rifkin, H. B. "Behavior Therapy with Compulsive Exhibitionism and Homosexuality." Unpublished manuscript, University of California, Santa Barbara, 1972.

52. Kanfer, F. H., and Phillips, J. S. *Learning Foundations of Behavior Therapy*. New York: John Wiley & Sons, 1970.

53. Kanfer, F. H., and Saslow, G. "Behavioral Diagnosis." In *Behavior Therapy: Appraisal and Status*, edited by C. M. Franks. New York: McGraw-Hill Book Co., 1969.

54. Kennedy, W. A., and Foreyt, J. P. "Control of Eating Behavior in an Obese Patient by Avoidance Conditioning." *Psychological Reports* 22 (1968): 571-76.
55. Kolb, D. A., et al. "Self-directed Change: Two Studies." *Journal of Applied Behavioral Science* 4 (1968): 353-71.
56. Kramer, H. C. "Effects of Conditioning Several Responses in a Group Setting." *Journal of Counseling Psychology* 15 (1968): 58-62.
57. Krasner, L. "Behavior Therapy." *Annual Review of Psychology* 22 (1971): 483-532.
58. Krasner, L., and Krasner, M. "Token Economies and Other Planned Environments." In *Behavior Modification in Education,* Seventy-second Yearbook of the National Society for the Study of Education, Part I. Chicago: University of Chicago Press, 1973.
59. Krumboltz, J. D. "Behavioral Counseling: Rationale and Research." *Personnel and Guidance Journal* 44 (1965): 383-87.
60. ———. "Behavioral Goals for Counseling." *Journal of Counseling Psychology* 13 (1966): 153-59.
61. ———. "Job Experience Kits." *Personnel and Guidance Journal* 49 (1970): 233.
62. Krumboltz, J. D., et al. "Non-Verbal Factors in Effectiveness of Models in Counseling." *Journal of Counseling Psychology* 14 (1967): 412-18.
63. Krumboltz, J. D., and Krumboltz, H. B. *Changing Children's Behaviors.* Englewood Cliffs, N.J.: Prentice-Hall, 1972.
64. Krumboltz, J. D., and Schroeder, W. W. "Promoting Career Exploration through Reinforcement." *Personnel and Guidance Journal* 44 (1965): 19-26.
65. Krumboltz, J. D., and Thoresen, C. E. *Behavioral Counseling: Cases and Techniques.* New York: Holt, Rinehart & Winston, 1969.
66. ———. "The Effect of Behavioral Counseling in Group and Individual Settings on Information-Seeking Behavior." *Journal of Counseling Psychology* 2 (1964): 324-35.
67. Lang, P. J. "Fear Reduction and Fear Behavior: Problems in Treating a Construct." In *Research in Psychotherapy,* Vol. 3, edited by J. M. Shlen. Washington, D.C.: American Psychological Association, 1968.
68. Lang, P. J., et al. "Physiological Analysis of Fear Modification Using an Automated Desensitization Procedure." *Journal of Abnormal Psychology* 76 (1970): 221-34.
69. Lang, P. J., and Melamed, B. G. "Avoidance Conditioning Therapy of an Infant with Chronic Ruminative Vomiting." *Journal of Abnormal Psychology* 74 (1969): 1-8.

70. Lazarus, A. A. "Aversion Therapy and Sensory Modalities: Clinical Impression." *Perceptual and Motor Skills* 27 (1968): 178.
71. ———. *Behavior Therapy and Beyond.* New York: McGraw-Hill Book Co., 1971.
72. Leitenberg, H. "Is Time-Out from Positive Reinforcement an Aversive Event: A Review of Experimental Evidence." *Psychological Bulletin* 64 (1965): 428-41.
73. Leitenberg, H., et al. "A Sequential Analysis of the Effect of Selective Positive Reinforcement and Therapeutic Instructions to Systematic Desensitization Therapy." *Journal of Abnormal Psychology* 74 (1969): 113-18.
74. Liberman, Robert. "A Behavioral Approach to Group Dynamics. Reinforcement and Prompting of Cohesiveness in Group Therapy." *Behavior Therapy* 1 (May 1970): 141-75.
75. Lindsley, O. R. "Therapy of Chronic Constipation in a Young Child by Rearranging Social Contingencies." *Behaviour Research and Therapy* 6 (1968): 484-85.
76. Lovaas, O., et al. "Experimental Studies in Childhood Schizophrenia: Analysis of Self-Destructive Behavior." *Journal of Experimental Child Psychology* 1 (1965): 99-109.
77. Magoon, T. "Innovations in Counseling." *Journal of Counseling Psychology* 11 (1964): 342-47.
78. Mahoney, M. J. "The Relative Efficacy of Self-Reward, Self-Punishment, and Self-Monitoring Techniques for Weight Loss." Ph.D. dissertation, Stanford University, 1972.
79. ———. "The Self-Management of Covert Behaviors: A Case Study." *Behavior Therapy.* In press.
80. ———. "Toward an Experimental Analysis of Coverant Control." *Behavior Therapy* 1 (1970): 510-21.
81. Mahoney, M. J., and Thoresen, C. E. "Behavioral Self-Control: Power to the Person." *Educational Researcher*, in press.
82. Mahoney, M. J., Thoresen, C. E.; and Danaher, B. G. "Covert Behavior Modification: An Experimental Analogue." *Journal of Behavior Therapy and Experimental Psychiatry* 3 (1972): 7-14.
83. Meichenbaum, D. H. "Cognitive Factors in Behavior Modification: Modifying What Clients Say to Themselves." A paper presented at the Fifth Annual Meeting of the Association for Advancement of Behavior Therapy, Washington, D.C., September, 1971.
84. ———. "Cognitive Modification of Test Anxious College Students." *Journal of Consulting and Clinical Psychology*, in press.
85. Meichenbaum, D., and Goodman, J. "Training Impulsive Children to Talk to Themselves: A Means of Developing Self-Control." *Journal of Abnormal Psychology* 77 (1971): 115-26.

86. Meyer, J. B., et al. "Behavioral-Reinforcement Counseling with Rural High School Youth." *Journal of Counseling Psychology* 17 (1970): 127-32.

87. Mischel, W. *Introduction to Personality.* New York: Holt, Rinehart & Winston, 1971.

88. Myrick, R. D. "Effect of a Model on Verbal Behavior in Counseling." *Journal of Counseling Psychology* 16 (1969): 185-90.

89. Patterson, G. R. "Behavior Intervention Procedures in the Classroom and in the Home." In *Handbook of Psychotherapy and Behavior Change*, edited by A. E. Bergin and S. L. Garfield. New York: John Wiley & Sons, 1971.

90. ————. "A Learning Approach to the Treatment of the School Phobic Child." In *Case Studies in Behavior Modification*, edited by L. P. Ullmann and L. Krasner. New York: Holt, Rinehart & Winston, 1965.

91. ————. "Reprogramming the Families of Aggressive Boys." In *Behavior Modification in Education*, Seventy-second Yearbook of the National Society for the Study of Education, Part I. Chicago: University of Chicago Press, 1973.

92. Patterson, G. R., and Gullion, M. E. *Living with Children: New Methods for Parents and Teachers.* Champaign, Ill.: Research Press, 1968.

93. Paul, G. L. *Insight versus Desensitization in Psychotherapy: An Experiment in Anxiety Reduction.* Stanford: Stanford University Press, 1965.

94. ————. "Outcome of Systematic Desensitization. I: Background, Procedures and Uncontrolled Reports of Individual Treatment." In *Behavior Therapy: Appraisal and Status*, edited by C. M. Franks. New York: McGraw-Hill Book Co., 1969.

95. ————. "Outcome of Systematic Desensitization. II: Controlled Investigations of Individual Treatment, Technique Variations, and Current Status." In *Behavior Therapy: Appraisal and Status*, edited by C. M. Franks. New York: McGraw-Hill Book Co., 1969.

96. ———— "Two Year Follow-up of Systematic Desensitization in Therapy Groups." *Journal of Abnormal Psychology* 73 (1968): 119-30.

97. Paul, G. L., and Shannon, D. T. "Treatment of Anxiety through Systematic Desensitization in Therapy Groups." *Journal of Abnormal Psychology* 71 (1966): 124-35.

98. Philips, E. L. "Achievement Place: Token Reinforcement Procedures in a Home-Style Rehabilitation Setting for 'Predelinquent' Boys." *Journal of Applied Behavioral Analysis* 1 (1968): 213-23.

99. Rachman, S., and Teasdale, J. *Aversion Therapy and Behaviour Disorders: An Analysis.* Coral Gables, Fla.: University of Miami Press, 1969.

100. Rank, R. C., et al. "Encouraging Affective Group Behavior by Social Modeling." *Counselor Education and Supervison* 11 (1972): 270-78.
101. Raymond, M. "Case of Fetishism Treated by Aversion Therapy." *British Medical Journal* 2 (1965): 854-57.
102. Rogers, C. R. "Psychotherapy Today or Where Do We Go from Here?" *American Journal of Psychotherapy* 17 (1963): 5-16.
103. Ryan, T. A. "The Influence of Counselor Reinforcement on Client Decision-Making and Deliberating Behavior." Ph.D. dissertation, Stanford University, 1963.
104. Shaw, D. W. "Social Modeling and Desensitization Approaches to Reducing Dentist Avoidance." Ph.D. dissertation, Stanford University, 1972.
105. Shoben, E. J., Jr. "Psychotherapy as a Problem in Learning Theory." *Psychological Bulletin* 46 (1949): 366-92.
106. Skinner, B. F. *Contingencies of Reinforcement: A Theoretical Analysis.* New York: Appleton-Century-Crofts, 1969.
107. ———. *Science and Human Behavior.* New York: Macmillan Co., 1953.
108. ———. *The Technology of Teaching.* New York: Appleton-Century-Crofts, 1968.
109. Staats, A. W. "Language Behavior Therapy: A Derivative of Social Behaviorism." *Behavior Therapy* 3 (1972): 165-92.
110. Staats, A. W., and Staats, C. W. *Complex Human Behavior.* New York: Holt, Rinehart & Winston, 1964.
111. Stampfl, T. G., and Levis, D. J. "Essentials of Implosive Therapy: A Learning Theory-based Psychodynamic Behavioral Therapy." *Journal of Abnormal Psychology* 72 (1967): 496-503.
112. Stevenson, I., and Wolpe, J. "Recovery from Sexual Deviations through Overcoming of Non-Sexual Neurotic Responses." *American Journal of Psychiatry* 116 (1960): 737-42.
113. Stilwell, W. E., and Thoresen, C. E. "Effects of Social Modeling on Vocational Behaviors of Mexican-American and Non-Mexican-American Adolescents." *Vocational Guidance Quarterly* 20 (1972): 279-86.
114. Stuart, R. B. "Behavioral Control of Overeating." *Behaviour Research and Therapy* 5 (1967): 357-66.
115. Tate, B. G., and Baroff, G. S. "Aversive Conditioning of Self-Injurious Behavior in a Psychotic Boy." *Behaviour Research and Therapy* 4 (1966): 281-87.
116. Thoresen, C. E. "Behavioral Humanism." In *Behavior Modification in Education,* Seventy-second Yearbook of the National Society for the Study of Education, Part I. Chicago: University of Chicago Press, 1973.

117. ———. "Relevance and Research in Counseling." *Review of Educational Research* 39 (1969): 263-81.
118. Thoresen, C. E., et al. "Determining Effective Models for Counseling Clients of Varying Competencies." *Journal of Counseling Psychology* 17 (1970): 369-75.
119. ———. "Sex of Counselors and Models: Effect on Client Career Exploration." *Journal of Counseling Psychology* 14 (1967): 503-8.
120. Thoresen, C. E., and Hamilton, J. A. "Peer Social Modeling in Promoting Career Behaviors." *Vocational Guidance Quarterly* 20 (1972): 210-16.
121. Thoresen, C. E., and Krumboltz, J. D. "Similarity of Social Models and Clients in Behavioral Counseling: Two Experimental Studies." *Journal of Counseling Psychology* 15 (1968): 393-401.
122. Thoresen, C. E., and Mahoney, M. J. *Behavioral Self Control.* New York: Holt, Rinehart & Winston, forthcoming.
123. Thoresen, C. E., and Stuhr, D. "Social Modeling and Counseling: Theory, Research and Practice." Paper presented at American Education Research Association, Chicago, April 1972.
124. Tooley, J. T., and Pratt, S. "An Experimental Procedure for the Extinction of Smoking Behavior." *Psychological Record* 17 (1967): 209.
125. Varenhorst, B. B. "Learning the Consequences of Life's Decision." In *Behavioral Counseling: Cases and Techniques*, edited by J. D. Krumboltz and C. E. Thoresen. New York: Holt, Rinehart & Winston, 1969.
126. Warner, R. W. "Alienated Students: Six Months after Receiving Behavioral Group Counseling." *Journal of Counseling Psychology* 18 (1971): 426-30.
127. Warner, R. W., and Hansen, J. C. "Verbal-Reinforcement and Model-Reinforcement Group Counseling with Alienated Students." *Journal of Counseling Psychology* 17 (1970): 168-72.
128. Weiner, H. "Some Effects of Response Cost upon Human Operant Behavior." *Journal of Experimental Analysis of Behavior* 5 (1962): 201-08.
129. Weitzman, B. "Behavior Therapy and Psychotherapy." *Psychological Review* 74 (1967): 300-17.
130. Wilkins, W. "Desensitization: Social and Cognitive Factors underlying the Effectiveness of Wolpe's Procedure." *Psychological Bulletin* 76 (1971): 311-17.
131. Wilson, T., and Davison, G. C. "Processes of Fear Reduction in Systematic Desensitization: Animal Studies." *Psychological Bulletin* 76 (1971): 1-14.
132. Winnett, R. A., and Winkler, R. C. "Current Behavior Modification in the Classroom: Be Still, Be Quiet, Be Docile." *Journal of Applied Behavior Analysis*, in press.

133. Wolpe, J. *The Practice of Behavior Therapy*. New York: Pergamon Press, 1969.
134. ———. *Psychotherapy by Reciprocal Inhibition*. Stanford: Stanford University Press, 1958.
135. Wolpe, J., and Lazarus, A. *Behavior Therapy Techniques*. New York: Pergamon Press, 1966.
136. Yates, A. J., *Behavior Therapy*. New York: John Wiley & Sons, 1970.
137. Zifferblatt, S. "Behavior Systems." *Behavior Modification in Education*, Seventy-second Yearbook of the National Society for the Study of Education, Part I. Chicago: University of Chicago Press, 1973.

CHAPTER V

Reprogramming the Families of Aggressive Boys

GERALD R. PATTERSON

Introduction

The recent developments in applications of social engineering technology described here were based within the framework of social learning "theories." Rather than a coherent theory, social learning might best be thought of as a hegemony of investigations under the general aegis of behavioristic tenets. Often the primary focus is upon reinforcement contingencies. Perhaps more of a strategy for constructing a theory than a theory itself, the general tenets of the approach have been outlined in detail by Skinner in the publications *Science and Human Behavior* (60) and *Contingencies of Reinforcement* (59). Social learning approaches particularly emphasize a functional analysis of the stimuli which control behavior. In the present context, these strategies for identifying determinants of behavior have been directed to the dual process of conceptualizing family interaction process, which produces aggressive child behaviors, and of devising a means for changing this system.

The power of such a simplistic strategy becomes particularly apparent when viewing a progression of studies attacking a single problem, such as family intervention. The problem defined by the earliest studies was to find a means for reducing the rates of aggressive child behaviors occurring in the home (18, 72). Aggression was operationally defined in such a way as to make it possible to observe the frequency of occurrence of these behaviors. Pre- and

Preparation of this report was supported in large part by Career Development Award MH-40, 518. Many of the ideas here were generated during the intensive interactions with colleagues in the continuing series of Tuesday discussions. In these interchanges the group process is such that it is impossible to extricate the individual contributions of R. Ray, D. Shaw, J. Cobb, N. Wiltz, H. Hops, H. Walter, K. Skindrud, S. Johnson, and V. Devine.

post-observation sessions in the home provided a basis for evaluating the outcome of the "treatment" procedures.

This early reliance upon observation data was crucial to the later developments in the evolution of the family intervention techniques. It was assumed that such data were not only reliable but were more sensitive reflections of changes in behavior than are the traditional self-report or parent-report measures (8, 84). But of equal importance was the fact that obtaining such data required a continued direct exposure to the *phenomenon* (aggression). This served as a basis for generating new hypotheses about both the determinants of aggressive behavior and additional means for changing it.

Operational definitions and high-quality data collected in a systematic fashion define the behavioristic system for changing the behavior of the psychologist. The concomitant fine-grained feedback possible in such an approach becomes a means for quickly identifying those hypotheses about behavior which are irrelevant and leads to a search for more powerful ones. Such changes in a number of investigators who have extensively explored family intervention have already led to the development of a social engineering technology which has some utility for clinical practice. After only six years of effort, it of course continues to evolve; presumably it will continue to improve in quality and utility. The present report summarizes the evolution of family intervention procedures during these first six years of their development. Because many investigators have chosen to work with families of aggressive boys, such problems become the primary focus for the present review.

Before describing the intervention procedures and outcome data, it will be necessary to consider some of the primary assumptions made within the social learning framework about the determinants of aggression and the determinants of behavior change within the family system.

Assumptions

REINFORCING CONTINGENCIES FOR DEVIANCY

Behavior is controlled by its consequences (60). When one applies such a simple hypothesis to a behavior such as "aggression," it is not immediately apparent as to what the "consequence" controlling the behavior might be. In fact, the statement that a mother is providing positive reinforcers for the very behaviors which cause her distress seems counterintuitive, to say the least. Observation data to be presented later in the discussion partially resolve this seeming paradox.

For discussion purposes, the term *deviant child behaviors* will include any one or more of the following observable responses: hit, tease, yell, negativism, disapproval, whine, humiliate, ignore, noncomply, destroy, dependent, and negative command. An unpublished study by S. Johnson showed that most parents reported it as unpleasant to be exposed to these child behaviors. A coding manual for operationalizing these and other responses occurring in family interaction is available (42).

Even the earliest family intervention studies noted that parents and other family members supplied a surprisingly rich schedule of positive social reinforcers for deviant behaviors (18). For example, observations in the homes of seven aggressive boys showed that, on the average, deviant child behaviors were "consequated" 26 percent of the time by such consequences as interest, approval, laughter, or physical positive (41). The family members also supplied aversive consequences for these behaviors 26 percent of the time. Shaw (56) analyzed the reinforcing contingencies for a new sample of fifteen families of boys who displayed high rates of deviant behaviors and fifteen displaying low rates. For the entire sample the deviant behaviors were consequated by positive consequences 33.7 percent of the time and by aversive consequences 24.4 percent. Johnson, Wahl, Martin, and Johansen (22) used a comparable coding system to observe thirty-three normal families of boys between the ages of four and six years. The percentage of consequences judged a priori to be positive for deviant child behaviors was 42.2 and for those judged aversive was 19.4.

For the older boys (six to thirteen) in the Patterson et al. (41) and Shaw (56) studies, there was a surprisingly consistent and *rich* schedule of consequences which seemed a priori to be positive reinforcers. It is of interest to note that the reinforcement schedules for younger (normal) boys' deviant responses were even richer (22).

It is of course necessary to demonstrate that the consequences

classed a priori as positive or aversive do indeed function as reinforcers. Currently, such analyses are being planned. Pending their
completion, the evidence from these studies is only suggestive.
Families may function in an "irrational" manner, by reinforcing
the very behaviors which contribute to their own discomfort.

Such findings lead to a consideration of the process by which
family members can become involved in supplying reinforcers for
deviant behaviors—the process was labeled "coercion" (43). Presumably it is based upon negative reinforcement as a mechanism to
strengthen the behavior of the aggressor and, in some instances,
of the victim as well. For example, one family member presents
an aversive stimulus to the child, such as "younger sister teases."
Over a series of trials, the older brother learns that if he hits his
younger sister, she will usually terminate the teasing; thus his hitting
behavior is strengthened.

Teasing produces hit responses a certain proportion of the time.
In effect, pain produces pain. Such a functional relation has been
noted by many other investigators (1, 46, 67). It was assumed by
Patterson and Cobb (35, 36) that aversive behaviors dispensed by
other family members were the stimuli controlling much aggressive
behavior in boys. It was also hypothesized that some exchanges become extended and that when this occurs there would likely be
an escalation in the intensity of the painful stimuli. It is assumed
that family systems which permit behavior control by the use
of pain will likely produce children who exhibit high rates of noxious responses.

Presumably, negative reinforcement is most likely to operate
in certain closed social systems where the child must learn to cope
with aversive stimuli. In such a family the boy's aggressive behavior
will be supported by *both* positive and negative reinforcement. His
hitting terminates much of the aversive stimulation. In addition, as
shown in the observation studies reviewed earlier, a fourth to a
third of his coercive behaviors will likely receive positive reinforcement as well.

SETTINGS AND BEHAVIORAL RATES

It is assumed that some children's behavior is under the control
of observable external stimuli. While the gross physical setting
probably exerts some control in determining whether or not ag-

gressive behavior will occur, it is assumed that the more powerful controlling stimuli are to be found in the behavior of other family members. Children's aggressive behavior, then, is thought to be social in the sense that it is generally under the control of social stimuli.

Observation data collected within the home demonstrate that the rate with which noxious behaviors occur is highly variable. Variability is the rule, even when sampling the *same child in the same physical settings* over time. These variations in rate are assumed to reflect covariations in the rates with which the controlling stimuli are presented. Presumably, there are certain things that, for example, the younger sister can do that will reliably produce a hit response from older brother. On days that the sister presents high rates of these controlling stimuli it would be assumed that brother's hit rate will be correspondingly high.

The first problem encountered is that of identifying the controlling stimuli for a given child's behavior. The data requisite for such analyses are based upon *in situ* observations describing the sequential dependencies holding between the behaviors presented by the child and those of other family members. In collecting such data the alternate samplings of environmental events and child behaviors are carried out for extended sessions over a number of days.

The details of the analysis of stimulus control for noxious responses have been outlined in two reports (35, 36). The identification of a stimulus as a significant one involves a two-step process. First, the conditional probability is calculated for p (noxious response/antecedent event X_i). X_i is the behavior of another person which occurred in the six-second interval immediately prior to the child's noxious response. This value is compared to the baserate value for that noxious response, given the presence of all other antecedents. This value is corrected by removing all incidents in which X_i was involved. If the two values were demonstrated to be significantly different, the stimulus was identified as either a "facilitating stimulus" or an "inhibitory stimulus." The report by Patterson and Cobb (36) identified extensive networks of controlling stimuli for thirteen different noxious responses exhibited by boys from both problem and nonproblem families.

The functional analysis of the stimuli controlling changes in behavior has direct implications for both intervention and prevention. Most intervention studies have focused upon reinforcement control exerted by the parents in altering rates of children's noxious responses. Within the present context such an approach would seem necessary but very incomplete. Additional efficiency should accrue from using information about stimulus control to focus specifically upon altering the behavior of the family agents who set the occasion for the boy's noxious behavior in the first place. The combination of stimulus control *and* reinforcement control in altering deviant behavior should enhance efforts to intervene. It should also give focus to attempts to design prevention programs.

The second implication of the emphasis upon stimulus control is perhaps not so direct. If one assumes that the behaviors of other persons are the main stimuli controlling behavior, then one would not expect the effects to generalize to settings in which other agents were present. In keeping with such a formulation, two studies have demonstrated that successful family intervention did *not* generalize to the classroom setting (58, 70). Similarly, Zeilberger, Sampen, and Sloane (86) showed for a single case that the effects of a successful classroom intervention did not generalize to the home. Brodsky (7) showed that successful manipulation of relevant verbal behavior did not generalize to social interaction patterns with peers. It seems, then, that because the social stimuli governing behavior vary from one setting to another, it may be necessary to devise separate engineering technologies for each setting.

Train the parents to change the child. Based upon the assumption that family members provide the reinforcement for the deviant child behaviors, it follows that the primary change agents in intervention would be the parents. Thus far there are no studies which compare the efficacy of training parents to carry out behavior-change programs versus employing a doctor-in-his-office working directly with the child. Similarly, no studies have compared the efficiency of training parents and siblings separately or working conjointly. Such studies are badly needed and would undoubtedly contribute much to our understanding of the family intervention process. For the moment, the family-intervention investigators seem to have gone along with the conventional wisdom in assuming that the parents are the primary agents of change for behaviors occurring within the home.

Typically, the parents are trained in a repertoire which has come to be labeled by some as "parenting skills." While not as yet tested systematically, it is assumed that all adults who are not severely retarded or psychotic can be trained to perform these skills. This would suggest, for example, that even parents involved in severe stress or psychiatric disturbance could be trained, as well as parents from lower socioeconomic levels.

PERFORMANCE MAINTENANCE

It was implied by some (40) that the reduction in aversive child behavior would strengthen the performance of parenting skills, such that they would be maintained following termination of the training program. Follow-up data were rarely provided in the earlier studies. They were presented for only one of the five cases treated by Hasting (17) and for single cases worked with by Wolf, Mees, and Risley (82). Comments by Walder, Cohen, and Daston (73) and Tharp and Wetzel (64), while based on nonsystematic follow-up, suggested that some families "slid back to their old ways" following termination of the training programs.

Systematic data were collected over a twelve-month follow-up for four of the five families trained in the study by Patterson et al. (41). The data showed that the gains had been maintained for three of the four families. In a replication study including thirteen families of aggressive boys, two left the community following termination (38). Of those remaining, eight showed the effects persisting during the follow-up study. However, it should be noted that these effects were obtained at an average cost of 5.7 hours of professional time for "booster shot" training during the follow-up.

These preliminary findings suggest that *some* parents do continue to perform their newly acquired or refurbished parenting skills. On the other hand, a substantial number (a third to a quarter) learn the skills but do *not* perform them consistently after training. Such findings underline the necessity for conceptualizing what are the reinforcers which *maintain the behavior of the parent*. Some speculations about these maintenance contingencies will be presented in a later section of this report.

REPROGRAMMING THE FAMILY SYSTEM

Parents are members of a small, relatively closed, social system which provides maintenance schedules for the behaviors of all members. It seems reasonable to suppose that changes in the reinforcement schedules being provided by one member would affect behaviors and schedules provided by other members. It was hypothesized by Patterson and Reid (43) that families maintain equity among members in the exchange of both positive and aversive consequences. In a test of this hypothesis, Reid (49) showed a median correlation of .65 in the rankings of family members for the giving and receiving of aversive stimuli and of .55 in the exchange of positive consequences.

There is another sense in which the data lead one to think of families as social systems. The entire *family* provides reinforcement for deviant child behaviors. Furthermore, it seems that it is not *just* the problem child who receives these reinforcers. The data showed that the problem child *and* his siblings displayed equally high rates of problem behaviors. The correlation between observed base-line rates of deviant child behavior for the identified problem child and for his siblings was .58 ($p < .05$) for one sample of problem families (38) and .48 ($p < .05$) for the replication sample. Data from both studies showed that there were in fact no significant differences in mean level between the "problem child" and his siblings in observed mean rates of problem behaviors.

A more sophisticated test of the reciprocity model was carried out with seven families of problem children in the 1968 study using a paired-composition model devised by Bechtel (4). This model tests the significance of deviation from equity among members of each family. The analysis showed that the exchanges of positive consequences were symmetric, or equitable, for each of the problem families. The analysis for the exchange of aversive consequences showed significant asymmetric exchanges for three of the seven families. In two of these instances the agents contributing most to the asymmetry were adults who dispensed more pain than they received (43:149).

These findings suggest that if one member of the family were trained to increase his rate of social reinforcers to another, this in turn could lead to an increased rate given by other family members. Wills (80) tested this hypothesis. After a base-line period, all of the husbands in a sample of married couples were instructed to double the rate of social reinforcers given to their wives. Not only did the wives' ratings of their "satisfaction with the relationship" significantly increase for those days, but also the rate of their social reinforcers given to their husbands showed corresponding increases.

It was hypothesized that reductions in the level of aversive behaviors exchanged vis-a-vis the problem child and other family members should be accompanied by changes in the verbal descriptors which they apply to his behavior. They should less frequently employ labels of deviant, bad, mean, hateful, disturbed, and so forth. A test of this assumption was made in the report by Patterson et al. (38), which showed significant improvement in the evaluative adjectives used to describe the problem child following intervention. However, no provision was made for testing changes in labels employed by siblings when describing the child.

One would also expect that changes in the reactions of family members to the problem child would be followed eventually by changes in the manner in which he describes himself and perhaps in the labels which he uses to describe family members. All of these assumptions, of course, rest upon the hypothesis that verbal labels used by family members to describe both each other and the problem child are partially anchored in observable behaviors. Given this, then, changes in behavior would be accompanied by corresponding changes in labels. As yet, no tests have been made of these hypotheses.

While these changes within the family system are directly related to the intervention procedures, there are some additional changes which, although less directly related, are certainly "hoped for" by most investigators; for example, that family members should shift from "pain control" techniques for shaping each others' behaviors to using positive social reinforcers. It would also be hoped that there might be significant increases in the amount of prosocial interaction occurring following intervention. While the latter effect was obtained for a mother-child pair in one family studied by

Patterson et al. (40), a comparable analysis for thirteen problem families following intervention showed such increases to be non-significant (38).

Parenting Skills

It is assumed that the presence of aggressive behavior within the home directly implicates the adults who permit such interchanges to occur. It is hypothesized that the parent must behave in certain ways to *allow the process to begin and to be perpetuated.* If parents are trained to apply parenting skills, dramatic changes in their children should follow. Deviant child behavior occurs *not* because of emotional conflicts within the parent, but because he or she omits the application of certain specific skills when interacting with the child.

Conventional wisdom about "mothering instincts" notwithstanding, it is hypothesized that effective parenting is based upon application of a systematic program of skills. These are skills which can be learned by women, men, or children, for that matter. First, an effective parent has clearly specified terminal behaviors for the child. They "work" on these behaviors on a *daily* basis. These goals are very specific and reflect in some sense child behaviors valued by the subculture in which the parent resides such as, "does his chores," "is polite," "is clean," "talks to people," "can play by self," "gets along with others," or "doesn't wet his pants."

If diurnal continence is the terminal behavior, it will require (a) monitoring the frequency of occurrence of wet and dry pants, (b) taking steps to set occasions in which the desired behavior is likely to occur, e.g., reducing the liquid intake, ask him to go to the toilet, buy training pants, and (c) providing consistent positive reinforcement for approximations to correct performance. The latter would include praising him for remaining dry even for a few hours and using mild aversive consequences (other than nagging) for errors, e.g., require that he wash his own pants when he wets them. Adequate socialization requires that the mother track, arrange, and consequate literally *hundreds* of such miniature programs.

Centuries of child rearing created a folklore which is moderately relevant for skills in the construction and application of such programs. The skills are taught to *some* young women via modeling and the mass media. However, it is our impression that even the most highly skilled of these mother-trainees could profit from more systematic instruction. It is also our impression that the majority of would-be mothers are relatively incompetent in such skills.

BEHAVIOR IS CONTROLLED BY CONTINGENCIES

The underlying assumption that behavior is controlled by contingencies is one of the most difficult things to teach parents. Much of the folk wisdom (and traditional psychology) supports the parental belief that the child's behavior reflects the outcome of an unfolding maturation or mysterious processes hidden within the child. A boy behaves aggressively because that is what three-year-old boys "naturally" do, or because he "once had the fevers" and that makes boys aggressive. Within-the-child assumptions typically relieve the parent of any responsibility for the maintenance or alteration of the child's behavior.

The alternative is to teach the parent that the younger child's behavior is a close, not perfect, reflection of the reinforcing contingencies supplied within the family. Such an assumption carries with it the clear statement that the parent and siblings are *responsible* for the child's behavior. In fact, each individual is responsible for his fellowman; the behavior of others with whom he lives reflects, in some part, the outcome of reinforcing contingencies supplied by himself. Most parents are amazed to discover that they can, in fact, alter the behavior of their child, their spouse, or themselves.

Several texts have been prepared as a means of teaching parenting skills within a social learning framework: *Parents Are Teachers* (2), *Families* (32), *Living with Children* (39), and *You Can Help Your Child Improve Study and Homework Behaviors* (87). All of them stress the importance of contingencies, pinpointing target behaviors, careful observation, and the consistent application of *positive* reinforcers.

THE PARENT AS OBSERVER

The research literature increasingly reflects a disbelief in the accuracy of parental recollections and descriptions of either their own child management practices or the behavior of the child (8, 84, 85). There are also data to suggest that parents are relatively inept observers of *concurrent* child behaviors. For example, a series of studies has compared parent ratings of current child behaviors with observations made in the home and found little correlation (14, 53, 55, 61). In this same vein, in a study by Peine (44), frequencies for the same child behaviors were tabulated by mother and by observers. The data showed the mothers consistently underestimated mean levels of deviant child behaviors obtained by observers from 50 to 700 percent!

To become effective child managers it is first necessary to be *specific* in describing what child behaviors are to be "managed." Relatively specific behaviors, e.g., "he yells," "he does not mind when I ask," or "he hits his little sister," are recorded together with the time during which they occurred. This precision is substituted for such vague or global terms as "he was ornery most of the time." In our own work with parents in problem families, it has been surprisingly difficult to teach them to refer to what the child actually does rather than to use such vague generalities.

Given that the parents have been trained to use more behavioristic language in describing their child, it is necessary that they actually spend some time observing him. Many parents spend surprisingly little time each day noting what it is that the child actually does. Some parents, on the other hand, seem to have a very accurate picture of what the child does in any given situation. This kind of careful observation is a *skill* and one which must be taught to those who would wish to become effective child managers.

PROGRAMS FOR BEHAVIOR CHANGE

The third skill area concerns the ability to plan a program for behavior change. This requires a number of subskills. The parent must clearly specify a terminal behavior, e.g., "I would like to have him study at least forty minutes each evening." Secondly, they should conceptualize the process of reaching that goal as involving a *series* of small steps taken by the child toward this goal. Third, the parent should specify the contingencies supplied to maintain the child's behavior during and after the program. While most parents can, with practice, conceptualize the shaping process involved in reaching a terminal goal, they may still have great difficulty working with the notion of reinforcing contingencies.

The idea of approval, praise, or attention being made contingent upon a response is of course a commonplace. However, many parents with their within-the-child perspective state that such contingencies will "weaken" the child and make him dependent upon other people. They would prefer that he perform out of a sense of duty or love.

Given that some parents do praise or approve, many *add* criticism. More often than not, however, they take the appropriate behavior for granted and do nothing at all. If they do agree to use reinforcers, they tend to use large-magnitude reinforcers, more appropriate for adults (e.g., money, dinners, movies) for which the child must work for weeks or months. The alternative, which is both more practical and effective, is to use affection—*often, contingently*, and *immediately*. The giving of contingent love, attention, and approval is a skill admired by everyone, claimed by many, but possessed by few.

Given that the parent has a program, it becomes necessary to *track* the behavior of the child as the program is applied. If the child behaves appropriately, he *must* be reinforced (occasionally) if that behavior is to be strengthened. For example, the study by Schutte and Hopkins (54) showed that under normal contingencies children followed the teacher's instructions 60 percent of the time. When the teacher reinforced compliance consistently, the classroom percentage increased to 78 percent. In doing this, the teacher tracked the sequence: teacher request–child compliance/noncompliance–teacher consequence. The tracking of such sequences is one additional facet of good parenting skills.

In most cultures, the mother decides which child behaviors are valued and then designs and constructs her own program. The study by Kriesberg (23) showed that mothers of poor families possessed general values and norms for child behavior which did not differ significantly from those held by parents in the upper socioeconomic classes. However, they did seem to differ in their skills in carrying out the child management programs necessary to reach these goals. Several observation studies have demonstrated that the lower- and middle-class mothers differ in the means by which they train younger children. The data from several studies showed that mothers from lower-class families used more aversive stimuli (5, 24). These findings are in agreement with some interview data from parents from lower socioeconomic classes which showed an emphasis upon the use of punishment to control child behavior (23, 83).

In addition, the observation by Hess and Shipman (19) made in a laboratory setting showed major differences in the skills of middle- and lower-class mothers as behavior managers. The unskilled (lower-class) mothers did not use prompts or modeling, tended not to break the problem down into manageable steps, and, finally, they reinforced correct behavior less often when it did occur. These unskilled mothers relied upon threats and commands for performance and on punishment for failure to meet the criterion. Their relative inability was also in keeping with the data from the interview study by Wortis et al. (83), which emphasized the lower-class mothers' lack of "how-to" managing skills.

It is assumed that *some* of the parents of aggressive children have not learned these parenting skills. Others have the skills but lack the contingencies from the environment necessary to maintain the behavior. For some, simply teaching them the skills will be sufficient to bring the behaviors under control. Perhaps simple skill training would be sufficient to help *some* mothers from lower-class families to become more effective. For others, the problem is more complex in that one must build in the reinforcers necessary to maintain good parenting behaviors.

Parent Training Techniques

SETTINGS

Beginning in the mid-1960s, a large number of studies focused upon developing a technology for training parents to deal with their own problem children. The locations for the training programs have been highly variable, ranging from well-structured laboratory situations (6, 16, 21, 27, 34) and office visits (63) to group seminars in which parents were supervised in applications of these techniques (26, 38, 48, 73). For others, the training programs have actually taken place in the homes of families (17, 18, 28, 40,

41, 86). Some investigators have trained lay personnel to make the home visits (64, 71). Others such as Ora and Reisinger (29) are training lay personnel to man a service clinic for preschool children with a wide range of problems. It is becoming clear that it is not necessary for treatment to occur in a clinic nor does one need an advanced degree in order to change the behavior of a child.

CONCEPTS

Most of the investigators have made some provision for teaching the language and concepts of social learning, observation procedures, and programming skills.

It is implied that the parents will acquire the specific skills more readily and generalize their use to a greater extent if they understand the general principles of social learning theory. Different modes of teaching the language and concepts have been used with varying degrees of sophistication and depth.

Parent seminars were used by Ray (48) and by Walder et al. (73). Some training programs have relied upon programmed materials prepared for the parent (17, 21, 40, 41, 48, 52). Occasionally investigators have supplemented lecture-discussion formats with actual laboratory training for the parents (H. Cohen, personal communication). As noted earlier, several programmed textbooks have been prepared for such parent training programs.

As yet, only a limited amount of field testing has been carried out to determine the impact of such programmed materials on parent effectiveness. In the Patterson et al. (38) studies, admission to the parent group meetings was made contingent upon the parents' first responding to a programmed textbook on social learning theory. The families were observed in the home for a minimum of six sessions prior to reading the book and for two consecutive sessions immediately following their responding to the programmed material. In the first study with thirteen problem families, the mean rate of observed deviant child behaviors for base line was .321, and after reading the book it was .199 (38). The behaviors included in the analysis were those targeted problems which the parents later included in their supervised child management training. The comparable data for a replication sample of eleven more families of aggressive boys were a mean targeted base-line rate of .410, and .318 for the posttest (33). Approximately 60 percent of the boys in the two samples showed some reductions in rate of deviant behavior. The Wilcoxon T value of 63.5 for the twenty-two (nontied) cases was significant at $p < .05$ (two-tailed).

The effects produced by simply reading the material were modest and may be shortlived, but certainly they were suggestive. Teaching the parents the language and concepts enabled them to design and implement their own programs sufficient to produce some reductions in noxious child behaviors. This could have major implications for the design of preventive programs. However, additional tests are needed to determine the persistence of such effects and the extent to which they generalize to nontargeted areas of child behavior.

OBSERVATION

The Kansas Medical Center group (26) was one of the first to emphasize "pinpointing behavior" and parents as observers in their training programs. The parent was not only taught to attend, but was also taught to graph the data as a means of summarizing the parental observations. Lindsley (26) stated that the simple act of counting behaviors produced significantly reduced rates for some deviant behaviors. Patterson et al. (38, 41), Tharp and Wetzel (64), and Walder et al. (73) also emphasized the training of the parent to observe and to collect data as being an integral part of the intervention program. Some of the training programs also made provisions for daily telephone monitoring of both the data collection and the application of programs. The daily calls served both as a prompt for the parent and as a positive consequence for effective performance.

To date, only one study has been carried out which evaluates the unique contribution of observing and recording behavioral control techniques. Peine (44) showed that when the mother was counting particular child behaviors, the rates did in fact decrease. However, on the following trials when the mother was counting a new response, the previously decelerated response returned to its base-line level. Whether or not future studies demonstrate that the decelerating effects for deviant behaviors are short-lived, even such temporary suppression effects could be useful in training programs. The fact that pinpointing and observing produce noticeable changes in their child's behavior should be reinforcing to many parents.

Most parents designed from two to ten programs; each focused upon a specified set of targeted behaviors. Some were designed to accelerate the occurrence of such prosocial behaviors as "talking to parents," "clean his room," "come home on time from school," or "play with siblings." Others were designed to decelerate problem behaviors ranging from "hit," "yell," and "tease" to "steal." Each of the initial programs made use of positive social reinforcers; some also included nonsocial reinforcers and "time out" as consequences.

REINFORCING CONTINGENCIES

It was implied by many investigators that parents of aggressive children would operate on lean schedules of positive reinforcement and use more negative reinforcement to strengthen prosocial behaviors. The mother, for example, might nag the child until he did his homework but then omit praise following his effort to study. For this reason, most parent training programs generally emphasize the importance of the parents' providing positive social reinforcers.

During the past year all training programs at the Oregon Research Institute began by having the parents role-play the use of positive reinforcers with children. They had practice periods during which they tracked and reinforced prosocial behaviors at home. These sessions were monitored by trips with parents, candy, pennies, toys, or special desserts. They were negotiated with the individual child and altered every few days to minimize satiation.

All investigators emphasized the importance of family members *not* reinforcing deviant behaviors. Some also made provisions for point losses each time a noxious response occurred. Other investigators emphasized the use of time-out procedures as a mildly aversive consequence which provided added control for behavior which must be decelerated rapidly (18, 41, 68, 86). To apply this technique the child was placed in a nonreinforcing setting immediately following the occurrence of a deviant response. Typically, he was left there for only five or ten minutes. White (78) showed that three minutes in time-out was as effective as thirty. The parent was instructed to remain calm and to apply this consequence each time the behavior occurred.

As an outgrowth of the pioneering efforts of Homme, Csanyi, Gonzales, and Rechs (20) in their application of Premack principles, there has been a growing emphasis upon contingency contracting. Such contracts are negotiated between parents and the child. They carefully pinpointed the behaviors to be accelerated or decelerated. The occurrence of a targeted behavior was immediately followed by recording a point gain or loss. The contract also specified the backup consequences which were to be earned for different point levels. These backup reinforcers could be earned on a daily basis by the very young child, or on a weekly basis by the more advanced. The backup reinforcers, point losses or gains, and targeted behaviors were continuously negotiated and rewritten. They were also signed by all participants. Examples of such contracts applied to family intervention can be found in the reports by Patterson et al. (38), Phillips (45), Ray (48), Stuart (62), and Stuart and Tripodi (63).

As yet there are no studies which evaluate the unique contribution of this component of family intervention. It does, however, seem so practical that it should eventually gain wide acceptance among practitioners. With practice in designing and carrying out single response programs, it is possible to expand the experience, through contracting, to cover a wide range of parental concerns. Such a contract might cover up to a dozen or more behaviors. In addition, the contract can be negotiated with the school or other community agencies, so that the teacher may record the child's daily performance on a check sheet carried by the child. In this fashion, the school and the parent can work together in monitoring and reinforcing the child's behaviors. Several investigators have used such arrangements to apparently good effect (12, 45, 63).

Evaluation Criteria

As shown in the review of evaluation studies of traditional child therapy (25), most investigators relied upon global descriptions by parents as necessary and sufficient criteria to determine treatment effects. It is the position of the writer that such complete reliance upon parent data is untenable in that there are now a number of studies which suggest consistent biases in such data. Of these, the most important bias is that parents report improvements whether or not the child's behavior changes.

It seems to be the case that global parent reports of changes in child behavior are under the control of variables other than just a desire to accurately describe child behavior. In the study by Collins (13), intervention was delayed unknown to the parents, and it was necessary to reassess the parents' perceptions of the child. The ratings showed significant improvement, even though treatment had *not* yet begun. A similar finding was obtained for a no-treatment control in a study by Clement and Milne (9). While it is conceivable that children's behavior improves simply as a function of the passage of time, it is also conceivable that parents perceived changes irrespective of what was happening to the children's behavior. However, a more adequately controlled study by Walter (76) showed that parents' global ratings of changes were unrelated to child behavior. In that study, families were randomly assigned to experimental and placebo groups. Multiple criteria were collected during base line and again after five weeks to assess changes in child behavior. Observation data collected in the homes showed significant decreases in observed rates of targeted deviant behaviors for families in the experimental group. There was a nonsignificant *increase* in rates for the families in the placebo group. Parents' global descriptions of improvement in their children revealed that all of the parents in the experimental group and two-thirds of the families in the placebo group believed that the child was improved.

The global ratings for the parents in the placebo group did not agree with the observers' tabulations in the home nor even with their own daily reports of occurrence of referral problem behaviors! Each parent, during base line and intervention, made daily reports on the occurrence/nonoccurrence of a list of behaviors for which they had come for assistance. The data showed a significant decrease in the reported frequencies of these behaviors for the families in the experimental group and an *increase* (nonsignificant) in these behaviors for the children in the placebo group. When the parents gave daily counts for specific behaviors, their reports correlated with data collected by observers. The correlation for base-line rates was in fact .63 ($p < .05$) (33). However, parents' global impressions did not correlate with either of these measures.

In the Walter study (76) two-thirds of the parents in the placebo group reported "improvement" for their children, even though the two criteria giving specific counts showed the rates of deviant behavior to be increasing. The poorly contrived control-group studies reviewed by Levitt (25) used global ratings from mothers and therapists to establish the fact that slightly more than two-thirds of nontreated emotionally disturbed children improved without treatment. The conclusion was that problem children improve as a function of the passage of time. Findings such as those in the Walter study would call such a conclusion into question and suggest an alternative hypothesis. Observation data collected in the home for both the Wiltz (81) and Walter (76) studies showed aggressive boys did not improve with the mere passage of time. Furthermore, it seems that the more global the rating elicited from the mother, the more likely she was to report improvements in her child's behavior.

One might say that at some abstract level mothers have a set to view their children optimistically. This set is largely unaffected by long-range increases or decreases in rates of child behavior. However, for whatever reasons, the set seems to exist; its presence suggests that global impressions simply should not serve as a primary criterion for evaluating treatment outcomes. It is urged that, as an alternative, investigators consider observation data collected in the home and/or parents' daily observations and tabulations of *specific* child behaviors. It is assumed by the present writer that these criteria will be shown to have long-range validity in terms of correlating with other measures of the child's adjustment. It is also assumed that they possess other psychometric assets, such as greater reliability.

Other than the study by Peine (44), little is known as yet about the reliability and validity of data obtained when parents observe and record the frequencies of their children's behaviors. Such methodological studies are badly needed. It is also true that data collected by observers within the home are not without their own unique set of measurement problems. For example, there are problems of observer-presence effects, observer bias, drift in observer reliability, and problems of data sampling, which have been reviewed in several studies (35, 50, 65, 77, 79). The exploratory studies completed thus far suggest that while problems of observers' presence, bias, and drift do exist, it is possible to collect high-quality observation data in settings such as the classroom and the home. It should be expected that the next few years will see marked increases in the number of methodological studies concerned with both parent-report data and field observations.

Efficiency of Family Intervention Technologies

While the single case studies such as those published in Ullmann and Krasner (66) demonstrated the feasibility of applications of social learning, they did not establish the *efficiency* of a social learning technology. The latter requires (a) estimates for magnitude of behavior change produced in *consecutive* cases, (b) estimates of time-cost to produce the effects, and (c) follow-up data to establish the persistence of the effects. These are the data required for the next phase of development of family intervention procedures. Following such data, it will be necessary to carry out carefully controlled comparative studies and parametric analyses of variables contributing to success. Group data for consecutive cases, estimates of professional time required, and systematic follow-up data are all characteristics which have begun to make their appearance in recent publications.

CONSECUTIVE CASES

As a rule of thumb, given perfect treatment outcome in comparing pre- and post-observations, six cases would be a sufficient sample size to establish an acceptable level of statistical significance, e.g., a t test for correlated means or the Wilcoxon (57). For the changes from base line to be significant at $p < .05$, each family would have to demonstrate improvements in the criterion measures. A series of studies, each using a minimum of six consecutive cases, could test the adequacy for each procedure being developed. During earlier stages when the procedures are less effective, larger samples would have to be used. In terms of our own family intervention procedures, which are far from perfect, it is necessary to use about twelve cases to achieve statistical significance.

Actually, there were a number of the earlier writers who worked with six or more cases (15, 16, 26, 52). Some effort was also made in these studies to specify the criteria for selecting cases, e.g., "retarded children" (15, 26) and "minimally brain damaged" populations in the case of the Hanf (16) and Salzinger et al. (52) studies. Criterion evaluation data were sometimes obtained from the parents (15, 26) and, in one study, by observers (16). Unfortunately, the data for these studies were not presented in such a manner as to permit careful evaluation of magnitude of change for individual cases, determination of the number of subjects changed, measurement of the amount of professional time required to bring about the changes, or persistence of effects.

In the same vein but with more comprehensive data, Rickert and Moore (51) trained six parents of retarded children from an initial sample of seventeen volunteers. While the dropout rate was very high (as it was also in the Lindsley [26] study), the procedures were very effective for those that remained. Of the behavior change projects attempted, 94 percent were successful. The criterion data were parents' tabulations of rate of occurrence of pinpointed problems. The fact that only selected portions of the data were presented makes evaluation of efficiency difficult. No systematic follow-up data were presented.

The study by Tharp and Wetzel (64) represented a substantial increment in sophistication. A large number of cases (seventy-seven) were treated by behavioral counselors. The counselors trained the parents to manage their own children. While the acting-out problems varied somewhat over the course of the study, the nature of the sample was reasonably well spelled out so that replication is feasible. The criterion data consisted of global ratings of improvement by therapists, parents, and teachers, and daily records for some pinpointed problems. Interestingly enough, the correlation between global ratings of improvement by parents and staff was not significant. While over half of the daily records were lost, the data that remained suggested substantial improvement in many of the families. This was a monumental effort to work with large samples of subjects using multiple criteria for evaluation. While the evaluation data were incomplete, they did suggest that the procedures had an impact.

Another large-scale pilot study was recently reported by Stuart and Tripodi (63). Seventy-six problem boys and girls were referred by the schools for failure to achieve and classroom disruptive behaviors. The children came from middle- and upper-class homes. A cadre of trained paraprofessionals trained the parents in the use of contingency contracting procedures. Careful records were kept on the amount of professional time required; the means among three treatment groups ranged from thirteen to thirty hours. These estimates did not include time spent in working with the schools or the time required for telephone contacts with family or school. The dropout rate from referral to completion of treatment was 19 percent.

In addition to the contribution involved in sampling a large group of moderately disturbed children, this study added the important feature of collecting several different types of criterion data to evaluate treatment outcomes. While the pilot study included no statistical tests of pre- and post-treatment comparisons, the trends were for improvement in the mothers' attitudes about their problem children as well as in mothers' global impressions about changes in certain problem behaviors.

The teachers perceived general improvements in classroom behavior. Other criterion data, such as number of days absent from school, showed a decrease from 15.4 to 10.1 for a group which had received intensive training. Data from school records for tardiness showed no improvements. However, grades showed a modest increase from 6.0 to 6.7, again for the intensive treatment group. The rather meager findings for the school criterion data were mitigated somewhat by the fact that the school population as a whole, for the same time periods, became markedly worse in absences and tardiness. Additional cases and follow-up data continue to be collected on this project. This long-term investigation should eventually provide a much needed analysis of outcome for a demonstration project actually providing community services for moderately disturbed children.

A comparable large-magnitude effort was made by a single individual working as a consultant in an Appalachian community (71). After training the social worker, who was in residence at the community mental health clinic, thirteen additional volunteers were trained and supervised. Observation data were collected by these volunteers prior to and following intervention for the sixty-six families which they treated. The data were collected in the classrooms or homes, whichever was appropriate. The initial referral problems ran the full gamut from retardation, autism, and academic failure to disruptive behavior in the home and classroom. From this population, certain cases were selected for treatment. The t tests comparing the pre- and post-observation measures were highly significant, particularly in such key variables as decreases in disruptive behavior in both the home and the classroom and increases in study behaviors in those two settings.

The sample size, completeness of the data, and significance of behavior changes point to this as a landmark study. The fact that it was carried out with minimal financial support adds further to its appeal as a field demonstration project. Unfortunately, data are not available on the amount of professional time invested per family. The fact that no follow-up data were collected and, in addition, the main criterion variable consisted of data collected by therapists on their own cases, suggests the possibility of bias in estimating success rates. It would have also been useful to have details on the problems dealt with, nature of the sample, which cases were selected for study and observation, and additional types of criterion data. However, as it stands, it is the most significant large-scale effort presented to date and clearly suggests the utility of such an approach when applied as a community service.

THE OREGON STUDIES

Experiences obtained with a long series of published and unpublished individual case studies (34, 40) led the author and his colleagues to work intensively with aggressive boys for a series of consecutive referrals. It was also decided to develop multiple criteria to evaluate the outcomes.

In the first study, parents of five out-of-control boys were trained, and the rudiments of a coding system appropriate for assessing family interaction were developed (41, 49). The observation data collected in the homes during base line, intervention, and follow-up showed modest changes in observed rates of deviant child behavior when comparing base line and termination. Twelve-month follow-up data were systematically collected for four cases (one family moved) and showed persistence of training effects for three of the families. On the average, 22.8 hours of professional time were required; this included time spent on intake interviews, staff conferences, training sessions, telephone contacts, and on transportation.

Thirteen consecutive referrals for extreme aggressive behavior constituted the sample for the next study (38). The cases were screened to include boys, ages six through thirteen, referred by the juvenile court, schools, and mental hygiene clinic. They represented a disproportionate sampling both of lower socioeconomic classes and families in which fathers were absent. The parents first learned the language and concepts of social learning theory and were then trained in group meetings to observe and collect data. In these sessions, they were also supervised as they designed and implemented programs to alter the behavior of the identified problem child. The targets often included behaviors of siblings and either one or both parents. These sessions for teaching parenting skills occurred once a week for a minimum of eight weeks. Each step of the program was contingent in that the parent must have performed successfully each step in order to earn the right to proceed to the next. For example, the parents first read and responded to a textbook on social learning theory (39) before they were given a training session on pinpointing problems. Such contingencies were employed throughout the training program in much the same manner as the parents employed them in training their children.

The average parent required 25.7 hours of professional time to become effective in *performing* the child management skills. Two criteria were used to evaluate the effects of the training. The first consisted of the observed changes in rates of "targeted deviant child behaviors." These included the behaviors targeted by parents for their child management programs. While each family worked with some behaviors unique to their situation, most included among them such problem behaviors as noncompliance, teasing, yelling, and hitting. After the study was underway, two kinds of parent-report data were added as additional criteria for evaluating outcome. The parents filled out an adjective checklist develped by Becker (3) prior to and following the training program. They also gave daily checklist data indicating whether or not the referral problems of greatest concern to them had occurred.

The observers' data for base line, fourth- and eighth-week treatment probes, and termination were subjected to an ANOVA for repeated measures. The analysis showed the changes in targeted deviant child behavior to be significant. The F was 4.31 ($p < .01$). The changes in mean level from base line to termination were in

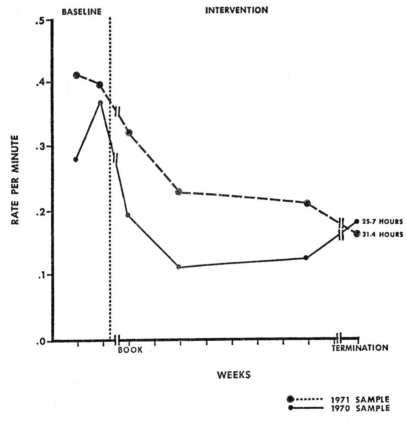

FIG. 1. Changes in targeted behaviors for two samples

close agreement with comparable changes in the 1968 pilot study
(41). For the latter, the mean base-line level for targeted deviant
behaviors was .27 responses per minute and .17 at termination.

The partial data available from parent-report measures also
showed significant changes. The mothers' descriptions of the problem children on the adjective checklist showed significant changes
in all five factors sampled by the ratings. In addition, for all five
cases in which parent data on frequency of occurrence of referral
symptoms were available, dramatic improvements were shown.

During the twelve-month follow-up two families moved to new
communities, and two refused to continue to participate. Of the
latter, one had been a "successful" case and the other unsuccessful.
Eight of the nine families in the follow-up study showed that the
gains made at termination had persisted. This persistence was reflected in both criteria—the observers' data and the parents' reports
on occurrence of referral symptoms.

Figure 2 summarizes the changes in the rate of targeted deviant
behavior for the nine families for whom data were available. The
data showed that the effects persisted for the majority of those
families for whom data were available. Taking into account the

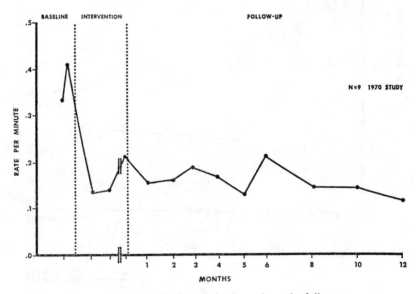

Fig. 2. Targeted deviant behaviors through follow-up

possibility that one of the two "refusals" might have been failures during this period would make this picture less sanguine.

It should also be noted that many of the families required some additional professional time during the follow-up period. An average of 5.7 hours of "booster shot" training was required; however, two or three of the families required extensive support in maintaining performance and contributed heavily to this figure. This experience suggests that some families may require *permanent* maintenance contacts costing two or three hours per month to keep the performance of parenting skills functioning at an adequate level. Women living alone with their children seemed particularly to need this type of contact.

The next report was a replication of these training procedures involving the same kind of sample of aggressive boys and their families. Eleven families were referred to the project by community agencies and required an average of 31.4 hours of professional time. They were trained in the procedures and by essentially the same set of behavior managers who had participated in the initial study. Three families dropped out prior to training; this dropout rate of 21 percent was comparable to that which obtained in the earlier study.

Two criterion variables were used to evaluate outcomes. As before, one consisted of estimates of targeted deviant child behaviors during base line and termination. These data were collected by professional observers. The second criterion was the frequency of occurrence of selected referral problems identified by the parents as being of primary concern to them. Of the two parent criteria used in the previous study, it was decided that this variable was probably a more sensitive and reliable estimate of changes in child behavior. The referral problem data were obtained on each of the days that the observers visited the home.

Nine of the eleven families showed large-magnitude changes of 30 percent or more drop from base-line level in observed rates of targeted deviant behavior. The ANOVA for repeated measures for the data from total base line, fourth-week probes, and termination produced an F of 3.77 ($p < .05$). This significant value replicated the findings from the earlier study. The data from both the original and the replication study are summarized in figure 1.

The second set of criterion data showed comparable changes from base line to termination. There was a steady decrease in occurrence of symptoms reported by parents at the fourth- and eighth-week probes. By termination, only 34 percent of the behaviors occurred on any given day. This percent was close to the 28 percent (for five cases) obtained at termination in the earlier study. In the current study over half of the subjects showed major reductions in parent-reported problem behaviors and an additional 18 percent showed modest reductions.

The ANOVA for repeated measures provided an *F* value of 2.92 ($p < .08$). The analysis showed the changes in the parents' reports of referral problem behaviors to be of borderline significance.

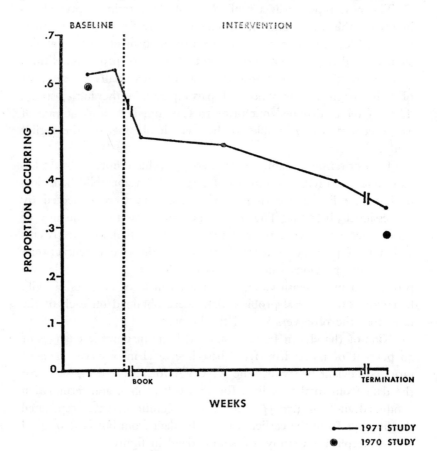

FIG. 3. Parents' reports on occurrence of referral problems

The two criteria also provided somewhat comparable base-line estimates for rates of deviancy. The correlation between the base-line rate of referral problem behaviors and targeted deviant behaviors was .63 ($p < .05$).

To date, two studies have been carried out which compare the effects obtained by application of the experimental procedures to nontreated control families (81) and to families enrolled in a placebo procedure (76). Both comparison studies used five-week intervals as the basis for comparison. At the end of this interval the families in the nontreated groups were assigned to the standard training procedures. The general assumption was that the experimental procedures would produce reliable decreases in observed rates of targeted deviant child behaviors within the relatively short period of training.

Wiltz (81) drew his sample from the first study (41). The first six referrals were placed in the experimental group, and the second six families were placed on a no-treatment waiting list for five weeks. A comparison of the pre- and post-observations of targeted deviant child behaviors showed no changes in the rates for the control group. There were significant decreases from the base-line measures for members of the experimental group. Incidentally, when the parents of the control group later received training, they were able to bring the behavior of their problem children under control.

The Walter (76) study involved the twelve families who participated in the replication study (33). Each family in the experimental group met for the standard training procedures used in the first four weeks of the program. Families in the placebo group met for weekly meetings and discussed tapes which they had made concerning their problems with their children. Parents in both groups rated their confidence in the treatment procedures being used before and after each session. There were no differences between groups in these expectancies nor did they change over time. There was, however, a nonsignificant *increase* in rates of targeted deviant child behavior for the placebo group. A comparable analysis for the experimental group showed a significant *decrease* in these rates. Similar changes in both groups were obtained when parents' data on referral problem behaviors were analyzed as criterion.

These two studies constitute a promising set of preliminary investigations attesting to the fact that there seems to be *something* (unspecified as yet) in the treatment procedures which produces reliable effects. The effect seems to be unrelated to the mere passage of time or to that placebo effect attributable to being "involved" in a parent group. More studies, using longer time intervals, will of course have to be carried out before these conclusions can be accepted with any great confidence. For the present, however, these findings suggest that the procedures warrant investigation and replication by other investigators.

DEMONSTRATION STUDIES

The general assumption is that much of children's social behaviors is under the control of external social stimuli. This, in turn, implies that different settings such as the classroom and the home may be under the control of different social stimuli. For example, the *in situ* analysis of stimulus control by Patterson and Cobb (35) showed that different classes of aggressive responses were controlled both by different agents and by different agent behaviors. Such being the case, then it would suggest that types of problem behaviors other than aggression might require rather different approaches.

Given that problems of social aggression are amenable to the social engineering procedures reviewed here, the question becomes one of the practical value of such coverage. In point of fact, only about a third of the problems for which children are referred for assistance are concerned with problems of aggression. What is needed, then, are groups of investigators, supported for extended periods of time, to develop technologies appropriate for working with the timid withdrawn child, the child who is an academic failure, and perhaps the immature or brain-damaged child. Actually, studies are currently being made to extend the coverage, e.g., the systematic work by H. Walker (personal communication) and by Clement, Roberts, and Lantz (10) with withdrawn children, or the work of Salzinger et al. (52) with brain-injured children. In each case a "problem" class would be defined not by the topography of the response but by the fact that the behaviors are under the control of the same stimuli.

Returning to an examination of the utilities which might accrue from the work currently completed in social engineering tailored for the aggressive child, there are several considerations of immediate import. To date, most of the large-scale efforts have collected incomplete data, no data at all, or data which are open to serious biasing effects. No large-scale comparative studies have been completed. The few carefully designed studies available have used only *very* small samples of aggressive children. While replication studies exist, they only confirm the fact that *one* (or two) groups of behavior modifiers are doing something (unspecified as yet) which produces reliable effects within the same laboratory. Further replications are necessary and, as a matter of fact, are forthcoming. For example, R. Stuart is replicating his earlier study. S. Johnson, at the University of Oregon, is replicating the Oregon Research Institute training procedures, using an independent group of behavior modifiers with a group of younger aggressive boys. E. Mash, at the University of Alberta, is also carrying out an independent analysis of some components of the training procedures. Needless to say, it is the efforts of these investigators to replicate the findings in their own laboratories which will constitute crucial tests for the procedures. The outcome of these and other replication studies will determine the readiness of such procedures for full-scale demonstration.

Given that the studies carried out within the next few years show the same modest success ratio, i.e., three out of four families, then it would be possible to design field demonstration studies.

As outlined by Patterson (31), such a demonstration center could be broadly conceived of as having both treatment and prevention missions. Only a few of the staff of such a "well child center" would require professional training. The bulk could consist of lay personnel drawn from the community and trained in the specific skills. In keeping with the precedents established by Wahler and Erickson (71) and Ora and Reisinger (29), these technicians would be supervised by the professional staff. While the initial goal for the well child center would be treatment, it could gradually shift its focus to include early training for young parents, high school students, and community professionals of all kinds in parenting skills. In effect, the primary mission for the treatment staff would be to put itself "out of business."

For such field centers, it would seem reasonable to use multiple criteria in evaluating outcomes. The parent *daily* reports of *frequencies* of occurrence of specified referral problems could be used as the primary criterion, although methodological studies should be carried out first to determine the adequacy of such data. Secondly, each well child clinic could have a group of two or three trained observers who spot-check random samples of the families; this would function as a quality check on parent data. Such observers could use simple code systems consisting of far less than the twenty-nine category codes used in our own work. Two or three observation sessions for base-line and outcome evaluations would be sufficient according to our preliminary estimates of data sampling requirements (38). The total cost of such assessment data would be less than what is now required for administration and presentation of a standard psychological workup. The dual set of criterion data would serve to keep the center accountable to the community, for such data would describe what changes, if any, occurred, and at what cost. The latter assumes that each intervention agent keeps careful track of how this time is spent.

Perhaps another five to ten years of work is required before such demonstration centers become feasible. This would allow for a series of replication studies and a series of studies defining which components of the training programs contribute to their efficacy. However, even the current level of development suggests to this writer that the promissory notes implied in the earlier N_1 case studies are becoming a reality which could lead to tomorrow's well child clinics.

REFERENCES

1. Azrin, N. H.; Hutchinson, R. R.; and Hake, D. F. "Pain-induced Fighting in the Squirrel Monkey." *Journal of Experimental Analysis of Behavior* 6 (1963): 620.
2. Becker, W. C. *Parents Are Teachers*. Champaign, Ill.: Research Press, 1971.
3. ———. "The Relationship of Factors in Parental Ratings of Self and Each Other to the Behavior of Kindergarten Children as Rated by Mothers, Fathers, and Teachers." *Journal of Consulting Psychology* 24 (1960): 507-27.

4. Bechtel, G. G. "The Analysis of Variance and Pair-Wise Scaling." *Psychometrika* 32 (1967): 47-65.

5. Bee, H. L.; Van Egeren, L. F.; Streissguth, A. F.; Nyman, B. A.; and Leckie, M. S. "Social Class Differences in Maternal Teaching Strategies and Speech Patterns." *Developmental Psychology* 1 (1969): 726-34.

6. Bernal, M.; Duryee, J.; Pruett, H.; and Burns, B. "Behavior Modification and the 'Brat Syndrome'." *Journal of Consulting and Clinical Psychology* 32 (1968): 447-55.

7. Brodsky, G. "The Relation between Verbal and Non-Verbal Behavior Change." *Behaviour Research and Therapy* 5 (1967): 183-92.

8. Burton, R. V. "Validity of Retrospective Reports Assessed by the Multitrait-Multimethod Analysis." *Developmental Psychology Monographs* 3 no. 3 (1970): part 2.

9. Clement, P. W., and Milne, D. C. "Group Play Therapy and Tangible Reinforcers Used to Modify the Behavior of Eight-Year-Old Boys. *Behaviour Research and Therapy* 5 (1967): 301-12.

10. Clement, P. W.; Roberts, P. V.; and Lantz, C. E. "Social Models and Token Reinforcement in the Treatment of Shy, Withdrawn Boys." *Proceedings, 78th Annual Convention*, pp. 515-16. *American Psychological Association*, 1970.

11. Cobb, J. A.; Ray, R. S.; and Patterson, G. R. "Increasing and Maintaining Appropriate Classroom Behavior of Aggressive Elementary School Boys." *A New Direction for Education: Behavior Analysis*, vol. 2, edited by E. A. Ramp and B. I. Happins. Lawrence, Kans.: University of Kansas, Department of Human Development, 1971.

12. Cohen, H. L.; Filipczak, J.; Slavin, J.; and Boran, F. "DICA: Programming Interpersonal Curricula for Adolescents." Paper presented at the meeting of the American Psychological Association, Washington, D.C., September 1971.

13. Collins, R. C. "The Treatment of Disruptive Behavior Problems by Employment of a Partial-Milieu Consistency Program." Doctoral dissertation, University of Oregon, 1966.

14. Crandall, V., and Preston, A. "Verbally Expressed Needs and Overt Maternal Behavior." *Child Development* 32 (1961): 261-70.

15. Galloway, C., and Galloway, K. "Parent Groups with a Focus on Precise Behavior Management." *IMRID Papers and Reports*, vol. 2, 1970. John F. Kennedy Center, George Peabody College, Nashville, Tenn.

16. Hanf, C. "Modification of Mother-Child Controlling Behavior during Mother-Child Interactions in Standardized Laboratory Situations." Paper presented at the meeting of the Association of Behavior Therapies, Olympia, Washington, 1968.

17. Hastings, A. S. "Operant Conditioning with Children in the Home with the Mother as the Experimenter." Master's thesis, Washington State University, 1967.

18. Hawkins, R. P.; Peterson, R. F.; Schweid, E.; and Bijou, S. W. "Behavior Therapy in the Home: Amelioration of Problem Parent-Child Relations with the Parent in a Therapeutic Role." *Journal of Experimental Child Psychology* 4 (1966): 99-107.

19. Hess, R. D., and Shipman, V. "Early Experience and the Socialization of Cognitive Modes in Children." *Child Development* 34 (1965): 869-86.

20. Homme, L.; Csanyi, A.; Gonzales, M.; and Rechs, J. *How to Use Contingency Contracting in the Classroom.* Champaign, Ill.: Research Press, 1970.

21. Johnson, S., and Brown, R. A. "Producing Behavior Change in Parents of Disturbed Children." *Journal of Child Psychology and Psychiatry* 10 (1969): 107-12.

22. Johnson, S. M.; Wahl, G.; Martin, S.; and Johansen, S. "How Deviant Is the Normal Child: A Behavioral Analysis of the Preschool Child and His Family," Paper presented at the meeting of the Association for the Advancement of Behavior Therapy, Washington, D.C., 1971.

23. Kriesberg, L. *Mothers in Poverty: A Study of Fatherless Families.* New York: Aldine Publishing Co., 1970.

24. Lafore, G. G. "Practices of Parents in Dealing with Preschool Children." *Child Development Monographs,* 1945, no. 31. Bureau of Publications, Teachers College, Columbia University, New York.

25. Levitt, E. E. "Research on Psychotherapy with Children." In *Handbook of Psychotherapy and Behavior Change,* edited by A. E. Bergin and S. L. Garfield, pp. 474-94. New York: John Wiley & Sons, 1971.

26. Lindsley, O. R. "An Experiment with Parents Handling Behavior at Home." *Johnstone Bulletin* 9 (1966): 27-36.

27. Martin, B. "Family Interaction Associated with Child Disturbance: Assessment and Modification." *Psychotherapy: Theory, Research and Practice* 4 (1967): 30-35.

28. O'Leary, K. D.; O'Leary, S.; and Becker, W. C. "Modification of a Deviant Sibling Interaction Patterns in the Home." *Behaviour Research and Therapy* 5 (1967): 113-20.

29. Ora, J., and Reisinger, J. J. "Preschool Intervention: A Behavioral Service Delivery System." Paper presented at the meeting of the American Psychological Association, Washington, D.C., September 1971.

30. Patterson, G. R. "Behavioral Techniques Based upon Social Learning: An Additional Base for Developing Behavior Modification Technologies." In *Behavior Therapy: Appraisal and Status,* edited by C. M. Franks, pp. 341-74. New York: McGraw-Hill Book Co., 1969.

31. ———. "A Community Mental Health Program for Children." In *Behavior Modification and Ideal Mental Health Services,* edited by

L. A. Hamerlynck, P. O. Davidson, and L. E. Acker, pp. 130-79. Calgary, Canada: University of Calgary, 1969.

32. ———. *Families. Applications of Social Learning to Family Life.* Champaign, Ill.: Research Press, 1971. (a)

33. ———. "Intervention for Families of Aggressive Boys: A Replication." Paper presented at the meeting of the American Psychological Association, Washington, D.C., September 1971. (b)

34. Patterson, G. R., and Brodsky, G. "A Behavior Modification Programme for a Child with Multiple Problem Behaviors." *Journal of Child Psychology and Psychiatry* 7 (1966): 277-95.

35. Patterson, G. R., and Cobb, J. A. "A Dyadic Analysis of Aggressive Behaviors." In *Minnesota Symposium on Child Psychology*, vol. 5, edited by J. P. Hill, pp. 72-129. Minneapolis: University of Minnesota Press, 1971.

36. ———. "Stimulus Control for Noxious Behaviors." In J. F. Knutson, ed., *The Control of Aggression: Implications from Basic Research*, Chicago: Aldine Publishing Co., (1972), forthcoming.

37. Patterson, G. R.; Cobb, J. A.; and Ray, R. S. "Direct Intervention in the Classroom: A Set of Procedures for the Aggressive Child." In *Implementing Behavioral Programs for Schools and Clinics*, edited by F. W. Clark, D. R. Evans, and L. A. Hamerlynck, pp. 151-201. Champaign, Ill.: Research Press, 1972.

38. ———. "A Social Engineering Technology for Retraining the Families of Aggressive Boys." In *Issues and Trends in Behavior Therapy*, edited by H. E. Adams and I. P. Unikel. Springfield, Ill.: Chas. C Thomas, 1972, forthcoming.

39. Patterson, G. R., and Gullion, M. E. *Living with Children: New Methods for Parents and Teachers.* Champaign, Ill.: Research Press, 1968.

40. Patterson, G. R.; McNeal, S.; Hawkins, N.; and Phelps, R. "Reprogramming the Social Environment." *Journal of Child Psychology and Psychiatry* 8 (1967): 181-95.

41. Patterson, G. R.; Ray, R. S.; and Shaw, D. A. "Direct Intervention in Families of Deviant Children." *Oregon Research Institute Research Bulletin* 8 (1968): no. 9.

42. Patterson, G. R.; Ray, R. S.; Shaw, D. A.; and Cobb, J. A. *Manual for Coding of Family Interactions*, 1969. Available from ASIS National Auxiliary Publications Service, c/o CMM Information Sciences, Inc., 909 Third Avenue, New York, N.Y. 10022. Document no. 01234.

43. Patterson, G. R., and Reid, J. B. "Reciprocity and Coercion: Two Facets of Social Systems." In *Behavior Modification in Clinical Psychology*, edited by C. Neuringer and J. Michael, pp. 133-77. New York: Appleton-Century-Crofts, 1970.

44. Peine, H. A. "Behavioral Recording by Parents and Its Resultant Consequence." Master's thesis, University of Utah, 1970.

45. Phillips, E. L. "Achievement Place: Token Reinforcement Procedures in a Home-Style Rehabilitation Setting for 'Predelinquent' Boys." *Journal of Applied Behavior Analysis* 1 (1968): 213-23.
46. Raush, H. L. "Interaction Sequences." *Journal of Personality and Social Psychology* 2 (1965): 487-99.
47. Ray, R. S. "The Relation of Interaction, Attitude Similarity, and Interpersonal Attraction: A Study of Reciprocity in the Small Group." Doctoral dissertation, University of Oregon, 1970.
48. ———. "The Training of Mothers of Atypical Children in the Use of Behavior Modification Techniques." Master's thesis, University of Oregon, 1965.
49. Reid, J. B. "Reciprocity and Family Interaction." Doctoral dissertation, University of Oregon, 1967.
50. ———. "Reliability Assessment of Observation Data: A Possible Methodological Problem." *Child Development* 41 (1971): 1143-50.
51. Rickert, D. C., and Moore, J. G. "Parent Training in Precise Behavior Management with Mentally Retarded Children." U.S. Office of Education Project 9-H-016, Final Report, 1970.
52. Salzinger, K.; Feldman, R. S.; and Portnoy, S. "Training Parents of Brain-injured Children in the Use of Operant Conditioning Procedures." *Behavior Therapy* 1 (1970): 4-32.
53. Schalock, H. D. "Observer Influence on Mother-Child Interaction in the Home: A Preliminary Report." Paper presented at the meeting of the Western Psychological Association, Carmel, California, 1958.
54. Schutte, R. C., and Hopkins, B. L. "The Effects of Teacher Attention on Following Instructions in a Kindergarten Class." *Journal of Applied Behavior Analysis* 3 (1970): 117-20.
55. Sears, R. R. "Comparison of Interviews with Questionnaires for Measuring Mother's Attitudes toward Sex and Aggression." *Journal of Personality and Social Psychology* 2 (1965): 37-44.
56. Shaw, D. A. "Family Maintenance Schedules for Deviant Behavior." Doctoral dissertation, University of Oregon, 1971.
57. Siegal, S. *Nonparametric Statistics for the Behavioral Sciences.* New York: McGraw-Hill Book Co., 1956.
58. Skindrud, K. "Generalization of Intervention Effects from Home to School Settings." Unpublished manuscript, Oregon Research Institute, Eugene, 1972.
59. Skinner, B. F. *Contingencies of Reinforcement: A Theoretical Analysis.* New York: Appleton-Century-Crofts, 1969.
60. ———. *Science and Human Behavior.* New York: Appleton-Century-Crofts, 1953.
61. Smith, H. T. "A Comparison of Interview and Observation Measures of Mother Behavior." *Journal of Abnormal and Social Psychology* 57 (1958): 278-82.

62. Stuart, R. B. "Behavioral Contracting within the Families of Delinquents." *Journal of Behaviour Therapy and Experimental Psychiatry* 2 (1971): 1-11.

63. Stuart, R. B., and Tripodi, T. "Experimental Evolution of Three Time Constrained Behavioral Treatments for Predelinquents and Delinquents." Paper presented at the meeting of the Association for the Advancement of Behavior Therapy, Washington, D.C., September 1971.

64. Tharp, R., and Wetzel, R. *Behavior Modification in the Natural Environment.* New York: Academic Press, 1969.

65. Thomas, D. S.; Loomis, A. M.; and Arrington, R. "Observational Studies of Social Behavior." *Social Behavior Patterns*, vol. 1, pp. 1-47. New Haven, Conn.: Yale University Press, Institute for Human Relations, 1933.

66. Ullmann, L. P. and Krasner, L. *Case Studies in Behavior Modification.* New York: Holt, Rinehart & Winston, 1965.

67. Ulrich, R. "Pain as a Cause of Aggression." *American Zoologist* 6 (1966): 643-62.

68. Wahler, R. G. "Behavior Therapy for Oppositional Children: Love Is Not Enough." Paper presented at the meeting of the Eastern Psychological Association, Washington, D.C., April 1968.

69. ———. "Behavior Therapy with Oppositional Children: Attempts to Increase Their Parents' Reinforcement Value." Paper presented at the meeting of the Southeastern Psychological Association, Atlanta, April 1967.

70. ———. "Setting Generality: Some Specific and General Effects of Child Behavior." *Journal of Applied Behavior Analysis* 2 (1969): 239.

71. Wahler, R. G., and Erickson, M. "Child Behavior Therapy: A Community Program in Appalachia." *Behaviour Research and Therapy* 7 (1969): 71-78.

72. Wahler, R. G.; Winkle, G. H.; Peterson, R. F.; and Morrison, D. C. "Mothers as Behavior Therapists for Their Own Children." *Behaviour Research and Therapy* 3 (1965): 113-24.

73. Walder, L.; Cohen, S.; and Daston, P. "Teaching Parents and Others Principles of Behavior Control for Modifying the Behavior of Children." Progress Report, 1967, U.S. Office of Education, no. 32-30-7515-5024.

74. Walker, H., and Buckley, N. K. "Investigation of Some Classroom Control Parameters As a Function of Teacher Dispensed Social Reinforcers." *Journal of Applied Behavior Analysis*, 1972, in press.

75. Walker, H. M.; Mattson, R. H.; and Buckley, N. "Special Class Placement as a Treatment Alternative for Deviant Behavior in Children." In *Modifying Deviant Social Behaviors in Various Class-*

room Settings, edited by F. A. M. Benson, no 1, pp. 49-80. Eugene, Oreg.: University of Oregon, 1969.

76. Walter, H. "Placebo versus Social Learning Effects in Parent Training Procedures Designed to Alter the Behaviors of Aggressive Boys." Doctoral dissertation, University of Oregon, 1971.

77. Weick, K. E. "Systematic Observational Methods." In *The Handbook of Social Psychology,* vol. 2, 2d ed., edited by G. Lindzey and E. Aronson, pp. 347-451. Reading, Mass.: Addison-Wesley Publishing Co., 1968.

78. White, G. "Time Out Duration and the Suppression of Deviant Behavior in Children." Master's thesis, University of Oregon, 1971.

79. Wiggins, J. S. *Personality and Prediction: Principles of Personality Assessment.* Reading, Mass.: Addison-Wesley Publishing Co., forthcoming.

80. Wills, T. "The Contribution of Instrumental and Affective Events to Perceived Pleasures and Displeasures in Marital Relationships." Master's thesis, University of Oregon, 1971.

81. Wiltz, N. A., Jr. "Modification of Behaviors of Deviant Boys through Parent Participation in a Group Technique." Doctoral dissertation, University of Oregon, 1969.

82. Wolf, M.; Mees, H.; and Risley, T. "Applications of Operant Conditioning Procedures to the Behavior Problems of an Autistic Child." *Behaviour Research and Therapy* 1 (1964): 305-12.

83. Wortis, H.; Bardach, J. L.; Cutler, R.; Rue, R.; and Freedman, A. "Child-rearing Practices in a Low Socioeconomic Group." *Pediatrics* 32 (1963): 298-307.

84. Yarrow, M. R.; Campbell, J. D.; and Burton, R. V. "Recollections of Childhood: A Study of the Retrospective Method." *Monographs of the Society for Research in Child Development,* 1970, 35(5), (Serial No. 138).

85. ———. "Reliability of Maternal Retrospection: A Preliminary Report." *Family Process* 3 (1964): 207-18.

86. Zeilberger, J.; Sampen, S.; and Sloane, H. "Modification of a Child's Problem Behaviors in the Home with the Mother as Therapist." *Journal of Applied Behavior Analysis* 1 (1968): 47-53.

87. Zifferblatt, S. M. *You Can Help Your Child Improve Study and Homework Behaviors.* Champaign, Ill.: Research Press, 1970.

SPECIFIC PROBLEM AREAS

CHAPTER VI

Behavior Analysis and Token Reinforcement in Educational Behavior Modification and Curriculum Research

ARTHUR W. STAATS

The devotion of a yearbook to behavior modification is of considerable gratification to the present author. It is now over a decade since he completed a general learning analysis of fields of human behavior investigation, including a chapter on educational psychology (45). At that time, unlike the present when a whole Yearbook can be devoted to this topic, the only available empirical material was that of programmed instruction and the behavior modification studies the author had himself conducted. As was indicated at that time, elaboration was needed along various lines. Several points included in that analysis will be stressed in this paper: (a) the need for the development of reinforcement principles and practices in education, (b) the need for behavior analysis, (c) the need to deal with basic areas of education such as reading, and (d) the need for a wider utilization of learning principles.

These suggestions were made originally in the context of a program of research that was already almost a decade in duration, and which has been continued up to the present. This program presents a methodological strategy itself, in addition to its specific findings and analyses. And it provides a basis for making additional projections. In part for these reasons, as well as for the specific content, the present chapter will describe some of the progress of this program, including descriptions of the principles, methods, apparatus, and some of the findings of this work.

Naturalistic Observations and Experimental-Naturalistic Research

With the development of a sophisticated experimental methodology in psychology came a disenchantment with the value of less formalized types of observational methods. With the experimental methodology, moreover, came a tendency to devalue as "applied" any psychological study that dealt with functional human behaviors. In the early 1950s, when the present work began, the study of learning principles was restricted largely to the laboratory. Only theoretical extensions in general areas had been suggested (11, 26) and these involved psychoanalytic theory. There were almost no direct applications of learning principles to specific human behaviors.

There were no accepted methods available, moreover, for studying or dealing with the significant behaviors of humans within a learning paradigm. The present author's learning approach thus began with the naturalistic observations of behavior and the interpretation of the behavior into stimulus and response terms—observations made in Veterans Administration hospitals with psychiatric patients (and, as will be referred to later, with children with learning and behavior problems in the UCLA Fernald Clinic). A major observation was that psychodynamic views led professionals to treat patients in ways that were just the converse of what would be prescribed from a reinforcement analysis. Because psychoanalytic theory suggested the abnormal behavior was the symptom of the individual's psychic disturbance, psychotherapists paid attention more to abnormal behavior than to normal behavior.

From a reinforcement viewpoint, however, one has to consider the effect of such treatment on the abnormal behavior itself. One has to be very interested in how one attends to the behavior of another person. For attention is usually a reinforcing stimulus. If one ignores normal behaviors and attends only to bizarre behaviors, then it would be expected that the bizarre behaviors of the patient would increase in frequency. Traditional psychodynamic conceptions actually fostered the social reinforcement of abnormal behavior and thus its maintenance.

The author used the first case that appeared in the literature that demonstrated what was generally happening in clinicians' interactions with individuals having abnormal behaviors to illustrate the common practices and to suggest behavior modification alternatives (41). The case was that of a schizophrenic patient who had confused speech which was characterized by saying the opposite of

the "appropriate" response. For example, the patient would reverse
language usages such as those of "yes" and "no." As was common
from the psychodynamic approach, the treating psychologists and
psychiatrists (24) were concerned with the patient's abnormal behavior as a sign of his supposed internal conflicts. Moreover, this
concern was reflected in how the patient was dealt with. Fortunately, the article had extensively quoted interviews with the patient
which clearly illustrated the process. It was clear in the interview
that the normal speech of the patient was of little interest. It was
only when the patient uttered one of his *unusual* statements that
the doctors became interested in what he was saying. Then they
would perk up, ask him questions concerning why he said that
instead of the other, did he really mean that, did he not mean the
opposite, and so on. In addition, the doctors also did other things
that would be counter to those recommended from reinforcement
analysis. For example, the patient was asked if he wanted a cigarette.
When the patient said "No," he was given the cigarette anyway,
which he accepted and smoked. The cigarette was a reinforcer and
would be expected to strengthen the abnormal behavior. In this
interaction, because of the theoretical orientation, there was no
realization of the fact that the psychotherapists were thus training
the patient to respond with his confused speech. That is, the learning analysis states explicitly that reinforcing the reversed speech
with the cigarette will train the patient to respond in a like way
in future situations. It should be clear that we could take any child
and train him in such confused speech.

The author's analysis suggested that reinforcement situations like
this would be unlikely to occur in the normal person's social environment. Thus, abnormal reinforcement environments could be
expected to produce abnormal behavior. Furthermore, it was suggested that abnormal behavior could be treated by changing the
reinforcement procedures. In this case the suggestion was that if the
abnormal speech of the schizophrenic patient was learned and
maintained by reinforcement, "then lack of such reinforcement
should lead to extinction of such behaviors. For example, withholding the cigarette should weaken the strength of the opposite speech,
and giving the cigarette to correct speech should strengthen that
type of response" (41:269). As this example indicates, the analysis

suggested that the normal behaviors of "abnormal" patients could be produced by reinforcing desirable behaviors and abnormal behaviors could be diminished by extinction.

As the first behavior modification analysis of abnormal behavior in the context of the principles of reinforcement, the rationale provided a foundation for early behavior modification developments. That is, the author (42), with the cooperation of associates—for example, J. L. Michael—also performed behavior modification work in the naturalistic situation, based upon his behavior analysis. The results were such as to verify the analysis and social reinforcing procedures involved.

Extensions to Formal Behavior Modification Studies

These developments to this point were tested in the work of T. Ayllon, Michael's student at that time, in their pioneering study introducing behavior modification to the hospital setting (4). This study gave formal evidence supporting the present author's 1957 analysis that reinforcement principles were important in molding abnormal behavior and could be used for treatment purposes. Several principles of the 1957 article were demonstrated; for example, that the social reinforcement from hospital personnel inadvertently could produce and maintain abnormal behaviors in patients, that desirable behaviors could be produced by positive reinforcement, and that abnormal behaviors could be removed through extinction procedures.

One example may be illustrated here. It was suggested in the analysis of the schizophrenic's opposite speech that the clinician's attention was reinforcing and thus maintaining the abnormal behavior. Ayllon and Michael made the same analysis of the abnormal behavior of the psychotic who would enter the nurses' office even though the behavior was considered to be obstructive. They reasoned that it was the attention of the nurses that reinforced the behavior and maintained it in high frequency.

The following instructions were given to the nurses: "During this program the patient must not be given reinforcement (attention) for entering the nurses' office. Tally every time she enters the office" (4:327). The results of the tally of the incidence of what may be considered a compulsive behavior are shown in figure 1.

The decreasing frequency of the behavior follows the pattern to be expected from use of the principle of extinction—when reinforcement is no longer provided for a behavior. In the same study Ayllon and Michael also showed again that abnormal speech that is characteristic of psychosis could be benignly decreased through positive reinforcement for normal speech and extinction of abnormal speech. These findings were dramatic support for the previous contention that abnormal behavioral symptoms could be manipulated by reinforcement principles and that learning theory indeed had something to offer clinical theory and practice and could no longer be ignored. One of the significant aspects of Ayllon and Michael's work, moreover, was methodological—i.e., obtaining the facilities and the cooperation of the hospital for research and the production of clearcut data. Their verification of the behavior modification principles and the demonstration of how to actually conduct behavior modification treatment gave impetus to many other investigations and to the development of the field.

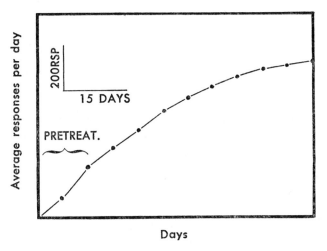

FIG. 1. Extinction of the response "entering the nurses' office." Record of a psychotic patient. From Ayllon and Michael (4:326).

Development of the Token-Reinforcer System

While these extensions were taking place, however, the author had gone on to the task of dealing with behaviors of greater complexity and of developing a reinforcer system for general use. It was evident that the short-term treatments of relatively simple behaviors—like the cases of the schizophrenic's opposite speech or the other psychotic symptoms Ayllon and Michael dealt with—while having very significant implications were only first steps towards understanding and dealing with complex human behaviors and behavior problems. Moreover, social attention as a reinforcer, while valuable for modification of simple behaviors in short-term procedures and for procedures involving infrequent learning trials, was not considered by the author to be adequate for complex cases involving many, many training trials and effortful responding and learning. A reinforcing system was needed that was powerful, flexible, long-lasting, even with repeated and massed use, and capable of employment with different subjects and different problems.

For example, in previous work in the Fernald Clinic with disturbed children who had problems of academic learning usually associated with emotional or behavior problems, it appeared to the author that such children did not learn because in a unit of time they made far fewer learning trials than did normal children. Their attentional and work behaviors were poorly maintained by the reinforcers that were usually effective. Under these conditions they learned new material at a very slow rate, even when given copious social approval and attention in a tutorial interaction.

In designing the first token reinforcer system for behavior modification in 1959, the immediate problem dealt with was the study and treatment of problems of learning in children who had special difficulties of one kind or another. In addition, the plan was to study the normal acquisition of important, complex cognitive (or language) repertoires—most of them of academic or preacademic significance. Studying and dealing with such behaviors demanded the type of reinforcer system described above.

One of the things we see on the basis of naturalistic observation is that tokens, like money, become excellent reinforcers for people, even when not subject to deprivation of primary reinforcers. This occurs because money is paired with or backed up by a large number of other reinforcers. Taking this tip from everyday life, a reinforcer system following the same principle was developed by the author (36:126).

In this first system, the child received plastic disks as tokens. Those disks could then be exchanged for an article which the child had selected to work for. The item might be a toy, an article of clothing, a piece of sporting equipment—anything the child selected. A central consideration was the infinity of backup reinforcers. The child's progress toward accumulation of sufficient tokens to get the backup reinforcer was also plotted daily so he had visual indication of his gain.

This reinforcement system was first tried on several children who were considered to be difficult problems in the traditional classroom and to be retarded in reading. The learning materials concerned reading and were designed to be simple to administer and to facilitate the recording of the child's progress.[1] That is, the child first learned the new words to be presented in a story: the word was presented singly and the child was told its name and was reinforced for looking at the word and saying its name. When the child could spontaneously read all the words, they were presented in the paragraphs of the story and then in the whole story. Better performance was reinforced with a higher value plastic disk (there were three values). The important result was the immediate change in the children's behavior. They became vigorous, attentive workers and they learned well.

This was the first use of a token-reinforcer system in clinical and educational behavior modification. Even later, investigators in programmed instruction were to suggest that learning and moving ahead are sufficient reinforcers to maintain the attention and work behaviors of children. "With humans, simply being correct is sufficient reinforcement" (18:278). As a consequence, those in that field did not systematically consider the question of appropriate reinforcers for children. They accepted the idea that achievement rewards are generally sufficient and did not consider the enormously important procedures of reinforcement. However, moving ahead, achievement, acquisition of skills, social approval, and so on, are all learned rewards. Whether or not and to what extent they will

1. Judson R. Finley and Karl A. Minke, as undergraduate research assistants in 1959, applied the token-reinforcer procedures in behavior modification sessions with individual children, and Richard E. Schutz also assisted in the conduct of the study which took place in a public junior high school.

be effective will depend upon the child's history of learning. The token-reinforcement system was developed to be effective with all children, including those for whom learning and other traditional rewards are not effective.

The success and potentiality of token-reinforcement procedures were communicated to J. L. Michael, and he and L. Meyerson attempted to strengthen the work behaviors of mentally retarded children, using the token-reinforcement system. P. Corke and S. Toombs, students of Michael, explored the token-reinforcer system with children in a remedial classroom. Ayllon also tried the present author's suggestion that the token system would have advantages in a psychiatric ward. In each case, the efficacy of the token-reinforcer system was quite dramatic in working with children and adults and the reinforcement system began to be broadly disseminated.

Behavior Modification with Academic Repertoires

After this first token study on remedial reading, the present author began to move in several directions in the extension of the learning theory and its application to the study of human behavior and to the treatment of the problems of behavior. An important part of this work, beginning in 1960, was the long-term study of the behavioral development of the author's own daughter, which was to continue for eight years. This involved the study of various aspects of language acquisition, sensorimotor skill learning, social behavior learning, the solution of problems of behavior, and so on (40, 37). As an illustration, training was conducted in number skills when the child was eighteen months of age. This training first involved learning the verbal discriminations between one, two, and three objects. Various objects had to be employed—such as raisins, pieces of popcorn, fingers, and marbles. Some of them, such as the raisins, were used both as objects to be counted and as the reinforcers. For example, the author would hold one raisin in one hand and two in the other hand and ask, "Do you want one raisin (displaying the raisin) or two raisins (showing the other hand)?" The child soon learned the number discrimination of saying "two" and pointing to the two raisins, being differentially reinforced by receiving the larger amount. As another example of the progressively advancing training, the author would hold up several fingers and ask, "How many fingers are there?" Reinforcement for a correct response would be social approval. After the basic number discriminations were learned, counting was added to her repertoire before she was two years of age, employing the token-reinforcer system. It was possible to study the learning of these number concepts while producing the early intellectual skills. The procedures and principles have since been employed and substantiated in systematic research (40, 46).

Controlled laboratory studies were begun in 1960 with preschool children to study the principles of reinforcement in the normal acquisition of central academic skills, especially reading acquisition, as well as number concept and writing development. Reading behavior was selected for special study because it was complex, demanded long-term training and innumerable training trials, was central in child development, was poorly understood, and was a frequent source of behavioral difficulty associated with a variety of educational and clinical problems. Therefore, principles and procedures verified with this behavior should be capable of general extension. These studies employed the token-reinforcer system, which the author had revised to be appropriate for very young children (see 39, 48, 50, 52).

Part of the results of the first formal study with young children (52) are shown in figure 2. The graphs show the learning curves of three children engaged in a reading learning task. The curves show the number of words learned per each training session, in which the words were first read singly and then in sentences and short paragraphs. The children were first reinforced for their reading responses for two training sessions. Strong attending and working occurred. At point *a* the reinforcement was discontinued. No reinforcement was given until the children requested that the reading game stop. This was at point *b*, when reinforcement was again introduced. Two of the children began to attend to the materials, to actively work at learning, and their learning curves began to rise again. One child had convinced his parents not to continue his participation in the study, and he never experienced the return to the reinforcement condition. Thus, the results show a strong reading learning behavior under reinforcement. When reinforcement is withdrawn, the reading learning behavior weakens (extinguishes) and the children finally request cessation of the activity. When reinforcement is reinstated, the behavior of remaining in the activity strengthens as does the reading learning behavior itself, as well as the products of such behavior—the acquisition of new words. As many behavior modification studies do today, the experimental design here varied the experimental conditions for each child and recorded the incidence of the behavior under the varied conditions. The results in figure 2 were supplemented by introducing another three children to the no-reinforcement condition first and then changing to the reinforcement condition when they had requested cessation of the reading activity. With no reinforcement the children voluntarily participated in the training only a very brief period, and then their attention and reading deteriorated. When reinforcement was introduced, they became attentive, active learners, began learning to read new words rapidly, and participated voluntarily in the study until it was terminated.

The results of the several studies with the preschool children showed clearly that learning itself, or even social reinforcement, is *not* sufficient to maintain the attention and work behaviors of

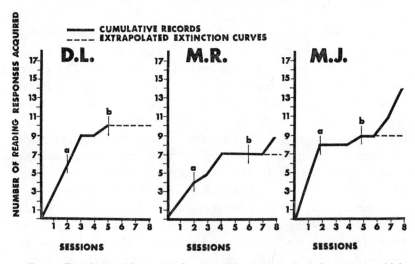

Fig. 2. For these subjects, the first condition included reinforcement, which was discontinued at point *a* and reinstated at point *b*. The dotted line commences at the point that the child would no longer remain in the experiment and depicts the learning curve which would have resulted if reinforcement was not reinstated. From Staats et al. (52:38).

normal young children engaged in arduous, extended learning tasks. Young children have come to be considered inappropriate subjects for formal learning procedures because of their inattention in traditional teaching situations. If there is sufficient reinforcement for the attentional and work behaviors, on the other hand, the learning proceeds smoothly and well and has general benefits to the child, as will be indicated further on.

As the first published use of the token-reinforcer system, this study has been referred to in terms of its implications for behavior modification work in clinical and educational settings (22:497, 28).

The experiment by Staats et al. was particularly significant because it demonstrated that with a token system and a variety of exchange items one is no longer dependent upon the power of a single backup reinforcer. That is, one is not limited to giving M&M candies whose power depends upon the momentary deprivation state of the child. Instead, the only limitation of backup reinforcer systems is the ingenuity of the experimenter (28:380).

The author was also suggesting at this time a number of ways the token-reinforcer system could be used in behavior modification work with children, thus providing a basis for various extensions:

These developments may be extended to the study of a number of types of significant behavior acquisitions, e.g., speech learning, arithmetic learning, etc., and to various special populations, such as deaf children, mutes, mental retardates, etc. Much operant research with humans has tended to involve only simple responses, such as knob-pulling and button-pressing, and simple controlling stimuli. The present facility would seem to be useful in the study of the acquisition of complex responses of more immediate significance to human adjustment. This could also involve work which had remedial objectives, e.g., remedial reading problems, the training of autistic children, general training problems in children resulting from deficient "motivation" (48:146-47).

This analysis was followed by a number of studies, in different settings, with different types of problems. For example, a research project was being conducted at the University of Washington with mentally retarded subjects. Programmed instruction materials were being employed in an effort to teach academic skills to these children who were difficult educational problems. Montrose Wolf, a graduate assistant in the author's work that involved employing the token-reinforcer system with four-year-olds, helped introduce that system to this program and also initiated a systematic series of studies of behavior modification with child behavior problems:

> Initially, the teachers attempted to strengthen desirable classroom behavior and correct answers to academic materials by following such behaviors with remarks of approval and by ignoring inappropriate responses. Little, if any, improvement in sustained studying behavior was obtained under these procedures. Evidently, verbal remarks in the form of approval and praise did not have reinforcing functions for these children. Consequently, a token-reinforcement system similar to that used by Staats, Staats, Schutz, and Wolf (1962) was added. This procedure did indeed establish and maintain higher rates of effective study and greater cooperation (Bijou, Birnbrauer, Kidder, and Tague, 1967, p. 316).

Ayllon and Azrin (3), Atthowe and Krasner (2), O'Leary and Becker (27), Wolf, Giles, and Hall (56), and Cohen and Filipczak (9), as examples, also began large scale applications of the token-reinforcer system, as did many others, to the study and treatment of behavior problems. Many of these extensions of the token-reinforcer system will be described elsewhere in the present volume and need not be dealt with here (see Krasner and Krasner and Zifferblatt chapters).

Early Cognitive Learning

Following the progress in these three areas, the author began to combine his experimental-naturalistic research findings on his own child with those of behavior modification studies with preschool children, in the study of the cognitive skills acquired in academic and preacademic training as well as in the study of children's problems in education. The experimental-naturalistic work had indicated that a learning theory analysis of writing, number concept learning, and especially reading, in combination with a token-reinforcement system, could be employed to study in detail the child's acquisition of complex cognitive repertoires. This could be done in long-term research in which very large numbers of learning trials were conducted. Moreover, the study could be done while the children were learning important, functional skills. The results suggested the methodology had general significance for studying and treating human behaviors.

It was important, however, to bring the principles, analyses, and procedures under detailed study. The procedures developed with the author's daughter were first extended in 1963 to several additional children, employing as the behavior modification technician a graduate student who had no special training in working with the complex learning of young children.[2] The results verified the previous findings, supported the general approach, and began to indicate the types of necessary information to provide the adult who is to serve as the trainer of a young child.

In 1965 the author set up a laboratory-classroom complex in Madison, Wisconsin, for twelve culturally deprived four-year-old children. (Later, a similar complex was established at the University of Hawaii.) The subjects were children expected to constitute learning and behavior problems when later entering school. They were given training in the laboratory attached to the classroom in the three areas of study—writing, number concept learning, and reading—using a token-reinforcement system. Again the methods and principles were supported. The children learned functional skills in the three types of cognitive development. At the same time, it was possible to systematically study the learning of young children. It is not possible to summarize the findings here (see 37, 40, 46) but a few examples may be given.

NUMBER CONCEPT LEARNING AND ORIGINALITY

The research with the various young children indicated that early number (quantitative) concept learning may be analyzed in very straightforward stimulus-response terms. The first phase of learning number concepts involves the discrimination of numerosity. The child has to learn to label objects by the stimulus of number, ignoring size, color, and other stimulus dimensions of the objects. Instrumental discrimination learning procedures can produce this type of learning standardly in young children (37, 40, 46)—at much earlier ages than past research and theory has suggested. When the child has learned to discriminate objects by number up to about four, then training in counting may begin. The number concepts of counting involve the learning of two types of skills, learned in coordinated action with one another. One skill is the

2. Karl A. Minke applied the procedures.

sensorimotor skill of responding to a group of objects one at a time (at least in the early stages of counting). The child can point to each object in succession or, better still, move one object at a time from a group. The other type of skill is to say successively one number as each object is moved or touched. The sensorimotor skill can be learned quickly. Also, the child who already has learned several numbers can learn easily to say them in succession. But it is necessary that the child learn to *coordinate* the two repertoires of skills, which is a task of some difficulty.

Once this coordination has been learned for a few counting responses, it should be stressed that the child has acquired a general skill that can be further developed on a purely verbal level. The general number skills, along with new verbal learning, may be employed creatively also where the child responds to novel stimuli on which he has never been trained. To illustrate, it has been shown (46) that after the child has learned a very small sensorimotor-verbal counting repertoire, the repertoire can be extended solely on the basis of verbal training (rote verbal learning). The child, who has only learned to count four objects, let us say, may be given verbal training by which he learns to say the numbers up to fifteen without ever being trained to count fifteen objects. On the very first time he is presented with fifteen objects, however, he will then be able to count them—a novel, original act on which the child has never been trained.

One criticism of stimulus-response learning theory has been that it is unable to account for originality in human behavior. The present results thus indicate that cognitive repertoires may be analyzed into their stimulus-response components and the repertoires can be produced in children through straightforward behavioral training, in an effective manner. Moreover, sophisticated analysis reveals how the cognitive repertoires, once learned, can be the basis for original behavior. This occurs when the individual has been given the basic repertoires through learning and then meets new situations that call out *original combinations* of already learned skills (37, 40, 45). The results provided by Staats et al. (46) also showed that a sophisticated learning analysis can indicate when rote verbal learning is productive and when it is not. That is, in number concept learning, rote learning inhibits the child's learning if he is taught to count verbally prior to being taught the sensorimotor-verbal skill coordination. After the coordination has been learned, however, the rote verbal learning of counting is effective. Without this understanding, programs for training the young child (like "Sesame Street") can err in teaching the child a rote verbal counting repertoire before the sensorimotor-verbal coordination is learned.

READING ACQUISITION AND CUMULATIVE-HIERARCHIAL LEARNING: A THEORY OF READING

The research on reading indicated that it is possible to begin to teach the child to read as soon as he has developed a good language repertoire (as is the case with number skills and writing). Children from various social backgrounds, including those who are culturally deprived, can be standardly trained to read the letters of the alphabet. This skill, incidentally, is the best predictor of how well the child will do in learning to read (8). Following the learning of the alphabet, which is a very difficult learning task for children with no previous training, the child may be trained to read whole words and sentences and to learn grapheme-phoneme units (phonics), and so on. When the token-reinforcer system is employed, the children can engage in such arduous, repetitive, cognitive learning tasks with enthusiasm in a voluntary manner. And the children can learn in a standard manner, a finding that has implications for contemporary educational and psychological conceptions of child development.

The author conducted experimental-longitudinal research with his own children in the area of reading until they had acquired full reading repertoires, and he conducted research with groups of children as well. The results of the two approaches have yielded a full learning theory of what reading is, how it is acquired, and how reading functions in the further cognitive development of the child (40). In summary, it is suggested first that reading actually consists of a number of repertoires. Cognitive development in children, including reading, is seen as a cumulative, hierarchical process in which children first learn foundation repertoires consisting of basic skills. These basic behavioral repertoires then enable the child to acquire higher level repertoires of skills which in turn constitute the basis for learning more advanced repertoires.

Reading, according to this theory, first depends upon the child having acquired the multiple repertoires that compose a functional language. While the analysis cannot be presented here, it is important to note that language itself consists of a number of repertoires that can be separately defined, the acquisition of each requiring many learning trials and years of learning for the child (37). Only if the child has acquired these basic behavioral repertoires will he be able to learn to read, and only if he has these language repertoires will reading be meaningful to him. For example, one of the language repertoires is that of "following instructions." The child's behavior, especially his attention, must be under the control of verbal stimuli if he is to attend to the materials the teacher presents and respond as directed. This repertoire is basic to all academic (and other) types of learning.

The first aspect of learning to read involves the child's learning to discriminate the stimuli involved, which at the most basic level are the letters. The child must have a distinctive verbal response to each letter, which can be taught according to strict instrumental conditioning principles.

Another repertoire that is important in learning to read is the grapheme-phoneme repertoire. The child must learn to say letters and syllables as they have to be pronounced in actually reading words. When he has a repertoire of such reading units and has learned how to respond to the letters and syllables of a word in order, from left to right, he is then able to sound out new words on which he has not been trained. This is another type of original, novel behavior that is built on the basis of a previously acquired repertoire of base stimulus-response units (see 40 and 46 for experimental demonstrations of originality through learning in this context). In any event, the child with this repertoire can continue to learn to read on his own. There has been short-sighted emphasis upon this type of learning to the exclusion of the others, but it *is* an essential aspect of reading learning and involves many learning trials.

It should be noted that the grapheme-phoneme repertoire is important in the learning stages of reading acquisition, but it is not a central skill for the accomplished reader. He rarely encounters a word that he has not learned to respond to as a whole word. The

essence of being an accomplished reader is the ability to instan-
taneously read a very large number of words (and phrases) with
but a glance. It is the recognition of this that has led some reading
approaches to emphasize whole-word reading training to the exclusion of other aspects.

The important point, however, is that there are a number of
repertoires the child has to acquire in learning to read. Fastening
upon one as the essential element is incorrect. The present theory
of reading shows that they are all important. Moreover, there is a
cumulative-hierarchical form to reading learning. Attention-dis-
crimination skills are basic to learning the alphabet. Being able to
discriminate and name each letter is basic to learning the grapheme-
phoneme repertoire. This repertoire is in turn basic to learning to
sound out words, which is basic to acquiring a large whole-word
reading repertoire. The theory of reading has considered the various
aspects of learning to read, in addition to those described here, and
formal and informal research has dealt with each to some degree
(40). Much additional research must be conducted to verify and
extend this theory.

One further point should be made in this context. Nonreading
(or alexia) or distortions or difficulty in learning to read (dyslexia)
are frequently considered to stem from biological defects. However, as the author has indicated (see 45:136-140, as an example),
it is erroneous to infer central nervous system defect in any case
of reading problem if the child has normal language. Analysis of
the two learning tasks reveals that the same principles of learning
and the same types of learning are involved in language acquisition
as in reading acquisition. If the child can learn the former, he can
learn the latter, *under appropriate learning conditions.* Difference
in frequency of problems of learning in the two areas arises because the conditions in learning language are customarily much
better than in learning to read.

THE COGNITIVE LEARNING ACCELERATION

One other finding is mentioned because of its importance to a
conception of child development and education. From the beginning work with the author's daughter it was observed that cognitive
learning became easier as the child progressed. This principle of

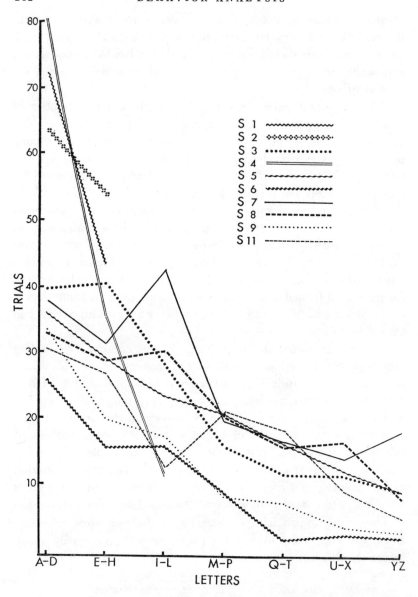

FIG. 3. The curves indicate the mean number of learning trials required for each of 10 children to learn succeeding groups of letters. The curves indicate that progressively fewer learning trials are required to learn additional groups of letters, demonstrating the cognitive learning acceleration principle. From Staats et al. (46:17).

accelerating cognitive learning was specifically studied (40, 46) with respect to learning to read the letters of the alphabet, as shown in figure 3. The graph shows the number of learning trials required to learn to read successive groups of four letters. There is a curve for each of ten children, seven of whom completed the alphabet learning task. Without exception, there is a systematic decrease in the number of learning trials required to learn to read the letters as the task progresses. Approximately four times as many trials are required to learn the first letters as the last. The maturational-developmental approach has warned us to be careful not to introduce learning to the child before he is ready. The present results, on the contrary, indicate that it is *learning that makes the child ready!* We must devise methods generally for producing this cognitive learning acceleration, especially with children who would otherwise miss such training. A revision in our accepted assumptions about child development is called for (see 37, 46) and is necessary to maximize our educational practices.

WRITING ACQUISITION AND THE COGNITIVE LEARNING ACCELERATION

The same types of findings have been obtained with the first learning of letter copying (an important imitation skill) and writing letters on command. Detailed stimulus-response study of the skills involved has shown the gradual course of this learning, the large number of learning trials that are necessary, and the general skills that result which finally enable the child to learn new letters almost immediately. The latter is another demonstration of cognitive learning acceleration and of originality through learning. Suggestive findings of a cognitive learning acceleration have also been found in early number concept learning (40, 46).

THE CHILD-LEARNING APPARATUS

Figure 4 schematizes the apparatus and token-reinforcer system that the author devised for work with children. The child sits in the chair to the left (by the tubes and toys). The experimenter, instructional-technician, or behavior modifier sits to the right, where he has his materials. The stimuli (like a letter or word in a reading learning task) are presented to the child on five- by eight-inch cards in the window slot in the top middle of the partition separating the child and adult. In addition, the child may also be presented with letters to copy in the space in front of him. Or, he can be presented with actual objects to count, or objects in picture form on cards. Or, as another example, the child may be given speech training.

Fig. 4. The child-learning and behavior modification apparatus. A general apparatus and reinforcement system for the study of various types of learning in children and for behavior modification in educational, child, and clinical psychology. From Staats (39:47).

When the child completes a response he is reinforced by delivery of a marble down the chute into the receptacle. (The behavior modifier has a plastic bowl which contains a number of marbles.) The child can then use the marble in one of several different ways. Depositing the marble in the small hole in the upper right of the partition (to fall into the behavior modifier's bowl) is the signal for the behavior modifier to deliver a unit from the trinket–edible mix (raisins, peanuts, M & Ms) into the chute. Or the child can deposit the marble into one of the tubes. When the tube is full the child receives the toy hung above it, the child having previously chosen the toy as one to work for. The smallest tube holds ten marbles and when it is full it will yield a very small reward (a pencil, a balloon, or a piece of bubble gum, for example). With preschool children the ten-marble tube and the trinket–edible mix provide sufficient reinforcement alternatives for a year's work. With older children all the alternatives may be used.

The behavior modifier can make data sheets and record every stimulus delivered to the child, every response made, and every reinforcer delivered. Time can also be recorded and objective records made of children's learning in a variety of tasks, employing only one adult. For precise experimental work various pieces of apparatus may be added to automatically present stimuli and record the child's responses, latency, and so on (see 40:240-62, 48).

This apparatus is described here because it has such a wide variety of uses. It can be employed for research purposes in a number of different ways on a number of topics—imitation, object discrimination learning, number discriminations, letter discriminations, learning in mental retardates, paired associate learning, verbal learning, the learning of Piagetian types of cognitive skills, and so on. Furthermore, the child-learning apparatus can be employed for behavior modification where the purpose is clinically or educationally remedial. Treatment for speech disorders, reading disorders or deficits, number skill deficits, retardation in various skills including language, and so on, may be conducted with the apparatus. It is difficult to imagine the behavior modification work and the basic studies that can be accomplished with this apparatus until it has been seen in use.

It is possible to employ the apparatus with children who because of age or behavior disorder would not ordinarily be amenable to treatment or research procedures. The apparatus and reinforcer system generally produce good attentional and working behavior and, with appropriate materials, unusual learning capabilities. The apparatus has been successfully employed with children down to the age of two. *It is suggested that because of its general-purpose features and effectiveness, the child-learning apparatus has the same utility and significance for study and treatment with children as operant conditioning apparatus has had for research with animals.*

ADDITIONAL RESEARCH IN EARLY COGNITIVE LEARNING

The need for extensions of this research to the analysis of cognitive skills and the opportunities to do so are quite large. Whitlock (54) applied the reinforcement procedures to the task of training a child to read who previously had had difficulty. Whitlock and Bushell (55) showed conclusively that a token (activation of a counter) that was redeemable by backup reinforcers (a token-reinforcer system) maintained the working and learning behavior of a child in a reading task better than did the token when presented without backup reinforcers. More recently, Coleman (10) has begun to employ a stimulus-response approach in the study of some of the processes involved in reading. He has conducted an experiment to establish the mean number of errors involved in learning to say the sounds of thirty-five letters (or letter combinations). In another experiment the difficulty involved in learning to blend two separate sounds together was studied, and the difficulty of each sound could be ascertained. In a third experiment the relative difficulty involved in copying different letters was studied.

The most extensive elaboration of the present behavior modification methods or analyses dealing with original reading in preschoolers, however, has been conducted by Hamblin, Buckholdt, Ferritor, Kozloff, and Blackwell (14). These researchers employed similar training procedures and reinforcement principles and obtained corroboratory findings in various areas. As examples, the acceleration in learning was demonstrated; it was shown that after a time, tokens, the backup reinforcer given after the training period, could be dispensed with (see 40:269-72) and that intelligence test scores were increased through the behavioral training, as were achievement test scores (see 40).

Recent work has also begun to address itself to the behavior analysis of the early learning of mathematics concepts (32, 53). Schimmel has employed the behavior analysis of early number concept learning, especially counting, and Wang, Resnick, and Boozer have incorporated the cumulative-hierarchical learning principle. Their hierarchy of learning tasks was different in some respects from those that have been described in the present work (40, 45, 46). The two analyses in this respect constitute opposing theories which require empirical test. Analysis of cognitive learn-

ing in stimulus-response terms, it is suggested, can be considered to
have only begun.

It is suggested that the principles of the cumulative-hierarchical
learning conception, linked with the research and behavior modification possibilities, has great potential for further extension. The
approach has been developed, for example, to a full analysis of the
child's language-intelligence development—as a central aspect of
personality—to provide an extensive basis for behavior modification
procedures (37).

Token Reinforcement and Treatment of Educational Problems

The first token-reinforcer system was used in the context of
treating children who had problems in learning to read. The system
was modified in the author's other work with early cognitive
learning. But the original token-reinforcer system and the method
of teaching remedial reading were employed in a formal study at
the first opportunity. This first study involved a juvenile delinquent
who was a severe behavior problem in school and who had never
passed a course in school. He was provided with four and one-half
months of training in reading based upon the token-reinforcement
system described earlier. His attention and work behaviors were
excellently maintained and he learned well. Moreover, he passed
his school courses at the end of the semester for the first time and
his misbehaviors in school decreased from ten the first month to
none the last month and a half (47).

Again, however, although it is necessary to begin long-term
study of complex human behavior with a single subject—and reliable data and principles can be established in this manner—it is
also necessary to demonstrate one's principles and methods with
other subjects. It is in this manner that support for general statements can be gained. Thus, the token-reinforcer procedures in
remedial reading were extended to group applications. Eighteen
junior high school children with reading learning problems, half
of whom were considered as educable retardates, were given the
behavioral reading treatment for a mean of 38.2 hours over a four-
and-one-half-month period. The behavior modification results with
a single subject were verified with the group.

The next study with thirty-two culturally deprived Negro children living in a ghetto area in Milwaukee and a control group of thirty-two yielded additional findings. As shown in the original and second studies, when an effective reinforcement system is employed and a learning analysis is made, the training materials may be relatively simple and yet effective. With explicit and simple procedures it was not necessary to have a trained teacher do the training. In the Milwaukee study the therapy technicians or instructional technicians were either unemployed black adults or black high school students who were literate. These instructional technicians themselves received only three hours of training in the administration of the materials and procedures and in recording the data. This training was administered and supervised by a teacher trained in the "motivated learning" procedures.

With an average of only $21.34 worth of reinforcers, the experimental subjects attended school better, learned to read more words, and scored better on reading and intelligence tests than did control subjects:

The results showed the procedures and reinforcement system to be effective in producing improved attention and work behaviors in these usually intractable children, and in the utilization and upgrading of unemployed black adults. However, 40.2 hours of training was not deemed sufficient to remediate long-standing cases of educational failure—although the results suggested that longer, more intensive programs of the present type could make important contributions to the solution of the social problems involved as well as to the study of human learning (49:331).

In a subsequent study Ryback and Staats (30) showed that the token-reinforcer system and the reading materials could be successfully used by parents with their own children, even when the children were considered to have special problems. The four children in the study, aged eight to thirteen, were diagnosed respectively as a mental retardate, an emotionally disturbed child, a case of learning disability with minimal brain dysfunction, and as a case of learning disability with a heart ailment. The results of the parental behavior modification nevertheless produced a mean increase on the *Diagnostic Reading Scales* (35); (a) on word reading ability from a grade level of 3.0 to 4.5, (b) on story reading from a grade level of 2.6 to 4.5, and (c) on silent reading and comprehension from a grade level of 3.0 to 4.7. The significance levels of these results were respectively .05, .005, and .025. It has generally been thought in clinical practice that parents cannot act as therapists to their children. The present results suggest, however, that the use of appropriate behavior modification principles and materials makes this possible. It may be suggested that extensions of these findings could have important implications for the solution of educational problems.

Camp (6) has further shown the token-reinforcer system and the reading materials to be effective in training children in a pediatric clinic. Camp and van Doorninck (7) found that children given the reinforced reading training in comparison to a control group did better on sight vocabulary reading tests but not on the *Wide Range Achievement Tests* (20). However, the reading training was brief and results in the study indicated that children with longer training did improve on the WRAT. Hamblin, Buckholdt, Ferritor, Kozloff, and Blackwell (14) have also employed the token-reinforcer system in the remedial treatment of children with learning and behavior problems.

One further outgrowth of the original behavior modification principles (41) as demonstrated by Ayllon and Michael (4) may be mentioned. A situation exists in education similar to that described in the context of psychiatric thought. There are concepts of child development that lead in many cases to solicitous attention being given to undesirable behaviors of children in the classroom. That is, when a child performs a response in the classroom that the teacher is concerned about, the teacher is likely to give the child solicitous attention, especially the young child. For example, a child who is isolated from other children is likely to be given such attention by the teacher, although this treatment would be likely to increase the frequency of isolate behavior. A child who cries is likely to be solicitously treated by the teacher, only to inadvertently be trained to additional crying. It has been shown in a series of studies that this does occur and that such behavior problems can be treated by application of reinforcement principles (1, 16, 17).

It is thus generally suggested that in the context of educational problems, as well as in the context of mental health problems, it takes more than benign motives to help a child with a behavior problem. Sympathetic feelings, no matter how well-intentioned, combined with a poor conception of human behavior, can actually create rather than remove problems of overt behavior and internal emotional states. This was the message of the analysis of the case of "opposite speech" in the psychotic patient presented earlier. The message is a very important one in the consideration of current educational practices. Where problems exist in behavior it is important to make a behavior analysis, such as of the practices of reinforcement that may be producing and maintaining the behavior. An understanding of the principles of reinforcement is requisite in this endeavor. Marked improvement in outcomes over those achieved with traditional conceptions and sympathetic feelings is obtainable. Many of the studies referred to elsewhere in the present volume utilize these principles of behavior modification in educational situations.

Moreover, as the next section will suggest, there are even more important potentialities for dealing with the general problems of education employing the principles of behavior.

Extensions of Token-Reinforcer Systems in Schools of the Future

The use of the principles of reinforcement in dealing with human behavior, in solving the problems of behavior, and especially the use of token-reinforcer systems and concepts in education has come a long way since this work began. But there are much more significant extensions to be made. The author's development of social- and token-reinforcement procedures for dealing with problems of behavior has been described (42). The use, primarily, of material backup reinforcers in token systems by no means utilizes the full potential of the token system, however. A passage the author wrote in the early 1960s may be quoted here:

. . . However, there has been little systematic study of the possible sources of reinforcers in school training or of the potential ways in which these reinforcers may be made contingent upon the learning behavior of the child.

As an example, consider the nursery school or kindergarten situation. Some of the reinforcers present in these school situations have been described—games, recesses, toys, snacks, rest periods, television, desirable activities of various kinds, and social approval. These are potent reinforcers but for the most part they are not made contingent upon the individual behaviors to be strengthened. Since most of these reinforcers occur only infrequently in the school day, however, even if they were made contingent upon a specific learning behavior, very few could be provided and thus only a few behaviors reinforced.

These reinforcers might prove to be very effective, however, if they were incorporated into a procedure involving a token system. For example, a recess could be exchanged for 100 tokens, and the tokens could be made contingent upon 100 appropriate responses. Through employment of such a token system effective use could be made of many reinforcers that are a natural part of early school training.

The development of such a system of reinforcers might necessitate some changes in school organization. For example, one way to use a token system might be to have a "work" room for the learning activities and other rooms for dispensing the "primary" reinforcers. . . . The child would stay in the work room until he accrued a given number of tokens and then go to one of the "reinforcer" rooms to receive his primary reinforcer. . . . (45:457-58).

This was the first outline of a general token-reinforcement system (token economy) for education or clinical purposes. Various aspects of these suggestions have since been tested. For example, it has been shown experimentally that access to a playroom may be used as the backup reinforcer for a token-reinforcer system (19). In this study the rate and quality of printing and writing was reliably increased with children in first- and second-grade classrooms.

The above outline of a token-reinforcer system for schools may be elaborated now. It is suggested that whole schools be designed on the basis of reinforcement principles and of the concept of the token-reinforcer system. The fact is that a public school has very strong resources for reinforcement of all students, including those who are now considered to be learning problems because of retardation, emotional or behavioral disturbances, cultural deprivation, and so on. Schools have special equipment for physical exercise, sports, games, dancing, painting, and the like. Most children do not have access to these sources of reinforcement at home and the activities that can occur in such facilities are very powerful reinforcers for them. In addition, schools offer some facilities for films and television, which could be expanded along with other reinforcing activities such as reading, special-interest clubs, and socializing.

When one examines the school situation, however, it becomes apparent that these strong reinforcers are largely wasted. The child has relatively long periods of restriction to the classroom and relatively brief access to the reinforcers. This system is ineffective for many reasons. First, the child's classroom behavior has no effect upon his receipt of the school reinforcers of play. Second, the time spent in the classroom by problem children is almost entirely a waste. They have a very low rate of learning responses. They do not attend to what is being said in class, they do not read, they do not work problems, and so on. *The reason that they do not learn is that they have very few learning trials.* Third, the length of the classroom period has been inviolate. This and other traditional procedures must be examined in terms of what is now known about the learning process. For example, when one works with an effective reinforcer systems, it soon becomes apparent that one can get many more learning trials out of the subject in a given period of time than under conditions of no reinforcement (40, 46). If the child acquired tokens for performing learning trials and if after enough had been acquired he could then go out and play, learning trials would occur more rapidly. The child would have to remain in the classroom for a much shorter length of time. On the other hand, he would be spending a greater amount of time in reinforcing activities in school. We would then see fewer problems in the child's attendance in school, as already suggested by the author's Milwaukee project.

To repeat, it is proposed that we develop a whole school which is designed on positive reinforcement principles.[3] The idea would be to provide reinforcing activities in the school which would maintain the child's coming to school. Within the school, the child would first report to a work-learning situation where he would perform work to a criterion, for which he would receive tokens.

After earning a certain number of tokens for work completed children would then be able to go on to a reinforcement period of their choice. This would be followed by another work-learning

3. Since this suggestion was advanced early in 1969 there has been movement towards the type of school described. A personal communication from James Breiling indicates that the St. Bride School on Chicago's South Shore will employ this approach on a schoolwide basis. Dr. Breiling has already organized parents and teachers in this program.

period, and so forth. It would be expected that for young children and for children who had not already learned better work-study skills, the work-learning periods would have to be relatively brief. As the child progressed, the ratio of work-learning time to reinforcement time would become greater. It would be expected that effective training of this type, even with problem children, would produce students who would spend as much time in work-learning activities in school as our better students do at the present time.

This plan suggests that a great deal of effort would be expended in the design of reinforcing activities within the school. In actuality, schools have only groped toward appropriate employment of their reinforcers in making them contingent upon learning behaviors. The same is true of effort to improve the reinforcers available. Lack of knowledge of behavior principles and the misconception that learning should occur for its own reward have held back progress. With systematic development and engineering and without the handicap of prejudice there could easily be an abundant source of reinforcement to maintain the effective learning of all children.

It should be noted that various types of training could be introduced into a school with such a reinforcement system. For children needing social learning or emotional learning or sensory-motor learning, in addition to intellectual learning, periods dealing with various subject matters could be designed. It would thus be possible to provide clinical treatment where it should occur—that is, in the situation where the child has to make his life adjustment—in a way not possible with a single class. We could design a school to treat a wide spectrum of child problems such as dropouts, incipient delinquents, children with school phobias, educational failures because of personal problems, cultural deprivation, motivational deficits, early cognitive deficits, deficits in social behavior, and the like.

The same types of training should be provided for adults in institutions, such as prisoners, hospitalized psychotics, and the clients of welfare clinics.[4] Analyses of such institutions, for example, in terms of their reinforcement systems would reveal a great deal about the

4. Cohen and Filipczak have recently completed a project in which a token-reinforcer system was applied to an institution for delinquent boys (9).

effects of the institutional practices and the resulting behaviors of their clients—as the author's early example of the psychiatric reinforcement of abnormal behavior indicated—and provide directives for improvement. Great potentialities in the application of token-reinforcement systems are yet to be realized.

General Concepts and Methods

This extended line of research was described in part because there are general methodological points involved which may be briefly mentioned here.

NATURALISTIC BEHAVIOR ANALYSIS AND EXPERIMENTAL-NATURALISTIC RESEARCH

Each of the major aspects of the research that has been described began on the basis of naturalistic observations and the analysis of the observations into the stimulus-response components and principles involved. Not enough import has been given to this aspect of behavior modification. However, perusal of the literature will reveal that the research and clinical work has ordinarily been preceded by such a behavior analysis (see 37, 40, 45). In the present paper the theory of reading is an illustration.) When an analysis has been made in terms of stimulus and response events and learning principles, it is possible to go into the naturalistic situation and conduct research. Principles may be validated in this manner prior to making formal experimental tests. Experimental-naturalistic research can be valuable for treatment purposes as well as a beginning toward the establishment of the data base needed for complete analysis. In a field with a strong tradition of laboratory research, these possibilities must be given recognition.

DEMONSTRATION STUDIES

Evidence in behavior modification, however, must be seen as an interlocking web. Formal laboratory research is an essential element. As the laboratory studies of reading indicated, it is necessary to test the main principles of learning involved, such as reinforcement, in a situation that is well-controlled and leaves little doubt that the findings are reliable. The laboratory is the place for primary concern with the basic principles.

ANALYTIC FIELD STUDIES AND EXPERIMENTAL-LONGITUDINAL RESEARCH

On the basis of the previously described types of research it is possible to develop materials and procedures for producing actual learning in educational institutions. Methods at this level also require innovation (see 40, 46). Traditional research has compared teaching methods by use of standardized tests, which is useful. But full understanding of the complexities of cognitive learning will come only when we have detailed data on the learning progress of individual children studied over long periods of time. There are still problems of methodology that must be worked out, but we will not know how children learn until we have that detail.

In conclusion, the methods that have been described in this chapter contain means for conducting basic and applied research on such repertoires. It is suggested that in addition to the reading repertoire there are other repertoires that must be subjected to detailed, systematic, long-term study. Number concept learning in young children (see 40, 45, 46), arithmetic skills (see Staats, 40, 45), and mathematics such as geometry and algebra (see examples of behavior analyses in this area in Staats [40, 45]) are several examples. The future of behavior modification in education must surely involve directing itself to an understanding of the major intellectual learning tasks it sets for its subjects. Only on the basis of specific and detailed analyses of these intellectual repertoires will principles and procedures be provided for producing the repertoires efficaciously, for the individual and the society. (See 37 for a comprehensive behavioral theory of intelligence, as one example.) Moreover, only on the basis of the learning conception that arises from this type of work will a rationale be provided for the general design of education. The major purpose of the present work, thus, is to move toward such understanding and to suggest methods for others to use in similar endeavors.

REFERENCES

1. Allen, K.; Hart, B. M.; Buell, J. S.; Harris, F. R.; and Wolf, M. M. "Effects of Social Reinforcement on Isolate Behavior of a Nursery School Child." *Child Development* 35 (1964): 511-18.
2. Atthowe, J. M. Jr., and Krasner, L. "A Preliminary Report on the Application of Contingent Reinforcement Procedures (Token Economy) on a 'Chronic' Psychiatric Ward." *Journal of Abnormal Psychology* 73 (1968): 37-43.

3. Ayllon, T., and Azrin, N. *The Token Economy*. New York: Appleton-Century-Crofts, 1969.
4. Ayllon, T., and Michael, J. L. "The Psychiatric Nurse As a Behavioral Engineer." *Journal of the Experimental Analysis of Behavior* 2 (1959): 323-24.
5. Bijou, S. W.; Birnbrauer, J. S.; Kidder, J. D.; and Tague, C. E. "Programmed Instruction As an Approach to Teaching of Reading, Writing, and Arithmetic to Retarded Children." In *Child Development: Readings in Experimental Analysis*, edited by S. W. Bijou and D. M. Baer. New York: Appleton-Century-Crofts, 1967.
6. Camp, B. W. "Remedial Reading in a Pediatric Clinic." *Clinical Pediatrics* 10 (1971): 36-42.
7. Camp, B. W., and van Doorninck, W. J. "Assessment of 'Motivated' Reading Therapy with Elementary School Children." *Behavior Therapy* 2 (1971): 214-22.
8. Chall, J. *Learning to Read*. New York: McGraw-Hill Book Co., 1967.
9. Cohen, M. L., and Filipczak, J. S. *A New Learning Environment*. San Francisco: Jossey-Bass, 1971.
10. Coleman, E. B. "Collecting a Data Base for Reading Technology." *Journal of Educational Psychology Monograph*, vol. 61, part 2, no. 4, 1970.
11. Dollard, J., and Miller, N. E. *Personality and Psychotherapy*. New York: McGraw-Hill Book Co., 1950.
12. Eysenck, H. J. *Behavior Therapy and the Neuroses*. New York: Pergamon Press, 1960.
13. Greenspoon, J. "The Effect of Verbal and Nonverbal Stimuli on Frequency of Members of Two Response Classes." Doctoral dissertation, Indiana University, 1950.
14. Hamblin, R. L.; Buckholdt, D.; Ferritor, D.; Kozloff, M.; and Blackwell, L. *The Humanization Process*. New York: John Wiley & Sons, 1971.
15. Hanley, E. M. "Review of Research Involving Applied Behavior Analysis in the Classroom." *Review of Educational Research* 40 (1971): 597-625.
16. Harris, F. R.; Johnston, M. K.; Kelly, C. S.; and Wolf, M. M. "Effects of Positive Reinforcement on Regressed Crawling of a Nursery School Child." *Journal of Educational Psychology* 55 (1964): 35-41.
17. Hart, B. M.; Allen, K. E.; Buell, J. S.; Harris, F. R.; and Wolf, M. M. "Effects of Social Reinforcement on Operant Crying." *Journal of Experimental Child Psychology* 1 (1964): 145-53.
18. Holland, J. R. "Teaching Machines: An Application of Principles from the Laboratory." *Journal of the Experimental Analysis of Behavior* 3 (1960): 275-87.

19. Hopkins, B. L.; Schutte, B. C.; and Garton, K. L. "The Effects of Access to a Playroom on the Rate and Quality of Printing and Writing of First- and Second-Grade Students." *Journal of Applied Behavior Analysis* 4 (1971): 77-87.
20. Jastak, J. F.; Bijou, S. W.; and Jastak, S. R. *Wide Range Achievement Test: Reading, Spelling, Arithmetic from Preschool to College*. Wilmington, Del.: Guidance Associates, 1965.
21. Kanfer, F. H. "The Effect of Partial Reinforcement on Acquisition and Extinction of a Class of Verbal Responses." *Journal of Experimental Psychology* 48 (1954): 424-32.
22. Krasner, L. "Behavior Therapy." In *Annual Review of Psychology*, edited by P. R. Mussen and M. R. Rosenzweig. Palo Alto: Annual Reviews, Inc., 1971.
23. ———. "Studies of the Conditioning of Verbal Behavior." *Psychological Bulletin* 55 (1958): 48-70.
24. Laffal, J.; Lenkoski, L. D.; and Ameen, L. "Opposite Speech in a Schizophrenic Patient." *Journal of Abnormal and Social Psychology* 52 (1956): 409-13.
25. Lindsley, O. R. "Operant Conditioning Methods Applied to Research in Chronic Schizophrenia." *Psychiatric Research Reports* 5 (1956): 116-39.
26. Mowrer, O. H. *Learning Theory and Personality Dynamics*. New York: Ronald Press, 1950.
27. O'Leary, K. D., and Becker, W. C. "Behavior Modification of an Adjustment Class: A Token Reinforcement Program." *Exceptional Children* 33 (1967): 637-42.
28. O'Leary, K. D., and Drabman, R. "Token Reinforcement Programs in the Classroom: A Review." *Psychological Bulletin* 75 (1971): 379-98.
29. Rotter, J. B. *Social Learning and Clinical Psychology*. Englewood Cliffs, N.J.: Prentice-Hall, 1954.
30. Ryback, D., and Staats, A. W. "Parents As Behavior Therapy Technicians in Treating Reading Deficits (Dyslexia)." *Journal of Behaviour Therapy and Experimental Psychiatry* 1 (1970): 109-19.
31. Salzinger, K. "Experimental Manipulation of Verbal Behavior: A Review." *Journal of General Psychology* 61 (1959): 65-94.
32. Schimmel, S. "Conditional Discrimination, Number Conception, and Response Inhibition in Two- and Three-Year-Old Children." Doctoral dissertation, Wayne State University, 1971.
33. Skinner, B. F. *Science and Human Behavior*. New York: Macmillan Co., 1953.
34. ———. "Teaching Machines." *Scientific American* 205 (1961): 90-102.
35. Spache, G. D. *Diagnostic Reading Scales*. Los Angeles: California Test Bureau, 1963.

36. Staats, A. W. "A Case in and a Strategy for the Extension of Learning Principles to Problems of Human Behavior." In *Human Learning*, edited by A. W. Staats. New York: Holt, Rinehart & Winston, 1964.

37. ———. *Child Learning, Intelligence, and Personality*. New York: Harper & Row, 1971.

38. ———. "Development, Use, and Extensions of Token Reinforcer Systems in Behavior Modification." In *Uses of Reinforcement Principles in Education*, edited by W. C. Becker. Champaign, Ill.: Research Press, forthcoming.

39. ———. "A General Apparatus for the Investigation of Complex Learning in Children." *Behaviour Research and Therapy* 6 (1968): 45-50.

40. ———. *Learning, Language, and Cognition*. New York: Holt, Rinehart & Winston, 1968.

41. ———. "Learning Theory and 'Opposite Speech'." *Journal of Abnormal and Social Psychology* 55 (1957): 268-69.

42. ———. "Motivational (Reinforcer) Systems in the Solution of Human Problems." In *Behavior Modification in the Classroom*, edited by G. A. Fargo, C. Behrns, and P. A. Nolen. New York: Wadsworth Publishing Co., 1970.

43. ———. "Social Behaviorism and Human Motivation: Principles of the Attitude-Reinforcer-Discriminative System." In *Psychological Foundations of Attitudes*, edited by A. G. Greenwald, T. C. Brokc, and T. M. Ostron. New York: Academic Press, 1968.

44. ———. "Social Behaviorism, Human Motivation, and the Conditioning Therapies." In *Progress in Experimental Personality Research*, edited by B. Maher. New York: Academic Press, 1970.

45. Staats, A. W. (with contribution by Staats, C. K.). *Complex Human Behavior*. New York: Holt, Rinehart & Winston, 1963.

46. Staats, A. W.; Brewer, B. A.; and Gross, M. C. "Learning and Cognitive Development: Representative Samples, Cumulative-Hierarchical Learning, and Experimental-Longitudinal Methods." *Monographs of the Society for Research in Child Development* 35 (1970): no. 8, serial no. 141.

47. Staats, A. W., and Butterfield, W. H. "Treatment of Nonreading in a Culturally Deprived Juvenile Delinquent: An Application of Learning Principles." *Child Development* 4 (1965): 925-42.

48. Staats, A. W.; Finley, J. R.; Minke, K. A.; and Wolf, M. M. "Reinforcement Variables in the Control of Unit Reading Responses." *Journal of the Experimental Analysis of Behavior* 7 (1964): 139-49.

49. Staats, A. W.; Minke, K. A.; and Butts, P. "A Token-Reinforcement Remedial Reading Program Administered by Black Therapy-Technicians to Problem Black Children." *Behavior Therapy* 1 (1970): 331-53.

50. Staats, A. W.; Minke, K. A.; Finley, J. R.; Wolf, M. M.; and Brooks, L. O. "A Reinforcer System and Experimental Procedure for the Laboratory Study of Reading Acquisition." *Child Development* 35 (1964): 209-31.

51. Staats, A. W.; Minke, K. A.; Goodwin, R. A.; and Landeen, J. "Cognitive Behavior Modification: 'Motivated Learning' Reading Treatment with Sub-Professional Therapy-Technicians." *Behaviour Research and Therapy* 5 (1967): 283-99.

52. Staats, A. W.; Staats, C. K.; Schutz, R. E.; and Wolf, M. M. "The Conditioning of Textual Responses Using 'Extrinsic Reinforcers'." *Journal of the Experimental Analysis of Behavior* 5 (1962): 33-40.

53. Wang, M. C.; Resnick, L. B.; and Boozer, R. F. "The Sequence of Development of Early Mathematics Behaviors." *Child Development*, in press.

54. Whitlock, C. "Note on Reading Acquisition: An Extension of Laboratory Principles." *Journal of Experimental Child Psychology* 3 (1966): 83-85.

55. Whitlock, C., and Bushell, D. "Some Effects of Back-up Reinforcers on Reading Behavior." *Journal of Experimental Child Psychology* 5 (1967): 50-57.

56. Wolf, M. M.; Giles, D. K.; and Hall, R. V. "Experiments with Token-Reinforcement in a Remedial Classroom." *Behaviour Research and Therapy* 6 (1968): 51-64.

57. Wolpe, J. *Psychotherapy by Reciprocal Inhibition*. Stanford: Stanford University Press, 1958.

CHAPTER VII

Behavior Therapy with Autistic Children

O. IVAR LOVAAS
and
ROBERT L. KOEGEL

The Autistic Child

If you are a special education teacher, a pediatrician, or a mental health professional, you will at one time or another be confronted with certain extremely deviant children who, if they already have received a diagnostic work-up, have been labeled either psychotic, autistic, or childhood schizophrenic. Sometimes this label is elaborated and has attached to it some other fine clause such as, with probable brain damage, or with probable retardation. If the child has been diagnosed in more than one clinic, he is likely to have more than one diagnosis—in one clinic, autistic, in another, brain-damaged, and so on. This happens because the exact guidelines for diagnosing a child as autistic, brain-damaged, or retarded are not yet well established.

AUTISTIC BEHAVIORS

A child so diagnosed will evidence behaviors described in the following paragraphs.

Apparent sensory deficit. This is perhaps the most striking feature about him. That is, one may move directly in front of him, smile at and talk with him, yet he will act as if no one is there. One may not feel that the child is avoiding or ignoring him, rather the

We express our thanks to the parents who entrusted their children to us and for the help and encouragement they have given. We also express our thanks to the staff at the children's unit, Neuropsychiatric Institute, UCLA. The preparation of this paper was supported by PHS Research Grant #11440 from the National Institute of Mental Health, and EHA Title VI-B, #42-00000-0000832/025, from the California State Departmen of Education to the office of the County Superintendent of Schools, Santa Barbara, California.

child simply does not seem to see or hear. Often the parents of such a child report that they did, in fact, incorrectly suspect the child to be blind or deaf and had at one time or another taken the child for a medical examination of his sight and hearing. As one gets to know the child better, one becomes aware of the great variability in this blindness and deafness. That is, while the child seems to give no visible reaction to a loud noise, such as clapping one's hands directly over his ears, he may respond appropriately to the crinkle of a candy wrapper or excessively to a distant, barely audible siren. Similarly, while he does not notice the comings or goings of people around him or other major changes in his visual field (turning off the lights may have no effect on his behavior), he will sometimes spot a small piece of candy on a table some twenty feet away from him. Obviously, he is not blind or deaf in the way we usually use these terms.

Severe affect isolation. Another characteristic that one frequently notices is that attempts to love and cuddle and show affection to these children meet with essential disinterest on the child's part. Again, the parents relate how their children seem not to know or care whether they are alone or in their parents' company. The children are indifferent to being liked by their siblings. As small babies they do not cup or mold when they are held and do not respond with anticipation to being picked up. They do not laugh or cry appropriately, if at all.

Self-stimulation. Another strikingly different kind of behavior of these children centers on very repetitive stereotyped acts, such as rocking their bodies in the sitting position, twirling around, flapping their arms at the wrists, or humming a set of three or four notes over and over again. The parents often report that their child may spend entire days gazing at his cupped hand, staring at lights and spinning objects, and so on.

Tantrums and self-mutilatory behavior. Although the child may not engage in self-mutilation when one first meets him, the parents may report that the child sometimes bites himself so severely as to bleed, or beats his head against walls or sharp pieces of furniture so large lumps rise and his skin turns black and blue. He may beat his face with his fists. Some of the children bear scars from their self-mutilation; for example, one can observe skin discolorations which remain from biting wounds on the inside of their wrists. One is likely to trigger self-mutilatory behavior in such a child if one imposes some restriction on their movement, such as holding them still. Often they will engage in self-destructive behavior if one attempts to impose even minimal standards for appropriate behavior, such as requesting the child to sit at his desk or table. Sometimes their aggression will be directed outwards, against their parents or teachers, in the most primitive form of biting, scratching, kicking, and other tantrum behavior.

Echolalic and psychotic speech. Most of these children are mute; that is, they do not talk. However, the speech of those who do talk may be echos of other people's attempts to talk to them. For example, if one addresses a child with the question "What is your name?" the child is likely to answer (preserving, perhaps, the exact intonation of the one who talked to him), "What is your name?" At other times the echolalia is not immediate but delayed, in that the child will repeat statements he heard that morning or the preceding day; or he may repeat TV commercials or other such announcements.

Behavioral deficiencies. While the presence of the behaviors we sketched above are rather striking, equally striking are the many behaviors the child does *not* have. That is, such a child has little if any self-help skills and needs to be fed and dressed. He may, in many ways, at the age of five or even ten years show the social or intellectual repertoire of a six-month-old baby. Very strikingly, he is mute, and has very likely the same deficiency in receptive speech as he has in expressive speech.

Meanings of Autism

It has been thought that the presence of all or most of these six categories of behavior denotes a distinct entity, a specific and unique problem, underlying disease, or process, which should have its own diagnostic label. Kanner (16) was the first to suggest treating such children as if they suffered from one single underlying problem, and he suggested the diagnosis "autism." He described eleven children who evidenced behaviors similar to those outlined above, noting in particular: their inability to relate themselves to other people ("extreme autistic aloneness"), a delay in acquisition of speech and other abnormalities of language (particularly reversal of pronouns and echoing), an excellent rote memory, and an obsessive desire for the maintenance of sameness.

Since Kanner's early article, numerous investigators have engaged themselves in a search for the etiology and treatment of what Kanner termed, perhaps prematurely, *autism*. In other words, almost all that has been written about autistic children has been based on the assumption that there is an underlying entity or a disease and that the behaviors one observes are expressive or symptomatic of this disease. It has also been thought that if this underlying process were changed, then the whole set of behaviors would also change.

Much of this search into autism has been characterized by repeated attempts to determine (and continuous disagreements about) exactly what behavioral grouping should constitute the diagnosis of autism. Thus, one investigator will insist on one kind of behavior grouping as being the "true" reflection of autism, while another will disagree with that and suggest a different kind of grouping. Some have attempted to increase the homogeneity among the children's behaviors in the hope of getting increasingly "pure" samples of the hypothetical process called autism. In general, these efforts to perfect a description of autism and to isolate its etiology and effective treatment have proven unsuccessful.

BEHAVIORAL VIEWPOINT

Perhaps it was a mistake to invest so much research on the guess that all these behaviors pointed to *one* underlying distinct process called autism. It is, for example, quite possible that the different behaviors are related to several different kinds of antecedent conditions. We do know that the behaviors which we enumerated above can be observed in other children too. For example, retarded and blind children self-stimulate a lot as do normal children if they have nothing else to do. Brain-damaged children sometimes echo while some retarded children have unusually well-developed rote memories.

It has been our point of view—and this is consistent with a behavioristic framework—that we could develop procedures to help these children overcome their pathological behaviors and develop healthy ones *without* having to postulate an underlying process such as autism. Instead, we have thought that we may be able to isolate the controlling conditions for each one of these behaviors, taken one at a time. We may then find that some of these behaviors interact in the sense that if you change one behavior, certain others will change concurrently. But one may also be prepared for the possibility that these behaviors are relatively independent of each other so that as one gains some control over one of them, one does not necessarily gain control over the others. For example, as one establishes the kind of relationship with a child which makes him affectionate to adults, he may not simultaneously show any improvement in his language. However, should a speech therapist be successful in teaching language to such a child, then one might observe a concurrent decrease in psychotic speech. Needless to say, we hope for large interacting response classes, since our treatment efforts would then become proportionately more efficient.

We would prefer to provide a diagnosis of the child in terms of the specific behaviors he does or does not have. Such a behavioral diagnosis may be productive for several reasons. First, if the variables which control a particular behavior are known, then the treatment is suggested by the diagnosis. If we do not know how to alter the behavior, then the diagnosis would suggest that further research need be attempted before these behaviors can be treated. Therefore, a prognosis is also included in the behavioral diagnosis. Finally, describing a child in terms of specific behaviors, since these are relatively public and visible to all, should help to facilitate communication between those who produce research and those who consume it.

TRADITIONAL VIEWPOINTS

Most teachers have been trained to approach these children from traditional viewpoints; perhaps it helps to clarify the behavioristic position by contrasting it to the more traditional ones. Since traditional interventions tie their treatment closely to supposed etiologies, the hypothetical etiologies and treatments will be considered together. There are three major theoretical approaches to autism. These are based on psychoanalytic theory, developmental theory, and physiological theory. We will discuss these theoretical orientations very briefly with the primary purpose of suggesting reference material appropriate to each for those who want to familiarize themselves with the various theories in more detail.

PSYCHODYNAMIC THEORIES

While the specifics of various psychodynamic theories on the etiology of autism may vary, they can be generally summarized as follows. When the child was an infant, he developed in an environment which was singularly cold and destructive. Both Kanner (16) and Bettelheim (4) implicate the parents in the development of autism. According to Bettelheim, the child believes that his parents wish to destroy him and he therefore withdraws into his inner autistic world as a defense against his frightening parents. Kanner specifies that the typical parents of autistic children are cold, detached, unaffectionate, and emotionally insulated. The child then fails to form a meaningful warm relationship with them and therefore never moves on to relate himself to ("cathect") the external world. The essential aspect and admittedly very simplified version of psychodynamic treatment approaches to autism consists of attempts by therapists or teachers to recreate the loving, accepting, and warm adult-child relationship which the parents failed to provide, in the hope that once the child accepts the adult, then he will move out toward the world, where his acquisition of new behaviors will follow naturally from the change in the emotional relationship he has to that world.

Large, comprehensive formulations like the psychodynamic attempt to understand autism have not been adequately evaluated; perhaps they never will be. In any case, on the purely empirical level the outcome studies on psychoanalytic attempts to treat these children have failed to produce significant results. Kanner and Eisenberg (17), Brown (6), and Rutter (41) all report data which suggest that autistic children treated with psychodynamic frameworks did not do significantly better than children who received no treatment. Similarly, more laboratory-like, experimental studies which were designed to test specific hypotheses derived from psychodynamic formulations have failed to find data which support the social, parental etiology. For example, the autistic's avoidance of social stimuli would seem to naturally follow from psychodynamic formulations. Hermelin (13), however, reports much data which suggest that autistic children do not selectively avoid social stimuli; rather, they show low visual fixations to almost all kinds of external stimulation. Finally, studies have failed to identify the parents as cold and detached or any other emotional type.

DEVELOPMENTAL THEORIES

There is considerable speculation that infantile autism arises on the basis of a developmental perceptual disorder. Goldfarb (11), Schopler (42), and Rutter (40) have all commented on this point. The term *developmental disorder* describes conditions in which there is an abnormal delay in the development of some normal function, so that what is abnormal at one age would be normal at a younger age. Basically, the theory is based on a developmental model of receptor preferences. It holds that there is a normal transition from preference and dependence on the near receptors (e.g., tactile, kinesthetic, and gustatory) in early life to a dominance of the far receptors (e.g., visual and auditory) in later years. It is speculated that autistic children fail to develop beyond the near receptors stage, and they therefore fail to comprehend the social, linguistic, and intellectual environments which are mediated primarily by the distance receptors.

There are several directions in treatment and education which are based on such models of faulty reception. Schopler and Reichler (44) have designed their teaching programs based on the child's "availability via his various receptor systems." The great emphasis on perceptual motor training in education, as exemplified in the work of people like Kephart (18) and Frostig (10), is also consistent with this theoretical orientation. It is too early to decide whether intervention based on this model has been successful, since no systematic data have been put forth to evaluate it. But it is important to note that experimental laboratory work designed to test the notion of distorted receptor hierarchies in autistic children (32, 33, 43) failed to support the notion of a distorted receptor orientation along the lines which we have outlined here.

Since it appears that the level of physiological arousal is an important determinant of how much an organism will be affected by environmental stimulation, a number of theories of abnormal arousal levels have surfaced in an attempt to account for autistic behavior. One theory suggests that autistic children suffer from a chronically high level of arousal (15); a second theory suggests that autistic children suffer from a chronically low level of arousal (37); and a third theory suggests that there are alternating periods of high and low levels of arousal (36). While these theories may in the future become supported in empirical work and provide suggestions for how to treat and educate these children, they have not as yet been adequately evaluated, nor have there been any systematic treatment-educational formulations which are clearly derived from these arousal hypotheses. Furthermore, as suggested by the comprehensive line of speculation, the relationship between arousal mechanisms and autistic behavior appears to be rather unclear.

Behavior Theory and Autism

The first succinct attempt to understand the behavior of autistic children within a behavioristic framework was carried out by Ferster (8). Ferster presented a very convincing argument of how it was that in the absence of acquired, symbolic rewarding aspects of social stimuli (and a general deficiency in acquired reinforcers), one might expect the very impoverished behavioral development one sees in autistic children. The primary contribution of Ferster's theoretical argument lies in the explicitness and concreteness with which he relates learning principles to behavioral development. There have been some general efforts to relate learning theory to psychopathology in the past but perhaps none presented the argument as directly as did Ferster.

Ferster's speculations on the etiology of the disorders are basically unnecessary in effecting behavior change and remain without experimental verification. The important part in his argument is the clear development of the relationship of the learning environment to the child's behavior. Shortly after he presented his theoretical notions about autism, Ferster and DeMyer (9) reported a set of experiments in which they exposed autistic children to very simplified but controlled environments where they could engage in simple behaviors such as pulling levers or matching to sample, for reinforcers which were significant or functional to them. The Ferster and DeMyer studies were the first to show that the behavior of autistic children could be related in a *lawful* manner to certain explicit environmental changes. What the children learned in these studies was not of much practical significance, but the studies did show that by carefully programming certain environmental consequences, these children could in fact be taught to comply with certain aspects of reality.

Shortly after Ferster's analysis of autism, Bijou et al. (5) pioneered in developing a token economy classroom for retarded children at Rainier State School in Washington. The Washington studies went a step beyond earlier work, since these children were exposed to "real-life" situations as is involved in adapting to and learning in school. Those psychologists and educators who had the good fortune to visit the classroom at Rainier were certainly inspired to see severely retarded children, given up for hopeless in the educational process, behave themselves well in the class, studiously reading or following instructions, constructing answers to problems, and showing delight in learning.

There were many other significant developments in the early sixties. Some of these concerned themselves with adult problems, but their technology became relevant for the treatment of children. For example, Ayllon (1) presented some data on how, again by carefully arranging and controlling reinforcing consequences, it was possible to move chronic schizophrenic, hopeless patients a bit of the way towards normalcy. Similar hope for understanding emerged in the data from Goldiamond's (12) laboratory in his work with stutterers.

All these studies had certain features in common: they employed procedures which we had learned about through the study of animals in controlled laboratory settings. They explicitly arranged certain relationships between their patient's behavior and his surroundings and immediate environment. The data which emerged from these studies were on the whole very regular and lawful, which is another way to say that one could understand the patient and be of help to him. Finally, because the majority of the patients who these investigators worked with had been so difficult to help before, a wave of optimism and enthusiasm was communicated about what might be done for the severely disturbed, such as psychotic and retarded children. It seemed, in these early studies, that the problem which faced us could be solved if we paid attention to perfecting our educational techniques for teaching appropriate behaviors, rather than making research efforts into some hypothetical entity within the child, such as brain damage or psychosis.

Let us now turn to a very brief summary of the essential points within that part of learning theory which we have relied upon to help us in our treatment projects with psychotic children. Using the concepts of learning theory, one can view a child's development as consisting of the acquisition of two events: (a) behaviors and (b) stimulus functions. If we look at the behavioral development of autistic children, perhaps the most striking feature about them centers on their behavioral deficiency. They have little if any behavior which would help them function in society. If one was going to treat autistic children based on this perspective, then one would try to strengthen behaviors, such as appropriate play and speech, by reinforcing their occurrence. When their occurrence is initially absent, those behaviors should be gradually shaped by rewarding successive approximations to their eventual occurrence. Similarly, one may attempt to treat certain behaviors, such as tantrums and self-destruction, by either systematically withholding those reinforcers which may be maintaining these behaviors or by the systematic application of aversive stimuli contingent on their occurrence. In other words, it would be possible to develop a treatment program where one worked directly with the child's behaviors, using whatever reinforcers were functional for that child. In the programs we have developed so far, we have usually developed behaviors, using primary reinforcers such as food.

The child not only acquires behaviors as he develops, but his environment also acquires "meanings" (stimulus functions) for him. One part of the meaning that the world has for a person centers on its perceived reward and punishment attributes. We speak here of symbolic rewards and punishments, which technically are referred to as secondary or conditioned reinforcers. That is, certain parts of the child's environment which were neutral when he was born come to acquire the function of rewarding and punishing him. One can think of many good examples to illustrate this point, and it is particularly obvious that within the social area much of this kind of learning takes place. The presence or absence of an approving smile, while neutral to the newborn infant, gradually assumes reinforcing functions as the child interacts with his parents. The primary reason that the acquisition of these secondary reinforcers is so important lies in their control over the acquisition of behavior. Normal children appear to acquire much of their behaviors on the basis of secondary reinforcers. If autistic children do not respond to praise, smiles, hugs, interpersonal closeness, correctness, novelty, and other such secondary reinforcers which support so much behavior in normal children, it would be logical to argue that their behavioral development should be accordingly deficient. Thus, much of an autistic child's failure to develop appropriate behavior could be viewed as a function of the total or partial failure of his environment to be meaningful to him, that is, to have failed in the acquisition of secondary reinforcers. This was the essence of Ferster's (8) theoretical analysis of autism.

In view of these theoretical notations, let us examine some of the early studies which emerged, applying reinforcement theory constructs, or what some refer to as operant conditioning, in an attempt to treat or educate autistic children.

EARLY STUDIES

Wolf, Risley, and Mees (47) published the first systematic attempt to use behavior modification with an autistic child. They worked with a three-and-a-half-year-old boy who did not eat normally, lacked normal social and verbal repertoires, and evidenced extreme tantrums and self-destructive behaviors, often leaving himself black and blue and bleeding. By systematically controlling the child's environment, these investigators were eventually able to bring the child's responding toward a more normal level of functioning. Tantrum behavior was treated by a combination of mild punishment and extinction. That is, the child was placed alone in his room contingent upon each tantrum, the door remaining closed until the tantrum behavior ceased. Since the child was in danger of losing his vision if he would not wear his glasses (and he would not), the authors used a shaping technique to teach the child to wear his glasses. That is, the child was first reinforced for holding a pair of empty glass frames, then for bringing the frames closer to his eyes, then for wearing the empty frames, and eventually for wearing the prescription glasses. The authors initially rewarded each approximation with candy, but reported that progress was slow until they placed the child on food deprivation and rewarded him with bites of his breakfast and lunch.

Prior to treatment the child had no appropriate speech, evidencing instead large amounts of delayed echolalia. That is, the child had speech, but it was not under the control of the people in his environment. The treatment consisted of first rewarding the child if he echoed the speech of his therapist, while he held a picture of the object she was labeling. Eventually, the therapist was able to drop her verbal prompt and the child would continue to label the pictures. As the child's speech developed he was required to use it appropriately before the therapist would meet his demands. Thus, the child gradually acquired the meanings of language. Wolf, Risley, Johnston, Harris, and Allen (46) also presented a follow-up study of this boy, showing that he continued to improve after his discharge from this program. Since the child, however, still evidenced some of his previous symptoms (e.g., tantrums, whining, etc.), the investigators provided an extension of the treatment program. After a total of three years of intensive application of operant behavior modification techniques, Dicky progressed from "hopeless" to the point where he was able to take advantage of a public school education program. According to his parents, he made a good adjustment and learned to read at the primary level quite well.

Wolf, Risley, and Mees (47) reported that their success was greatly facilitated by the child's initial delayed echolalia. That is, the therapist had a behavior to work with; it just needed to be brought under appropriate stimulus control. In 1965, Hewett described a procedure for working with children who were initially mute. In the first phase of treatment the child was reinforced for making eye contact with the therapist, since the child's attending to the therapist was a prerequisite for his learning to imitate. The child sat in a booth looking at the therapist through a small window. When the child attended to the therapist, he was rewarded with food; when he did not attend, a shutter closed over the window leaving him in darkness. After visual attending behavior was established, the therapist used a shaping procedure which may have triggered imitative behavior. For example, the child was initially able to produce only a few vowel sounds but did not produce any speech. Thus, the authors first rewarded the child for producing the vowel sounds made in response to the therapist's vocalizations, and then gradually insisted on more precise imitations of the word the therapist produced before delivering reinforcement. Using this procedure, the child acquired a thirty-two-word vocabulary. In phase four of the treatment, the therapist taught the meanings of the words to the child in a manner similar to that reported by Wolf, Risley, and Mees (47). That is, the child was required to use speech before his demands were met. For example, he had to use the word "go" to get the therapist to take him off the ward, or say "I want water" if he wanted a drink, and so on. By the termination of the study, the child had a usable vocabulary of one hundred and fifty words.

What the studies of Wolf, Risley, and Mees (47) and of Hewett (14) showed was that it was quite possible to take learning theory principles, move outside the laboratory setting and into the child's day-to-day environment, and begin to work with behaviors which were directly and clinically relevant, such as reducing tantrums and atavistic behavior and establishing meaningful social behaviors. These studies relied on what was known already within learning theory to carry out their therapeutic programs. Their use of extinction, shaping by successive approximations, and similar principles had all been isolated in animal research.

When one works with children who have severe behavioral deficiencies, it soon becomes apparent that there are some real limitations in the degree to which one could build complex behavior repertoires into children by using direct shaping procedures. Observations of the development of normal children suggested that the acquisition of complex behaviors was facilitated through imitation of such behaviors in adults and peers (3). When one works with autistic children, one soon discovers that these children are greatly deficient in imitative behavior, seeming to learn little if anything on an observational basis. Therefore, to make significant progress in the acquisition of complex repertoires, we needed to know more about the conditions under which imitation occurred. Fortunately, Baer and Sherman (2) published a very important study which showed that if one reinforced a child for imitating some of a model's behavior, the child would also begin to emit other of the model's behaviors, even though he had not been explicitly reinforced for imitating them. They viewed imitation as a discrimination, a situation in which the child discriminates the similarity between his and the model's behavior as the occasion for reinforcement. Although the Baer and Sherman study dealt with normal children who already imitated, its results gave rise to procedures for building imitative behavior in nonimitating children. Thus, Metz (35), using reinforcement theory principles, presented the first study to show how one could use reinforcement theory principles to build nonverbal imitative behavior in nonimitating autistic children. Lovaas et al. (26) showed how it was possible, through the use of a discrimination learning paradigm, to build imitative verbal behavior in previously mute autistic children.

In reviewing the history of this development it is apparent that barely ten years have elapsed since Ferster (8) published the first theoretical article which attempted a behavioral analysis of autism and that not more than seven years have elapsed since the first treatment study was published. Obviously this is a very new field that has experienced a promising start.

RECENT DEVELOPMENTS

We will now go on to illustrate some of the more recent developments within the behavior modification approach to autistic children. As we do so it will become apparent that a behavioral approach to autism has not addressed itself to the "total" child or "autism" as an entity, whatever that means. Neither has this behavioristic approach committed itself to a particular etiology of autism. It is important to point out that it would be very significant to discover whether there is a phenomenon called autism and to discover a specific etiology of such a problem. However, the search for answers to such questions is severely restricted because of limitations on research methodology. So, for the time being, we refrain from posing questions to which it seems impossible to obtain answers today. On the other hand, the children present certain immediate problems which we can attempt to ameliorate on the basis of what we know today.

Analysis of self-destructive behavior. One of the most bizarre and most profoundly sick behaviors which one will ever meet is self-mutilation, which is characteristic of so many psychotic and retarded children. One can see children who tear with their teeth large amounts of tissue from their shoulders and arms, who chew off part of their fingers, hit their heads so violently against the wall that they detach their retinas, and (accidentally) would kill themselves unless they were somehow sedated or restrained. Many of these children, although they may be only eight or nine years old, have spent most of their lives in restraints, being tied down both by their feet and arms.

Irrational as these behaviors may appear, the studies which were conducted to better understand these behaviors show self-mutilation to be a very "lawful," understandable phenomenon. Rather than the self-destruction being an expression of some tenuous internal state, such as a shattered, guilty, worthless self, we found it to be rather straightforward learned behavior. By that we mean that when we gave sympathetic comments contingent upon the child hurting himself, then his self-destruction increased in strength, only to return to base-line levels when these comments were no longer administered. It looked like the self-mutilation was reinforceable, like operant behavior. If the self-mutilation was an operant, then it should also decrease in strength if one made sure that there were no extrinsic consequences such as social attention contingent upon it.

This is exactly what happened. When the children were left free to injure themselves without parents or nursing staff intervening, the self-destructive behavior fell off in a very gradual but lawful manner from, for example, a high of some four thousand self-destructive acts in the first hour to thirty-five hundred the second hour, then three thousand, and then slowly to zero by the tenth session. What most convinced us that self-mutilation was in fact operant behavior pertained to its highly discriminated nature. For example, the child would not hurt himself in a room where he had been "run to extinction" but would resume self-destruction at full strength in another situation only feet and seconds away *if* he had been comforted for self-destructive behavior there. Clinically speaking, the children did not waste any blows unless there was a payoff for it, and they were very discriminating as to which situations paid off. Technically speaking, we say that self-mutilation was under the control of discriminative stimuli (S^D).

Although extinction may work to reduce self-destruction, there are serious limitations to extinction procedure since some of the children hurt themselves severely during extinction. Therefore, we tried out ways of delivering aversive stimuli (such as painful electric shock) contingent on self-destruction. The data we reported (31, 34) showed an immediate and very dramatic termination of the self-destructive behavior, even in children who had been self-destructive for years. It is unclear why a relatively innocent averse stimulus should terminate self-destruction, considering the very severe physical abuse the children inflicted upon themselves. It is possible that the children had adapted themselves to the pain from their self-inflicted injuries, while the electric shock was new, offering no opportunity for adaptation. Several people have now published on the control of self-destructive behavior (7, 38, 45, etc.) and the data are remarkably consistent.

It is likely that we understand self-destructive behavior better than any other of the behaviors which psychotic children bring to treatment. It is also significant to point out that the analysis we have presented for self-destructive behavior is the kind of analysis which behavior modifiers undertake; that is, trying to understand one behavior at a time, identifying the conditions which control the behavior, and observing how changes in one behavior may alter others. Surprisingly, and disappointingly, the reduction in self-destructive behavior did *not* bring with it a simultaneous change in large classes of other behaviors. The children who stopped mutilating themselves did not simultaneously become normal.

Self-stimulatory behavior. By far the most common form of behavior exhibited by psychotic and retarded children centers on the self-stimulatory behavior we described earlier. This includes a great deal of spinning, twirling, rocking, and gazing, as well as other very repetitive and stereotyped movements which seem to have no particular relationship to what is happening in the child's day-to-day life.

Our understanding of this behavior class is very limited. From clinical observation, and not so much based on systematic research, it appears that this behavior disappears or is supplanted when more normal behaviors are acquired. We do know also that the presence of certain forms of self-stimulation makes the child more difficult to teach, apparently because he is less attentive to external cues. For example, in a study by Lovaas, Litrownik, and Mann (30) autistic children were taught to respond to an auditory input in order to obtain candies and other sweets. If the child was presented with this auditory stimulus when he was involved in self-stimulatory behavior, then frequently he would fail to respond to the auditory input, either completely missing the opportunity to obtain his reinforcer or responding after some delay. In another study by Koegel and Covert (20) autistic children were taught a very simple discrimination task such as responding on a machine (depressing a lever) in the presence of a light stimulus. They observed that the children failed to acquire this very simple discrimination as long as they were allowed to self-stimulate. When given disapproval (either verbal or with a slap on the hand) resulting in the suppression of self-stimulation, the children did learn. It appears, then, that the self-stimulatory behavior may interfere with one's efforts to teach these children, and for the sake of helping them acquire new behaviors one may initially decrease self-stimulatory behavior.

The teaching of appropriate behaviors. Since these children have such limited repertoires and since many are essentially without any social or intellectual behavior, they present a great challenge to educators. In a sense, one has the opportunity to start building a person from the beginning in regard to social and emotional, as well as intellectual, development. In the short amount of space allotted here we can only point to certain examples to illustrate the techniques which have been employed in our attempts to build new behaviors.

Simultaneously with the suppression of self-stimulatory behaviors, the teacher generally begins her work by attempting to establish some early forms of stimulus control. That is, the teacher may request of the child some simple behavior such as sitting quietly in a chair. Since even such a minimal request often evokes tantrums of self-destructive behavior, the establishment of this basic stimulus control and the reduction of aggression and self-destructive behaviors generally proceed together. It is generally impossible to work on the acquisition of appropriate behaviors until one has achieved some reduction of the pathological behaviors.

When one attempts to educate children who are so deficient in behavioral development, theoretically one has two alternate paths to follow. For example, instead of building behaviors piece by piece, one could decide to teach a child to value interpersonal interactions, intellectual achievement, curiosity about the world, and so on. Technically speaking, one could attempt to place these children in a situation where one optimized the child's motivational system to help them acquire conditioned reinforcers. We have pointed out before (27) that in many ways this would be an optimal strategy because the child, being properly motivated, would learn much without explicit attempts to teach him. To illustrate this point, if a child was strongly reinforced by a large range of social reinforcers, he would probably learn to behave in social ways, that is, to talk, play with peers, and so on, so as to come in contact with these stimulus events. It is unfortunate that this alternate path to teaching is not open to us since we do not know how to establish conditioned reinforcers or to build motivation in autistic children. No doubt one of the great challenges in the years ahead will be to achieve a better understanding of how motivation is acquired.

Given this limitation on the child's motivational system, the alternative is to proceed to build behaviors with the reinforcers which are functional. One can always fall back upon basic reinforcers such as food and pain, and as one works with any one child, one discovers idiosyncrasies in their motivational structures, such as a particular liking for a certain piece of music, a toy, etc., which can be partitioned in various ways and delivered to the child *contingent* upon certain desirable behaviors. The acquisition of new behaviors is accomplished in a step-by-step program. Let us turn to efforts to build language to illustrate how these programs have worked out.

Building language. Using a shaping procedure, several investigators (14, 24) have provided procedures for developing speech in previously mute autistic children. The procedure relied heavily on developing *imitative speech.* Let us illustrate the procedures from our language program. This program has been presented on film (23) and in outline form (25). Briefly, the verbal imitation training involves four steps of successive discriminations. In step 1 the therapist increases the child's vocalizations by reinforcing him (usually with food) for such behavior. In step 2 the child's vocalizations are reinforced only if they are in response to the therapist's speech (e.g., if they occur within five seconds of the therapist's vocalization). In step 3 finer discriminations are reinforced. That is, the child is reinforced for making successively closer approximations of the therapist's speech until he can match the particular sound given by the therapist (e.g., "a"). In step 4 the therapist replicates step 3 with another sound (e.g., "m") demanding increasingly fine discriminations and reproduction from the child. In this manner starting with sounds which are discriminably different (such as "m" and "a"), the child is taught to imitate an increasingly large range of sounds, words, and sentences. Imitation, then, is a discrimination where the response resembles its stimulus. Once he can imitate, the previously mute child becomes similar to echolalic autistic children. That is, they both imitate the speech of others, but neither knows the meaning of the words he utters. Their speech exists without a context.

A program for the establishment of meaningful speech involves establishing a *context* for speech, which consists of two basic discriminations. In the first discrimination the stimulus is nonverbal and the response is verbal, as in "expressive" speech (e.g., the child may be taught to label a food). In the second discrimination the stimulus is verbal, but the response is nonverbal, as in language "comprehension" (e.g., the child learns to follow instructions, obey commands, and so forth). Most language situations involve components of both discriminations, such that both the stimulus and response have both verbal and nonverbal components. The speech program, based on these two discriminations, begins with simple labeling, which is made functional as soon as possible. For example, as soon as a child knows the label for a food, he is fed contingent upon asking for food. The program gradually moves on to make the child increasingly proficient in language, including training in more abstract terms (such as pronouns, time, etc.); some grammar, such as the tenses; the use of language to please others, as in recall or storytelling, and so forth. These later levels are only rarely reached by mute children, but are almost always reached by echolalic children. Other investigators using similar procedures report similar data on language training (39).

Throughout the treatment program there is an emphasis on teaching the child behaviors which are both socially desirable and useful to him. Thus, while the majority of the research has focused on attempts to build language, there have also been several attempts to facilitate social and self-help skills. Lovaas et al. (28) published a procedure for building nonverbal imitation which proved particularly useful for the purpose of developing social and self-help skills. It includes methods for building those behaviors which make the child easier to live with, such as friendly greetings and shows of affection, dressing himself, feeding himself, brushing his teeth, and so on. Again the method is based on shaping procedures where the child is rewarded for making closer and closer approximations to the attending adult's behavior. As the children learn to discriminate the similarity in their own and the model's behaviors, they gradually acquire imitative behavior, as they did in the speech program.

GENERALIZATION AND FOLLOW-UP RESULTS

We now have some data which provide an estimation of the changes one might expect in autistic children undergoing behavior therapy (30). We examined three measures of the generality of treatment effects: (a) stimulus generalization, the extent to which behavior changes that occur in the treatment environment transfer to situations outside that treatment; (b) response generalization, the extent to which changes in a limited set of behaviors effect changes in a larger range of behaviors; and (c) generalization over time (or durability), that is, how well the therapeutic effects maintain themselves over time.

Let us illustrate the kinds of treatment changes and follow-up data we have collected by presenting certain data on the first ten children we treated. We recorded five behaviors in a free-play situation, which was different from the treatment environment, and in the presence of people who had not treated the child. Two of these behaviors were "sick" behaviors—*self-stimulation* and *echolalia*, which we have described earlier. Three of the behaviors were "healthy"—*appropriate verbal*, which was speech, related to an appropriate context, understandable, and grammatically correct; *social nonverbal*, which referred to appropriate nonverbal behavior that depended on cues given by another person for its initiation or completion; and *appropriate play*, which referred to the use of toys and objects in an appropriate, age-related manner. The recordings were made before treatment started, at the end of treatment (after twelve to fourteen months), and in a follow-up some one to four years after treatment. The children were divided into two groups—those who were discharged to a state hospital and those who remained with their parents.

The data are presented in figure 1. Percent occurrence of the various behaviors is plotted on the ordinate for before "B" and after "A" treatment and shows the latest follow-up "F" measures. "I" refers to the average results for the four children who were in-

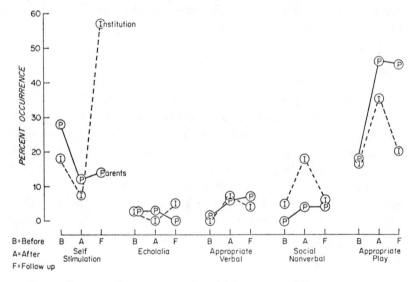

FIG. 1. Percent of occurrence of multiple-response follow-up measures

stitutionalized (discharged to a state hospital), and "P" refers to the six children who lived with their parents after their discharge from treatment. For all the five behaviors the trends are the same: the children who were discharged to a state hospital lost what they had gained in treatment with us; they increased in their psychotic behavior (self-stimulation and echolalia); they appear to have lost all they had gained of social nonverbal behavior, and they lost much of their gains in the area of appropriate verbal and appropriate play. The children who stayed with their parents, on the other hand, maintained their gains or improved further. For the children who regressed in the state hospital, a brief reinstatement of behavior therapy could temporarily reestablish the original therapeutic gains.

Since we assessed these behaviors in environments other than that of the treatment, we know that our procedures produced stimulus generalization. The children's Stanford-Binet IQ scores and Vineland Social Quotient scores also showed large gains during the course of treatment, and since we did not train the children on these tests, they provide explicit measures of response generalization.

These findings clearly emphasize an important point underlying the use of principles of behavior modification. That is, there may be important differences in the procedures for the production and maintenance of behavior. Thus, it does not appear to be enough to help the child acquire appropriate behaviors and to overcome the inappropriate ones; it is also important to provide maintaining conditions which ensure that the improvements will last.

CONTEMPORARY RESEARCH

Behavior therapy for severely psychotic children requires extensive teacher involvement; it is incremental and slow and the therapeutic gains are reversible. Many very important questions still remain unanswered. Why do certain autistic children show much larger improvements than others? Why does a given autistic child show relatively large and rapid improvements in some areas and slow, minimal gains in other areas? Why do so few autistic children become normal? Can autistic children function in public schools? Let us conclude this chapter by reviewing some current research which will hopefully suggest improvements in the use of behavior modification with autistic children.

Many researchers and clinicians have emphasized the extreme inconsistency with which autistic children respond to sensory input. At one time they appear to be blind and deaf, while at another time they show extremely fine visual and auditory acuity. In one situation they respond correctly to an instruction, while at another time they appear to have learned nothing about how to respond. Such peculiarities in the children's responding led us to conduct the following studies.

In the first study (30) we trained normal children and autistic children to respond to a complex stimulus involving the simultaneous presentation of auditory, visual, and tactile cues. Once this discrimination was established, elements of the complex were presented separately to assess which aspects of the complex stimulus had acquired control over the child's behavior. We found that the autistics had primarily come under the control of only one of the cues while the normals responded uniformly to all three cues. We also found that we could arrange conditions such that a cue which had remained nonfunctional when presented in association with other cues could be established as functional when trained separately. Thus, the autistic children did *not* appear to show a deficit in any particular sensory modality. Rather, when presented with multiple sensory input, a restricted range of that input gained control over their behavior.

In a teaching situation, when the child can both see the teacher's face as well as hear him talk, the autistic child may solve the verbal-imitation problem by attending only to the teacher's face. We referred to this finding as "stimulus overselectivity," and pointed out that it had many implications for understanding the behavior and learning problems of autistic children. For example, if autistic children are generally overselective in their response to multiple cues, they may be functionally blind in those situations where they are "hooked" on auditory cues and functionally deaf in those situations where they are "hooked" on visual cues. We have many similar studies in progress. For example, in one study autistic children were trained to discriminate between a boy doll and a girl doll. The results showed that for some children this discrimination would diminish to chance level when a specific stimulus (such as the shoes) was removed from the dolls, pointing out the extreme selectivity with which autistic children respond to their environment.

Such stimulus overselectivity also has implications for understanding why autistic children learn certain tasks so slowly. A necessary condition for much learning involves a contiguous or near contiguous presentation of two or more stimuli. If autistic children do not respond to one of the stimuli, certain acquisitions may then fail to occur. For example, their acquisition of affect may be retarded, as well as their development of meaningful speech. The establishment of meaningful speech involves establishing a *context* for speech and thus requires response to multiple inputs. For example, in attempting to teach a child to say the word *book*, the most common training procedure ("this is a book") involves a cross-modality shift. If the child responds to the auditory input, he may fail to perceive the visual referent, and hence not associate the appropriate label.

We now have data which bear directly on this problem of shifting stimulus control. These data show that autistic children often selectively respond to prompt stimuli to the exclusion of training stimuli (19). Two groups of children (autistic and normal) were pretrained on a color discrimination task. Later, the colors were presented simultaneously with training stimuli (e.g., two geometric forms, two tones) in a prompt-fading procedure. Gradually fading the color prompt generally produced acquisition of the training discrimination for normal S's but not for autistic S's. The autistic S's continued to selectively respond to the prompt until it was entirely faded out, at which point they began to respond at chance level. They had learned nothing about the training stimuli (e.g., forms). Surprisingly, the autistic S's acquired these same training discriminations when prompts were not used. That is, the usual technique of providing the children with extra stimuli to guide their learning may be exactly what makes it so difficult for them to learn.

It is interesting to note that while the autistic children generally failed to transfer from the color prompt to the training stimuli, they became very good at discriminating minute differences in the color prompts. That is, perhaps stimulus overselectivity may have benefited the autistic children's acquisition of the very difficult faded color discrimination. Once trained on the color cue in the initial pretraining, stimulus overselectivity may have functioned to decrease the children's acquisition of discriminations along continuums other than color but to increase their acquisition of discriminations along the color continuum. Thus, it might be a better procedure to use a training technique such as transfer along a continuum (22) which would actually take advantage of an autistic child's overselectivity. A study currently in progress in our lab examines this hypothesis. Preliminary results show that when the prompt stimuli fall along the same continuum as the training stimuli, prompting facilitates the acquisition of a very difficult discrimination which the children show no evidence of acquiring, either without or with a prompt in a continuum other than the training stimuli.

CLASSROOM TREATMENT

Little if any systematic research has been carried out on the education of autistic children in classroom settings. Research to date has focused primarily on the treatment of autistic children in a one-to-one teacher-child ratio. Economically, this makes the treatment unfeasible in many hospital and school situations. Therefore, we have currently begun a research program concerned with the teaching of autistic children in groups (21). Let us illustrate this research by citing a study where the emphasis is on establishing a teacher as a discriminative stimulus (S^D) for appropriate behavior even though the child is in a large group of children. To achieve this end we began working with two children, using one teacher and two teacher aides. The teacher provides commands and instructions and the aides deliver contingent rewards and punishments. As the children become more and more proficient, reinforcement for appropriate behaviors becomes increasingly intermittent, and additional children are introduced into the group, one at a time. If behaviors deteriorate at any one time, the size of the class is immediately reduced, reinforcements become more dense, and shortly thereafter, we begin building again. Through a process like this, then, it is hoped that the autistic child will be able to behave appropriately in a more average (normal) classroom.

Summary Comment

In the very short span of ten years, behavior modification has contributed in a major way to the education of the autistic child. Its major contribution lies in its demonstrated effectiveness. As such, it is the only intervention which has been empirically demonstrated to offer help. Each child who underwent treatment made measurable progress, even though the progress was slow and incremental and few children became "normal." We know more about some behaviors than others. For example, we know more about self-destructive behavior than self-stimulation. We were of more help to some children than to others. If the child possessed a verbal topography at the beginning of treatment, even if it was socially nonfunctional (such as echolalia), then we could help him substantially in developing a meaningful language. But we were less proficient in establishing new behavioral topographies in autistic children when none existed. For example, if the child was mute, his progress with behavior modification procedures was very limited. Follow-up data showed that in order to maintain the gains which the child made in treatment, he had to remain within an extension of the therapeutic environment. For example, to continue showing improvement his parents had to be taught behavior modification principles. The delivery of contingent, functional reinforcers has repeatedly been demonstrated to be a most significant feature, both in providing for learning and in maintaining the behavioral gains.

As we worked with these children, it became more apparent that they possessed certain deviations in perceptual functioning, particularly in responding to multiple stimulus inputs, which necessitate revisions of the usual manner of presenting educational material. Only additional research will enable us to structure such optimal learning environments.

While the first ten years in behavior modification relied heavily on learning principles derived from the animal laboratory, and their ready application resulted in rapid progress, it is likely that the next ten years will demand considerable new research directed specifically to the autistic child in order to help him develop appreciably further.

REFERENCES

1. Ayllon, T. "Intensive Treatment of Psychotic Behavior by Stimulus Satiation and Food Reinforcement." *Behaviour Research and Therapy* 1 (1963): 53-61.
2. Baer, D. M., and Sherman, J. "Reinforcement of Generalized Limitation in Young Children." *Journal of Experimental Child Psychology* 1 (1964): 37-39.

3. Bandura, A. *Principles of Behavior Modification*. New York: Holt, Rinehart & Winston, 1969.
4. Bettelheim, Bruno. *The Empty Fortress*. New York: Free Press, 1967.
5. Bijou, S. W.; Birnbrauer, J. S.; Kideler, J. D.; and Tague, C. "Programmed Instruction As an Approach to Teaching of Reading, Writing and Arithmetic in Retarded Children." *Psychological Record* 16 (1966): 505-22.
6. Brown, J. L. "Prognosis from Presenting Symptoms of Preschool Children with Atypical Development." *American Jounral of Orthopsychiatry* 33 (1960): 382-90.
7. Bucher, B., and Lovaas, O. I. "Use of Aversive Stimulation in Behavior Modification." In *Miami Symposium on the Prediction of Behavior, 1967; Aversive Stimulation*, edited by M. R. Jones. Coral Gables, Fla.: University of Miami Press, 1968.
8. Ferster, C. B. "Positive Reinforcement and Behavioral Deficits of Autistic Children." *Child Development* 32 (1961): 437-56.
9. Ferster, C. B., and DeMyer, M. "A Method for the Experimental Analysis of the Behavior of Autistic Children." *American Journal of Orthopsychiatry* 32 (1962): 89-98.
10. Frostig, M., and Home, D. *The Frostig Program for the Development of Visual Perception*. Chicago: Follett Publishing Co., 1964.
11. Goldfarb, W. *Childhood Schizophrenia*. Cambridge: Harvard University Press, 1961.
12. Goldiamond, I. "Stuttering and Fluency as Manipulatable Operant Response Classes." In *Research in Behavior Modification*, edited by L. Krasner and L. P. Ullmann. New York: Holt, Rinehart & Winston, 1965.
13. Hermelin, B. "Recent Psychological Research." In *Early Childhood Autism*, edited by J. K. Wing. London: Pergamon Press, 1966.
14. Hewett, J. M. "Teaching Speech to an Autistic Child through Operant Conditioning." *American Journal of Orthopsychiatry* 35 1965): 927-36.
15. Hutt, S. J.; Hutt, C.; Lee, D.; and Ounsted, C. "A Behavioral and Electroencephalographic Study of Autistic Children." *Journal of Psychiatric Research* 3 (1965): 181-97.
16. Kanner, L. "Autistic Disturbances of Affective Contact." *Nervous Child* 2 (1943): 217-50.
17. Kanner, L., and Eisenberg, L. "Notes on the Follow-up Studies of Autistic Children." In *Psychopathology of Childhood*, edited by P. Hoch and J. Zubin. New York: Greene & Stratton, 1955.
18. Kephart, N. C. *The Slow Learner in the Classroom*. Columbus, Ohio: Charles E. Merrill Books, 1960.
19. Koegel, R. L. "Selective Attention to Prompt Stimuli by Autistic and Normal Children." Doctoral dissertation. University of California, Los Angeles, 1971.

20. Koegel, R. L., and Covert, A. "The Relationship of Self-Stimulation to Learning in Autistic Children." *Journal of Applied Behavior Analysis* 5 (1972): in press.
21. Koegel, R. L., and Rincover, A. "Classroom Treatment of Autistic Children." Unpublished manuscript, University of California, Santa Barbara, 1972.
22. Lawrence, D. H. "The Transfer of a Discrimination along a Continuum." *Journal of Comparative and Physiological Psychology* 45 (1952):511-16.
23. Lovaas, O. I. "Behavior Modification: Teaching Language to Psychotic Children." (Instructional film, 45 min. 16 mm. sound) New York: Appleton-Century-Crofts, 1969.
24. ———. "A Program for the Establishment of Speech in Psychotic Children." In *Early Childhood Autism*, edited by J. Wing. London: Pergamon Press, 1966.
25. ———. "Teaching Language to Psychotic Children." Unpublished manuscript, University of California, Los Angeles, 1972.
26. Lovaas, O. I.; Berberich, J. P.; Perloff, B. F.; and Schaeffer, B. "Acquisition of Imitative Speech by Schizophrenic Children." *Science* 151 (1966): 705-7.
27. Lovaas, O. I; Freitag, G.; Kinder, M. I.; Rubenstein, B. D.; Schaeffer, B.; and Simmons, J. Q. "Establishment of Social Reinforcers in Two Schizophrenic Children on the Basis of Food." *Journal of Experimental Child Psychology* 4 (1965): 109-25.
28. Lovaas, O. I.; Freitas, Lorraine; Nelson, Karen; and Whalen, Carol. "The Establishment of Imitation and Its Use for the Development of Complex Behavior in Schizophrenic Children." *Behaviour Research and Therapy* 5 (1967): 171-81.
29. Lovaas, O. I.; Koegel, R. L.; Simmons, J. Q.; and Stevens, Judy. "Some Generalization and Follow-up Measures on Autistic Children in Behavior Therapy." *Journal of Applied Behavior Analysis*, in press.
30. Lovaas, O. I.; Litrownik, A.; and Mann, R. "Response Latencies to Auditory Stimuli in Autistic Children Engaged in Self-stimulatory Behavior." *Behaviour Research and Therapy* 9 (1971): 39-50.
31. Lovaas, O. I. Schaeffer, B.; and Simmons, J. Q. "Experimental Studies in Childhood Schizophrenia: Building Social Behavior in Children by Use of Electric Schock." *Journal of Experimental Research in Personality* 1 (1965): 99-109.
32. Lovaas, O. I., and Schreibman, Laura. "Stimulus Overselectivity of Autistic Children in a Two-Stimulus Situation." *Behaviour Research and Therapy* 9 (1971): 305-10.
33. Lovaas, O. I.; Schreibman, Laura; Koegel, R.; and Rehm, R. "Selective Responding by Autistic Children to Multiple Sensory Input." *Journal of Abnormal Psychology* 77 (1971): 211-22.

34. Lovaas, O. I., and Simmons, J. Q. "Manipulation of Self-Destruction in Three Retarded Children." *Journal of Applied Behavior Analysis* 2 (1969): 143-57.
35. Metz, J. R. "Conditioning Generalized Imitation in Autistic Children." *Journal of Experimental Child Psychology* 2 (1965): 389-99.
36. Ornitz, E. M., and Ritvo, E. R. "Perceptual Inconstancy in Early Infantile Autism." *Archives of General Psychiatry* 18 (1968): 76-98.
37. Rimland, B. *Infantile Autism*. New York: Appleton-Century-Crofts, 1964.
38. Risley, T. "The Effects and Side Effects of Punishing the Autistic Behaviors of a Deviant Child." *Journal of Applied Behavior Analysis* 1 (1968): 21-34.
39. Risley, T., and Wolf, M. M. "Establishing Functional Speech in Echolalic Children." *Behaviour Research and Therapy* 5 (1967): 73-88.
40. Rutter, M. "The Description and Classification of Infantile Autism." In *Infantile Autism*, edited by D. W. Churchill, G. D. Alpern, and and M. K. DeMeyer. Springfield, Ill.: Charles C Thomas, 1971.
41. Rutter, M. "Prognosis: Psychotic Children in Adolescence and Early Adult Life." In *Childhood Autism*, edited by J. K. Wing. London: Pergamon Press, 1966.
42. Schopler, E. "Early Infantile Autism and Receptor Processes." *Archives of General Psychiatry* 13 (1965): 327-35.
43. Schopler, E. "Visual versus Tactile Receptor Preference in Normal and Schizophrenic Children." *Journal of Abnormal Psychology* 71 (1966): 108-14.
44. Schopler, E., and Reichler, R. J. "Psychobiological Referents for the Treatment of Autism." In *Infantile Autism*, edited by D. W. Churchill, G. D. Alpern, and M. K. DeMeyer. Springfield, Ill.: Charles C Thomas, 1971.
45. Tate, B. G., and Baroff, G. S. "Aversive Control of Self-injurious Behavior in a Psychotic Boy." *Behaviour Research and Therapy* 4 (1966): 281-87.
46. Wolf, M. M.; Risley, T.; Johnston, M.; Harris, F.; and Allen, E. "Application of Operant Conditioning Procedures to the Behavior Problems of an Autistic Child: A Follow-up and Extension." *Behaviour and Research and Therapy* 5 (1967): 103-11.
47. Wolf, M. M.; Risley, T.; and Mees, H. "Application of Operant Conditioning Procedures to the Behavior Problems of an Autistic Child." *Behaviour Research and Therapy* 1 (1964): 305-12.

CHAPTER VIII

Behavior Modification in Teaching the Retarded Child

SIDNEY W. BIJOU

Behavior modification was first incorporated into the teaching of the retarded child in the early 1960s. Now, a little more than ten years later, it is considered by many ranking educators to be the approach with the greatest promise (30, 33). This chapter will (a) describe briefly the theoretical and methodological foundations of this approach, (b) present a behavior analysis of the retarded child, (c) describe the behavioral concept of teaching (and training) the retarded child, (d) describe examples of programs based on behavior analysis, and (e) discuss some problems and issues.

Theoretical and Methodological Foundations

The behavior modification model discussed here has four features which have been critical in shaping the technology of teaching the retarded child.

1. Both basic and applied research focus is on the individual, i.e., the interactions between a total-functioning, biologically unique person and the observable actions of people and objects. Changes in interactions are functionally related to environmental events, past and present, and external and internal. (The hereditary history of a person is influential in determining, in part, his biological equipment and his internal physiological environment.) Even when an investigator is concerned with the behavior of groups, he nevertheless studies the behavior of individuals as they interact with observable stimulus events.

The research described here is supported by the U.S. Office of Education, Division of Research, Bureau of Education for the Handicapped, Project No. 23-2030, Grant No. OEG-0-9-232030-0762 (032).

2. The concepts and principles of the system are empirical and functional. Observable stimuli are defined in terms of their effects on an individual's responses; observable responses, in terms of their effects on stimuli—the responses and the stimuli are reciprocally related. Hence, behavior analysis is always concerned with the relationships among stimulus functions (e.g., discriminating stimuli and reinforcing stimuli), response functions (e.g., attending behavior and escaping behavior), and setting events (e.g., fatigue and deprivation of reinforcing stimuli) in the situation and in the history of the person. These relationships, derived from over sixty years of research, have been organized into a theoretical system (e.g., 50, 52).

3. Much of the research is directed toward discovering the functional relationships between behavior and stimulus events. Reliability of findings is demonstrated by replicating the conditions of the experiment for the same individual; generality of the findings is demonstrated by replicating the same study on other individuals (48). The data gathered, whether in natural or laboratory situations or for descriptive (ecological) or experimental purposes, are usually in terms of rate of occurrence. The advantages of a rate measure in basic research have been reviewed by Skinner (51) and in educational applied research by Kunzelmann (34).

4. The concepts and principles in both basic and applied research are exactly the same. The objectives of the two endeavors differ. Basic research seeks to discover the behavior changes that occur when environmental conditions are rearranged; applied research aims to find out the practical value of making specified environmental changes. One advantage of a common set of terms for basic and applied research is that products resulting from the former can be applied directly to the latter, i.e., there is no need for paradigms, metaphors, or analogies. Ignorance about the conditions which cause complex behavior is recognized as the "state of the art" and not as an occasion for creating new terms.

Behavior Analysis of the Retarded Child

Despite advances in the biological and behavioral sciences, the concepts of retardation and the retarded child have remained surprisingly static. In one way or another the retarded child is still described as lacking some mental ability or function, such as the ability to see relationships, to abstract, or to generalize. And the conditions postulated as causes of retardation have been variations on a dualistic theme, e.g., hereditary and environment, or endogenous and exogenous factors. We shall first review the current concept of retardation and then look at a version that is more consistent with a behavioral approach.

According to the American Association for Mental Deficiency, "Mental retardation refers to subaverage general intellectual functioning which originates during the developmental period and is associated with impairment in adaptive behavior" (27:3). The American Medical Association concurs, offering a definition that differs only slightly: "Mental retardation refers to significantly subaverage intellectual functioning which manifests itself during the developmental period and is characterized by inadequacy in adaptive behavior" (19:1).

The conditions responsible for subaverage intellectual functioning, according to the AMA formulation, fall into three categories: (a) *biological*—intrinsic neural organization, biochemical enzyme efficiency, perception (neurophysiological), motor disorders, sensory disorders (visual, auditory, kinesthetic, etc.), language pathways, seizures, other somatic handicaps, and combinations of these conditions, (b) *sociocultural*—child-rearing patterns, economic level, housing, urban-rural locale, subculture (minority group, prejudice, educational facilities, employment opportunities, medical care, social services, and combinations of these factors), (c) *psychological*—sensory deprivation, infant-maternal interaction (insufficiency, distortion, and discontinuity), perception (psychological), adaptation patterns, cognitive capacities, anxiety, self-concepts, and combinations of these factors.

The view that retardation is a symptom of pathology caused by biological, sociocultural, and psychological factors dominates the thinking not only of clinical psychologists and physicians but also of educators. In special education this belief is manifested in the so-called defect and deficit theories of exceptionality. There are two kinds of defect theories. In one, subaverage intellectual functioning is said to be caused by *organic* conditions such as those listed above in the biological category. In the second, subaverage intellectual functioning is attributed to a *hypothetical* entity or process such as those listed in the psychological category. In either case, the strategy for teaching retarded children depends on whether the presumed cause can be remediated. Defect theories which assume organic causes (e.g., clinically inferred brain injury or psychoanalytical, constitutional personality types) lead to practices that "teach around the defect." Defect theories which assume hypothetical causes such as perceptual or learning disability theories attempt either to work around or to correct the cause depending on the child's responsiveness to the treatment.

The deficit theories of retardation, on the other hand, attribute subaverage intellectual functioning not to organic or hypothetical defects but to histories of poverty, neglect, and racial discrimination, or to conditions very similar to those in the sociocultural category and, in some cases, in the psychological category. According to this view, special education should be designed to compensate for such lacks and losses as early and as extensively as possible.

Instructional programs for the retarded child based on both the defect and deficit theories have not fared well (16, 18, 20, 29, 37, 44) for they have two shortcomings: (a) Each is limited in scope, and (b) each treats retardation as a symptom of mental pathology.

BEHAVIORAL ANALYSIS OF RETARDED DEVELOPMENT

Retardation, from a behavior analysis view, is conceived to be a description of a person's behavior which, like all other behavior, is a function of his genetic and personal history. The specific behaviors said to define retardation, or "inadequate adaptive" behavior, are of major concern not as indicators of pathology, but as the basis for planning a teaching program, remedial or compensatory.

It is undeniable that the biological factors listed in the AMA formulation, insofar as they are observable, are among the conditions that may produce retarded behavior. However, they must be viewed functionally, that is, as (a) *limiting the person's response equipment* (sensory, motor, and the neurological connecting system) so that he cannot respond normally, and (b) *providing an abnormal internal environment* (some of the usual stimuli are absent or they occur with unusual intensities and durations), thereby generating abnormal reactions. Hence, the important thing about biological factors for a functional analysis is that they may reduce the response potential of the person and may distort his internal environment.

Sociocultural factors also contribute to retardation. In more general terms than those in the AMA formulation, sociocultural factors are considered as the institutional practices of the culture, together with the unique behaviors of parents, peers, teachers, and others, in direct interaction with the child in the form of child-rearing practices, teacher-pupil-school relationships, and so forth. Sociocultural factors must also be viewed functionally. For example, child-rearing practices which produce strong anxiety and aversive reactions may hinder the normal development of the child. Furthermore, the physical environment, consisting of the natural and man-made objects of the culture, is included in the sociocultural category. Hence, prolonged absences of the usual objects in the cultures constitute restrictions in opportunities for the child to develop normal behavioral repertoires.

The factors in the AMA's psychological category are not parallel to those in the biological and sociocultural categories. Some refer to sociocultural phenomena (e.g., sensory deprivation), some to the behavior of an individual (e.g., adaptation patterns), some to hypothetical concepts (e.g., cognitive capacity), and most to the interactions between the responses of a unique biological individual and biological and sociocultural stimuli.

To summarize, *retardation* or, better yet, *developmental retardation* (4, 5, 17) is a term used to describe a person with limited behavior repertoires resulting from his genetic and personal history. The so-called normal individual, with his normal anatomy and smooth physiological functioning, develops as a consequence of interactions with a succession of normal sociocultural events. His progression is established as the norm for his culture. The retarded person, on the other hand, develops as he does from interactions with a variety of deviant conditions. Some may be in the response equipment of the individual and some may be in the biological and sociocultural environments. The more deviant the conditions in his interactional history, the more extreme the retardation.

Behavioral Concept of Teaching

Of the many ways in which teaching has been conceptualized, the one most compatible with a behavioral approach is that teaching (and training) is the arrangement of conditions to expedite learning in an individual. Skinner (53) elaborates thus:

> Teaching is the arrangement of contingencies of reinforcement under which students learn. They learn without teaching in their natural environments, but teachers arrange special contingencies which expedite learning, hastening the appearance of behavior which would otherwise be acquired slowly or making sure of the appearance of behavior which might otherwise never occur (pp. 64-65).

"Contingencies of reinforcement" and "special contingencies" refer to: (a) conditions antecedent to responses (e.g., the presentation of an arithmetic problem), (b) conditions consequent to responses (e.g., "That's right"), and (c) setting or contextual factors (e.g., mother's presence in the classroom). Many of these conditions and factors are under the control of the teacher and her assistant. However, some originate in the behavior of others in the teaching situation and some in the internal environment of the child (e.g., a severe cold). These conditions and factors determine the changes that occur in the child's motor, academic, and social behaviors, some transitory and some durable. The child's feelings, emotions, attitudes, and interests are not ignored, as is sometimes believed, nor are they considered beyond the ken of the approach. They are analyzed in behavioral terms and programmed as a part of the curriculum.

ARRANGING CONDITIONS ANTECEDENT TO RESPONSES

Arranging conditions antecedent to responses consists of (a) presenting the materials of the curriculum or training program, and (b) using techniques that facilitate responding to the tasks presented. There is little disagreement over the general content of training programs and curricula for the retarded child. For the severely retarded individual, the programs are usually limited to training in self-care and simple management skills; for the moderately and mildly retarded, the programs resemble those of the regular class: basic academic subjects (reading, writing, spelling, arithmetic, language, arts and crafts, and knowledge relating to here-and-now objects and events), ancillary academic behaviors (appropriate study habits and positive motivation for school subjects), and appropriate personal-social behaviors (personal hygiene, acceptable social behavior, and appropriate behavior toward property).

According to behavior analysis, all instruction should be individualized. How else can the teacher arrange contingencies to expedite the learning for each of her pupils? This requirement of individualized instruction should not be interpreted to mean that all instruction must be on a one-to-one relationship with the teacher. It does mean, however, using materials, devices, and other individuals to manage the teaching situation so that the child attends to the task, responds, and is reinforced appropriately. It is a well-known fact that lessons designed for a group or a class, even when prepared by a sensitive teacher, "reach" only the children who constitute the "middle" group.

Individualized instruction for the retarded child is usually programmed. Some programs are systematic sequences of academic materials on expendable sheets of paper (some requiring devices for their presentation) and others are merely outlines of teaching procedures. All told, only a limited number of workable programs are commercially available at present. It is entirely possible for schools, districts, or state education departments themselves to develop programs for their teachers' use. The specific steps to be adhered to for each program are to (a) identify the specific behavior to be learned, (b) analyze the components of the behavior and arrange them into sequences with the aid of teachers and specialists in the content area, (c) evaluate the program on the children who will be using it, and (d) modify it in whatever ways the children's responses indicate.

The effectiveness of the individualized program frequently depends on the techniques that help a child make responses to a task. Too often the teacher resorts to "common sense" and outmoded concepts of retardation and learning. Thus, one finds teachers who fill the child's time with low-level activities or extensive drills. In a behaviorally oriented program the procedures are designed to encourage responses to new material in a wide variety of settings. Techniques for this purpose include manding (telling or instruct ing), prompting and fading, modeling, and priming (getting the response to occur by means of other stimuli).

The second class of conditions that are arranged to expedite learning are those that occur after responses. Stimuli that strengthen the antecedent behavior by increasing its probability of occurrence on a given occasion (e.g., answering a question) or in a given form (e.g., writing letters of the alphabet) are called reinforcers. Some reinforcing stimuli are described as organismic (e.g., food, water, air, aversions) and some as ecological (e.g., sensory stimulation from water play or excitement generated by games). Organismic and ecological stimuli are rarely used as contingencies for learning academic and self-help skills. However, ecological stimuli are enthusiastically endorsed as a natural part of the teaching situation in the form of play, arts, crafts, and the like. Other reinforcing stimuli are described as "acquired" since they are developed through relationships with people, physical objects, and activities. Unfortunately, some acquired reinforcers, especially those associated with activities, are thought by teachers and administrators to be "natural" and therefore no provision is made to develop or to modify them. Such a conception works to the disadvantage of the child who has not had the opportunity to develop interests in activities associated with school and school learning.

A class of acquired reinforcers called "contrived" reinforcers because they are not considered to be natural to the school situation is often used in remedial education to (a) initiate academic and social learning and (b) endow or reendow social and academic stimuli with reinforcing properties. The main technique in (a) is the use of an increasing ratio schedule of reinforcement (social reinforcers are given less and less frequently), and in (b) it is the employment of a percentage schedule of reinforcement (the contrived and social reinforcers are given together less and less frequently [9]).

Response consequences not only increase the reliability of responding on the proper occasion and shape responses, but they also maintain the behavior acquired, i.e., improve retention and recall. It is well known that schools, in general, devote more attention to the acquisition of new behavior than to the maintenance of acquired behavior. In contrast, special educational programs tend to stress maintenance because the retarded child is often said to be deficient in this respect. Regardless of the reason for including maintenance exercises in programs for the retarded, it is a desirable feature, for when behavior is functional under a variety of circumstances it becomes a viable part of the child's repertory.

Finally, demonstration that a stimulus class (e.g., praise) has reinforcing properties for a child does not guarantee permanence since these properties, like all others, are derived from and dependent upon other conditions called setting factors. Food does not always reinforce seeking, getting, and eating behaviors. When a person is "stuffed" after a bountiful Thanksgiving dinner, an offer of more pumpkin pie or more of anything is most likely to lead to avoidance behavior ("No, thanks, I've had enough").

SETTING FACTORS

Setting factors, or conditions that endow stimuli with a functional characteristic such as a reinforcing property, may come from the child, the teacher, the classroom, and the society. Those originating in a child include his health, his emotional disposition (e.g., a constant state of anxiety), his need for food, rest, or sleep, and so forth. Setting factors from the teacher include her general emotional disposition (the serious, stern teacher versus one who is relaxed and pleasant) and her attitude toward the learning potentiality of the children in her class. She expresses the latter by the way she deals with failures in learning (e.g., attributing failure to a deficiency in the child rather than to poor programming). Setting factors in the classroom include the physical appearance of the room itself, the social atmosphere generated by the teacher and children, and classroom routines. Finally, setting factors in the society itself which affect children's performances include activities associated with holidays, parent-teacher programs, and the like. The setting factors generated by society interact with setting factors that are unique to each child. Thus, the Christmas season affects each child according to his own personal history together with factors operating at the moment. For example, a serious illness in the family, anticipation of the arrival of favorite grandparents, an unemployed father, an unexpected goodly sum of money to be spent on Christmas gifts—all set the stage for different kinds of behaviors at Christmas.

ASSESSMENT OF LEARNING PROGRESS

An approach to teaching that views instruction as the arrangement of conditions to enhance learning requires a three-phase assessment procedure. The first involves determining the entrance repertories of the child by means of inventory or criterion-referenced tests (23). Standardized tests of intelligence, ability, and personality may be used, but they do not furnish the kind of information the teacher needs for planning a program of instruction. They sample behavior and yield scores (e.g., IQs, percentiles, and school-grade equivalents) which rank the child's performance with respect to a reference group. Results of psychometric tests may be used profitably to select and classify children for school placement and to predict performance on an actuarial basis but, unfortunately, they are frequently used for purposes for which they were not intended. For example, many educators treat psychometric results as though they were medical laboratory tests which identify the basic nature of the pathology and thereby lead to a diagnosis and an appropriate and specific treatment program. The parallel does not hold. Psychometric tests do not measure the functioning of a bodily organ (including the brain) or system. They measure the behavior of a total-functioning organism. Furthermore, specific treatment programs for specific diagnostic categories have not been determined. We cannot say that an educable child with "perceptual confusion" should be treated only with a prescribed program and that all other treatment programs would be harmful. Many "minimally brain-damaged" children have benefited from programmed instructional materials developed on children who do not carry this label.

The second phase of assessment deals with monitoring the child's learning behavior. Much has been written about the need for keeping daily objective records of progress, and several methods have been suggested (e.g., 34). Descriptions of most of the methods will be included in the examples of behavior modification programs in the next section.

The third phase of assessment is concerned with evaluation of the outcome. Here, assessment consists of a summary of findings from program posttests, psychometric tests, achievement tests, and statements about the child's personal-social behaviors and the effective reinforcing contingencies. Assessment of outcome sometimes also includes measures of the child's achievement after leaving the special class. Findings indicating that the child has continued to progress lead to praise for the program; findings indicating that he has remained about the same or that he has regressed lead to a critical evaluation of the program. Such conclusions are unwarranted since the child's performance at any point after training is a joint function of the treatment program *and* the contingencies in the interval between termination of treatment and the time of the follow-up assessment. Hence the follow-up assessment should evaluate both (10).

Examples of Behavior Modification Techniques with Retarded Children

Teaching objectives and techniques in various programs for the retarded depend to a considerable extent on the child's level of development. We therefore distinguish between the retarded child over five years of age with a fair command of language (the school age "educable" child with an IQ above 50) and the retarded child over four years of age with practically no linguistic skills (the "trainable" child with an IQ below 50). Among retarded children more than two-thirds are deemed educable. For that reason and because of space limitations, we shall focus on the larger group. We should point out in passing, however, that the trainable group has received substantial attention, as the following references suggest: Azrin and Foxx (1) on toilet training; Bensberg (2) and Bensberg, Caldwell, and Cassell (3) on self-care training, including dressing and undressing, eating, and toileting; LeBlanc and Lent (35) and Lent (36) on training adolescent girls in personal, social, educational, and vocational skills; Mackay and Sidman (39), Sidman (47), Sidman and Stoddard (49) on perceptual and basic academic learning; and Meyerson, Kerr, and Michael (42) on training basic motor skills. Gardner (22) summarized behavior modification as applied to the training of the retarded adolescent and adult.

EXPERIMENTAL CLASS IN A RESIDENTIAL SCHOOL

The Experimental Class at the Rainier School, Buckley, Washington, established in 1961, is an example of one of the early efforts to apply behavior principles to retarded children (8, 12). The children in the initial program were between eight and fourteen years of age; their average IQ was about 60 (*Peabody Picture Vocabulary Test*); their academic achievement ranged from no academic achievement (*Wide Range Achievement Test*) to upper first grade; and their clinical diagnoses included brain-damaged, mongoloid, cultural-familial, and unknown or undifferentiated. Many were further classified as school behavior problems.

The children attended the experimental class only for academic work; the remainder of the school day was spent in their regular classrooms. At first, class time was limited to fifteen to twenty minutes a day. As the children learned the prerequisite classroom behaviors and began to show progress in school achievement, class time was increased to an hour or more.

For most of these institutionalized children the contingencies ordinarily used in academic classrooms proved not to be effective for strengthening behaviors in reading, writing, and arithmetic. Consequently, a contrived contingency was explored. In its final form it consisted of marks on small sheets of paper. Full sheets were exchangeable for "backup" reinforcers, such as toys, candy, and social events. The giving of a mark was accompanied by positive comments from the teacher. The "backups" in the mark system were gradually extended to include activities and objects intrinsic to the classroom, e.g., serving as tutor. All response contingencies— natural, acquired, and contrived—were also used to support and develop appropriate classroom social behavior and study habits (14, 15).

Throughout the project and particularly during the later years, reading, writing, and arithmetic programs were developed. All began with preacademic tasks (simple discriminations, naming, conceptualizing, etc.) and ended with complex behaviors (e.g., reading and following directions and solving practical arithmetic problems). Instructional manuals for teachers and aides describing techniques for presenting the material, for responding to correct and incorrect responses, for recording progress, and for modifying the programs were also prepared (13).

At this writing, the class is still in operation under the direction of C. Tague Harper. Children in the present class, like their predecessors, come to school cheerfully, are academically productive, and advanced pupils help the new students. The "time-out" contingency, which in the early days had been used to weaken disruptive behavior, is no longer in operation. Advanced pupils now only occasionally exchange their marks for candy bars and notions, saving them, for the most part, for special outings at the end of the school year.

Demonstration of the workability of the experimental class has led to the development of a schoolwide program, the Rainier School Behavior Curriculum (55). This staff venture, under the direction of the teacher who pioneered the experimental class, is designed to provide a record of skills and behaviors already acquired by the children in a form that is easily communicated to teachers as well as a system of individual instruction which depends on precise descriptions of each child's skills. When completed, the curriculum will have three components integrated into a single system. The first is a comprehensive series of statements in behavioral terms of what the student can do in various areas of instruction. Referred to as the "Behavior Assessment Statement," it includes (a) *arithmetic* (number system, addition, subtraction, multiplication, and division); (b) *arts and crafts* (shapes, drawing skills, colors, crayons, scissors, pasting, painting, collage, finger crochet, printing, stitchery, enameling, and clay modeling); (c) *music* (songs by rote, music theory, enunciation, playing musical instruments, rhythm band, musical games, action songs, and folk dancing); (d) *language arts* (writing, composition, letter recognition, phonetic spelling); (e) *oral language* (articulation, nouns, verbs, adjectives, adverbs, language structure, word combinations, *is* and *was* verbs, verb endings, and retelling stories); (f) *physical skills* (calisthenics, gross motor movements, locomotor skills, presport and games skills, self-help—dressing, hygiene, classroom eating, getting to and from school); (g) *social skills* (telephone directory, home telephone, pay telephone, restaurant, and postoffice); and (h) *classroom management* (sitting, raising hands, remaining quiet, pointing, manipulative skills, matching colors, matching shapes, matching pictures, matching letters and words).

The second part of the Rainier School Behavior Curriculum, the "Skill Description and Criterion Test," provides definitions of the behaviors listed in the "Behavior Assessment Statement" and specifies the standards for assessment. The third part (in process) is the "Procedures Manual," which will contain suggested materials and specific teaching techniques for teaching those behaviors rated "no" in the Behavior Assessment Statement. All items in the "Behavior Assessment Statement" will be numbered in a decimal system, and corresponding items in the "Skill Description and Criterion Test" and in the "Procedures Manual" will have the same numbers.

The areas included in the present form of the "Behavior Assessment Statement" and the "Skill Description and Criteria Test" are those that are most widely used. Specialized areas are being developed and some now included are being revised.

SPECIAL CLASSES IN COMMUNITY SCHOOLS

Santa Monica, California. In California's Santa Monica Unified School District, Hewitt and his colleagues have established special classes for educable mentally retarded children based on the experience they have had with educationally (learning) handicapped children (28). In this program, called the engineered classroom, the special child is viewed as a learner whose competencies must be assessed and treated in a flexible and multifaceted learning setting. Hence, the teachers are trained to:

(a) Create a classroom environment as invitingly different as possible from those the educationally handicapped child has failed in previously and gradually reintroduce him to the demands of a regular classroom. (b) Provide within the new clasroom a full range of direction-following, exploratory, social, and academic activities so that it is possible to assign each child at all times a level of task he is ready for, needs to do, and can be successful doing. (c) Create as many positive associations to learning and accomplishments in the classroom as possible and truly make every effort to guarantee all children success. (d) Maintain a predictable learning environment in which the child knows exactly where he stands through regular contacts with the teacher and some feedback system (e.g., checkmarks) that helps him understand the relationship between his social and academic behavior and classroom consequences (28:7).

The classroom for educationally handicapped children, which serves as the model for teaching the class for retarded children, has four centers: (a) mastery (student desk area), (b) communication (social), (c) exploratory (science and art), and (d) order (pre-academic attention, response, and direction-following activities). Where perceptual-motor training is desired, the order center is extended to accommodate the needed materials and activities. Academic emphasis is increased by scheduling individual students into the mastery center instead of other centers. The children are reintegrated into regular classrooms as soon as they show that they can work effectively in the mastery center.

In the engineered classroom for educable retarded children, the emphasis on science at the exploratory center is reduced and greater stress is placed on perceptual-motor training and simple concrete experiences with a wide variety of visual, auditory, and tactual materials. Discovery science tasks are replaced with activities involving animal care, color-matching, size and form discrimination, story and music-listening, and arts and crafts. Science and art are merged in the exploratory center. The space devoted to the order center is doubled to provide opportunities for more children to work with direction-following tasks such as puzzles, pegboards, letter-by-letter printing, and typing. In general, group instruction prevails, especially in phonics and basic arithmetic concepts.

The checkmark system provides a maximum of five checkmarks for each fifteen minutes of work: one for starting, one for working, and three as a bonus for some stated goal. The checkmark card, exchangeable for goodies, accommodates sixty marks. The checkmark system is also used to improve social behavior outside the classroom, e.g., on the school bus.

Durham, North Carolina. The Durham Educational Program, Durham, North Carolina, is designed to modify the behavior of disadvantaged young children on the twin assumptions that adverse socioeconomic conditions may produce retardation and that learning laws apply to this group as well as to any other. "The teacher seeks to apply learning principles with the intent of treatment and change of maladaptive, deficient, or undesirable pupil behavior.

Such studies involve systematic programming of the environmental consequences of a child's behavior" (46).

General behavior modification procedures are employed with all the children who represent a cross-section of residents in Durham poverty areas. The children exhibiting the most severe behavior problems are referred to personnel within the project to consult in developing individual modification programs. The referrals, most of whom are boys, range in age from two to eight and typically exhibit "problem behavior" including aggressions, failure to follow directions, and lack of participation in school work. Each child's behaviors are classified on a rating scale (54) as desirable, inappropriate, and/or unacceptable, and the teacher's interaction with each child is assessed as positive, social, neutral, structuring, questioning, redirecting or restructuring, and/or negative. The monitoring system is similar to the one reported by Lovaas, Freitag, Gold, and Kassorla (38).

During the base-line period, a behavior modification consultant and a technician prepare a tentative treatment program. After a base-line performance has been obtained, typically in two weeks, the consultant, technician, and teacher decide on the behavioral goals and the techniques to be employed. The program is modified primarily on the basis of the data gathered.

The behavior modification plan itself is a series of contingency statements for the teacher. Desirable and undesirable behaviors and potential reinforcers and punishers are defined, and the action to be taken by the teacher contingent upon a child's particular behavior is described. When necessary, contrived reinforcers (tokens exchangeable at a miniature store) are used.

When a teacher is assigned a child for treatment, she is given training as a behavior therapist for that child. Through consultation and data analysis she learns to analyze his behavior over time and how to apply appropriate consequences. She may be required to increase or decrease the behaviors she displayed to the child during the base-line period or to modify drastically her interactions with the child. The research personnel help the teacher by reinforcing her behavior, giving sympathetic recognition of the problems she encounters, and providing her with information on the progress of each child. Signals from the researchers, videotapes, and remote radio setups are frequently used as training aids. Finally, the teacher is responsible for compiling her own data on a daily basis and discussing the findings with members of the staff.

CLASSES IN UNIVERSITY-AFFILIATED LABORATORY SCHOOLS

University of Illinois. The project at the University of Illinois, initiated in 1965, is concerned with (a) preparing programmed instructional materials and manuals for teaching preacademic and primary school subjects, (b) studying procedures for modifying personal-social behaviors, and (c) devising individualized assessment procedures for the teacher (6, 9).

The children, five to eight years old and viewed by teachers as severe behavior problems or extreme learning disability cases, are referred primarily by school psychologists. The curriculum designed for them consists of two interrelated programs. One emphasizes basic academic skills and knowledge; the other, precurrent academic behavior ("study habits"), self-control, and those necessary personal-social behaviors prescribed by the classroom culture. The class structure consists of five study periods, a language period, story time, and recess. Each child's assignment in each subject for each study period, prepared by the teacher and her assistant the afternoon before, is contained in a color-coded folder in the child's desk. Since the work is completely individualized, the children do not necessarily work on the same subject at the same time, and those who do happen to be working on the same subject are generally working on different units. The teacher helps some children, the assistant helps others, and some work alone, depending on their achievement levels and study skills.

The materials and procedures for teaching basic academic skills and knowledge are developed cooperatively by the laboratory staff. Alterations in the programs result mainly from monitoring the individual performances of children. The reading program, a revision of the work at the Rainier School (8, 24), consists of an attending sequence and twenty-seven sets of graded verbal and pictorial materials. Each subset has four components: (a) picture identification, (b) reading discrimination, (c) oral reading, and (d) reading comprehension. A fifth component—stories—is included in some of the subsets. The vocabulary portion of the reading program is keyed to a graded series of stories in the *Bank Street Readers,* so that the child is familiar with the words when he encounters them in his reading. The arithmetic program aims to teach both prearithmetic and primary-level addition and subtraction operations. The prearithmetic component involves (a) shaping attending behaviors, (b) stimulating initial arithmetical responses through imitative prompting procedures, (c) chaining numbers, (d) responding to written numbers, objects, and representations of objects, and (e) bringing oral number responses under the control of printed or written materials. After mastery of the prearithmetic skills, the child is introduced to the primary operations in addition and subtraction. The next unit of the program transfers stimulus control of simple single-digit addition and subtraction problems to the vertical format. The final component of the program involves establishment and maintenance of stimulus control of complex arithmetical chains involving simple problem-solving, place-value groupings, and carrying and borrowing operations. In the writing and spelling program the child acquires the ability to (a) hold the pencil, (b) discriminate between acceptable and unacceptable models of writing, (c) develop finer differentiated manual responses, (d) work without having models to depend on, and (e) write from dictation in both manuscript and cursive forms. When the child has achieved this goal and has made at least minimal progress in reading, he moves into the spelling program, which has as its core the vocabulary list from the reading program. The language program (still in the developmental stage) aims to sharpen and refine the child's "requesting" repertory and to increase his descriptive skills. As part of the daily activities the teacher prompts the child in requesting things in a socially acceptable manner, to say "thanks" when helped and so on. To improve the child's descriptive skills, the teacher emphasizes knowledge about things and events in the immediate environment.

Teaching study behaviors (precurrent) and personal-social behaviors is not different from a procedural point of view from teaching academic subjects. The steps involved are (a) specifying the target behavior in behavioral terms, (b) assessing the present relevant behavior, (c) planning the treatment sequence, (d) assessing progress, (e) revising the sequence as indicated by the data, and (f) maintaining the acquired behavior.

The desirable precurrent behaviors for reading, arithmetic, writing and spelling, and language are incorporated in their respective programs. Techniques for weakening behaviors which interfere with precurrent behaviors include extinction (ignoring) and teacher "time out" (looking away, contingent on the child's distracted behavior, and looking back, contingent on resumption of the desirable behavior). Techniques for strengthening desirable precurrent behaviors include (a) primes (e.g., modeling: "I like the way Jimmy is working") and prompts (e.g., "Try doing it this way"), and (b) reinforcement of successive approximations to desired precurrent behaviors (praising him for writing his words closer to the lines on the paper).

The target behaviors of the personal-social curriculum center on self-care, social relationships with adults and peers, sexual behavior, and the treatment of property. Also included are intellectual "traits" such as positive motivation for academic learning. To attain these objectives it is frequently necessary to cope with behaviors that are antithetical to acceptable personal-social behaviors and which range from mild to severe on a scale of disruptiveness. Severe forms include hitting, biting, spitting, throwing objects at a person, pulling hair, damaging property, intruding upon another child's ongoing activity, ridiculing a child's problem or physical handicap, and running out of the classroom, play yard, or school building. Milder forms are those behaviors that impinge upon the rights of the other children. Programming the replacement of severe forms of interfering behavior with acceptable behavior necessitates (a) weakening or eliminating the undesirable behavior by the use of techniques that do not generate detrimental side effects and (b) simultaneously strengthening desirable behaviors in ways that are likely to maintain and generalize them. The procedures used to weaken or eliminate problem behavior include extinction, removing the occasion for the response, contingent loss of positive reinforcers and time out from all opportunities for positive reinforcement, and setting up conditions that compete effectively with the undesirable behaviors. Techniques that strengthen desirable behaviors and promote their maintenance and generalization involve reinforcement contingencies. If the positive reinforcers that are intrinsic to the classroom are ineffective, then contrived reinforcers are introduced not only to strengthen desirable behavior but to develop reinforcing properties in the stimuli generally indigenous to the classroom situation.

Assessments of a child's academic repertory at entrance, his daily progress, and his terminal behaviors are made by the teacher and her assistant. The entrance assessment is based on observational data obtained by a laboratory teacher on the child's last day or two in the public school classroom from which he is being removed and during his first week in the laboratory classroom, on pretests from the reading, arithmetic, writing, and spelling programs, on reports and interviews, and on standardized intelligence tests (Slosson) and achievement tests (*Caldwell Preschool Inventory, Wide Range Achievement Test*). All except the standardized tests are taken into consideration when the teacher prepares the initial instructional program for the child.

Information about the child's daily progress comes from five sources. The first is the teacher's subjective impressions. The second is the actual products of the child's performance, e.g., completed writing assignments, sheets of arithmetic problems, and written spelling pages. The third source, primarily from tutoring, yields data on the frequencies of correct and incorrect responses and the pattern of response contingencies, i.e., social comments and marks. The fourth is the pretests and posttests from the programs. And the fifth is the observational data, usually frequency counts of personal-social behavior (11).

The terminal assessment consists of the results from readministration of the standardized tests of intelligence and achievement, a description of the mastery level achieved in each of the academic programs, and a reassessment of the problem behavior given as the reason for the original referral. The final report contains an objective description of the child's actual academic skills and knowledge in terms of his final performances on the programs, his social behavior at the end of the school year, and the contingencies that proved successful with him.

University of Arizona. The Center for Early Childhood Education, University of Arizona, also focuses on the young developmentally retarded school child (41). The goals of the center are to (a) decrease or eliminate disruptive or inappropriate behaviors and establish and elaborate appropriate behaviors to enable each child to return to a public or private school, (b) carry out research on behavior modification, and (c) train students, teachers, and parents in behavior modification techniques.

Sixteen children were in the program during the first year of operation, 1969-1970. Ten were referred by public and private schools and six by social agencies because of marked deviant behavior. Five had never been enrolled in school.

A modified activity curriculum was used to capitalize on the children's interests, hence manipulating, constructing, and dramatizing activities were used as aids to learning. The academic program was dictated by the needs of the children and at the same time took cognizance of the public school district's first-grade curriculum and the programs to which the children would return. Emphasis was placed upon integration of speaking, listening, reading, and writing. A daily reading period focused specifically on the skills needed for comprehension and word attack. For the children requiring a readiness-oriented program there was stress on speaking and listening. The more advanced children were taught a basic sight vocabulary and word-attack skills by a modified Grace Fernald technique, the phono-visual phonics program, and others. Mathematical concepts were taught with the Science Research Associates program in group situations, which features games and manipulation. When individual instruction was required, workbooks were used. Science and social studies were taught through activities in and outside the classroom.

Behavior modification techniques were applied to all aspects of the program. For example, classical conditioning methods (stimulus pairings) were used to develop new reinforcers or to strengthen weak ones. Modeling, prompts, and props (physically moving the child through the reinforceable behavior) served to actualize operants. In addition, the usual school reinforcers were supplemented by a token system with material and activity "backups," and extreme forms of disruptive behaviors resulted in a "timeout" contingency.

Assessment began before the child was enrolled and included observations in public school classrooms, interviews with public school teachers and with parents, a parent attitude survey, observation of a parent in a teaching task, and informal observations of the child during an orientation visit. Behavioral repertories of the children were analyzed as (a) inappropriate behaviors which should decrease; (b) appropriate behaviors which required strengthening; and (c) academic skills. Observations of the child's behavior were made during the entire period of his attendance, and follow-up observations were made in the school to which the child returned.

The home intervention program, as that portion of the project is known, was designed to help parents with the behavior problems of their children and involved fourteen families. The parents were interviewed about their child-rearing practices, were observed teaching their child a standard task, and were given the *Parent Attitude Survey* (40). The program began with parents visiting the classroom, participating in guided observations, and reading *Living with Children* (43). Then a succession of contacts (home visits and phone calls) was initiated to discuss principles of behavior modification. These ranged from several brief conversations during transportation to the school to a high of twenty-six home visits. The average number of home visits was eleven. In addition, there were numerous supportive phone calls to the mother. Although the details of each family contact differed, most of the parents needed help in observing behavior, withholding attention for undesired behaviors, and reinforcing desired behaviors. The conclusions regarding the home intervention program were that (a) the parents came to see in varying degrees that their children's behaviors were a function of their own behaviors, (b) the parents liked the methods, although some had reservations, and (c) success with a child in class was closely associated with success in the home intervention program.

Of the ten children referred from schools, all but two were reintegrated with good or fair success. One was retained by agreement in the laboratory classroom but entered the public school second grade in the following school year. With reference to grade placement, of the six children referred from schools, two were successfully integrated into public school first grades, one entered public school first grade in the following school year, and three entered special classes. One remediation was carried out in the public school instead of removing the child from his regular class. Of the children who were originally considered behavior problems, all but one showed marked improvement. The behaviors remediated were inattentiveness, refusal to participate, unintelligible speech, disruptiveness, excessive crying, aggression, noncooperation, lack of social skills with peers, lack of proper eating and toileting habits, defiance, thumb-sucking, poor hand-eye coordination, deficient motor skills, infantile and helpless behaviors, fearfulness, slowness, low rates of verbalization, inappropriate verbalization, persistent inappropriate attention-getting behaviors, and a lack of academic and preacademic skills.

University of Washington. In the Experimental Educational Unit at the University of Washington, Seattle, Washington, there are fourteen classes for retarded children between the ages of one and eighteen years, all referred by the local school districts and by pediatricians in the metropolitan area. On the basis of intensive case studies, the children are diagnosed as mentally retarded, brain-injured, or emotionally disturbed.

The view at Washington is that teaching effectiveness results from precision in measurement of the target behaviors, systematic manipulation of the instructional program, and the proper use of reinforcing contingencies. Consequently, the teachers are trained to (a) establish the entering behaviors of the child, (b) specify the behavioral objectives for him, (c) plan his instructional program, and (d) continually evaluate his responses to the program (25).

There are two classes for preschool age children. In one class, with six children, the program centers on the development of communication skills. A speech therapist and a preschool teacher, together with a consultant from speech pathology and audiology and one from the instructional materials center, prepare materials and procedures. The curriculum in the other preschool class, with eight children, consists of the usual preschool and preacademic activities in writing, language, and number skills.

In the single primary class, the curriculum is an integration of materials and techniques from speech therapy and special education. It consists of a reading readiness sequence leading into a reading series with emphasis on phonetics. Examples of materials are the *Sullivan Programmed Reading Series* (Buchanan) and the *Michigan Successive Discrimination Reading Program* (Smith). The mathematics program, comprised of many manipulative-type skills, uses speech techniques to overcome language difficulties encountered in teaching number concepts and in naming number skills. Materials include *Word Problems Programmed* (Armstrong, Porter, and Spitzler). The writing program is based on *Handwriting with Write and See* (Skinner and Krakower) and *Phonics with Write and See* (Bishop), and the spelling program is based on *BRL Spelling* (Buchanan).

With the aid of devices such as the language master, instruction is individualized or carried out in a near tutorial presentation within a group setting. "The teacher allows the child to function and progress at his own level and rate of development on each program presented without interfering with the progress of the total group's social behavior. Although there exists a wide range in skill development among the children in any one group, by using these techniques the social activities remain common to all, thus providing a naturalness in the setting and permitting common group and social behaviors" (26:51).

The progress of each child is charted on six-cycle graph paper. Base-line measures are taken, changes in the program are introduced, and changes in the child's progress are assessed. "Evaluating response data using procedures of experimental analysis accomplishes several purposes. First, it provides information on the type and amount of influence specific conditions have on specific behaviors. Second, it enables experimental control over extraneous learning conditions as well as over the independent variables being investigated" (25:18).

The Experimental Educational Unit is also devoted to research and professional training, utilizing technological devices for recording information on the learning environment and for analyzing the information obtained. "Such situations allow for a systematic investigation of the many facets of the classroom that in the past have been without definition or have not been within the realm of researchable ideas. These learning environment records form the basis for research designs which can be carried out with student trainees as an integral part of their collegiate program" (26:53).

Problems and Issues

The proper application of behavior modification to the teaching of the young, educable, retarded child, even in its present pristine state, may be seriously delayed because of misunderstandings about behavior theory, requirements for training teachers to use it, and the need for additional programs to maintain and extend the learning acquired in school. We shall discuss each of these problems.

MISUNDERSTANDINGS

Many school administrators and teachers have reservations about behavior modification for diametrically opposed reasons: (a) It is too superficial to be really effective, and (b) it is too effective and will lead to abuses.

Those who regard behavior modification as superficial identify it as a modern version of the old reward and punishment prescription for teaching, i.e., when a child is good, reward him; when he is bad, punish him. On this basis they claim that behavior modification cannot deal with such essentials of human existence as feelings, emotions, aspirations, and needs, and at best it can be helpful merely in teaching habits. It is understandable that one might take this position considering that learning theory was once expressed in mechanistic, plus-and-minus terms. However, a clear-cut distinction should be made between behavior modification and learning as the consequence of rewards and punishment. Recent advances in behavior theory and technology and the emergence of a philosophy of science which integrates psychology with the natural sciences (31, 32) make this distinction obvious. It should be apparent from our discussion in the first section of this chapter that behavior modification is the application of a large number of concepts and principles which make up an empirical system with built-in provisions for corrections, refinements, and extensions (7, 21, 45, 50, 52). Continued engineering research, inspired by findings from the laboratory and problems from the classroom, makes the approach potentially capable of dealing with all aspects of a child's behavior and personality.

The other reservation about behavior modification—that it is too effective and will lead to abuses—is certainly not a characteristic of the approach but refers rather to the possible behavior of teachers. The assumption is that if teachers are trained to teach effectively, they may be tempted to use their knowledge to their own advantage. They might, for example, find it convenient to keep children quiet and passive and thereby make teaching a totally effortless job. This is like saying that it is dangerous to teach medical students how to heal because they may use their therapeutic knowledge for personal gain rather than for curing the sick. Society recognizes that some professional people will misuse their specialized skills and it therefore attempts to prevent such abuse by programs of professional indoctrination and by imposing, through laws and codes of ethics, aversive contingencies for malpractice. In other words, the members of our society who are in a position to control others in prescribed or institutionalized ways are subject to conditions of countercontrol. To be cognizant of this safeguard and still to be wary of the effective teacher is to cast serious aspersions on the way in which teachers are selected, trained, and supervised. Finally, while effective teaching may expose teachers to charges of misuse and abuse, ineffective teaching may serve to protect them against such charges. No matter what they do, including assigning endless hours of busywork, they can claim that the practice is good for the personality and adjustment of their pupils. Who can say otherwise?

TRAINING TEACHERS AND AIDES

To apply behavior modification appropriately to the teaching of retarded children, it is essential to have well-trained teachers. Well-designed and carefully prepared programs, manuals, and procedural outlines are worthless in the hands of teachers not trained to use them; contrariwise, well-trained teachers can perform creditably even with poorly developed materials and guides.

Teacher training emerges as an issue because the training which student teachers currently receive differs sharply in many respects from the concepts and principles of behavior modification (see McDonald's chapter in this yearbook). Hence, there must be special training programs for teachers who want to learn behavior modification techniques and these programs must be more than the two- to five-day workshops or institutes now so prevalent. Even minimal training should include supervised practice in individualizing instruction, managing contingencies, monitoring learning, and modifying programs.

One is tempted to believe that if no provision is made for such specialized teacher training on a large scale, widespread application of behavior modification to teaching the retarded will take at least twenty years, the time it usually takes for any new technique to seep into the classroom through publication channels—from journal articles to textbooks to college courses and, finally, to supervised practice teaching. Other modes of dissemination are also possible and it is encouraging to learn that some are being tried. For example, the Council for Exceptional Children is launching a training program called the "Invisible College" (Jordan, 1971) which will provide school administrators and teachers with reading materials and cassettes prepared by educators who have applied behavior modification techniques in their work with all types of exceptional children. It will be interesting to see whether this approach will help to shorten the time gap between what we know and what we practice.

MAINTAINING AND EXTENDING BEHAVIOR ACQUIRED IN THE SPECIAL CLASSROOM

Maintaining and extending learning acquired in the special classroom is a problem created by specialization in our social and educational structure: teaching self-care and social behaviors in the home and teaching academic behaviors in the school; teaching normal children in regular classes and exceptional children in special classes. The problem of maintaining and extending learning acquired in the classroom looms up as a far more serious one than the problem of retardation itself. It is not unrealistic to assume that in the future a moderately retarded child in a behaviorally oriented special class will be able to make reasonable progress in his academic programs, considering that the classroom procedures are basically the same as those for changing any behavior: assess the child's entering repertories, provide him a program appropriate for his repertorial status, manage contingencies to produce and strengthen appropriate behaviors, monitor progress, and modify the conditions on the basis of the data collected. On the other hand, the problem of maintaining and extending the behavior a child acquires in the special class has not been faced because it demands changing conditions both in the home and in the classes to which he is subsequently assigned. The solution, although extensive in scope, is straightforward: establish school-adjunct programs to teach rudimentary behavioral techniques to parents and individualize instruction in elementary classes. The former has been explored on a small scale with preschool and primary-grade children at the Universities of Arizona, Kansas, and Illinois; the latter, in at least three community schools, e.g., in Orange County, California; Pittsburgh, Pennsylvania; and Urbana, Illinois.

Summary

Behavior modification has been applied to the teaching of the young retarded child for over ten years with gratifying results. Its principles and methodology are currently being extended and refined in research and demonstration centers throughout the country. The behavior modification approach is based on the application of the experimental analysis of behavior which focuses on the observable behavior of an individual in relation to the observable actions of the people, processes, and objects in his environment.

Those whose programs use behavior modification in the teaching of the retarded child conceptualize the retarded child not as one with symptoms of subnormal mental functioning, but as one with limited behavioral repertories resulting from inadequate biological equipment and/or restrictions and limitations in his biological and sociocultural environment. These programs, furthermore, view teaching not as communication, but as the arrangement of conditions to expedite learning. The concrete manifestations of these conceptions give the approach its distinctive features: individualization of instruction, programmed subject matter and learning sequences, explicit prompting techniques, contingency management, assessment of individual behavior repertories, monitoring methods of evaluating progress in academic and social learning, and systematic program modification. Basically, then, behavior modification is environmental modification.

The serious problems and issues that arise in applying behavior modification to the education of the young retarded child center on conditions that may delay its incorporation into school systems on a large scale. These include (a) misunderstanding the nature of behavior modification, (b) the strategy for training teachers and teachers' aides in behavior modification principles and techniques, and (c) the approach to establishing parent programs and modifying primary-grade curricula to enable the child to maintain and extend the skills and knowledge he has acquired in the behavior modification special class.

REFERENCES

1. Azrin, N.H., and Foxx, R. M. "A Rapid Method of Toilet Training the Institutionalized Retarded." *Journal of Applied Behavior Analysis* 4 (1971): 89-100.
2. Bensberg, G. J., ed. *Teaching the Mentally Retarded: A Handbook for Ward Personnel.* Atlanta, Ga.: Southern Regional Education Board, 1965.
3. Bensberg, G. J.; Caldwell, C. N.; and Cassel, R. "Teaching the Profoundly Retarded Self-Help Activities by Behavior Shaping Techniques." *American Journal of Mental Deficiency* 69 (1965): 674-79.
4. Bijou, S. W. "Functional Analysis of Retarded Development." In *International Review of Research in Mental Retardation,* edited by N. Ellis, I, pp. 1-19. New York: Academic Press, 1966.
5. ———. "The Mentally Retarded Child." *Psychology Today* 2 (1968): 47-51.
6. ———. *Application of Behavioral Principles to the Remedial Instruction of Retarded and Emotionally Disturbed Young Children.* Final Report, Project no. 23-2030, Grant no. OEG-0-9-232030-0762 (032). U.S. Department of Health, Education, and Welfare, Office of Education, Bureau of Education for the Handicapped, Washington, August 1971.
7. Bijou, S. W., and Baer, D. M. *Child Development: A Systematic and Empirical Theory.* Vol. I. New York: Appleton-Century-Crofts, 1961.
8. Bijou, S. W.; Birnbrauer, J. S.; Kidder, J. D.; and Tague, C. "Programmed Instruction As an Approach to Teaching of Reading, Writing and Arithmetic to Retarded Children." *Psychological Record* 16 (1966): 505-22.
9. Bijou, S. W., and Grimm, J. A. "The Education and Training of the Retarded Child." In *Amplifications of Reinforcement Principles in Education,* edited by W. C. Becker. Champaign, Ill.: Research Press, forthcoming.

10. Bijou, S. W., and Peterson, R. F. "The Psychological Assessment of Children: A Functional Analysis." In *Advances in Psychological Assessment*, vol. 2, edited by P. McReynolds, pp. 63-78. Palo Alto, Calif.: Science & Behavior Books, 1971.

11. Bijou, S. W.; Peterson, R. F.; Harris, F. R.; Allen, A. K.; and Johnston, M. S. "Methodology for Experimental Studies of Young Children in Natural Settings." *Psychological Record* 19 (1969): 177-210.

12. Birnbrauer, J. S.; Bijou, S. W.; Wolf, M. M.; and Kidder, J. D. "Programmed Instruction in the Classroom." In *Case Studies in Behavior Modification*, edited by L. P. Ullmann and L. Krasner, pp. 358-63. New York: Holt, Rinehart & Winston, 1965.

13. Birnbrauer, J. S.; Kidder, J. D.; and Tague, C. E. "Programming Reading from the Teachers' Point of View." *Programmed Instruction* 3 (1964): 1-2.

14. Birnbrauer, J. S., and Lawler, J. "Token Reinforcement for Learning." *Mental Retardation* 2 (1964): 275-79.

15. Birnbrauer, J. S.; Wolf, M. M.; Kidder, J. D.; and Tague, C. "Classroom Behavior of Retarded Pupils with Token Reinforcement." *Journal of Experimental Child Psychology* 2 (1965): 219-35.

16. Blackman, L. "The Dimensions of a Science of Special Education." *Mental Retardation* 5 (1967): 7-11.

17. Cameron, N., and Margaret, A. *Behavior Pathology*. Boston: Houghton Mifflin Co., 1951.

18. Connor, L. "The Heart of the Matter." *Exceptional Children* 34 (1968): 579.

19. Covert, C. *Mental Retardation: A Handbook for the Primary Physician*. Report of the American Medical Association Conference on Mental Retardation. Chicago: American Medical Asssociation, 1964.

20. Dunn, L. M. "Special Education for the Mildly Retarded—Is Much of It Justifiable?" *Exceptional Children* 35 (1968): 5-22.

21. Ferster, C. B., and Perrott, M. C. *Behavior Principles*. New York: Appleton-Century-Crofts, 1968.

22. Gardner, W. I. *Behavior Modification in Mental Retardation: The Education and Rehabilitation of the Mentally Retarded Adolescent and Adult*. Chicago: Aldine-Atherton, 1971.

23. Glaser, R. "Instructional Technology and the Measurement of Learning Outcomes: Some Questions." *American Psychologist* 18 (1963): 519-21.

24. Greene, F. M. "Programmed Instruction Techniques for the Mentally Retarded." In *International Review of Research in Mental Retardation*, edited by N. R. Ellis, II, pp. 210-39. New York: Academic Press, 1966.

25. Haring, N. G. "Behavior Modification and Special Education I: The Experimental Unit—University of Washington." *Fourth Annual Education Engineering Conference*. School of Education,

UCLA; Santa Monica Unified School District; University Extension, UCLA, 1968.

26. Haring, N. G., and Hayden, A. H. "Program and Facilities of the Experimental Unit of the University of Washington Mental Retardation and Child Development Center." In *Special Education Programs*, edited by M. V. Jones. Springfield, Ill.: Charles C Thomas, 1968.

27. Heber, R. "A Manual on Terminology and Classification in Mental Retardation." *American Journal of Mental Deficiency* (Monogr. Suppl.; 2d ed.), 1961.

28. Hewett, F. M.; Taylor, F. D.; Artuso, A. A.; and Stillwell, R. J. "The Engineered Classroom: Progress Report I." *Fourth Annual Education Engineering Conference*, School of Education, UCLA; Santa Monica Unified School District, University Extension, UCLA, 1968.

29. Johnson, G. O. "Special Education for the Mentally Handicapped— a Paradox." *Exceptional Children* 29 (1962): 62-69.

30. Jordan, J. B. "Dial G for Grapevine: A Conversation in Exceptional Child Research." In *Dimensions*, edited by J. B. Jordan and P. L. McDonald, pp. 5-17. Arlington, Va.: Council of Exceptional Children, 1971.

31. Kantor, J. R. *The Aim and Progress of Psychology and Other Sciences*. Chicago: Principia Press, 1971.

32. ———. *The Scientific Evolution of Psychology*, vol. 2. Chicago, Ill.: Principia Press, 1969.

33. Kirk, S. A. "Behavioral Research: What Is It—What It Can Mean." *Mental Retardation News* 20 (1971): 7.

34. Kunzelmann, H. P., ed. *Precision Teaching*. Seattle, Wash.: Special Child Publications, 1970.

35. LeBlanc, J., and Lent, J. R. *Progress Report: A Demonstration Program for Intensive Training of Institutionalized Mentally Retarded Girls*. Parsons State Hospital and Training Center, Parsons, Kansas, 1967.

36. Lent, J. R. "Minosa Cottage: Experiment in Hope." *Psychology Today* 2 (1968): 51-58.

37. Lilly, M. S. "Special Education: A Teapot in a Tempest." *Exceptional Children* 37 (1970): 43-48.

38. Lovaas, O. I.; Freitag, G.; Gold, V. J.; and Kassorla, I. C. "Recording Apparatus and Procedure for Observation of Behaviors of Children in Free Play Settings." *Journal of Experimental Psychology* 2 (1965): 108-20.

39. Mackay, H. A., and Sidman, M. "Instructing the Mentally Retarded in an Institutional Environment." In *Expanding Concepts in Mental Retardation*, edited by G. A. Jervis. Springfield, Ill.: Charles C Thomas, 1968.

40. Martin, M. *Attitude Change After Behavioral Training*. National

Laboratory on Early Childhood Education, Document no. 70706-A-00-U-12, 1969.

41. Martin, M.; Hoecker, P.; and Hildebrandt, J. "A Laboratory Classroom for Behavior Modification and Reintegration of Children Excluded from the First Grade." Unpublished manuscript, Arizona Center for Early Childhood Education, College of Education, University of Arizona, Tucson, Ariz., 1970.

42. Meyerson, L.; Kerr, N.; and Michael, J. L. "Behavior Modification in Rehabilitation." In *Child Development: Readings in Experimental Analysis*, edited by S. W. Bijou and D. M. Baer, pp. 214-39. New York: Appleton-Century-Crofts, 1967.

43. Patterson, G. R., and Gullion, M. E. *Living with Children*. Champaign, Ill.: Research Press, 1968.

44. Quay, H. C. "The Facets of Educational Exceptionality: A Conceptual Framework for Assessment, Grouping, and Instruction." *Exceptional Children* 35 (1968): 25-36.

45. Reynolds, G. S. *A Primer of Operant Conditioning*. Glenview, Ill.: Scott, Foresman & Co., 1968.

46. Sibley, S. A. "Behavior Modification with Disadvantaged Pupils." Paper presented at the American Educational Research Association Convention, Chicago, Ill., 1968.

47. Sidman, M. "Reading and Auditory-Visual Equivalence." *Journal of Speech and Hearing Research* 14 (1971): 5-13.

48. ———. *Tactics of Scientific Research*. New York: Basic Books, 1960.

49. Sidman, M., and Stoddard, L. T. "Programming Perception and Learning for Retarded Children." In *International Review of Research in Mental Retardation*, edited by N. Ellis, II, pp. 151-208. New York: Academic Press, 1966.

50. Skinner, B. F. *Contingencies of Reinforcement: A Theoretical Analysis*. New York; Appleton-Century-Crofts, 1969.

51. ———. "Operant Behavior." In *Operant Behavior: Areas of Research and Application*, edited by W. K. Hong. New York: Appleton-Century-Crofts, 1966.

52. ———. *Science and Human Behavior*. New York: Macmillan Co., 1953.

53. ———. *The Technology of Teaching*. New York: Appleton-Century-Crofts, 1968.

54. Spaulding, R. *A Social Learning Approach to the Education of Disadvantaged Children in Durham, North Carolina*. Education Improvement Program Publication, Duke University, Durham, N.C., 1967.

55. White River School District. *The Rainier School Behavior Program*, Rainier School, Buckley, Wash., 1970.

CHAPTER IX

Behavior Modification and Socially Deviant Youth

HAROLD L. COHEN

This chapter is concerned with the options available to a democratic society in maintaining law and order and especially in dealing with disruptive and delinquent youth. It attempts to define prevalent concepts of "normalcy" and "deviancy" and to account for the national youth dilemma that has given rise to our present, acute delinquency problems. It discusses the social institutions and conditions responsible for shaping behavior and explains why punitive measures have been ineffective as rehabilitation directives. It submits the proposition that options are prime requisites for a democratic way of life and offers examples of a remedial program conducted in a correctional institution and a delinquency prevention program presently operating in a public school.

What Is Deviant Behavior?

Newspapers bombard the public daily with reports of what society considers "deviant" behavior. "Deviancy" in these reports is generally interpreted as denoting a departure from "normal" legal, social, or moral standards. All societies have an unwritten code, and most of them also a written code, specifying what that society accepts as normal behavior. However, these specifications vary widely with a number of factors, including geographic location, ethnic origin, religious tradition, economic condition, and time.

DEFINITIONS OF NORMALCY AND DEVIANCY

"Normalcy" can be defined in statistical, moral, medical, legal, or conventional terms. The classification of any specific behavior

Preparation of this paper and much of the IBR research described herein was supported by Grant No. 5, RO1 MH14443 03-CD, 1968, from the Center for Studies of Crime and Delinquency, National Institute of Mental Health.

as "normal" or "deviant" depends upon the type of definition used.

Normal behavior in the statistical sense is defined in terms of the incidence of a particular type of behavior in the population— i.e., the central tendencies of the population distribution. Yet some behaviors sufficiently common to be accepted as "normal" from the *statistical* standpoint—e.g., smoking, excessive use of alcohol and other drugs—are considered abnormal or deviant from the *medical* standpoint, since they depart from a standard of healthful behavior. *Legal* standards of behavior differ markedly from time to time and from place to place. Dueling, once the only acceptable response to insult or injury among gentlemen, is now forbidden. Today, homosexual behavior between two consenting adults in the privacy of their own dwellings is legally permissible in some states—Illinois, for instance—but a criminal offense in other states. *Conventions* and *moral codes* are less rigid than the law, but even more pervasive in setting the standards by which a behavior is judged normal or deviant; in fact, laws are the formulations of moral codes and conventions into legally enforceable regulations. Thus, different laws, moral codes, and customs in different localities and times can change the *consequences* of the behavior without in any way altering the behavior itself.

Historically, the most widespread of legal and moral standards has been that forbidding the taking of human life. Every government has established laws against murder, yet there has scarcely ever been a time when war was not being waged somewhere in the world. A declaration of war is tantamount to a license to commit murder, with the government deciding whom it is legally and morally correct to kill as a matter of national defense or in fulfillment of its political and social objectives.

APPROPRIATENESS OF BEHAVIORS

As one examines these different kinds of environments and standards, it becomes apparent that no behavior of which a human being is capable is, in itself, normal or deviant, good or bad, sane or insane. It is simply *appropriate* or *inappropriate* to the environment and social milieu in which it occurs. Every group defines what it considers acceptable behavior. Every environment has "go" and "no go" signals indicating to the behaving individual whether his behavior is appropriate or inappropriate for that group (4).

The contingencies that the environment provides for certain kinds of behaviors stimulate and maintain those behaviors. We recognize this intuitively, if not intellectually. We question odd behavior—behavior not generally appropriate to the setting. If we cannot understand why an individual behaves as he does, what he gets out of it, we tend to label his behavior abnormal, deviant, or crazy. If we understand his motives but judge that his behavior conflicts with the interests of the group, we call the behavior criminal. Most behaviors are classified as socially acceptable or deviant on this basis. Yet, when someone pursues an acceptable goal—for instance, money and the success and material goods that money represents, through an unacceptable behavior, e.g., stealing—we seldom stop to examine the alternative behaviors society has made available to him for attaining this goal.

BEHAVIORAL PROBLEMS OF YOUTH

Today we are concerned with the escalating rate of crime in our society. According to the FBI *Uniform Crime Reports*, the crime rate per 100,000 rose by 35 percent in the period from 1960 to 1965 and by another 45 percent between 1965 and 1970 (7). We are dismayed by the evident failure of our criminal justice system to deal equitably and constructively with persons who commit crime. We are aware that approximately one million persons are incarcerated in our correctional institutions, including federal, state, and local prisons, jails, workhouses, reformatories and training schools, and other institutions for delinquents (2). We realize that only six cities in the country have populations larger than our incarcerated population. We learn that this huge prison population represents only about 2 percent of the reported criminal acts in the country. Moreover, studies of the prison population indicate that it consists largely of people who not only had the bad luck to be caught, but further compounded the felony by having previously had the bad luck to be poor, black, or young.

While the number of persons from the lower socioeconomic groups, the minority groups, and the inner city areas is disproportionately high, the most alarming aspect of today's crime statistics is the tremendous increase in crime among the young. Between 1960 and 1970, when the rate of violent crime per 100,000 increased by 66.9 percent in persons over eighteen, it leaped 166.8 percent in the under-eighteen group—nearly three times faster. Moreover, the growth rate in other types of serious crime was 113.7 percent for youths under eighteen, as compared to 16.9 percent for the adult population. And it must be realized that these figures are based on reported crime only. In 1971, youths under twenty-one committed 40 percent of all crimes of violence (homicide, aggravated assault, forcible rape, robbery) and 69 percent of the serious property crimes (burglary, larceny over fifty dollars, and auto theft). People in this age group were thus responsible for 63 percent of the serious crime in this country.[1]

Drug abuse—now a national issue—is also spreading more rapidly among young people than among their elders, and the rate is growing faster in suburban areas than in urban centers. The FBI reports that state and local arrests of persons under eighteen for drug offenses in the 1965-1970 period increased by 2,832 percent, as compared to 1,200 percent in urban localities (7). Of the active narcotic addicts recorded by the Bureau for Narcotics and Dangerous Drugs in 1965, 3.4 percent were under twenty-one years of age; by 1970 this percentage had grown to 11.6 (3). Of the eighteen-to twenty-five-year-old group questioned in a survey by the National Commission on Marihuana and Drug Abuse, 39 percent said they had used marihuana at one time or another, and 17 percent said they were using it currently. The percentage drops off rapidly in the over–twenty-five group (12). Alcohol, too, is a growing problem among young people. In a large study of fifteen- to twenty-year-old students, it was found that 43 percent of the girls and 57 percent of the boys drank alcoholic liquors (14).

National statistics on social problems such as crime and drug abuse are difficult to interpret, but all indicators point to sharp increases in the nation as a whole and a downward shift in the age level of the people involved. They also show that these undesirable behaviors are not concentrated in low income, poorly educated, inner-city urban, and minority groups; they pervade every sector of our society.

1. Information supplied by Dr. Rose Yaryan, Law Enforcement Assistance Administration, Washington, D.C., in a telephone interview.

What Social Institutions Shape Behavior?

The dominant shapers of behavior in our society are the family, the religious group, the school, the peer group, and the mass media. To understand what is happening to our youth today, we have to analyze what has happened to these institutions in the last half century.

THE FAMILY

The family sets the pattern of behavior for the child and establishes the mode with which he will seek to resolve his problems. But the twentieth-century family is a markedly different social institution from the family of earlier times. In the nineteenth century and the opening years of the twentieth century—roughly up to the time of World War I—the family was structured around the authoritarian figure of the father in a contained and restricted environment. Lack of transportation limited the child's opportunities for interpersonal and social transactions to his parents, siblings, close relatives, neighbors, and a select set of friends. All the people with whom the child had regular contact were likely to share much the same ethnic background, religious convictions, moral standards, and life values. The child grew up accepting these as absolute. In time, he matured, married, and founded a family of his own, sometimes remaining in the paternal home and usually remaining in the neighborhood in which he was born. World War I created the first serious fissure in this structure. It stimulated a technological development that was to have a revolutionary effect on transportation and communications.

The Second World War produced a fantastic explosion in the child's opportunities and options. No longer was he limited to home and neighborhood. Cars, planes, and other modern means of transportation afforded him greatly increased physical mobility, but they were as nothing compared to the expansion of his ability to move through space and time by means of television. For good or for ill, he was brought into contact with images and situations far removed from his family. The fantasy world of television has become a powerful part of his real environment. So has the documentary side of television. On the one hand, he witnesses in a single week of viewing westerns and mysteries more acts of violence than his parents saw in their entire lives preceding the advent of television. On the other hand, he is given exposure to the achievements of other cultures and often finds in them values lacking in his own. He is subjected to the crosscurrents of religious and racial developments. He no longer accepts the ways of his parents as the *only* right ways—or even the right ways at all.

The concept of permanence, of a closely hedged and family-directed social life, and of an absolute sense of values is no longer operative in most American families (9:268-70). Therefore, the kinds of social rules that were established under that concept have lost their influence on the child. Most children are inclined to set up their own approach to problem-solving. They don't use the family as a total model. Papa no longer necessarily knows best. Mom is no longer the indisputable moral arbiter. Today, the child wants to participate at the family round table as a codirector. He talks about creating his *own* life-style, changing the furniture in his *own* room, choosing his *own* friends, establishing himself as a person with rights equal to those of the adults. We now talk about teen-agers' rights and responsibilities. We talk about a world that has indeed shifted away from the pattern of single or dual authoritarian leadership. The helpless and submissive children of Charles Dickens's day are gone.

The alienation of children from their families and schools is reflected in the composition of the inmate population in our juvenile correctional institutions. More of these are "children in need of supervision" rather than children who have committed serious offenses. In 1970 the proportion of children institutionalized for such status offenses as running away from home and truancy was 54 percent, as compared to 31 percent for more serious offenses. Moreover, the disposition of the cases for children who commit status offenses is harsher than for those who commit serious crimes (15).[2] Again, however, the representation of the poor, the black, and the urban children in the incarcerated population is disproportionately high. While reliable data are not readily available, there is good reason to believe that the incidence of problem behaviors of the

2. Information confirmed by Dr. Rose Yaryan, Law Enforcement Assistance Administration.

"status offense" type is at least as prevalent among the affluent and middle-class children, who are able to avoid adjudication as delinquents, as among the disadvantaged. In one study of preventive delinquency programs for students of junior high school age in a middle-class community, now being conducted by the Institute for Behavioral Research, the findings at the end of the first eighteen months indicate that running away from home is the most frequent offense reported (11).

Many of the youth who run away from school and home are establishing communes where they make the rules. They are living together out of wedlock and thus creating (for America) a new concept of family. They are attempting to raise their children as a group rather than as separate families. We do not know yet whether this "Easy Rider" concept of living—the commune and the common-law family—will survive. But the break with the past is essentially an attack against the authoritarian social institution, whether this is the family or the government.

Indeed, the government is in a sense the larger family and is experiencing the same kind of revolt as the biological family. A reversal in roles has taken place. Instead of regarding the government as the source, judge, and enforcer of legality and morality, many young people are attempting to bring the government to trial at the bar of morality. Slogans such as "My country, may she always be right, but, right or wrong, my country!" and "Westward the tide of empire rolls" have lost their appeal. National self-interest is not regarded by many as a consideration that overrides their repugnance for human slaughter. They question such time-honored American institutions as the university, the church, and the corporation. They regard the police as instruments of oppression rather than as protectors. They are skeptical when their parents are outraged if they are caught shoplifting, since they remember that these same parents not only cheat on their income tax, but boast about their cleverness in doing so. They reject the values of the society which the family and the government have created. The antiestablishment movement is in a larger sense an antifamily movement.

THE RELIGIOUS GROUP

Formerly a strong shaping influence, the religious group has been losing most of its effectiveness for many of the same reasons that have weakened the hold of the family on young people. The decline of religious isolationism has had many diverse effects. On the one hand, it has destroyed a formerly powerful deterrent to forbidden behaviors—the belief that the infallible consequence of such behaviors will be divine retribution. On the other hand, it has created a ferment of questioning that is altering the very nature of church institutions. Ministers of all religious denominations are attacking their churches for nonrelevancy. Clerical participation in civil disobedience demonstrations is becoming commonplace. Church institutions whose basic doctrines have been accepted for hundreds of years are undergoing change (10).

Young people are asking: Does God exist or is man his own shaper and controller? The existentialists contend that man shapes himself and that the contemporary environment is a condition of his own making. Man, not God, is responsible for war, racial hatred, and economic deprivation; to change the world condition, he must change himself.

Another contemporary religious phenomenon is a movement toward familiarization with God. God is my brother, he's "Jesus Christ Superstar." An attempt is being made to bring God down to the experiential level of youth and the young adult world. The goal is to feel and experience a God who is familiar to young people, a God of their own making, who is worshipped with their own music and art, and in their popular gathering places, a God in the vernacular, rather than one of church spires and formal prayer.

THE SCHOOL

At present, of the traditional social institutions the public school has the greatest potential for shaping and maintaining acceptable behavior patterns in youth. But the schools have been far from exempt from the influences that have changed other institutions and are themselves channels for these influences. Bussing, the mobility of the American family, the existence of a large, transitory school population of the children of servicemen and diplomatic personnel —these and a host of other factors have made the school experience of today's youth far different from that of their parents. Modern schools have lost their parochiality. They present children with opportunities for a wide diversity of social relationships and expose them to an unprecedentedly wide range of ideas and values.[3]

Within the educational system, however, too much emphasis has been placed on specific, traditional kinds of subject matter and too little on the effect of teaching methods and on the behavioral results of the methods. When serious "disruptive behavior" occurs, the school often abrogates its responsibilities, turning the problem over to the medical profession and the social agencies (the police and eventually the courts). When the twentieth-century family lost most of its power as a social institution, the school became the major program for socialization. If wisely used, it can be a potent instrument for conveying the attitudes and shaping the behaviors that will enable children to live satisfying lives as law-abiding, productive citizens of a viable democratic society. But the school must change to adapt itself to its new, all-important task.

It must be recognized that the classroom is only one of the places where the behavior of the school children is being shaped. The major environmental arena consists of the hallways, lounges and cafeterias, and the parks and shopping centers in the proximity of the school. This is where the interpersonal, the hidden, curriculum is being shaped and maintained by the students themselves. Despite this, the public school still maintains its old curriculum, divided into artificial hourly or forty-minute periods of subject matter. To combat the kinds of codes of behavior being established by the students, it sets up its own internal police. But the threat implicit in the presence of the police and other school authorities is proving far less potent in shaping behavior than the pressures brought upon the children by their contemporaries.

THE PEER GROUP

The practice of grouping children in school by chronological age has greatly strengthened the power of the peer group at the expense of the influence of tradition and authority. The home is no longer the primary gathering place for young people; they seek their companionship, entertainment, and life-style in the shopping plaza. And this is an environment that they have in a very real sense designed for themselves. With generous allowances and opportuni-

3. Testimony before the Equal Educational Opportunity Committee, Senator Walter Mondale (D-Minn.), Chairman (1970-72).

ties for remunerative work, youth now has something it never had before to the same degree—purchasing power (8:16-19). It has used this purchasing power to change the culture. Because commercial institutions cater to them as customers, the young people have created new clothing styles, music styles, styles of speech, styles of behavior, and styles of environmental design. All of these are now visibly affecting the adult world. The young people are preempting areas of activity that used to belong to their elders. In their world, the Beatles, the Rolling Stones, and a barrage of youthful entertainers set the fashions—the long hair, the miniskirt, the peace beads, the poncho, the food, the music—the whole way of life. The shopping center is the place where all this is concentrated. It is the place where one promenades, where one is on exhibit. When school is out, the hamburger "joints" are jumping. Everything that is happening is at the mall, at the shopping centers, at the business centers. Is it any wonder, then, that the peer system is more potent than the parental or governmental structure?

How Do We Deter Antisocial Acts?

What are we to do about all this? It is one thing to understand some of the conditions that are responsible for the youth culture and its antisocial aspects, but we cannot abdicate our responsibility for maintaining an orderly society. Why are our traditional instruments of social control failing us now?

Fundamental to the Judeo-Christian ethic and to Roman and English law are the concepts of the responsibility of each individual for his acts and the protection of the rights of individuals and minorities. Traditionally, the law has required that behavior contrary to these concepts must be punished. The concept of punishment as a means of shaping behavior to desirable ends is not, however, peculiarly Judaic or Christian, Roman or English; it is universal. It is the concept that is operative in our educational and legal systems today. We have elected the punishment option in dealing with individuals who deviate from what society establishes as the norm.

One reason for the prevalence of punitive systems is that punishment results in the immediate, if temporary, suppression of the undesired behavior, thus reinforcing the punisher. But another reason is the frustration of society with other means of reshaping deviant behavior, which have largely lacked the immediate benefits of punishment and have been equally ineffective in the long run. Thus, while the punishments inflicted on the guilty have become less savage with the passage of time—we no longer cut off the hands of thieves or stone adulteresses—the punitive approach remains, combined with another concept—that of reform. Our practice is to imprison those who commit antisocial acts, to remove them from society until they learn their lesson. Our purpose is to reshape the deviant one so that his behavior is attuned to the pattern of the law-abiding majority. The sinner is expected to become a penitent, effectually concurring in his punishment. The trouble with this approach is that it has failed. The present rate of delinquency, violence, and recidivism is proof enough of this failure (2).

What Is the Behavioral Approach?

"SLOT-MACHINE" REINFORCEMENT

Behavioral research has cast some light on the reasons for the failure of the punitive approach. Punishment, we have learned, is most effective in suppressing an undesired behavior when it is inflicted every time the behavior occurs. Otherwise, it produces "avoidance" or "escape" behavior. The individual who has been punished attempts thereafter to avoid the presence of the police or other enforcing authorities, or at least to refrain from exhibiting the punishable behavior in their presence. But his needs and wants are strong; he is poor, and if the forbidden behavior is the only, or the most attractive, option he has, he will continue to resort to it as the opportunity offers. And each time that the behavior remains undetected or is not punished, it is being reinforced.

Much inappropriate behavior—and much appropriate behavior, too—is maintained by this "slot-machine" type of reinforcement schedule. Las Vegas is thronged by people who understand full well that, over the long run and over the mass of gamblers, the house always wins. Yet they lose their money cheerfully because of the possibility that, for an individual, a lucky number or card will mean a big windfall. Similarly, the thief is maintained in his behavior by a variable schedule of rewards. One theft may net him one or two dollars, several may net him nothing at all, the next may result in his apprehension, but there is always the possibility that on the next try he will hit the jackpot.

One of the most difficult tasks we face is that of eliminating antisocial and criminal behavior that has been reinforced by such a variable success schedule, particularly if the successes have occurred under a variety of environmental conditions, thus creating a larger stimulus support system. The power of this kind of supporting contingency is manifest in the continuation of our democratic, free enterprise society. Such a society is dependent on the scattered availability of an eventual jackpot for a variety of subject areas and a variety of citizens. The fulfillment of a variable reinforcement schedule for America's millions of immigrants—the successful performance payoff for effort expended—has been one of the greatest sources of this country's strength. But when such a schedule reinforces an antisocial behavior, it is hard to combat. To change an antisocial behavior once it has been shaped, society must make available to the offending individual alternative responses that can successfully earn him a similar or larger payoff, or teach him behaviors that are competitive and incompatible on an equally powerful schedule of reinforcement.

One of the disadvantages of punishment as a control technique is that it can effectually suppress many other behaviors besides the one it is intended to suppress. A student expelled from school for disruptive behavior loses his opportunity to learn to behave more acceptably. A youthful delinquent who is confined to a correctional institution seldom learns any skills that will enable him to function more acceptably in his community. An adult offender who is confined to prison does not support himself or his family, educate his children, or participate in community activities.

The majority of Americans do not steal or commit other crimes to gain their reinforcements. The present aversive control system—the religious and moral codes with their delayed payoffs; the police, law, and courts with their delayed payoffs—has been able to direct most of them to seek safer means of getting their rewards. But these people do have other repertoires of skills and behavior that enable them to gain success with a payoff commensurate with that of crime and with less risk. Since most youthful offenders sentenced to correctional institutions do not have a variety of rational options available to them (such as employable skills with a reasonably high payoff), they resort to the one choice that they are equipped to use—unlawful behaviors.

If we are to minimize the antisocial behaviors of our poor delinquent youths, we need to teach them competitive skills which, in our society, produce desirable payoffs: money, self-respect, prestige, security, and so forth. If we are to minimize the antisocial behavior of the middle-class youths, we need to teach them a variety of interpersonal skills. If the payoffs for new, socially acceptable behaviors are programmed properly, these behaviors will gain in strength and the incompatible, deviant behaviors will diminish. Programs on a national scale to achieve these ends are becoming more necessary than ever as the advance of technology eliminates the unskilled jobs that once provided many uneducated people with at least a minimal livelihood, and as national developments plunge even highly educated, specialized people into unemployment on a massive scale.

A LEARNING ENVIRONMENT IN A PENAL INSTITUTION

Some beginnings have been made; I have participated in several of them. For instance, for two years I directed a project that the Institute for Behavioral Research conducted at the National Training School for Boys (NTSB), a correctional institution for youthful offenders located in Washington, D.C. (5). The project involved forty-one incarcerated teen-age delinquents whose crimes ranged from auto theft and housebreaking to rape and homicide. Eighty-five percent of them had dropped out of public school, and most of them were equally unresponsive to the educational program within the federal penal system at NTSB. The CASE (Contingencies Applicable to Special Education) Project was designed to positively expand the academic and social repertoires of these adolescents through the use of operantly formulated contingency systems and the design of a special environment. The goal was to prepare as many students as possible for return to the public school system within one operational year.

To attain this goal, we converted an old cottage on the Training School grounds into a twenty-four-hour learning environment, established new systems of operations, and set up an economy based on academic achievement and special schedules of reinforcement.

The students were hired to work for the CASE "corporation"; their product was intellectual wealth in general and academic achievement in particular. They worked on programmed courses and regular texts, and attended programmed classes and lecture classes. When they performed on tests at the 90 percent level or better, they were paid off in points that could be exchanged for material goods, services, and special privileges.

Programmed instruction was used extensively in order to tailor the academic programs to the widely varied needs of the individual students. Upon entering the project, the student inmate was given a battery of tests designed to assess his standing in various school subjects—his present repertoire. Actually, the purpose of the tests was to aid in the selection of the materials that would be appropriate for him. (A student, for instance, might score at the high school level in mathematics and the third-grade level in reading. His programs in each subject or skill would be determined by his achievement in that subject, not by some average "class level.") Upon consultation with his adviser, the student would be assigned programs. If he had the necessary prerequisites for a class, he would pay his entrance fees, using points advanced to him as working capital or earned by taking tests or completing programs.

Note that the classes were not free; as in the outside world, it was necessary to pay tuition for education as an investment. In this and other respects, the project environment was designed to make available to the student inmates the choices and perquisites normally available to average wage-earning Americans but usually denied to youths in a prison.

Because of prison conditions of admission, parole, etc., only thirty-six of the forty-one student participants were present in the project for ninety days or more. The assessment of general student progress in the academic curriculum was based on the records of these thirty-six students. Table 1 shows the academic achievement levels of students in various curriculum areas at the times of their entry and exit from the program. It can be seen that the proportion of students achieving at the lower half of the traditional twelve grades of school at the time of entry shifted in the direction of successful achievement with curricular materials suited to the upper half of the twelve grades. In English, for example, all of the students were functioning approximately within the range of the elementary school grades at the time of their entry. By the time of their departure from the project, 59 percent of them were functioning at an eighth- to twelfth-grade level. The average mean growth rate of the CASE students was twice the average for American public school students, with individual growth rates ranging as high as four times the national average.

TABLE 1

ACADEMIC ACHIEVEMENT LEVELS OF CASE STUDENTS IN VARIOUS
CURRICULUM AREAS AT TIMES OF ENTRY AND EXIT

Curriculum Area	Entrance Placement In Curriculum Level				Terminal Achievement In Curriculum Level			
	F # %	S # %	JR. # %	SR. # %	F # %	S # %	JR. # %	SR. # %
Reading	8 – 26	13 – 37	14 – 37	1 – 0	1 – 6	10 – 28	14 – 40	11 – 26
English	35 – 97	1 – 3	0 – 0	0 – 0	3 – 8	12 – 33	9 – 26	12 – 33
Science	8 – 18	28 – 82	0 – 0	0 – 0	5 – 9	10 – 29	16 – 44	5 – 18
Mathematics	26 – 75	10 – 25	0 – 0	0 – 0	5 – 17	3 – 8	19 – 50	9 – 25
Social Studies	12 – 33	24 – 67	0 – 0	0 – 0	2 – 6	13 – 36	7 – 19	14 – 39

F = Freshman = grades 1–4   JR = Juniors = grades 8–10.5
S = Sophomores = grades 5–7   SR = Seniors = grades 10.6–12

More importantly, we were able to effect attitudinal changes that improved the preparation of these young people for life in a competitive, industrialized society. An essential for success in such a society is the ability to make wise choices among the available options. In penal systems the inmates are told what to do and when and how to do it. They are never given an opportunity to make decisions for themselves. The student inmates who participated in the CASE program made their own decisions on a number of matters. They could choose to work at their studies or not to work. If they chose not to work, no punishment was inflicted, but their living conditions then remained the same as those of the other juveniles in the training school; that is, they wore the NTSB uniform, ate whatever meal was served in the NTSB mess hall, showered in the communal shower rooms, and slept in dormitories. If they chose to work—and all of them did, most of the time— they had considerable latitude in spending their earned points for the amenities of life. They could purchase recreational time in a lounge equipped with a pool table, games, and candy and soft-drink dispensing machines; they could buy paperback books, magazines, clothing, and most types of merchandise available through mail-order houses. They could exchange points for a private shower, an extremely small but nevertheless private room for sleeping and entertaining their friends, or meals with a choice of menu served in a restaurant-type setting. According to a set schedule, they were permitted to purchase time away from the institution to enable them to shop, sight-see, or visit with their families. It was gratifying to see that the CASE students, after a brief initial period, consistently selected rewards that contributed to their dignity—privacy, meals in pleasant surroundings, and gifts for relatives and friends.

Purchasing power, an essential ingredient in any society, can be a powerful agent of change. The CASE students were from poor and uneducated families. Poverty and ignorance produce a tight subculture within which the means to economic change are limited. Lack of the educational skills necessary to participate in the mainstream of American life had forced these young people—white and black alike—to "self-ghetto" themselves in small communities on the periphery of the larger society. But they responded dramatically to the CASE program. Not only was their academic progress impressive, but their improvement in interpersonal behavior (though not in this project measured objectively) was commended by the staff of NTSB and other observers. Even though, because of the institutional conditions, none of them was in the program for the full two years of the project (the range was from three to eighteen months), their recidivist rate during the first year after their release was two-thirds less than the norm for the NTSB. By the end of the third year, their recidivism rate approached the norm (5).

The CASE program evidently delayed the delinquent's return to incarceration, but most of the young offenders returned to home and community situations where the new behaviors were not reinforced. As adjudicated delinquents, young men who had spent time in a correctional institution, they would have even fewer employment opportunities than other youths with similar social and educational backgrounds—the ones who did not get caught and stigmatized. Nevertheless, the CASE project demonstrated what could be achieved with specific learning procedures, environmental controls, and appropriate consequences for performance. It has influenced the nation's juvenile correction system. The new Kennedy Youth Center in West Virginia, which replaces the old National Training School, has retained much of the CASE academic program. Other youth centers whose personnel attended a CASE Training Institute in 1967 have also instituted contingency management programs.

My experience with troubled young people, both in and out of institutions, has convinced me that most of the youths who exhibit "deviant" behaviors are neither evil nor sick (i.e., in need of psychiatric care). Neither do they reject the values and material goals of middle-class society; they are eager to share them. (By middle-class values and goals, I do not mean status symbols like minks, yachts, or country-club memberships, but, rather, decent housing, the comforts associated with the American standard of living, and upward social mobility.) These young people are simply incompetent to obtain their share of the good things of life through socially acceptable means.

The CASE Project demonstrated the effectiveness of contingency management in a controlled penal environment. I am opposed, however, to the whole concept of institutionalization for young delinquents. It is my conviction that it is undesirable to remove a juvenile, for rehabilitative purposes, from the community in which he lives. He needs help in adjusting his behavior to this environment, not to that of a correctional institution. I believe that all rehabilitative programs for juveniles should be carried out in the community, where situations requiring decisions and appropriate behavior abound. Only in the "real world" of the community can young people be given guidance and practice in making sound decisions and establishing viable relationships with other people.

I am not alone in this belief. Several projects are currently being conducted in attempts to institute such attenuative programs. The Achievement Place model developed in Kansas is an example (13). Achievement Places are residential treatment facilities for delinquent or dependent, neglected youths who are (or are about to be) suspended from school, or are in trouble in the community, and who are considered "uncontrollable" by their parents. Six to eight such boys or girls live in family style in a home environment under the supervision of a pair of "teaching parents." The teaching parents are professionally trained in behavior modification procedures, remedial education techniques, juvenile law, and community relations. The program and the treatment are community based. Each youth's problems are dealt with in his community, his school, his home, and his peer group. A token reinforcement system is used to help maintain discipline without reducing the quality of social interaction and instruction which is necessary if the child is to achieve stable and normal behavioral adjustment. The point system is also employed to strengthen and increase the frequency of desirable behaviors.

The State of California has been experimenting extensively with work-release programs for older offenders (1) and with community-based programs for juveniles (16). I believe that a major reason for the good results obtained with these programs is that inmates, upon release, have established roles and noncriminal associates in their communities.

Even more strongly, I believe that the ideal arena for prevention or modification of deviant behaviors is the school. The public school is a made-to-order vehicle for preventive programs that will equip young people to solve their problems and attain their reasonable personal goals within the legal and social framework established by our society. I do not underestimate the difficulty of the task of providing this kind of academic and interpersonal education to young people. But I believe it can be done—must be done. We must stop investing money in prisons for youth and begin investing our funds and energy to establish preventive systems within our schools and community centers. As a nation, we can scarcely afford to support, simultaneously, a high rate of crime and a large population of incarcerated, unproductive convicts. We *can* afford to develop effective academic and interpersonal programs within the nation's public schools.

A LEARNING MODEL FOR PUBLIC SCHOOLS

For the past three years, the Institute for Behavioral Research has been engaged in developing a public school learning model called PICA (Programming Interpersonal Curricula for Adolescents) (6). The general purpose of the PICA project is to develop remedial procedures for adolescents with scholastic problems which are part of a larger pattern of problem behaviors that may presage a future of delinquency. The model was developed with delinquent and predelinquent ("problem") students who were referred to the Institute's laboratories by their school jurisdictions. The number of participating students was small—about a dozen each year—but the curricula and other materials, the methods and procedures were designed for extension to whole school systems as a preventive delinquency measure. Note that PICA is an *educational* model, designed to be administered by teachers, not a therapeutic model for the use of clinical psychologists or other therapists.

Contingency management is a key to the PICA model, as it was to the CASE project. Students are rewarded for academic achievement in two basic subjects, language and mathematics, and for appropriate behaviors in the school, the home, and the community. The academic program is tailored to each student's individual needs through the use of programmed instructional materials. The behavior management procedures clearly define for the students what behaviors are considered appropriate and inappropriate.

The heart of the PICA project is its Interpersonal Skills Program, dealing with subjects, issues, and behavior-shaping activities in areas of importance to teen-agers. This program consists of 180 class lessons, organized into seven courses. These include a course in law—Teen-Agers' Rights and Responsibilities (TARR)—designed to provide students with information and skills relevant to preventing or avoiding a wide range of problems and to responding to community responsibilities. Preventing the Abuse of Drugs (PAD) is an informational program designed to prevent or deter teen-age use of harmful drug agents. Still other courses deal with sex education, operant behavior, problem-solving in the family, the contemporary scene, and "how to's"—skills required in both academic and everyday life. Two more courses, one in verbal behavior and the other in vocational education, are under development.

The interpersonal skills courses help the students develop self-discipline and self-control and aid them in setting up procedures for adapting their own behavior so that it is acceptable to their peers, parents, teachers, and other people in the community, while providing satisfaction to themselves.

The results from the 1970-71 school year—the last in which the PICA project was conducted in the laboratory school setting before moving into the public schools—are presented below. In assessing these results, it must be remembered that the PICA students who aided in the laboratory development of the program were young people whom the schools had designated as extremely disruptive, unmanageable, predelinquent, and on the verge of either dropping out, being expelled, or being sentenced by the juvenile court.

The standard grade-score increase for a student during a ten-month school year is considered to be 1.0 on a nationwide basis. Figure 1 compares the average grade-score increase of the PICA

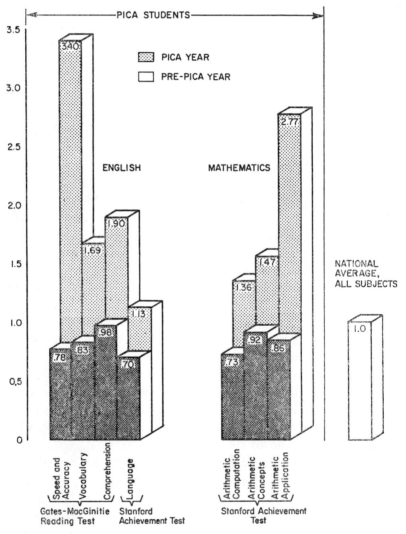

FIG. 1.   Comparison of student grade level increases; PICA year and pre-PICA years

students during the PICA year with their growth the preceding year and with the national average. The improvement over the preceding year was dramatic, and in all cases they exceeded the national average.

Of the standard academic subjects, only two—language and mathematics—were taken as part of the PICA program; the students attended their regular classes for other subjects. Figure 2, based

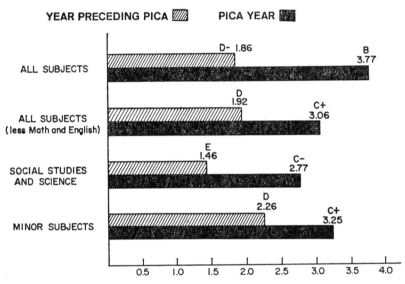

Fig. 2. Comparison of student school grades: PICA year and year preceding PICA

on a numerical evaluation of the letter-grades A through E, shows clearly that PICA students increased their school grades significantly over the previous year, from a D-minus level to a B level. The total grade figures are partially biased in that they incorporate the PICA English and mathematics grades as well as the grades for subjects taught only at the schools. However, the three following classifications do not contain the PICA grades in English and mathematics:

	Mean Grade	
	Pre-PICA	During PICA
Total grades (less math and English)	1.92 (D)	3.06 (C+)
Social studies and science	1.46 (E)	2.77 (C—)
Minors (art, music, phys. ed.)	2.26 (D)	3.25 (C+)

While these grade increases cannot be ascribed directly to a particular PICA function, it is reasonable to assume that PICA's academic and interpersonal skills program contributed to the change. Further, considering the relationship that exists between a student's academic grade and his social behavior in the classroom, it may be inferred that PICA students presented fewer discipline problems than formerly. This was the unanimous opinion of the regular school teachers of PICA students, and it was corroborated by the students' daily behavioral ratings.

At the beginning of the current school year (1971-72), the PICA project was transferred from the Institute for Behavioral Research laboratories to a public junior high school in Silver Spring, Maryland, where it is operating with thirty teen-agers designated as "problem students" by their teachers. Although the program has been in operation there for only a few months, the students are responding in much the same way as did those with whom the laboratory development work was done, i.e., with better attendance, improved academic performance, and more appropriate behavior. The school is now making plans to convert a larger proportion of the student body to the PICA program.

NEXT: THE COMMUNITY AND THE CITY

The next step is to carry the concept into the community and we have already begun. BPLAY (Behavioral Programs in Learning Activities for Youth) is a project designed to provide after-school programs for teen-agers. The objective is to reduce teen-agers' opportunities and inclination for delinquent behavior. The method is to attract them to a learning environment and educational programs during their nonschool hours by providing rewards for their attendance and performance. For the simple reason that one cannot be in two places at the same time—cannot be shoplifting while taking a course in auto mechanics—these leisure-time activities should reduce the incidence of delinquent acts in the target population. But the BPLAY programs are designed to do more than this. They are intended to increase the youngsters' repertoires of skills that bring social and material rewards and provide personal satisfaction. The project is being conducted in an inner-city neighborhood comprising a population of a quarter of a million, including approximately 22,000 young people of junior or senior high school age.

An industrialized democracy places high demands for skills on its citizens—and not only for skills, but for overall competence. They must have a repertoire of behaviors that allow them to adapt to the changing requirements of changing times.

PICA and BPLAY are examples of ways to bring contingency management and educational technology into the public schools and the community. We are looking forward to the time when the principles these projects employ—environmental design and behavior modification through contingency management—will be incorporated not only in the schools but in all those facets of work and leisure that make up the design and management of our cities.

REFERENCES

1. Bagdikian, Ben H. "An Agenda for Reform of a Hell Behind Walls." *Washington Post*, February 6, 1972.
2. ———. "A Human Wasteland in the Name of Justice." *Washington Post*, January 30, 1972.
3. Bureau for Narcotics and Dangerous Drugs. *Active Narcotic Addicts Records*. Washington, 1971.
4. Cohen, H. L. "Behavioral Architecture." *Architectural Association Journal*, London, June 1964.
5. Cohen, H. L., and Filipczak, J. A. *A New Learning Environment*. San Francisco: Jossey-Bass, 1971.
6. Cohen, H. L.; Filipczak, J. A.; Slavin, J.; and Boren, J. *Programming Interpersonal Curricula for Adolescents (PICA)—Project Year Three: A Laboratory Model*. Silver Spring, Md.: Institute for Behavioral Research, October 1971.
7. Federal Bureau of Investigation. *Uniform Crime Reports: Crime in the United States*, Washington, August 31, 1971.
8. "Forty-Four Million Young Adults—A New Wave of Buyers." *U.S. News and World Report*, January 11, 1972.
9. Fuller, R. Buckminster. *Utopia or Oblivion: The Prospects for Humanity*. New York: Bantam Books, 1969.
10. Gray, Francine du Plessix. *Divine Disobedience*. New York: Alfred A. Knopf, 1970.
11. Institute for Behavioral Research. *Behavioral Programs in Learning Activities for Youth* (BPLAY). Silver Spring, Md., forthcoming.
12. National Commission on Marihuana and Drug Abuse, Washington, Newspaper release, January 21, 1972.

13. Phillips, E. L. "Achievement Place: Token Reinforcement Procedures in a Home Style Rehabilitation Setting for 'Pre-Delinquent' Boys." *Journal of Applied Behavior Analysis* 1 (1968): 213-23.
14. Rutgers Center for Alcohol Studies. *Selected Statistics on Consumption of Alcohol and Alcoholism.* Rutgers, New York, 1970.
15. Velie, Lester. "The Child Trappers." *Readers Digest,* Pleasantville, N.Y., February 1972.
16. Warren, Marguerite Q. *Project Summary: Center for Training in Differential Treatment.* NIMH, Public Health Service, U.S. Department of Health, Education, and Welfare, 1971.

See also the informal references in notes 1, 2, and 3.

BEHAVIORAL SYSTEMS

CHAPTER X

Behavior Systems

STEVEN M. ZIFFERBLATT

One of the more significant advances in education in the past ten years has been the incorporation of "systems approaches" in management and instructional contexts (6). A systems approach makes possible the development of an empirically based process model directed at representing and controlling the complex inter-relationships of the teacher-student instructional environment. Empirical models are not new in education but they have typically been employed in a piecemeal additive fashion rather than from a perspective of dealing with the total environment.

A need for precision, relevance, and accountability in education for both learning and social behavior has been expressed by communities within education as well as without (60). Systems approaches have already been successful in dealing with total environments in fiscal, personnel, and administrative contexts in education (6). The DEPS (Data-based Educational Planning Systems) characterizes current attempts to incorporate program-planning–budgeting systems into educational programs. "In short," writes Banghart, "DEPS is a planning system designed particularly for educational problem-solving. It can be used to

Set educational priorities
Measure program performance
Relate educational outcomes to budgetary inputs
Translate objectives into costs
Analyze and update programs and costs on a continual basis
Provide a data base for future planning
Compare various instructional processes in terms of both outcomes and costs

This chapter is dedicated to Clay Gerken, a man of warmth, flexibility, and vision.

Match ongoing school activities with school board and community goals
Make school costs more visible
Improve information flow
Increase community and staff involvement
Promote accountability . . ." (6).

Needless to say, the social and learning environment in a given school is no less complex and demands precise, integrative, and empirically based procedures. The tools and techniques of systems approaches, already successful with time, numerical, and fiscal referents, can be invaluable in dealing with learning and social events, especially if employed with *behavioral referents*. Nonbehavioral systems approaches are currently dealing with learning and social variables vis-a-vis instructional systems technology (5, 38). However, these systems usually emphasize inferential relationships to actual learning behavior, e.g., written performance, attitude change, normative tests, and *possibly* actual learning and social behavior. The distinguishing characteristic between conventional instructional systems approaches and a "behavior system" is that the latter focuses solely on the actual student behavior and its contingency arrangements. These differences will be discussed more explicitly in another part of this chapter.

Thus, while there has been a great deal of systems-oriented behavior on the part of educators, very little of this activity has actually attended to the most important product of any educational program: actual student learning and social behavior. Education abounds with systems innovations such as "cost-effectiveness, accountability, modular scheduling, individualized curricula, instructional technology" (11). It is asserted here that while these new techniques are important to students, the means-end relationship must be kept more carefully in perspective, i.e., what are the effects of such "contingency arrangements" on student behavior? The appropriate objective of all educational programs concerns student behavior. Too often we may well have engineered an exquisite bathtub environment without examining its effects on the baby!

Why have we failed to concentrate our efforts and enthusiasm in developing a systems approach aimed directly at student behavior? There are some historical and knowledge biases concerning how we understand behavior and value it as a legitimate referent of professional activity. Our efforts have carried us under and over, in front of, and behind behavior via the use of constructs and operational definitions. Rarely, however, have we focused directly on behavior. The characteristics of a systems approach require a great deal of precision in specifying program operations and in using empirically derived data. Recent developments in behavior modification, i.e., the applied analysis of behavior, suggest that observable operant behavior and its contingency arrangements have attributes that might enhance the use of a systems approach (27).

What Is a System?

The term *system* encompasses a multitude of sins (and euphemisms), e.g., we are products of the system, our taxation system needs overhauling, and we have excellent photographic and stereo systems. We even have a system for poker, horse racing, and bingo, and our upset stomach tells us that something is wrong with our system. Recently a new shaving system was advertised. We are bombarded with conceptual jargon referring to our biological, economic, political, psychological, and social systems. Yet, underlying all these systems references is a common dimension of expressing interrelations, that of looking at the whole by observing how all components function together. A system is a structural or conceptual entity which helps us comprehend that an entity functions or operates as a whole by virtue of the interdependence of its parts (16, 51). A systems approach helps us to examine how all these parts work together or might work together to accomplish a specific mission or set of objectives.

KNOWLEDGE UNDERPINNINGS OF SYSTEMS APPROACHES

At this time there are four distinct discipline areas which contribute conceptually and methodologically to systems approaches:

General systems theory (GST). GST originated from an analysis of the existence of an interrelatedness of various biological processes in the human body. From this analysis an attempt was made to generalize this quality and its component processes to more complex events such as groups of people, cultures, organizations (8). A number of descriptive studies of hospitals, governments, and business have emerged attempting to isolate lawfulness and uniformity in interrelationships (4, 7, 15, 25). Examples of some of the principles of GST that have attempted to explain this "lawfulness" within complex social entities are nucleation, adaptation, differentiation, centralization, equilibrium, and open and closed systems (8).

At this point, GST has made little progress toward empirical and scientific confirmation of GST principles (29). The language and principles of GST are so abstract and general that their scientific manipulation and thus their practical relevance in understanding and controlling educational systems are of limited value. Nevertheless, the deliberate emphasis on understanding structure and function in any entity as a product of interaction and interdependent components does provide an overall useful premise for understanding behavioral systems.

Cybernetics. The term *cybernetics* (meaning steersman or governor) was employed by Norbert Weiner (69) to identify the main characteristic of any systems approach—control. Weiner advocated control of a system through the use of information via feedback and feedforward loops (69). When all the components of a given complex entity are working towards accomplishing an objective, the internal communication and control devices have organized into a system. The terms *information, communication, control, feedback*, and *feedforward* in their operational sense are also fundamental to behavior systems.

Engineering and business systems. Weiner's cybernetic concepts were derived within mathematical and philosophical contexts and set the stage for the technological development of complex control mechanisms in engineering science. A variety of complex electronic instrumentation, as well as all of computer technology, is largely predicated on the technological consequences of the thought of Weiner and a few others (54).

Many advances in management information and control in business and industry have been made through the extrapolation or logical extension of cybernetic concepts. Among these are flow charts, PERT and GANTT charts, CPM, cost benefit analysis, simulation techniques, and operations research strategies. Many of the systems approaches developed in business and industrial contexts have been employed effectively in education for the same kinds of problems (6:2). A number of these systems procedures are important to systems dealing solely with behavior.

Psychosocial systems. The popular notion of man as an ongoing adaptive organism in a continually changing environment set a challenge for behavioral scientists that was eventually "conquered" by systems extrapolations. There is a plethora of psychosocial theories which purport to study man's psychological state (system) as a function or product of a variety of interrelationships. Recall the homeostatic notions of Freud and his component and balance constructs (id-ego-superego, eros-thanatos, defense mechanisms, countertransference) predicated upon a physical and biological notion of homeostasis. Lewin's Field Theory is essentially systems-based, the "field" being defined as the totality of coexisting facts which are conceived of as mutually interdependent (41:240). Kurt Goldstein's Organismic Theory emphasizes the "organism as an organized system" and depicts various psychological states as a function unity—integration, consistency, and coherence of intra-psychic and physical elements (30:298). It is apparent that a great deal of the dynamic and substantive aspects of personality theory is predicated on concepts originally derived in physical and biological systems.

GENERAL CHARACTERISTICS OF SYSTEMS APPROACHES

While systems concepts appear to have developed separately in a variety of contexts (basic science, philosophy, social science, business, and technology), there are a certain number of common attributes.

Specification of objectives or mission orientation. All systems approaches are mission- or objective-oriented. A mission is initially specified and then the system boundaries are defined to comprise all components that must be interrelated to accomplish a mission. A system is usually a functional, rather than structural, entity (16). For example, different system components would be delineated within the public "school system" if the mission of the system is to improve personnel cost effectiveness, rather than achieving a given learning level in math.

A systems approach thus requires (a) the specification of objectives and (b) the examination of all events related to achieving these objectives. The importance of specifying precise, measurable objectives has been repeatedly stressed by systems approach proponents (16, 44, 52, 63). Loughary commented: "without carefully defined objectives, the use of a systems approach is likely to be educational nonsense" (44:733). The systems approach, like the computer, is a way of thinking (16) and is only as useful as the validity of the data introduced to its processes. Designing precise and measurable objectives is one of the most critical steps of the systems approach.

The use of models. Another task of a systems approach is to represent through models all the components and their functions that are related to the mission of the system. Ryan (52) identifies this characteristic of systems approaches as analysis and synthesis. All components and functions are detailed and a process model is developed which will achieve the mission. Well-developed systems models are usually mathematically or electronically based. Graphic models involving descriptions and flows of activities related to the mission are also employed. The flow-chart model is typically employed in education. Figure 1 presents a flow-chart model. This type of model describes activities, graphically depicts their interrelationships, and suggests the most effective flow of activity to achieve the objectives.

Procedural control towards objectives. Since the objectives of a system are usually the consequence of many complex interactions, when possible it is desirable to design intermediate checkpoints to see how the product is progressing. Waiting until the product is finished might involve untimely and costly mistakes. Decisions are made at these checkpoints as to whether progress is satisfactory. An information path is designed to either feedback the product if it does not meet criteria, or feedforward the product if it meets criteria. Naturally, if a product is feedback, another decision has to be made involving possible system modification. This continuing and redundant process of decision-making and feedback–feedforward is called system "control" and is perhaps the most critical aspect of the systems approach. This might be termed a "fail-safe mechanism" (72).

Maximization of product-process relationships A necessary collateral of internal system control is identification of a more optimal procedure for accomplishing the mission. This is especially important in systems where products take a long time to produce and are costly. Very often a mission has been accomplished or the objectives already met. The next problem is efficiency-effectiveness ratios. Maximization strategies are usually employed in industrial contexts (67), yet their relevance to education (learning) might be extremely important (e.g., successful problem solutions using less staff, less time, and more self-instructional material). Maximization and control define the internal attributes of systems approaches. The notion of alternative strategies is implicit in maximization.

Continual monitoring and ongoing revision (adaptation). A systems approach gives adaptive capabilities to programs. Adaptation is obviously critical to any organismic attributes projected on a system. A system is only as good as its responsiveness to current and future needs. New information and priorities are always developing in education and it is important to insure responsiveness and modification. Adaptivity in education is often incorporated into an ongoing system by a continual needs assessment procedure (38). Ongoing evaluation of the relevance of the systems mission is thus an integral step in the systems approach.

Explicit design, development and procedural phases. Before a system has anything to process it must be sure it has gathered the relevant data, components, and personnel. Also, after the system has assembled all of the above prerequisites, it must be organized into several explicit procedural phases in order to get the job done. There is a variety of ways in which the entire systems procedure is characterized. Banathy (5) and Gagné (27) have designed representative strategies for instructional systems which are more specific and more germane to applying a systems approach to learning and social behavior in education. Gagné's strategy developed a systems procedure paradigm in a military training context (27). His emphasis upon man-machine components previously limited his paradigm's application in public instruction when the inclusion of the term *machine* in education was aversive to educators. *Today it is perhaps the most distinguishing characteristic of his systems paradigm.* A general procedure paradigm for systems is depicted and is comprised of inclusions by Corrigan (20), Gagné (27), and Banathy (5) and represents the "systematic process of the systems process" (figure 1).

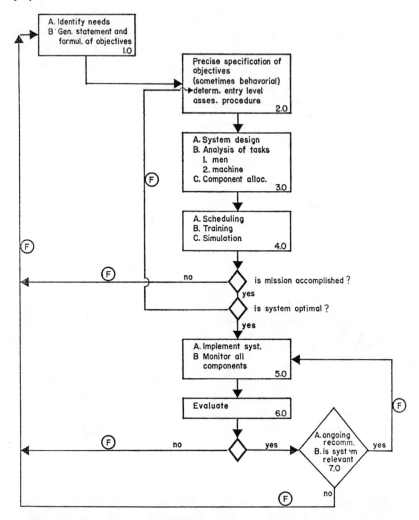

Fig. 1. A general paradigm of systems procedures. Adapted from Banathy (5), Corrigan (20), and Gagné (27).

Modular versatility. Many learners of varied capabilities and histories undertake learning experiences in a large-scale educational system. It is important that a learning experience or an educational program be maximally utilized by each individual if the program is to be maximally effective. Systems approaches in education attempt to control for this variability by designing small independent, yet interdependent, instructional units (modules). In this way each learner might enter the instructional system at *his* appropriate level and progress at his appropriate rate. The contrasts in capabilities between linear and branching program paradigms represent an appropriate analogue (45). The systems approach corresponds more closely with the paradigm of branching programs. Modal structures obviously increase the capabilities of systems by providing versatility to the system.

Thus, there are seven characteristics which are general to systems approaches: (a) specification of objectives, (b) the use of models to represent structure and function, (c) procedural control, (d) maximization strategies, (e) adaptation, (f) explicit process phases, (g) modular versatility.

Current systems approaches incorporate degrees of these characteristics in numbers and completeness rather than all characteristics in an absolute sense.

A Behavioral Systems Approach and Instructional Systems

We have seen that systems approaches in education have been most successful and popular in empirical contexts, i.e., where precise data, objectives, and operations can be employed. Most of these "successes," with the exception of instructional systems, have been related to events other than the student learning and social behavior of students, since such referents as time, money, materials, and computer operations have precise data attributes. Instructional systems have indirectly dealt with student learning and social behavior by erecting inferential bridges to behavior with curriculum manipulations, achievement tests, and higher-order constructs such as intelligence and aptitudes. In contrast, a behavior system deals directly with student behavior per se, rather than its relationship to tests or "measurable constructs." All objectives in a behavior system, whether intermediate or terminal, have attributes similar to that specified for operant behavior (see 34).

In a behavior system all operations, such as curriculum arrangements, media, teacher behavior, physical environment arrangements, motivation, and time, are defined as contingency arrangements in the sense of a three-term contingency (57), i.e., the antecedents, behaviors, and consequences. The contingency arrangements are defined solely in terms of their functional relationship to behavioral objectives of each student. How does a behavior system differ from its nearest relative, the instructional system, and what advantages does it offer? It differs in several ways:

1. Nearly all instructional system designers advocate the employment of behavioral objectives in specifying the mission of the system (5, 20, 38, 46, 52). A number of vocational guidance instructional systems also incorporate specification of mission in behavioral objective terms (14, 36, 19). However, the context in which a behavioral objective is designed may be quite different. For instance, an instructional system specifies the curricula and media for a set of objectives, e.g., reading. This is quite different from a behavior system where a particular reading behavior is defined as a three-term contingency (antecedents-behavior-consequences). The latter implies an *observed functional relationship* using a base-line, observation and manipulation procedure within an operant framework rather than an arbitrary assignment of "what should be" antecedents and consequences of behavior. Thus, the types of decision made about curricula, media, etc., or contingency arrangements may be quite different. The operational and functional contingencies of a behavior objective in an instructional system are not as tightly related to the behavior as they are in a behavior system.

2. In instructional systems the term *behavioral objective* is quite often developed within a logical positivist or operationalism context. This is in contrast to the actual referent quality of a behavior objective in a behavior system. For example, in an instructional system a well-developed practice is to treat a cognitive-based construct behaviorally through its operational definition, e.g., learning, self-concept, attitude, via various tests. In behavior systems the behavior is the sole referent and object of measurement. See Skinner (56) for further discussion of this point.

Actually, many instructional systems rely heavily upon test batteries which validly and reliably measure achievement and learning for a variety of objectives (figure 2). Often these tests are only inferentially related to actual behavior via some notion of validity—construct, concurrent, empirical, and so forth (21).

Thus validity-related tests are often used to measure student behavior *in lieu of* the actual student behavior. It is important to note the current differences and implications of instructional and

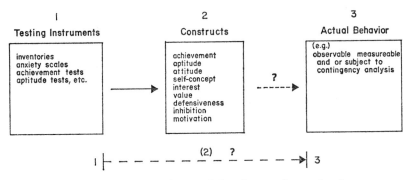

Fig. 2. Inferential bridges characteristic of most instructional systems

behavior systems. A behavior system is predicated upon the simple notion that if one is designing an environment for the acquisition, discrimination, and maintenance of certain behavior, one should monitor the actual behavior as a dependent variable, subject to a variety of contingency arrangements (independent variable).

3. There is a plethora of verbal behavior among educators and systems advocates concerning the meaningfulness, relevancy, and motivational aspects of education. There is, however, very little that most educators can provide in the way of systematic insurance (short-term or life) that behavioral objectives are functionally and operationally related to these concepts. Behavior systems, in employing a three-term contingency definition, use empirical operations on all behavior to make positive consequences available for behavior and to enable others to be selected if modification is called for. Thus, a behavior system "cares enough to do the very best" in very explicit ways for its students.

BEHAVIOR SYSTEMS: A NEW DIRECTION

The attributes of behavior systems include those of both systems procedures and the applied analysis of behavior.

In recent years the applied analysis of behavior (behavior modification) has provided empirical, systematic, and generalizable techniques for describing and controlling behavior-environment relationships in education (71). Operant behavior offers an almost unique example of how, at an empirical and predictable level, a unit behavior enters into a variety of orderly relationships with its environment. The stage is set for the expansion of behavioral strategies, coupled with systems procedures, into a larger, more complex context involving many behaviors, levels of behaviors, and settings (61).

Operant analysis of behavior: a systems analogue. In a previous section some of the fundamental characteristics of a systems approach were delineated. A number of these are an integral methodological component of the operant analysis of behavior (34). Some of these operant characteristics are as follows:

1.   Specification of objectives: Precision and specificity of the unit of behavior is a necessary prerequisite of the operant analysis of behavior. An analysis of a topographical description of a behavior and the conditions under which the behavior is emitted represents the basic operant.

2. Procedural control: Systems approaches employ feedback and feedforward paths to control progress towards objectives. The operant analytical procedure is comparable to control. The use of base-line and continuous observation procedures makes possible the monitoring of progress towards goals. When an independent variable is introduced, the effect on the dependent variable is immediately observable. The investigator is then able to make decisions concerning the recycling of the behavior and the possible introduction of another independent variable. This is the essence of the operant analytical procedure: the continuing cycle of observation—base line, treatment, base line. If treatment has the desired effects, the analytical procedure feeds forward to ongoing monitoring procedures. If the treatment does not have the desired effect, the entire analytical strategy feeds back until the desired effect is attained. For a more complete discussion of operant analysis and n=1 methodologies see Browning and Stover (13).

3. Explicit process phases: One characteristic of a systems approach (treatment) is the explication of operations in all phases of system design, development, implementation, and analysis. Operant treatment procedures (phases) and the conditions under which a specific phase is implemented are equally as explicit. For example, the methodology of behavior diagnosis and treatment (10, 37) involves detailed specific procedures. Figure 3 illustrates these phases.

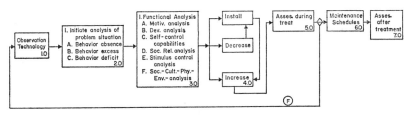

Fɪɢ. 3. Procedural flow chart for behavioral analysis, diagnosis, and treatment

There are a number of methodological compatibilities between operant and systems procedures. The capabilities of each approach diverge at this point. Operant analysis can provide a precise method of inquiry concerning the relationship of a number of responses to its environment. It is molecular or atomistic in a sense. Current attempts to extend this method of inquiry to many and concomitant classes of behavior and to many and concomitant environments requires additional knowledge concerning (a) the interrelationships of behaviors and environments and (b) an empirical methodology for controlling these relationships. A systems approach supplies such a conceptual and methodological superstructure. The coupling of these two knowledge systems produces a method of inquiry that has both rigor and comprehensibility. With the use of behavior systems we can analyze total environments and generate capabilities that extend far beyond the range of single classrooms and curricula. The empirical and scientific inclusion of home, recreational, vocational, medical, and social contexts into the educational process may provide the total and relevant educational experience that we are striving for today. There are a number of behavior systems in operation currently that are exploring these possibilities.

In summary, while the behavior of students has been analyzed with success by application of principles of behavior on an individual basis, there is every reason why further avenues should be explored applying the same principles to many students across a variety of settings. A number of successful explorations into complex contexts have already been launched.

Current behavior systems in education. Behavior systems in education and special education range from the "minisystem" of programmed instruction to complex macrosystems encompassing an entire school (45). Conceptually and methodologically, programmed instruction can be viewed as a minisystem. Recall the basic systems attributes mentioned earlier. In a micro sense, many of these principles are embraced in the programmed instruction paradigm (57).

Differential entry levels and progress rates are accounted for in branching types of programs (57). A great deal of programmed instruction is based upon cognitive referents with observable written responses. Yet, if a cognitive referent is defined as private behavior rather than as indicative of a mentalistic structure and analyzed with respect to its contingency arrangements, the behavior is then under the scrutiny of an operant analysis strategy (23). Programmed instruction viewed in this sense is a behavior system.

The applications of programmed instruction in education are far too numerous to mention here. A major source of information on systems applications in programmed instruction is Ofiesh and Meirhenry (49).

In recent years several investigators (2, 10, 28) have extended the laboratory analysis of behavior to actual human situations. This work is characterized by a degree of experimental control and objective measurement uncommon to the traditional study of human behavior (26). What seems to be emerging in a laboratory context is increasingly greater ability to extend the control of laboratory situations to human environments. It is conceptually quite possible to investigate a person's entire behavioral repertoire, the "metastasis" of contingencies and contingency arrangements (behavior system) in a laboratory context. This is in contrast to programmed instruction, which usually attends with precision to one behavior class at a time. An approximation of this was recently initiated by Findley (26). He set up a complete laboratory-based behavior system (all contingencies and contingency arrangements) for a single subject and studied the response attributes of the individual in an operant manner.

(1) The environment was designed to be as comfortable and livable as possible, approximating ordinary household furnishings, in contrast to furnishings of a space chamber or medical laboratory. (2) The subject was not given elaborate instructions, nor asked to perform in a given manner, nor even asked to remain within the chamber for a given period. Instead he was introduced to an environment which placed de-

mands and required certain behaviors, however crude, for the obtaining of life's necessities and other conditions for as long as he remained. (3) The specific program provided some degree of flexibility for the subject by way of options and some opportunities for altering the environment by means of the introduction of new materials and the like. . . . (p. 113)

Findley studied the management of the total environment through the operant analysis of a variety of responses such as work tasks, activity groups, cigarette usage, music activity, and cleaning activities. Findley's comprehensive analysis did reveal a number of contingent relationships which are akin to the interrelationships of behaviors in a system. In addition, Findley suggested the possibility of extending such analytic procedures to two or more individuals in larger "laboratory" settings. Such control over environments offers a desirable analogue for the future study of behavior in a system.

Token economy systems. The most prevalent use of behavior systems is through what is termed the *token economy system.* (See chapter 11.) In contrast to Findley's work, the token system may be viewed as an "applied laboratory" (2) Token economy systems, in contrast to programmed instruction and programmed environments, attempt to analyze and control the many behaviors of many individuals in a given environmetal context(s). It should be noted that loosely structured and noncontingent educational programs exist under the guise of token economy systems.

Token systems are comprehensive in that they profess to engineer the current, more natural contingency arrangements to a greater degree than programmed or laboratory-based environments. The functional relationship between the teacher, the learning environment, and student behavior is continually engineered so as to better insure the acquisition and maintenance of desirable student behavior. A great deal of emphasis is placed upon insuring adequate reinforcement in the form of a generalized reinforcer and upon its access for behavior.

Token economy systems vary considerably on six basic dimensions:

1. The number of topographies programmed (e.g., does the system program reading behavior, arithmetic behavior, task attention, social behavior, etc.?)

2. The levels of the topographies programmed (e.g., does the system engineer or shape increasingly complex topographies for a given behavior?)

3. The interrelationships of topographies (e.g., does the system arrange for the occurrence of topographies concomitantly, or design one topography as a contingency arrangement for another?). An example of this would be programming reading and mathematic problems concomitantly, or designing an environment where criteria performance in reading is a prerequisite for access to a social contingency program.

4. The programming of topographies in several different settings (e.g., what types of mathematical contingencies are programmed in the classroom, home, library, in recreational, vocational, or economic contexts?)

5. The programming of staff as maintenance agents (e.g., does the program analyze staff behavior in a similar manner?)

6. The shaping of maintenance schedules (e.g., does the program shape the reinforcement schedule for students in reference to either fixed or variable, ratio or interval, or token or more appropriate reinforcement modalities?)

The "systemness" of token or similar behavior systems can be evaluated with reference to these six dimensions. Single response programming, by itself, contains many systems attributes. However, many of the response gains made in single programming efforts might be lost due to failure to acknowledge these gains in other related contexts.

It is important to remember that human behavior does occur in the context of a social-environmental system regardless of systematic programming. While control of the program is a worthwhile goal, a systems approach's most important feature is that it lends itself to the control of complexity. The most important asset of a behavior system is that it can approach the complex, rich, and broad human experience with conceptual and methodological rigor. Very few current behavior systems encompass all these six dimensions. Some merely design separate contingency arrangements around a number of unrelated behaviors (2, 3a, 31, 32, 68). Others not only specify contingency arrangements for a number of topographies but specify levels of the contingency in an increasingly complex direction (13, 48, 53, 58, 66). Lindsley (43), who has devoted much effort to data collection and technological training, extends his particular notions about contingency arrangements beyond the classroom to resource personnel, teachers, parents, administrators, and his own colleagues. This extension insures that classroom programs "work" to a greater degree.

Another breed of behavior systems is developing through the work of Harold Cohen and his colleagues (17). The system installed by Cohen and his colleagues embraces virtually every aspect of the student's environment. All academic, personal, social, and recreational events are embedded within contingency arrangements. Moreover, each of these behaviors is related to the others in the sense that criteria in one are a requisite for activity in others. The student has the opportunity for self-selected contingencies and contingency arrangements. Students' progress through many levels of each behavior and each contingency becomes more complex. Staff behavior is functionally related to student contingencies. Novel or creative responses, visiting privileges, and an increasing skill in the area of self-control are designed as open-ended contingencies. One of the most novel aspects of the program is Cohen's systematic inclusion of architecture and the physical environment as part of many contingency arrangements.

Other equally novel extensions of behavior systems are being conducted. Behavior systems are now being extended to a community rather than institutional base. Achievement Place (see chapter 9) is investigating the effects of a behavior system in a home and community context with predelinquent boys. The residential community base provides house parents, reinforcers and contingencies are usually available in the home, and programmed contingency arrangements are extended to the school and community at large (47, 50).

Counselor behavior systems. Recent developments in counselor training have extended the behavior systems approach to professional education (39, 59, 72). In a recent paper Thoresen (61) outlined the essential operations of a systems approach to counselor training and the counseling process (figures 4 and 5). Thoresen indicated that the powerful tools of behavior modification and a systems approach raised a number of issues and controversies concerning (a) precise specification of objectives and methodology (b) relevance of traditional courses and practicums and (c) the use of instrumentation for both data collection and counseling. He concluded that "the synthesizing of social learning rationales for counseling with a systems approach to training holds exciting promise for creating powerful ways of helping individuals deal effectively with their problems" (61:22).

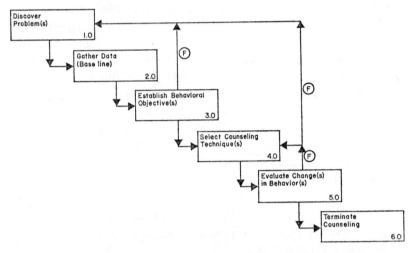

Fig. 4. Flow chart of behavioral counseling events (Thoresen, 61)

A similar though more detailed behavior system for the behavioral counseling process is under development at Michigan State University. In both cases the training system for counselors is functionally linked to the specific behaviors required for competencies in counseling. In addition, the training and counseling systems are designed by the same guiding behavioral and systems principles and are singular in the "practice what we preach" sense. Designing a training system for counselors with the same principles that the counseling system employs has obvious advantages for trainees.

In summary, behavior systems are increasing in scope and are being developed in an increasing number of contexts. There is a great variance in their degrees of systemness, but all are predicated upon an operant methodology.

BEHAVIOR SYSTEMS: TOWARD A COMPREHENSIVE MODEL

Behavior systems are at a crossroad in their development. As they increase in scope, size, cost, and complexity, there will be

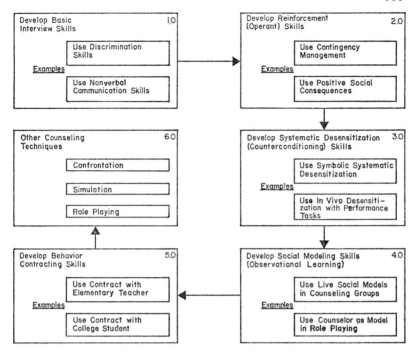

FIG. 5. Flow chart of specific counselor skills (Thoresen, 61)

a need to develop models to insure systemness and contingency arrangements. There are several models available to insure the attributes of a system (38, 52) and behavioral attributes (34:chap. 1). Efforts to develop a comprehensive model synthesizing behavioral and systems approaches might prove extremely useful to educators in view of the new and unique tasks of design analysis.

A behavioral system model should: (a) have the capability of representing all interrelationships between different contingencies (e.g., reading, math, social behavior), (b) specify all interrelated context or setting contingencies (home, library, classroom, etc.), (c) specify all operations (contingency arrangements) required to generate and maintain behavior (e.g., time, media, teacher behavior, cost), and (d) describe the progress of flow of activities in conducting the program. Thus, the model must take into consideration all learning objectives, all settings, all operations, and all progress towards the goal(s) of the program. While the precise content of such a model is yet to be developed, its general parameters are fairly simplistic and are immediately available to us.

Analysis and evaluation. The analysis and evaluation strategies of a behavior system might be somewhat different than and less amenable to current evaluation strategies in education due to size, cost, and duration of a program. Current evaluation and analysis models in education are largely derived from laboratory- or statistically based methodologies in the social sciences. While their effectiveness in deriving solutions in experimental or laboratory-based settings is widely acknowledged, the types of decisions and analysis that might be of concern to systems educators in applied settings might not lend themselves well to traditional methodologies. Evaluation or analysis in education is typically terminal in nature, i.e., the program (independent variable) is successful or unsuccessful. These questions are usually answered by statistically based decisions at predetermined levels of significance. In many instances analysis is performed by separate teams and is a post hoc operation. Sometimes evaluation is anecdotal and in other instances evaluation teams use or design separate measures or tests, which are linked conceptually to a program. It is a well-accepted procedure to contract the "dirty business" of evaluation to separate "objective" firms which specialize in such activities. Rarely is analysis and evaluation integrated in an ongoing manner into the design and operation of a program. Evaluation modes in education characterized by the above are extremely costly in terms of student losses, time, and money. Over and above this, such methodologies may not be revelant to a behavior system which, although complex, has immediately observable ongoing data available. It is quite possible that the "costly baby can be thrown out with the costly bath" in using traditional methodologies. Rarely, for instance, is an entire system incompetent—merely parts of it. The internal dynamics of a behavior systems approach eliminate terminal decisions and instead uses ongoing and continual feedback types of decisions.

There are alternative strategies for analysis and evaluation available in technological fields. The term *analysis and evaluation* as employed in technology encompasses a more in-depth approach to evaluation. It is an integral and ongoing part of a technological program. An analysis model attempts to represent all relevant variables in a program in relation to a prespecified mission or criteria.

Technological models of analysis are usually directed toward system control in the cybernetic sense. The goal of analysis or ongoing evaluation is maximization of efficiency-effectiveness ratios. In education, analysis is usually concerned with the level of a product achieved by a given process. Questions seem to center more on the variable outcomes of various processes, rather than precise specification of mission and the variables required to achieve it. Thus, in technology the dependent variable or mission to be accomplished is held steady, while in education the dependent variable is encouraged to vary in order to make decisions about several independent variables. For example, in educational evaluation the question asked as to the mean difference between groups of learners on a standardized test is in relative terms. Is the difference significantly different? In technological evaluation the question often asked is what proportion of units meet the predetermined criterion level? (See Thoresen [62] for a discussion of predetermined vs. relative criteria in counseling research.)

The difference in emphasis seems to relate to the applied base of analysis of technology as opposed to the statistical-analysis base of education. Both strategies have strong merits in different situations. The important question seems to be whether educators are aware that alternatives exist and of the appropriate occasions to employ them.

In technological analysis, specific system control rather than causal attribution (experimental-statistical context) is the priority. It is essential that an analysis model fully represent all variables of the system. This complexity is deliberately included. Accomplishment of the mission rather than "why is it working?" is of prime importance. Technology is more concerned with how a specific combination of numbers and levels of personnel, types of machines, and systems priorities can be made more efficient and effective. These analytic goals seem quite appropriate to human behavior in education (21).

Another important difference between technological and educational analytic models concerns the concept of variability. In conventional educational approaches using comparative group methodologies, the goal of causality depends largely on attempts to control for all relevant experimental or quasi-experimental conditions. Variability is usually "controlled" since it is considered somewhat irrelevant to the experimental question, or it is controlled statistically in an attempt to produce "generalizable" data. A technological model is more concerned in representing with maximum fidelity (27) whatever sources of variability operate. Interestingly, the n = 1 experimental methodology also looks carefully at variability, treating it as valuable data rather than as "error variance" or a nuisance to be minimized. In actual operations, the sources of variability cannot be easily controlled or ignored and will be present in actual conditions.

As has already been stated, accomplishment of mission in the most efficient and effective manner rather than "why is it working?" is of prime importance. Education typically employs research and evaluation models based upon theoretical validation and causal attribution. It might be more useful, however, to maximize what a given system can do with its idiosyncratic curricula, personnel, and students rather than to formulate generalizations or causal statements. The important goal in behavior systems is to accomplish the mission in the best way possible. Behavior systems evaluation attends to the following concerns: (a) mission specification in a way that it can be analyzed, (b) mission accomplishment, (c) efficiency-effectiveness ratios (contingency arrangements), (d) differential effectiveness with given populations. In other words, what is happening in the *specific* program, how can this be explicitly represented (interrelationships), and how can operations be continually refined while holding the mission constant?

Thus there are a number of tactical and methodological differences between evaluation and analysis priorities for behavior systems and those currently employed in education. These differences might be accounted for simply on the basis of applied systems priorities in contrast to experimental and attribution priorities. Educational programs as well as behavior systems are at a stage of importance where full knowledge of the systems priorities and the consequences of certain evaluation strategies is of critical importance. Our educational programs are at a point where the consequences of ill-applied and perhaps rudimentary evaluation and analysis strategies are very costly to individuals and to society.

We cannot afford to bask in the sunshine of tradition and imprecision. There are conceptual and certainly methodological alternatives available to us if we (a) choose to change our way of thinking about relationships between events and (b) look to other, "newer" disciplines for guidance.

An Analogue for Analysis

OPERATIONS RESEARCH

There are a number of conceptual and methodological models presently available that might guide model development for a behavior system. Operations research, or management science, is a very successful systems-based model for analyzing complex systems in technology (1). A scientific method is employed in analyzing the actual operations of a specific setting with emphasis upon the solution of problems relating to flow inventories and cost-benefit analysis (65). Operations research (OR) strategies emphasize the need for a system-wide view of evaluation. OR takes the systems view by developing a model and simulating process to represent the entire system and its interrelationships in relation to a prespecified mission. The mission of the model is usually to represent optimal solutions (1). The analytical strategy in OR involves seven steps (67):

1. Formulating the problem (mission)
2. Constructing a model to represent system variables possibly related to the problem or affected by it
3. Deriving an optimal solution
4. Deriving alternative solutions
5. Maximizing a solution
6. Implementing and maintaining a solution
7. Ongoing recycling of steps 1-6

Most important, the OR paradigm is system specific and usually does not attempt to generalize across systems. Idiosyncracy among systems is readily recognized and the analysis model is usually applied to one program at a time. Such an overall analytical strategy seems responsive to the needs of a behavior system.

An operations research strategy can provide an excellent strategy for the design and analysis of any or all aspects of a system, i.e., the superstructure of the system. The operant analysis of behavior provides a precise base for the analysis of all contingencies and contingency arrangements, regardless of systems context. These two analytic tools in combination—OR for the systemness and operant analysis for the components—can provide a precise systematic base for the analysis and design of a behavior system.

The Structure of the Model

Mission specification. Since the context in which analysis occurs is system-based, a behavior system is defined in terms of its mission. The mission of a behavior system is comprised of a number of distinct behaviors with operant attributes. Whenever possible, the operant behaviors (mission) should be divided into small distinct units and sequenced in terms of complexity and chronology. These behaviors provide the base of the model (figure 6).

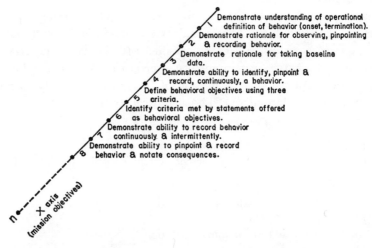

Demonstrate understanding of operational definition of behavior (onset, termination).
Demonstrate rationale for observing, pinpointing & recording behavior.
Demonstrate rationale for taking baseline data.
Demonstrate ability to identify, pinpoint & record, continuously, a behavior.
Define behavioral objectives using three criteria.
Identify criteria met by statements offered as behavioral objectives.
Demonstrate ability to record behavior continuously & intermittently.
Demonstrate ability to pinpoint & record behavior & notate consequences.

X axis (mission objectives)

Fig. 6. Specification of mission objectives (behaviors)

The systems context. Behavior systems, as well as all programs in education, are presently responding to a need for greater inclusions and integration of instructional settings. No longer is the classroom seen as the sole context of learning. Schools and institutions are pressing for inclusive enrichment, facilitative, supportive, and other relevant environments where learning typically occurs but is not integrated into the educational environment (40). Learning is increasingly viewed as a total environment experience and the burden of synthesis rests with competent professionals. Picture for a moment the school with a community base, where a mission is specified and the total environment is analyzed in relation to its contribution to the mission. Here the child moves about a variety of settings depending upon the mission behavior and contingency arrangements. The school house provides curricula, and management or settings provide some of the appropriate learning experiences. Such an approach is both conceptually, operationally, and analytically possible with a behavior system and its design and evaluation model. Figure 6 depicts the systemness of the basic behaviors comprising the mission of the behavior system. However, each basic behavior occurs either in a specific setting, or in a number of additional settings, whether in part or in a supportive manner. This interrelationship of behaviors and their many contexts provides another dimension of the systemness of a behavior system (figure 7).

The intersection of these two dimensions of a behavior systems model enables the behavior systems engineer to ask useful questions of the behavior system:

1. Is there a logical sequence to mission behaviors (x axis analysis)?
2. How many intermediate objectives exist in a supportive, facilitative, or enrichment context (y axis analysis)?
3. How many additional intermediate or settings objectives might be installed to increase mission achievement probability or to develop "in-depth" skills?
4. How do all the x-y objectives relate to each other? Is there redundancy?
5. Are the intermediate objectives of the x–y axis all sequenced correctly horizontally and vertically to measure maximum potential for achievement?

The x-y axis present behavior content and its systems interrelationships in a simplistic graphic manner. The emphasis in this graphic model is threefold: design, analysis, and continual modification. Additional implications will be mentioned at a later point.

A third dimension of the model responds to the operational attributes of the behavior system. This dimension represents all operational collaterals that generate and maintain a specific unit

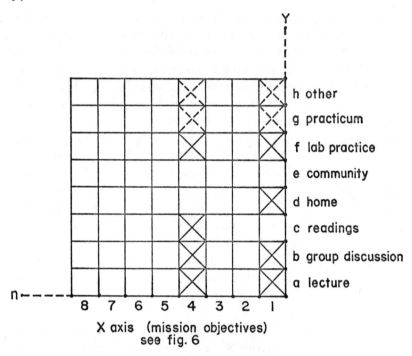

X-Y axis intermediate objectives

1a. Listen to lecture and notate in programmed workbook
1b. Participate in group feedback discussion and make corrections in work-book
1c. None
1d. Read two case descriptions and recipes and pick onset and termination of two problematic behaviors and recipe behaviors
1e. None
1f. Pick out two behaviors from videotape and specify onset and termi-nation (100% criteria)
1g. Relates to practicum counseling procedure #6 (alternative client actions utilized to solve problems)
1h. (Onset termination skill is prerequisite of objectives 4, 18, 19, 29, 34, 10)

FIG. 7. Delineation of specific behavior in settings in context with mission objectives

of behavior delineated on the *x-y* axis. In this sense the model repre-sents all units of behavior and their systemness (*x-y* axis) as a func-tion of various specified and analyzable contingency arrangements (figure 8).

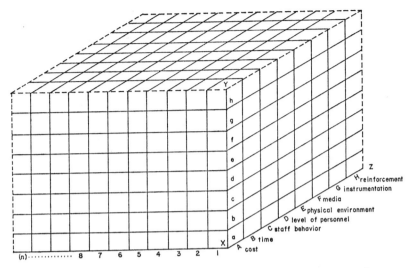

Fɪɢ. 8. Behavior systems analytic model (behavior, settings, contingency arrangements)

A number of useful questions about a behavior system may be asked through the above three dimensions:

1. What is the overall cost of achieving (a) each objective, (b) all the supportive objectives for a given mission objective, (c) all the objectives for a given setting, and (d) for the entire program?
2. How much time is required to achieve (a), (b), (c), and (d)?
3. What are the specific staff behaviors required to achieve (a), (b), (c), and (d)?
4. What physical environment and architectural components are required to achieve (a), (b), (c), and (d)?
5. What types of curricula and media are needed to achieve (a), (b), (c), and (d)?
6. What are the consequating events for (a), (b), (c), and (d)?

Figure 9 illustrates how a staff training program may be designed as a consequence of analyses of student objectives.

All the analytical questions mentioned in the previous section reflect the systems-based and operations research character of design, implementation, and analysis of a behavior system. A number of specific additional questions characterized solely by an OR strategy (system optimization and ongoing comparison of alternatives) might be asked:

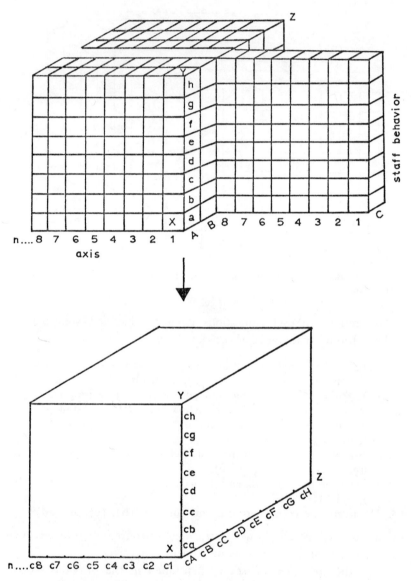

Fig. 9. Extraction of staff behavior from behavior system. Model and design of staff behavior system in a like manner.

1. What are the effects on the mission objective(s) of increasing or decreasing the number of supportive, facilitative, experiential, or enrichment facilities?

2. What are the effects on the mission objective(s) of modifying the number of sequenced units of behavior?
3. What are the effects of modifying any or combinations of the operational collaterals (contingency arrangements) of the z axis?

In other words, if the mission is held steady, how can the maximum efficiency-effectiveness ratio be achieved in the behavior system?

CAPABILITIES OF THE MODEL

It is important to note the capabilities of such a model for a behavior system. The model represents (a) mission objectives (x axis), (b) the systemness of behaviors (x-y axis), and (c) the contingency arrangements of behaviors (z axis). Many pragmatic questions concerning the design, operation, and analysis of a behavior system may be asked with the use of such a model. However, it by no means offers a solution to all behavior system problems. For instance, the delineation of the entire procedural flow of events in the behavior system, with the appropriate control processes, might best be accomplished with the use of a procedural flow-chart format (see figures 4 and 5). This might be accomplished by developing a flow-chart format for all the behavior specified on the x-y axis (figure 7). The advantage of developing a flow chart from the model is simply that each behavior or activity is automatically referenced to contingency arrangements (z axis) in case modifications are to be made.

In addition, there is an analogy between the operant clinical research design ($N=1$) and OR and systems strategies in determining the validity of a clinical treatment strategy. In the operant single-case strategy, great emphasis is placed upon explicating the independent variable(s) and representing the variety of responses (topographies) and attributes (variability, latency, frequency, etc.) that are dependent upon it. The representation of all response variability and treatment operations has its analogue in behavior system design and analysis. A design and analysis model for a behavior system would have as its first goal *representing all responses and their attributes* as they actually occur. Secondly, there is a compatibility in analysis goals. Both operant and OR strategies are *analysis*-oriented, rather than causally oriented. Thus, both models readily recognize the current limitations of causal inference strategy models as a way of knowing and doing research about human behavior. They are more concerned with specific analysis and maximization of effect than with generalization and standardization of knowledge.

Furthermore, the cybernetic loop mechanism of systems design roughly parallels the direct, immediate observation (feedback and feedforward) decisions in operant analysis (34).

A behavior system combines the conceptual, methodological, and empirical attributes of operant and systems techniques. These two disciplines have had remarkable success in their own right in dealing with environmental control. We have seen that the analysis demands of a behavior system have changed qualitatively with the synthesis of both behavioral and systems priorities. A model such as the one presented above simply suggests that it is feasible to develop a new and required analytic capability for systems of human behavior, a need that has been pressing in education for some time. Both operant and systems knowledge are predicated upon the notion that it is not appropriate, useful, or scientific to divorce design, implementation, and analysis. This point of view has thoroughly justified itself in the "harder sciences" and is a way of thinking that has important implications for behavior systems and education. The implications of a marriage of these two disciplines are dramatic.

REFERENCES

1. Ackoff, R., and Sasieni, M. *Fundamentals of Operations Research.* New York: John Wiley & Sons, 1968.
2. Ayllon, T., and Azrin, N. "The Measurement and Reinforcement of Behavior of Psychotics." *Journal of Experimental Analysis of Behavior* 8 (1965): 357-83.
3. Ayllon, T., and Michael, J. L. "The Psychiatric Nurse as a Behavioral Engineer." *Journal of Experimental Analysis of Behavior* 2 (1969): 323-34.
3a. Axelrod, Saul. "Token Reinforcement Programs in Special Classes." *Exceptional Children* 37 (1971): 371-81.
4. Baker, F. "An Open-Systems Approach to the Study of Mental Hospitals in Transition." Paper presented at American Psychological Association, September 1966.

5. Banathy, B. *Instructional Systems.* Palo Alto, Calif.: Fearon Publishers, 1968.

6. Banghart, F. *Educational Systems Analysis.* London: Macmillan & Co., 1969.

7. Berrien, F. K. *General and Social Systems.* New Brunswick: Rutgers University Press, 1968.

8. Bertalanffy, L. von. "General System Theory: A Critical Review." *General Systems,* vol. 7, 1962.

9. Bijou, S. W. "Operant Extinction after Fixed Interval Reinforcement with Young Children." *Journal of Experimental Analysis of Behavior* 1 (1958): 371-81.

10. Bijou, S. W., and Paterson, R. "The Psychological Assessment of Children in Functional Analysis." In *Advances in Psychological Assessment,* vol. 2, edited by P. McReynolds. Palo Alto: Science & Behavior Books, 1968.

11. Boulding, K. "Expecting the Unexpected Future of Knowledge and Techniques." *Prospective Changes in Society by 1980,* edited by E. L. Morphet. Denver: Designing Education for the Future: An Eight State Project, 1967.

13. Browning, R., and Stover, D. *Behavior Modification in Child Treatment.* Chicago: Aldine-Atherton, 1971.

14. Campbell, R. E., et al. "The Systems Approach: An Emerging Behavioral Model for Vocational Guidance." *Research and Development Series,* 45. Ohio State University, January 1971.

15. Chin, R. "The Utility of Systems and Developmental Models for Practitioners." In *The Planning of Change,* edited by W. Rennis, K. Benne, and R. Chin. New York: Holt, Rinehart & Winston, 1961.

16. Churchman, C. W. *The Systems Approach.* New York: Delta, 1968.

17. Cohen, H.; Filipczak, J.; and Bis, J. *Case I: An Initial Study of Contingencies Applicable to Special Education.* Silver Spring, Md.: Institute for Behavior Research, 1967.

18. Coleman, J. S., and Karweit, M. L. *Multi-Level Information Systems in Education.* Santa Monica: RAND Corporation, 1969.

19. College Entrance Examination Board. *Youth Guidance Systems.* Palo Alto, Calif., 1971.

20. Corrigan, R. E. *A System Approach for Education (SAFE),* Garden Grove, Calif., 1969.

21. Cronbach, L. "Evaluation for Course Improvement." *Teachers College Record* 64 (1963): 672-83.

22. D and R Report. "Education and Administration." *Conference for Educational Development and Research Newsletter,* (DEPS CASEA Progress Report) vol. 1, 6, p. 2.

23. Day, W. F. "On Certain Similarities between the Philosophical Investigations of Ludwig Wittgenstein and the Operationalism of B. F. Skinner." *Journal of Experimental Analysis of Behavior* 12 (1969): 489-506.

24. ———. "Radical Behaviorism in Reconciliation with Phenomenology." *Journal of Experimental Analysis of Behavior* 12 (1969): 315-29.
25. Emery, F. E., and Trist, E. L. "The Causal Texture of Organizational Environments." *Human Relations* 18 (1965): 21-32.
26. Findley, J. "Programmed Environments for the Experimental Analysis of Human Behavior." *In Operant Conditioning: Area of Research and Application*, edited by W. Honig. New York: Appleton-Century-Crofts, 1966.
27. Gagné, R., ed. *Psychological Principles in System Development.* New York: Holt, Rinehart & Winston, 1966.
28. Goldiamond, I. "Stuttering and Fluency as Manipulatable Operant Response Classes." In *Research in Behavior Modification*, edited by L. Krasner and L. P. Ullmann.
29. Hall, A.D., and Fagan, R. E. "Definition of a System." *General Systems*, vol. 3, 1958.
30. Hall, C., and Lindzey, G. *Theories of Personality*. New York: John Wiley & Sons, 1957.
31. Haring, N.; Hayden, A.; and Nolen, P. "Accelerating Appropriate Behavior of Children in a Head Start Program." *Exceptional Children* 35 (1969) 775-84.
32. Hart, B., and Risley, T. "Establishing Use of Descriptive Adjectives in the Spontaneous Speech of Disadvantaged Pre-School Children," "*Journal of Applied Behavior Analysis.* 1 (1968): 109-20.
34. Honig, W. K., ed. *Operant Behavior: Areas of Research and Application.* New York: Appleton-Century-Crofts, 1966.
36. Jones, G. B.; Nelson, D. E.; Ganshaw, L. H.; and Hamilton, J. A. *Development and Evaluation of a Comprehensive Career Guidance System.* Palo Alto, Calif.: American Institutes for Research, 1971.
37. Kanfer, F., and Saslow, G. "Behavioral Diagnosis." In *Behavior Therapy: Appraisal and Status*, edited by C. Franks, pp. 417-45. New York: McGraw-Hill Book Co., 1969.
38. Kaufman, R. A. "A System Approach to Education: Derivation and Definition." *AV Communication Review* 16 (1968).
39. Krumboltz, J.; Thoresen, C.; Zifferblatt, S.; and Stewart, N. "Behavioral Systems Counselor Training: Processes and Products." Symposium presented at the American Educational Research Association, New York: February 1971.
40. Levin, H., ed. *Community Control of Schools.* New York: Clarion Press, 1970.
41. Lewin, K. *Field Theory Social Science: Selected Theoretical Papers.* D. Cartwright, ed. New York: Harper & Bros., 1951.
43. Lindsley, O. "Precision Teaching." Paper presented at the University of Nebraska, Spring 1968.
44. Loughary, J. W. "Instructional Systems—Magic or Method?" *Educational Leadership* 25 (1968): 730-34.

45. Lumsdaine, A. A., and Glaser, R. *Teaching Machines and Programmed Learning: A Source Book*, vol. 1. Washington, D.C. Department of Audiovisual Instruction, 1960.
46. Mager, R. *Preparing Instructional Objectives*. Palo Alto: Fearon Publishers, 1962.
47. Mahoney, M. "A Residential Program in Behavior and Modification." Paper presented at Annual Meeting of Association for the Advancement of Behavior Therapy, Washington, D.C., September 1971.
48. Moore, O. K. "Autoletic Response Environments and Exceptional Children." In *Experience, Structure and Adaptability*, edited by O. J. Harvey, pp. 169-216. New York: Springer Publishing Co., 1966.
49. Ofiesh, G., Meirhenry, W., eds. *Trends in Programmed Instruction*. Washington: National Association for Programmed Instruction and National Education Association Department of Audiovisual Instruction, 1964.
50. Phillips, E. "Achievement Place: Token Reinforcement Procedures in a Home-Style Rehabilitation Setting for Pre-Delinquent Boys" *Journal of Applied Behavior Analysis* 1 (1968): 213-23.
51. Rapoport, A. "The Promise and Pitfalls of Information Theory." In *Modern Systems Research for the Behavioral Scientist*, edited by W. Buckley, pp. 132-42. Chicago: Aldine Publishing Co., 1968.
52. Ryan, T. A. "Systems Techniques for Programs of Counseling and Counselor Education." *Educational Technology* (1969): 7-17.
53. Scriven, C.; Straka, J.; and LaFond, R. "Applied Behavioral Technology in a Vocational Rehabilitation Setting." In *Behavior Modification in Mental Retardation*, edited by W. Gardner, pp. 315-61. Chicago: Aldine-Atherton, 1971.
53a. Sidman, M. *Tactics of Scientific Research*. New York: Basic Books, 1960.
54. Singh, J. *Great Ideas in Information Theory Language and Cybernetics*. New York: Dover Books, 1966.
55. Skinner, B. F. *The Contingencies of Reinforcement*. New York: Appleton-Century-Crofts, 1969.
56. ———. "The Operational Analysis of Psychological Items." *Psychological Review* 52 (1945): 270-77.
57. ———. *The Technology of Teaching*. New York: Appleton-Century-Crofts, 1968.
58. Staats, A.; Minke, K.; and Butts, P. "A Token-Reinforcement Remedial Reading Program Administered by Instructional Technicians." In *Wisconsin Research and Development Center for Cognitive Learning, Technical Report No. 127*, Madison, 1970.
59. Stewart, N. "A Systems Approach to Counselor Education." In *Behavioral Goals and Methods in Counselor Education*. Symposium presented at the American Psychological Association, Washington, D.C., September 1971.

60. Thompson, R. *A Systems Approach to Instruction*. Hamden, Conn.: Linnet Books, 1971.

61. Thoresen, C. E. "Behavioral Systems Approach to Counselor Education." Paper presented at the Invitational Planning Conference: Counselor Education Models for the Seventies. The City University of New York, May 1970.

62. ———. "Relevance and Research in Counseling." *Review of Educational Research* 39 (1969): 263-81.

63. ———. "The Systems Approach and Counselor Education: Basic Features and Implications." *Counselor Education and Supervision* 9 (1969): 3-18.

64. United States Air Force. *Systems Analysis: Procedures for Systems Definition*. Headquarters Ballistic Systems Division, Air Force Systems Command. Washington, D. C.: United States Air Force, 1962.

65. Van Dusseldorp, R.; Richardson, D.; and Foley, W. *Educational Decision-Making through Operations Research*. Boston: Allyn & Bacon, 1971.

66. Villars, T. "Using Operant Techniques to Teach Handwriting." In *Operant Conditioning in the Classroom*, edited by C. E. Pitts, pp. 329-36. New York: Thomas Y. Crowell Co., 1971.

67. Wagner, H. *Principles of Operations Research*. Englewood Cliffs, N.J.: Prentice-Hall, 1969.

68. Walken, C. "Accelerating Classroom Attending Behaviors and Learning Rate." *E R I C E D* 026-695, 1968.

69. Weiner, N. *The Human Use of Human Beings*. New York: Avon Books, 1950.

71. Zifferblatt, S. M. "Architecture and Human Behavior: Toward Increased Understanding of a Functional Relationship." *Educational Technology*, in press.

72. ———. "A Fail-Safe Competency Assessment Procedure for Counselor Trainees." In *Behavioral Goals and Methods in Counselor Education*. Symposium presented at the American Psychological Association, Washington, D.C., September 1971.

CHAPTER XI

Token Economies and Other Planned Environments

LEONARD KRASNER AND MIRIAM KRASNER

Introduction

The purpose of this chapter is to present a view of the classroom as a planned learning environment. We will focus on the token economy procedures which illustrate this approach within the context of behavior modification (6, 21, 29, 33) and its linkage with other planned environments such as the "open classrooms," and explore the consequences of this viewpoint for teacher training and education.

The criteria for including material in this chapter involves its pertinence for the educational process. We will concentrate on those studies in which there is deliberate application of principles of behavior modification and environmental design using tokens (generalized reinforcers) *to represent* positive reinforcement. The use of token reinforcement opens up the possibility of wider and more encompassing environmental planning, which is the major theme of this chapter. Thus, studies using direct reinforcement and other behavior modification procedures will not be included since they are covered elsewhere in this yearbook.

An arbitrary distinction is made in emphasizing investigations in which tokens are utilized since they are no more than a facet of an approach to human behavior and as such *should not be studied in isolation.* We are doing so as a matter of convenience of presentation, hence we are continually emphasizing the interrelation between the use of token economy and other techniques in planning a learning environment.

Preparation of this chapter was supported in part by Research Grant No. 11938 from the National Institute of Mental Health, United States Public Health Service.

In presenting the token economy as a planned environment in social institutions, especially in the classroom, the notion that we are reviewing a brand *new* procedure, radically departing from the past, implicitly promising salvation for the many problems of education and of society, should be dispelled. Token economy developed in mental hospitals, then spread to other social institutions including the classroom. The general notion of *planning the environment* so as to shape and maintain "desirable" behavior was an integral part of the planning of the first mental hospitals (and other "correctional" institutions) in this country in the early nineteenth century (59). Nor can the use of positive reinforcement (the major, but not the only, element in token economy) in the classroom be considered as new since the use of rewards for academic performance has a long educational history. Further, the principles of a token economy are the same as those of the money economy within which we all function. Yet a token economy program as a *systematic* and *planned* approach should help clarify and influence the educational and social issues that are implicitly and explicitly part of the classroom scene.

The term *behavior therapy* was first used in the literature in a status report by Lindsley, Skinner, and Solomon (40) on the application of operant conditioning to the behavior (a plunger-pulling response) of psychotic patients. Independently of this early report, Lazarus (38) used the term to refer to Wolpe's (84) application of reciprocal inhibition techniques to neurotic patients, and Eysenck (17) used the term to refer to the application of modern learning theory to maladaptive behavior. Despite the use of the term *behavior therapy* by the early investigators who applied operant conditioning to human behavior, a subsequent trend was to utilize the term *behavior modification* as being more descriptive of what they were actually doing and as indicative of the movement away from the medical connotations of the term *therapy*.

Ullmann and Krasner (75) describe behavior therapy as "treatment deducible from the sociopsychological model that aims to alter a person's behavior directly through application of general psychological principles." This is contrasted with *evocative psychotherapy*, which is "treatment deducible from a medical or psychoanalytic model that aims to alter a person's behavior indirectly by first altering intrapsychic organizations." Another similar conceptualization is given by Patterson (56): "It seems to me that future trends will, of necessity, involve a greater reliance upon principles available from social learning. The term *social learning* as used here refers to the loosely organized body of literature dealing with the changes in learning, or performances which occur as a function of contingencies which characterize social interaction." Of most relevance for viewing behavior modification (we will be using this term rather than behavior therapy or social learning throughout this chapter) applied to the educational sphere is that it represents a way of conceptualizing the impact of *environmental* events on human behavior. Krasner (33) has argued that behavior modification is rapidly moving in the direction of coalescing with aspects of sociology and economics into a broadly conceived field of environmental psychology.

Another context into which the use of token programs in education must be placed is the very recent growth of alternative models of what constitutes a classroom and a school. In the past several years there has developed a plethora of new approaches to education illustrated by the notions of the "free school" and the "open classroom." The open classroom approach in the United States, influenced by the British infant schools (58, 62), emphasizes the importance of a carefully planned environment and, as such, is both *compatible* with and *complementary* to the behavior modification approach. On the other hand, the concept of the "free school," to the extent that it is based upon the hypothesis that behavior is determined by the inner forces of autonomous individuals, is not compatible with the behavior modification and open classroom approaches which emphasize environmental planning.

DEVELOPMENT OF TOKEN ECONOMIES

Token economy, as eventually applied in the classroom, derives from the behavior modification streams of operant conditioning and utopian planning (33). The landmarks in the operant conditioning stream are: the early laboratory studies of Skinner (63); application to simple behaviors of psychotic patients in a state hospital (40); applications to preschool and retarded children by Bijou and his co-workers (e.g., 7); token economy classrooms with retardates

(8, 9), with delinquents (16), and with delinquent retardates (24, 39); application of operant conditioning to autistic children by Ferster (19) and by Lovaas (43); and the use of tokens as reinforcers in a reading program with children by Staats et al. (69). Ayllon, first at a Canadian hospital (4) and later at Anna State Hospital in Illinois (2, 3), applied these general principles to psychiatric patients and established the first token system on a hospital ward. Becker and his associates, at the University of Illinois, moved token systems into the classroom, initially with disturbed children (51). In the late 1960s, a University of Kansas group moved the concept of token systems into the community (see 49).

A second stream in the development of behavior modification out of which token economy developed can be labeled as utopian and has been influenced primarily by Skinner's utopian novel, *Walden Two* (66). The planning for a token economy is analogous to planning a society. This will be emphasized in a later section when we relate token economy to economic planning and the designing of social systems.

Basic Elements of Token Economy Programs

We start with a definition of token economy in terms of the operations involved in planning for it, setting it up, and carrying it out. First, there is *systematic observation* of the behavior of the people for whom the program is intended and the consequences of this behavior in the specific situation in which it is occurring. This observation may be in the classroom, on a hospital ward, in the home, or in the community. The unit of observation goes beyond the specific act of an individual to include the response elicited by the behavior from the environment. Thus it is insufficient to observe that a child "left his seat." The full observational unit is that the child left his seat, the teacher said, "go back to your seat," three children laughed, and another child started to leave his seat.

Second, there is the *designation* of certain specific behaviors as *desirable*, hence reinforceable. This may include behaviors on a hospital ward, such as dressing oneself or making a bed, or, in a classroom, staying in one's seat or raising a hand. These behaviors are usually those which someone (the teacher, ward nurse, or the individual) determines are socially useful and of initial low frequency. Later we shall stress the value decisions implicit in deciding that a certain behavior (e.g., remaining in seat) is desirable.

The third element is the determination of what environmental events may serve as *reinforcers* for the individual. What are the good things in life for these individuals? What are they willing to work for? For the hospitalized adult, it may include a bed, a pass, or a chance to sit in a favorite chair. For the child in the classroom, it may include candy, toys, or a chance to go on an interesting trip.

The fourth element is the *medium of exchange,* the token, which connects elements two and three. The token *stands for* the backup reinforcer. It can act as a discriminative or reinforcing stimulus or both. The token may be a tangible object such as a plastic card or a green stamp that one can handle, or it may be a mark on a piece of paper, or a point scored which the individual knows is there but to which he has no direct access. Despite the label of *token economy*, the tokens themselves are merely a gimmick, a training device to help teachers and others in the classroom (or hospital ward) to learn how to observe behavior and its consequences, how to use their own behavior in a reinforcing manner, how to respond contingently, and how to arrange the environment so as to maximize the possibility of the individual child receiving reinforcing stimuli at the appropriate time.

The fifth element is the *exchange rules*. The planning of a token economy must specify the economic relationship between the amount of tokens an individual may earn and the cost of the good things in life. If a person can earn only (at most) ten tokens a day and the cheapest item he can purchase costs one hundred tokens, the system will not work. Conversely, if he can earn a hundred tokens and he can take care of all his desires for only ten tokens, this system will not work either. We must take into consideration the economic constraints which determine the value and effects of specific reinforcers. At this point, we begin to develop a very complex relationship which is analogous to what occurs to all of us in our everyday life as we try to determine various ways of budgeting money in our real-life economic system.

EXAMPLES OF TOKEN ECONOMIES

The most comprehensive recent review of the token economy program in the classroom is that of O'Leary and Drabman (53). They conclude that "these programs have demonstrated effectiveness in changing the academic and social behavior of very diverse child populations. However, the use of token and backup reinforcement is but one procedure within a complex constellation of factors within the overall token reinforcement program" (p. 379).

The use of reward itself in the classroom is, of course, not new, but the *systematic* use of contingent reinforcement by a teacher trained in the procedure does represent a basic change. The principles behind the use of tokens in the classroom, contingency reinforcement of desirable alternative behaviors, is the same as in mental hospitals but there are problems unique to the nature of the classroom.

We start with a description of the early studies in order to present some of the general principles and problems involved which apply in whatever situation this procedure is used.

Use in hospital settings. Ayllon and Azrin (2) reported the results of the first token economy program in a psychiatric hospital ward. The behaviors selected for reinforcement included serving meals, cleaning floors, sorting laundry, washing dishes, and self-grooming. The reinforcers included such items as: rooms available for rent; selection of people to dine with; passes; a chance to speak to the ward physician, chaplain, or psychologist; opportunities for viewing television; candy, cigarettes, and other amenities of life. Tokens served as acquired reinforcers that bridged the gap between behavior and an ultimate reinforcement. These investigators placed particular emphasis on the objective definition and quantification of the responses and reinforcers and also upon programming and recording procedures.

The Ayllon and Azrin token economy was used on a ward for long-term female patients in a midwestern state hospital. Another token economy program (1, 35) was set up in a Veterans Administration hospital in California with male patients (average age, fifty-eight years) having median time of hospitalization of twenty-four years. Most of these patients had been labeled as chronic schizophrenics and the rest as having organic cerebral disease. As a group, their behavior was apathetic and indifferent; the patients showed inactivity, dependency, and social isolation. The procedures used were similar to those developed by Ayllon and Azrin except that this program was designed to be used on an *open ward* where patients could come and go—if, of course, they had the right number of tokens for the gatekeeper. The token economy had to compete with the economy (which used dollars and cents) outside the ward, the "real" world outside. Many kinds of economic problems had to be faced and special procedures were developed to deal with them, e.g., a banking system to foster savings, a monthly discount rate to cut down hoarding, and colored tokens to prevent stealing.

This program was a success as measured by changes in specified behavior, observers' ratings, and reactions of hospital staff. The changes in behaviors, such as attendance at group activities, were a function of the number of tokens (value) given for the activity. Group attendances increased as more tokens were given for them and decreased when the "pay off" returned to its previous value. The greatest change was in the staff expectations of what the patients were capable of. The morale of the staff increased enormously when they found that their participation in the token economy program had a therapeutic effect on the behavior of the patient; it became a matter of prestige throughout the hospital to work on the token ward.

Schaefer and Martin (60) described the effects of a token economy program on the apathetic behavior of patients in a California state hospital. Other successful token economy programs with adult psychiatric patients have been reported by Steffy and co-workers (70), Marks, Sonoda, and Schalock (45), Gericke (23), Lloyd and Garlington (42), and Sletten et al. (67). Token economy programs have been extended to other groups including retardates, delinquents, adolescents, and children who have classroom behavior problems. (See Kazdin and Bootzin [31] for an evaluative review.)

Token economy in the classroom. O'Leary and Becker (51) introduced the use of a token reinforcement program in a large class ($N = 17$) of children with behavior problems in a public school. Observations were focused on the eight most disruptive children. Two observers recorded behaviors labeled deviant (e.g., pushing, talking, making a noise, and chewing gum) every thirty seconds for an hour and a half three days a week. Behaviors manifested during the observation periods were classified as either disruptive or non-disruptive.

On the first day of training, the experimenter put the following words on the blackboard: In Seat, Face Front, Raise Hand, Working, Pay Attention, Desk Clear. The experimenter then explained that tokens would be given for these behaviors and that the tokens could be exchanged for backup reinforcers of candy, comics, perfume, and so on. The teacher, during several brief class interludes, rated the extent to which each child had met the criteria.

For the first three days, tokens were exchanged at the end of each period; tokens were then accumulated before being cashed in, first for two days, then three days, and finally for four days. The process was designed gradually to fade out the backup reinforcer so that the more traditional acquired reinforcers of teacher's praise would become effective. In addition, group points (exchanged for ice cream) were awarded for quietness of the group during the rating period. Further techniques of verbal praise, ignoring (extinction), and time-out-from-reinforcement were used as appropriate. During the base-line observation period, the disruptive-deviant behavior ranged from 66 to 91 percent of the observations. The daily mean of observed disruptive-deviant behavior dropped to a range of from 4 to 32 percent during the period of token training. The authors concluded that "with the introduction of the token reinforcement system, a dramatic, abrupt reduction in deviant behavior occurred . . . The program was equally successful for all children observed, and repeated anecdotal evidence suggested that the children's appropriate behavior generalized to other situations" (51:637).

This program contained most of the elements that were to characterize future token programs in the classroom and which had appeared in the earlier mental hospital and retardation applications, namely: systematic observation; explicit selection of the desired behaviors with the assistance of the teacher, as alternatives to undesirable behavior; the exchange system; the training of the teacher in her new role; the use of additional behavior influence techniques such as social reinforcement; and the careful charting of behavior by trained observers.

O'Leary et al. (52) replicated the earlier study in a more systematic manner to determine the separate effects of the various variables utilized in the previous study. They worked with seven children in a second-grade class of twenty-one children. After a period of base-line observations, they successively introduced *classroom rules* (e.g., on the blackboard the rule, "we sit in our seats"), *educational structure* (e.g., the teacher structured her program into four sessions of thirty minutes each), and *praising appropriate behavior while ignoring disruptive behavior*. None of these procedures consistently reduced disruptive behavior in six of the seven target children; the three procedures were successful with one of the children. When a token reinforcement program was introduced, the frequency of disruptive behavior declined in five of the remaining six children.

Withdrawal of the token program then resulted in increased disruptive behavior in these five children. The reinstatement of the token program reduced disruptive behavior in four of the five children. Follow-up data indicated that the teacher was able to transfer control from the token and backup reinforcers to the reinforcers existing within the educational setting, such as stars and occasional pieces of candy. Improvements in academic achievement during the year may have been related to the token program, and attendance records appeared to be enhanced during the token phases. The token program was utilized only in the afternoon and the data did *not* indicate any generalization of appropriate behavior from the afternoon to the morning.

This particular study is cited because it illustrates many important points about token economy programs in the classroom that become more focused by the observations of the same investigators replicating their earlier work. Clearly there are many complex and subtle variables involved in this kind of program which become more obvious in the authors' comparison of the results of the two studies:

Although a token reinforcement program was a significant variable in reducing disruptive behavior in the present study [1969], the results are less dramatic than those obtained by O'Leary and Becker (1967). A number of factors probably contributed to the difference in effectiveness of the programs. The average of disruptive behavior during the base period in the 1967 study was 76%; in the present study it was 53%. The gradual introduction of the various phases of the program was probably less effective than a simultaneous introduction of all the procedures, as in the previous study. In the earlier study, the children received more frequent ratings. [Also] the class could earn points for popsicles by being quiet while the teacher placed ratings in the children's booklets; in the present study, group points were not incorporated into the general reinforcement program. In the 1967 study, the teacher attended a weekly psychology seminar where teachers discussed various applications of learning principles to classroom management. An *esprit de corps* was generated from that seminar that probably increased the teacher's commitment to change the children's behavior. . . . A number of children in the present study had an abundance of toys at home and it was difficult to obtain inexpensive prizes which would serve as reinforcers; in the earlier study, selection of reinforcers was not a difficult problem since the children were from disadvantaged homes (52:11-12).

Thus, selected considerations must be added to any evaluation of token programs, such as base-line levels of the target behaviors, the phasing of the program, the frequency of certain teacher behaviors, the use of group reinforcers, the consequences of a teacher training program (and available reinforcers for the teacher), and the availability of reinforcers for the children in their total environment. There are still more complexities as we shall note after descriptions of other programs.

Another example of a token reinforcement program is elaborated in the research of Hewett, Taylor, and Artuso (28). Fifty-four children with learning and behavior problems, most of whom had been labeled emotionally disturbed, were assigned to six different classrooms of nine students each. The ages of the children ranged from eight to eleven. Hewett and his group describe their program as involving an "engineered classroom" rather than a token economy. However, the principles of both are the same. The experimental condition of the project involved rigid adherence to the engineered classroom design and systematic reliance on the giving of *check marks*. The control condition of the project consisted of any approach the teacher chose to follow, including aspects of the engineered design, except use of tangible or token rewards. Conventional grading, verbal praise, complimentary written comments on completed assignments, and awarding privileges for good work were all acceptable. The independent variable was adherence to the engineered design. The dependent variable was the student "task attention" and academic functioning level in reading and arithmetic. Specific criteria for a student's task attention, as measured by observers, were established.

The student's task was significantly facilitated by use of a token system, i.e., check marks. Reading achievement was not significantly affected by either the experimental or control condition, but gains in arithmetic fundamentals were significantly correlated with the presence of the experimental condition.

The Hewett et al. study (28) was a forerunner and prototype of attempts to apply token programs to disturbed children. This program was more complex in its involvement of more teachers, the use of comparative control groups rather than its own control base lines, a focus on academic target behaviors, and the testing of the removal and reinstatement of the token programs.

Wolf, Giles, and Hall (83) reported a token economy designed to develop and maintain the academic behavior of children with low scholastic achievement in a community setting. This report described the results of the first year of after-school remedial education for such children from the fifth and sixth grade in a poor, urban area. The remedial program incorporated standard instructional material, the mastery of which was supported by token reinforcements.

The reinforcement procedure resembled a trading-stamp plan. Each child was given a folder containing groups of four pages of different colors divided into squares. The different colors signified different sorts of rewards. After a child had completed an assignment correctly, he was given points by the teacher, who then marked the appropriately colored squares. At first, points were given after each problem that was worked correctly. As the student acquired a more accurate output, the amount and/or difficulty of work needed to obtain points was gradually increased.

The number of points to be given to a child for particular work was decided by the teacher. This decision was sometimes determined partially through negotiation with the child—a unique feature of this program. Filled pages of points were redeemable, according to their color, for a variety of goods and activities including weekly trips to outdoor events or to the cinema, food, money, articles that were available in the store, and long-range goals such as clothes, inexpensive watches, and second-hand bicycles. The children could earn tokens in each of three areas: regular classroom work; work completed in the remedial classroom; and work represented by their six-week report-card grades.

With this basic paradigm, Wolf, Giles, and Hall (83) performed several experimental analyses of the token procedures. In the overall program, they compared the academic achievement of their experimental students during the year with that of a matched control group (fifteen in each group). The results indicated that the remedial group gained 1.5 years on the *Stanford Achievement Test* as compared to 0.8 of a year for the control group; these differences were significant ($p < .01$). There was a similar significant difference in report-card grades. The authors concluded:

The remedial program's effectiveness in maintaining the children's participation was indicated by the high attendance record, and the fact that whenever the opportunity was given them the children chose to attend class on regular school holidays. . . . The cost of the program, which was substantial, must be contrasted with the long term cost to society in terms of human as well as economic resources lost by not educating these children adequately. The cost could be reduced significantly by utilizing the potential reinforcers which already exist in almost every educational setting. Properly used, such events as recess, movies, and athletic and social activities could be arranged as consequences for strengthening academic behavior (83:63-64).

Thus we see in this study the introduction of token economy to the disadvantaged of our population, changes in price structure to shape the quality and quantity of classroom work, the child entering the decision-making process, the introduction of long-range goals, and the practice of utilizing reinforcing events beyond the classroom as well as a greater utilization of the "natural" reinforcers of the classroom.

Other token programs have used receipts for money with institutionalized female adolescent offenders (48); given tokens for good performance on a "news" test (73); used plastic washer tokens as tickets for special events (13); given tokens to school dropouts in a

Neighborhood Youth Corps who were "hired" to complete remedial workbook assignments (15); used contingent tokens in a remedial reading program (26); given points as tokens, along with time-out procedures and parental involvement, in working with disruptive fourth- to sixth-graders (76); used poker chips to increase instruction-following behavior in retardates (85); used peers to dispense tokens to individualized reading programs (79); and given tokens to extinguish tantrum behavior (47).

ON REINFORCERS

Tokens per se serve as discriminative stimuli which stand for, or are symbolic of, some other object or event. Theoretically, the tokens take on reinforcing properties because of the desirability of the backup reinforcers which they represent. Yet, it is clear from observation that tokens do take on reinforcing properties of their own. The clearest analogue of this is the individual who works for money far beyond his needs. The token money becomes highly desirable for itself.

Among the variety of actual tokens used are check marks, stars, rings, chips, and tags. O'Leary and Drabman (53:389) offer a list of the desirable properties of the tokens themselves: their value should be readily understood; they should be easy to dispense; they should be easily transportable from the place of dispensing to the area of exchange; they should be identifiable as the property of a particular child; they should require minimal bookkeeping duties for the teacher; they should be dispensable in a manner which will divert as little attention as possible from academic matters; they should have some relevance to real currency if one's desire is to teach mathematical or economic skills which will be functional outside the classroom; and they should be dispensed frequently enough to insure proper shaping of desired behavior.

Every conceivable object or event that can be considered desirable as a backup reinforcer can be and has been used. These include such diverse items as candy, food, clothing, watches, and access to events such as movies, sports events, and circuses.

Once it becomes clear that reinforcers do not necessarily mean material objects but can include the opportunities to do certain things, to go places (e.g., movies or dances), then it is clear that reinforcers are stimuli in the sense of stimulation. Stimulation is

364 TOKEN ECONOMIES AND PLANNED ENVIRONMENTS

basic to living. We could even argue that stimulation, unless it is aversive, is rewarding per se.

The planned or open classroom represents a way of organizing the natural reinforcers in the environment so as to maximize the likelihood that learning will take place. The introduction of tokens per se may hasten the process or may make it more explicit for those who have not yet learned or who have mislearned the relationship between their behavior and its environmental consequences.

ON GENERALIZATION EFFECTS

Behavior changes only in a social context. The question is whether a change in behavior generalizes from one situation to another. Although both laboratory and individual case studies with operant procedures have attempted to approach problems of generalization across time (do changes in the morning carry over to the afternoon?) and across situations (does change in the classroom extend to the home?), most of the token economy programs have not examined generalization effects.

The key observation on the problem of generalization is that of Baer et al. that ". . . generalization should be programmed rather than expected or lamented" (5:97). It seems clear that the token programs, with a few exceptions, do not result in generalized behavioral change. But most of the studies were not intended or designed to bring about change in other situations.

O'Leary and Drabman (53:395) offer a list of ten procedures which may be useful in enhancing the likelihood of obtaining generalization:

(1) Provide a good academic program since in many cases you may be dealing with deficient academic repertoires, not behavior disorders.

(2) Give the child the expectation that he is capable of doing well, by exaggerating excitement when the child succeeds and pointing out that if he works hard, he can succeed.

(3) Have the children aid in the selection of the behaviors to be reinforced and, as the program progresses, have the children involved in the specification of contingencies.

(4) Teach the children to evaluate their own behavior.

(5) Teach the children that academic achievement will "pay off."

(6) Involve the parents.

(7) Withdraw the token and backup reinforcers gradually and

utilize other "natural" reinforcers existing within the classroom setting, such as privileges.

(8) Reinforce the children in a variety of situations and reduce the discrimination between reinforced and nonreinforced situations.

(9) Prepare teachers in the regular class to praise and shape the children's behavior as they are phased back into the regular classes.

(10) Look at the school system as a large-scale token system with the distribution of token and backup reinforcers and extending from the school board to the superintendent, to the principal, to the teacher, and finally to the children.

Research Design

Implicit in the behavior modification approach is the emphasis on research evaluation of the success of the program. The problems of token economy research are at least as complex as those in any other area of human behavior change and probably more complex. Classroom research is particularly difficult because of the problems in controlling relevant variables.

It should be clear from our descriptions of the studies thus far that this approach involves many more concepts over and above reinforcement. This would include role modeling, expectancy, demand characteristics, and probably others, in addition to positive reinforcement per se. The goal of the research investigator using a token economy is to demonstrate, first, significant behavioral change, and, second, that the change is due to the specific techniques used in the program.

Token economy programs can be divided into the following categories according to the research design used:

(1) Programs that are primarily demonstration projects in which no attempt is made to control variables. Although change may be observed, it cannot with certainty be attributed to the tokens per se.

(2) Programs using the subject's behavior before the program is started as a base line, that is, subjects as their own controls. Operant measurement is taken of the subject's behaviors for a specific period of time. The token program is introduced and the same behaviors continue to be measured. The token contingencies may be removed and again the behavior continues to be measured. Then the token contingencies are reintroduced. This is called the ABAB design or treatment reversal: base line, token–base line, token. One problem with this design is the difficulty in reproducing identical base lines after treatment since the experimental program itself may result in real changes.

(3) The effectiveness of the token economy procedure can be

tested by the use of control groups which receive either no specific treatment or a different treatment (83). The problem with this design is that a token economy involves a multitude of variables so that it is difficult to match groups on all but one variable.

(4) Performance in the token economy is related to performance in another learning task. Panek (54) worked with thirty-two chronic schizophrenics. He conditioned common word associations with positive and negative contingencies of verbal and token reinforcement, and then compared success in associated learning with the total number of ward/token transactions. Rankings of the rate of learning were significantly correlated with rankings of the total use of tokens. This suggests that the conditioning task could be used as a predictor of the response to token programs.

Behavior Theory and Economic Theory

Winkler (81) reported the first investigations of the relationship between economic variables, such as prices, wages, and savings, in a token economy program in a psychiatric hospital. Linking the social learning principles of token programs with economic theory, Krasner (32) pointed out that "token economy procedures need a combination of social and economic planning. When an economist (e.g., Galbraith, 1967 [22]) relates a 'general theory of motivation' to the economic structure of society, he is presenting hypotheses that can be tested in small social units such as hospital wards, by means of a token economy" (32:172). Such linkages are also possible and necessary in the classroom.

The concepts of token economy and of economics interact in three ways: (a) economic principles (e.g., law of supply and demand) can be used to understand why existing traditional token economies work or do not work; (b) economic and behavioral principles can be used in the design of innovative economies; and (c) token economies can be used to test economic theory. Winkler and Krasner (82), to clarify these interactions, report research using token economies with chronic psychiatric patients. The implications of this type of economic research go beyond the treatment of psychiatric patients to any token economy which operates with similar rules, be it in a classroom, correctional institution, or a delinquent rehabilitation unit.

Various simple principles that have been well established in operant laboratories, such as reinforcement, can be found to operate in token economies. It should also be possible to demonstrate in token economies the operation of at least simple economic principles. The phenomena found in token economies fit into the economic principles developed in the analysis of national economies.

In addition to augmenting the theoretical base for understanding token economies, the investigation of economics can provide ideas for the design of new, perhaps more effective, token economies. Research on the interface between economic theory and token economics would, therefore, seem to be essential to a complete understanding of token economies and valuable in the design of innovative token programs, particularly in the classroom.

THE TOKEN ECONOMY AS A "REAL" ECONOMY

A modified use of a token economy program which extends the possibility of utilization of these programs in the classroom has been reported by Krasner (34). This is a unique token program which took place in a fifth-grade classroom. Previous token programs have emphasized remedial goals. In this classroom, the token economy was a program in which the development of the economy served as a learning experience itself. A fifth-grade teacher [1] initiated a token program in the form of a *simulated society*. He started the program in the role of a king with divine rights, and with an initial royal treasury of a dozen bottle caps as the total capital. The token economy developed and soon took on a life of its own.

The behavior of the children was determined by the shifting directions of the economy as it progressed from a system of slavery to capitalism and then to socialism. The initial goal of this program, as determined by the teacher, was for the children to learn about and be more appreciative of historical and economic processes by reproducing them, to some extent, via the concept of a token economy. The children learned that prices and wages have a strong influence upon their behavior. The children then were able to control the program by introducing new and increasingly more complex relationships between "prices" and "wages" in much the same manner as in the world outside the classroom. This was evidenced by the spontaneous development of a welfare program to take care

1. Gerald Martin of Three Village Central School District, Setauket, New York.

of those who didn't earn enough tokens to function in the economy. As a result of this program a considerable sophistication in economic functioning and human behavior developeed on the part of the children.

It may seem paradoxical to discuss the two concepts of token economy and open classroom in the same chapter since both derive from different, if not antithetical, frameworks. Yet both sets of procedures represent approaches to the classroom as a planned environment which are not only compatible with but complement each other in a complete environmental program. Both represent sharp departures from traditional thinking about the nature and function of education. Both emphasize the teacher's role in carefully and systematically planning classroom stimuli in a manner to elicit and sustain specified behavior of individual children. A discussion of the value decisions in determining what are target behaviors will follow in a later section.

To date there is a paucity of experimental data as to behavior change within the aegis of the open classroom concept. Most of the published literature on the open classroom is enthusiastic but anecdotal (18, 58, 62, 78). These investigations have observed that the major elements of the open classroom approach are the integrated day, individualized instruction, family grouping, and the use of much "stuff" or material.

The integrated day encompasses a notion of a total environment attempting to break down distinctions between work and play, between subject matters, and between the inside and the outside of the classroom. Weber (78) describes it this way:

In planning for the free day there is no separation of activities or skills and no separate scheduling of any one activity other than the fixed points . . . designed for all children in the school. As a result, one might see all aspects of the environment—reading, writing, numbering, painting, acting, music—in use at all times. A group getting the teacher's special help or stimulus could be found at any time. . . . The English viewed a child's use of the environment as cutting across subject areas in pursuit of his interests. This kind of scheduling not only supported a child's integration of experience but also sustained his involvement (pp. 90-91).

The integrated day involves a concept of having available in the environment a wide variety of stimuli and learning conditions which should make the learning situation more interesting, exciting, meaningful, and reinforcing to the child. Family or vertical grouping is a nongraded grouping which may span, for example, three years, placing five-, six-, and seven-year-olds together in the same classroom. The word *family* is used to describe the process because the classroom is deliberately calculated to resemble a family. Older children help with the teaching of younger children, and the classroom environment is designed as an extension of the home and family. The rationale behind this arrangement is that children learn from each other; peers are important sources of reinforcement. The core of individualized instruction is that the planning of the classroom involves setting up twenty-five separate and specific sets of stimuli so that each child learns at his own pace. Finally, wide use is made of inexpensive materials readily found in most environments, such as water, sand, and common household working utensils, as stimuli to shape and maintain behaviors such as decision-making and self-direction.

Implications for Teacher Training

It is clear that viewing the classroom as a planned environment (encompassing an open classroom and/or a behavior modification token economy) has major implications for the training of teachers, an area which has barely been explored. From its inception, the initiation of token programs has stressed the importance of teacher training. The core of setting up a token economy involves the use of tokens as a device for training the teacher in the principles and techniques of behavior modification and the technique of utilizing her own behavior in a contingently reinforcing behavior.

As the concept of a planned environment develops, the teacher's responsibility broadens to include the planning of the total environmental stimuli to which the individual children are exposed. This includes value decisions as to what kinds of behavior are most desirable on the part of the children, e.g., in seat versus purposeful movements or competitive versus cooperative behavior. The teacher is continually making such decisions. The thrust of the investigations cited is that such decisions are made deliberately or inadvertently in class every day. The problem is how to train the teacher to be aware of the consequences of these decisions and to learn how to involve the children in the decision-making.

The first step, perhaps the most important one, in the training process is the avowed acknowledgment on the part of those responsible for teacher training that the behavior of *making value decisions* is basic. This means acceptance of the view that there is no inherently correct structure to the classroom. Setting up a classroom with five straight rows with six desks in each is, in itself, a value decision with implicit expectancies of certain kinds of behavior. Whether these behaviors are good or bad is not the issue. Rather, it is how to train the teachers (a) to become aware of and state their goals and (b) to utilize their role as an environmental organizer to achieve these goals.

Bussis and Chittenden (14) offer a useful conceptualization of the classroom environment as a two-dimensional scheme based on the extent to which the individual teacher and the individual child are active contributors to decisions regarding the content and process of learning in the classroom. "A popular dimension in early education research postulates that a classroom can be located somewhere on a scale of 'child-centeredness to adult-centeredness.' At one extreme is a classroom completely controlled by the teacher and organized around formal curricular requirements; and, at the other end, a classroom in which the children are theoretically setting the entire course of learning, with a wide variety of positions in between" (14:20).

It is clear that the goal of the open education approach is to have the child behave along the active end of the continuum with high contribution. "From a pedagogical standpoint, it is believed that the growth of personal knowledge and the organization of experience can best take place when the child himself is located at the command center of the proceess" (14:20). Where does the teacher role stand insofar as contribution is concerned? There is much controversy about this role, especially since the advocates of "free" education relegate the teacher's role to nil, at most to that of an understanding, supportive adult. However, almost every reviewer of the British infant schools and of their attempted counterparts in this country emphasize the very high active involvement of the teacher. Thus the open classroom is one in which there is a considerable amount of *both* student and teacher behavior and in which both have control over environmental contingencies. The same is true for the token economy classroom as it would be for any planned classroom environment.

Social and Ethical Implications

TARGET BEHAVIORS

We have indicated in the previous section that the second step in setting up a token program is the specification of the behavior which is to be changed. Implicit in such a specification is the *value judgment* as to the desirability of the alternative behaviors which are replacing the undesirable ones. The behaviors that are to be shaped tell us much about the values of the teacher (and/or investigator) as to what is good behavior. For example, Bushell, Wrobel, and Michaelis (13) used as dependent variables the behaviors of attending quietly to instructions, working independently, or in cooperation with others as appropriate, remaining with and attending to assigned tasks, and reciting after assignments had been completed (13:55). Conversely, the undesirable behaviors were "disrupting others who are at work, changing an activity before its completion, and engaging in 'escape' behaviors such as trips to bathroom or drinking fountain, or gazing out the window . . ." (13:55).

In determining what are to become target behaviors, token systems may be making their greatest social contribution and also may encounter strong controversy. In a critique of the goals of behavior modification in the classroom, Winett and Winkler (80) reviewed publications in the *Journal of Applied Behavior Analysis* from 1968-1970 in which behavior modification was applied to relatively normal classrooms. "Our purpose was not to evaluate specific techniques but rather to investigate the kinds of target behaviors that were either reinforced or in various ways proscribed." They cited as illustrative a study by Thomas, Becker, and Armstrong (72) which sought to rigorously classify "appropriate" and "inappropriate" behavior. Labeled as *inappropriate* were such behaviors as: getting out of seat, standing up, walking around, running, hopping, skipping, jumping, moving chairs, racking chairs, tapping feet, rattling papers, carrying on a conversation with other children, crying, singing, whistling, laughing, turning head or body toward another person, showing objects to another child, and looking at another child. *Appropriate* behavior included: attending to the teacher, raising hand and waiting for the teacher to respond, working in seat on a workbook, following in a reading text. A later study by some of the same group (46) followed the above guidelines in determining their target behaviors. Bushell, Wrobel, and Michaelis (13) and O'Leary et al. (52) used similar criteria and also, respectively, prohibited the behavior of singing a Spanish song during the wrong time-period and talking in the hall. Ward and Baker (77) added a further general category under inappropriate behavior: doing something different from that which one had been directed to do.

It is quite clear that the desirable behaviors tend in the direction of quietness and nonmovement whereas the undesirable behaviors tend in the direction of movement and interactive stimulation. It would appear that the behavior modification approach in the classroom as typified by token economy has been used to support the implicit behaviors held desirable as part of the traditional school approach. Winett and Winkler draw this bleak picture of current goals: "Just what do those present goals seem to be? Taken as a fairly accurate indicator of what public schools deemed as the 'model' child, these studies described this pupil as one who stays glued to his seat and desk all day, continually looks at his teacher or his text/workbook, does not talk to or in fact look at other children, does not talk unless asked to by the teacher, hopefully does not laugh or sing (or at the wrong time), and assuredly passes silently in halls" (80).

The issue of target behavior is not peripheral but rather central to the application of token economy in the classroom. Many of the early applications of behavior modification in the classroom, particularly in the mid-sixties, were attempts at demonstrating that indeed the application of learning principles could change behavior. The particular behavior selected was done on the basis of its being readily observable, countable, and of importance to the teacher.

Little regard was given for evaluating the desirability of the behaviors themselves. The social and ethical implications of target behavior have increasingly become more focal.

ETHICAL IMPLICATIONS

Viewing the classroom as a planned environment with emphasis on token economy is in an early stage of development. A hardheaded reviewer could conclude from the research evidence that the traditional token economy which we have been describing in this chapter is indeed an effective technique for modifying behaviors labeled by somebody as deviant or undesirable. Beyond that, the implications of viewing the ordinary classroom as a planned environment have just begun to be explored and hard research evidence is virtually nil. Investigators are beginning to pose more appropriate questions. For example, it is more meaningful for the teacher to ask, "What is the desirable behavior for child A in environmental situation X?" rather than, "What can I do to keep these children in their seats so that I can teach them?" It may be more meaningful to ask, "How may this environment be arranged so that the child, as well as the teacher, can make decisions with real consequences for the child's control of his own behavior?" Posing the question in this manner implies that decision-making and self-control on the part of the child is desirable.

The notion of education as involving a group of children seated in front of and paying attention to a teacher who imparts wisdom and knowledge is fading into a concept of a carefully planned process (planning involving teacher, administrator, parents, and students) involving the total environment of the child and including the child, peers, teachers, parents, and the community.

Conclusion

We close this chapter by returning to our historical introduction in which we placed token economy and planned environments within the context of the development of behavior modification, which, in itself, can be viewed as a social movement (74). The fact that token economies belong within the utopian stream of development has important social implications. Token economy programs, because of the issues involved, may be compared to utopian planning. The questions that must be answered when a token economy is set up are similar to those that must be answered in the planning of the "good" society. First, what are the goals of the society, the desired behaviors to be reinforced? Second, what training or educational procedures are necessary to shape or maintain these behaviors in this society? Third, how can the current way of life be modified so that there is a reasonable chance of initiating the new planned program?

Walden Two (66) is of special interest because in this book a behavioral scientist attempts to foresee and, to some extent, control the consequences of his scientific endeavors. Further, the principles of token economy and *Walden Two* are both based on the operant conditioning principles developed by Skinner (63, 65) which have permeated the classroom through programmed learning procedures and, more recently, through the token programs described in this chapter. In fact, *Walden Two is* a token economy. Individuals in the community work for "labor credit"—entries in a ledger. Several of the token programs in the classroom use the same technique, avoiding physical tokens. The allocation of specific credits for specific tasks is based on principles suggested by Edward Bellamy in 1888 (6a). The different credit values for different kinds of work are adjusted from time to time on the basis of demands. This principle is also used in several token economy programs (e.g., see 2). Thus, pleasant jobs have lower value and must be worked at for long periods to earn tokens, whereas unpleasant jobs (cleaning sewers, for example) have high value and hence little work time. In *Walden Two* each member of the community must earn twelve hundred labor credits in order to maintain status in the community. But tokens are not needed for specific good things in life—all goods and services are free. The number of labor credits needed to maintain oneself in the community may be changed according to the needs of the community. The aim of the society is to obtain enough work from its members to enable that society to maintain itself "with a slight margin of safety."

Skinner (64) has recently reemphasized the importance of "survival" behavior and makes a strong case for behaviorally oriented "planned" environments. Krasner (32) has argued that planning and individual choice are not *antithetical*: "Token economy programs are far from deterministic or mechanistic. Systematization does not mean mechanization. In fact, the major element in these programs is flexibility. Unless the program continually changes by incorporating new behaviors, changing values, and bringing in new 'good things,' it becomes as static as any traditional program. When a token program begins, it is impossible to predict contingencies that may be available within a year" (32:120).

Token economy programs incorporate all the principles of behavior modification, which includes most experimental techniques of changing human behavior. Learning a new behavior may be influenced by operant and classical conditioning, modeling, placebo, or expectancy. All these procedures may be objectively described in behavioral terms, measured and controlled. Some of the descriptions of token programs have used oversimplified reinforcement concepts. Reinforcement is operating but it is more than just a question of a token reinforcing a behavior and thus increasing the likelihood of its occurrence. There are many more cues in any one situation, e.g., the tokens being accompanied by social reinforcements such as, "I'm pleased," "That's very good," or smiles and head nods. The purpose of these extra reinforcements is to develop the eventual effectiveness of social reinforcement by pairing them with the tokens. The aides, nurses, and teachers who give these social reinforcements have been trained to expect them to be highly effective in producing change and, also, to respond positively to minimal change. Whatever cues are involved in high expectancy, these cues are maximized to enhance the social influence process (36). Demonstrations of appropriate behavior are given by aides or by other patients; in other words, modeling is used (6). Whatever variables are involved in the placebo effect (20) are also present in these programs, as in all behavior modification. But the evidence is that the specific technique of *token reinforcement* adds something in addition to all other effects.

The evidence is strong that behavior modification applications in the classroom are indeed useful for remediation purposes. However, our view is that the next step in the development of research and application will involve planning for the regular school programs by utilizing behavior modification token economies within the context of the open classroom in a new pattern of educational practice, an avowedly planned environment. The disruptive discipline behaviors which early token programs were designed to ameliorate (e.g., leaving seat) have been designed *out* by the nature of the environment of an open classroom.

REFERENCES

1. Atthowe, J. M., and Krasner, L. "A Preliminary Report on the Application of Contingent Reinforcement Procedures (Token Economy) on a 'Chronic' Psychiatric Ward." *Journal of Abnormal Psychology* 73 (1968): 37-43.
2. Ayllon, T., and Azrin, N. H. "The Measurement and Reinforcement of Behavior of Psychotics." *Journal of Experimental Analysis of Behavior* 8 (1965): 357-83.
3. Ayllon, T., and Azrin, N. H. *The Token Economy: A Motivational System for Therapy and Rehabilitation.* New York: Appleton-Century-Crofts, 1968.
4. Ayllon, T., and Michael, J. L. "The Psychiatric Nurse as a Behavioral Engineer." *Journal of Experimental Analysis of Behavior* 2 (1959): 323-34.
5. Baer, D. M.; Wolf, M. M.; and Risley, T. R. "Some Current Dimensions of Applied Behavior Analysis." *Journal of Applied Behavior Analysis* 1 (1968): 91-97.
6. Bandura, A. *Principles of Behavior Modification.* New York: Holt, Rinehart & Winston, 1969.
6a. Bellamy, E. *Looking Backward: 2000-1887.* Boston: Ticknor, 1888.
7. Bijou, S. W.; Peterson, R. F.; Harris, F. R.; Allen, K. E.; and Johnston, M. "Methodology for Experimental Studies of Young Children in Natural Settings." *Psychological Record* 19 (1969): 177-210.
8. Birnbrauer, J. S., and Lawler, J. "Token Reinforcement for Learning." *Mental Retardation* 2 (1964): 275-79.
9. Birnbrauer, J. S.; Wolf, M. M.; Kidder, J. D.; and Tague, C. E. "Classroom Behavior of Retarded Pupils with Token Reinforcement." *Journal of Experimental Child Psychology* 2 (1965): 219-35.
10. Broden, M.; Hall, R. V.; Dunlap, A.; and Clark, R. "Effects of Teacher Attention and a Token Reinforcement System in a Junior High School Special Education Class." *Exceptional Children* 36 (1970): 341-49.
11. Burchard, J. D. "Residential Behavior Modification Programs and the Problem of Uncontrolled Contingencies: A Reply to Lachenmeyer." *Psychological Record* 19 (1969): 259-61.
12. Burchard, J. D. "Systematic Socialization: A Programmed Environment for the Habilitation of Antisocial Retardates." *Psychological Record* 17 (1967): 461-76.

13. Bushell, D., Jr., Wrobel, P. A.; and Michaelis, M. L. "Applying 'Group' Contingencies to the Classrom Study Behavior of Pre-school Children." *Journal of Applied Behavior Analysis* 1 (1968): 55-61.

14. Bussis, A. M., and Chittenden, E. A. *Analysis of an Approach to Open Education*. Princeton, N.J.: Educational Testing Service, 1970.

15. Clark, M.; Lachowicz, J.; and Wolf, M. "A Pilot Basic Education Program for School Dropouts Incorporating a Token Reinforcement System." *Behaviour Research and Therapy* 6 (1968): 183-88.

16. Cohen, H. L. "Educational Therapy: The Design of Learning Environments." In *Research in Psychotherapy*, vol. 3, edited by J. M. Shlien. Washington: American Psychological Association, 1968.

17. Eysenck, H. J. "Learning Theory and Behaviour Therapy." *Journal of Mental Science* 105 (1959): 61-75.

18. Featherstone, J. *Schools Where Children Learn*. New York: Liveright, 1971.

19. Ferster, C. B., and DeMyer , M. K. "The Development of Performance" in Autistic Children in an Automatically Controlled Environment." *Journal of Chronic Diseases* 13 (1961): 312-45.

20. Frank, J. D. *Persuasion and Healing*. Baltimore: Johns Hopkins Press, 1961.

21. Franks, C. M. *Behavior Therapy: Appraisal and Status*. New York: McGraw-Hill Book Co., 1969.

22. Galbraith, J. K. *The New Industrial State*. Boston: Houghton Mifflin Co. 1967.

23. Gericke, O. L. "Practical Use of Operant Conditioning Studies in a Mental Hospital." *Psychiatric Studies and Projects* 3 (1965): 1-10.

24. Girardeau, F., and Spradlin, J. "Token Rewards on a Cottage Program." *Mental Retardation* 2 (1964): 345-51.

25. Gripp, R. F., and Magaro, P. A. "A Token Economy Program Evaluation with Untreated Control Ward Comparisons." *Behaviour Research and Therapy* 9 (1971): 137-49.

26. Haring, N. G., and Hauck, M. A. "Improving Learning Conditions in the Establishment of Reading Skills with Disturbed Readers." *Exceptional Children* 35 (1969): 341-51.

27. Henderson, J. D. "The Use of Dual Reinforcement in an Intensive Treatment System." In *Advances in Behavior Therapy, 1968*, edited by R. D. Rubin and C. M. Franks. New York: Academic Press, 1969.

28. Hewett, F. M.; Taylor, F. D.; and Artuso, A. A. "The Santa Monica Project: Evaluation of an Engineered Classroom Design with Emotionally Disturbed Children." *Exceptional Children* 35 (1969): 523-29.

29. Kanfer, F. H., and Phillips, J. S. *Learning Foundations of Behavior Therapy*. New York: John Wiley & Sons, 1970.

30. Kaufman, K. "The Differential Effects of Reward and Cost Procedures in Token Programs with Disruptive Adolescents in a Psychiatric Hospital School." Doctoral dissertation, State University of New York, Stony Brook, New York, 1971.

31. Kazdin, A. E., and Bootzin, R. R. "The Token Economy: An Evaluative Review." *Journal of Applied Behavior Analysis*, in press.

32. Krasner, L. "Assessment of Token Economy Programmes in Psychiatric Hospitals." In *The Role of Learning in Psychotherapy*, edited by R. Porter. London: Churchill, 1968.

33. ———. "Behavior Therapy." In *Annual Review of Psychology*, vol. 22, edited by P. Mussen. Palo Alto, Calif.: Annual Reviews, 1971.

34. ———. "Token Economies." In *Uses of Reinforcement Principles in Education*, edited by W. C. Becker. Champaign, Ill.: Research Press, forthcoming.

35. Krasner, L., and Atthowe, J. M. "The Token Economy As a Rehabilitative Procedure in a Mental Hospital Setting." In *Behavioral Intervention in Human Problems*, edited by H. C. Rickard. New York: Pergamon Press, 1971.

36. Krasner, L., and Ullmann, L. P. *Behavior Influence and Personality: The Social Matrix of Human Action*. New York: Holt, Rinehart & Winston, 1973.

37. Kuypers, D. S.; Becker, W. C.; and O'Leary, K. D. "How to Make a Token System Fail." *Exceptional Children* 35 (1968): 101-09.

38. Lazarus, A. A. "New Methods in Psychotherapy: A Case Study." *South African Medical Journal* 32 (1958): 660-63.

39. Lent, J. R. "Mimosa Cottage: Experiment in Hope." *Psychology Today* 2 (1968): 51-58.

40. Lindsley, O. R.; Skinner, B. F.; and Solomon, H. C. *Studies in Behavior Therapy: Status Report I*. Waltham, Mass.: Metropolitan State Hospital, 1953.

41. Lloyd, K. E., and Abel, L. "Performance on a Token Economy Psychiatric Ward: A Two Year Summary." *Behaviour Research and Therapy* 8 (1970): 1-9.

42. Lloyd, K. E., and Garlington, W. K. "Weekly Variations in Performance on a Token Economy Psychiatric Ward." *Behaviour Research and Therapy* 6 (1968): 407-10.

43. Lovaas, O. I. "Some Studies on the Treatment of Childhood Schizophrenia." In *Research in Psychotherapy*, vol. 3, edited by J. M. Shlien. Washington: American Psychological Association, 1968.

44. Mandelker, V.; Brigham, T. A.; and Bushell, D., Jr. "The Effects of Token Procedures on a Teacher's Social Contacts with Her Students." *Journal of Applied Behavior Analysis* 3 (1970) 169-74.

45. Marks, J.; Sonoda, B.; and Schalock, R. "Reinforcement versus Relationship Therapy for Schizophrenics." *Journal of Abnormal Psychology*, 73 (1968): 397-402.

46. Madsen, C. H.; Becker, W. C.; and Thomas, D. R. "Rules, Praise, and Ignoring: Elements of Elementary Classroom Control." *Journal of Applied Behavior Analysis* 1 (1968): 139-50.

47. Martin, M.; Burkholder, R.; Rosenthal, T. L.; Tharp, R. G.; and Thorne, G. L. "Programming Behavior Change and Reintegration into School Milieux of Extreme Adolescent Deviates." *Behaviour Research and Therapy* 6 (1968): 371-83.

48. Meichenbaum, D. H.; Bowers, K. S.; and Ross, R. R. "Modification of Classroom Behavior of Institutionalized Female Adolescent Offenders." *Behaviour Research and Therapy* 6 (1968): 343-53.

49. Miller, L. K. "Freedom Money: A Token Economy Approach to Organizing Self-Help Activities among Low Income Families." O. E. O. Grant CH. 8719 A/O. Annual Report no. 1, 1969.

50. Miller, L. K., and Schneider, R. "The Use of a Token System in Project Head Start." *Journal of Applied Behavior Analysis.* 3 (1970): 213-20.

51. O'Leary, K. D., and Becker, W. C. "Behavior Modification of an Adjustment Class: A Token Reinforcement Program." *Exceptional Children* 33 (1967): 637-42.

52. O'Leary, K. D.; Becker, W. C.; Evans, M. B.; and Saudargas, R. A. "A Token Reinforcement Program in a Pubic School: A Replication and Systematic Analysis." *Journal of Applied Behavior Analysis* 2 (1969): 3-13.

53. O'Leary, K. D., and Drabman, R. "Token Reinforcement Programs in the Classroom: A Review." *Psychological Bulletin* 75 (1971): 379-98.

54. Panek, D. M. "Ward Association Learning by Chronic Schizophrenics on a Token Economy Ward under Conditions of Reward and Punishment." Paper presented to Western Psychological Association, San Francisco, 1967.

55. Parrino, J.; George, L.; and Daniels, A. C. "Token Controlled Pill Taking Behavior in a Psychiatric Ward." *Journal of Behaviour Therapy and Experimental Psychiatry* 2 (1971): 181-85.

56. Patterson, G. R. "Behavioral Techniques Based upon Social Learning: An Additional Base for Developing Behavior Modification Technologies." In *Behavior Therapy: Appraisal and Status*, edited by C. M. Franks. New York: McGraw-Hill Book Co., 1969.

57. Phillips, E. L. "Achievement Place: Token Reinforcement Procedures in a Home-Style Rehabilitation Setting for 'Pre-delinquent' Boys." *Jounral of Applied Behavior Analysis* 1 (1968): 213-23.

58. Plowden, L., Ch. *Children and Their Primary Schools, A Report of the Central Advisory Council for Education* (England), vol. 1. New York: British Information Services, 1967.

59. Rothman, D. J. *The Discovery of the Asylum.* Boston, Mass.: Little, Brown & Co., 1971.

60. Schaefer, H. H., and Martin, P. L. "Behavioral Therapy for 'Apathy' of Hospitalized Schizophrenics." *Psychological Reports* 19 (1966): 1147-58.
61. Shean, G. D., and Zeidberg, Z. "Token Reinforcement Therapy: A Comparison of Matched Groups." *Journal of Behaviour Therapy and Experimental Psychiatry* 2 (1971): 95-105.
62. Silberman, C. E. *Crisis in the Classroom.* New York: Random House, 1970.
63. Skinner, B. F. *The Behavior of Organisms.* New York: Appleton-Century-Crofts, 1938.
64. ———. *Beyond Freedom and Dignity.* New York: A. A. Knopf, 1971.
65. ———. *Science and Human Behavior.* New York: Macmillan Co., 1953.
66. ———. *Walden Two.* New York: Macmillan Co., 1948.
67. Sletten, I. W.; Hughes, D. D.; Lamont, J.; and Ognjanov, V. "Work Performance in Psychiatric Patients: Tokens versus Money." *Diseases of the Nervous System* 29 (1968): 261-64.
68. Staats, A. W. "Reinforcer Systems in the Solution of Human Problems." In *Behavior Modification in the Classroom,* edited by G. G. Fargo, C. Behrns, and P. Nolen. Belmont, Calif.: Wadswoth Publishing Co., 1971.
69. Staats, A. W.; Minke, K. A.; Finley, J. R.; Wolf, M.; and Brooks, L. O. "A Reinforcer System and Experimental Procedure for the Laboratory Study of Reading Acquisition." *Child Development* 35 (1964): 209-31.
70. Steffy, R. A.; Hart, J.; Craw, M.; Torney, D.; and Marlett, N. "Operant Behavior Modification Techniques Applied to a Ward of Severely Regressed and Aggressive Patients." *Canadian Psychiatric Association Journal* 14 (1969): 59-67.
71. Stuart, R. B. "Operant-Interpersonal Treatment for Marital Discord." *Journal of Consulting Clinical Psychology* 33 (1969): 675-82.
72. Thomas, D. R.; Becker, W. C.; and Armstrong, M. "Production and Elimination of Disruptive Classroom Behavior by Systematically Varying Teacher's Behavior." *Journal of Applied Behavior Analyses* 1 (1968): 35-45.
73. Tyler, V. O., and Brown, G. D. "Token Reinforcement of Academic Performance with Institutionalized Delinquent Boys." *Journal of Educational Psychology* 59 (1968): 164-68.
74. Ullmann, L. P. "Behavior Therapy as Social Movement." In *Behavior Therapy: Appraisal and Status,* edited by C. M. Franks. New York: McGraw-Hill Book Co., 1969.
75. Ullmann, L. P., and Krasner, L. *A Psychological Approach to Abnormal Behavior.* New York: Holt, Rinehart & Winston, 1969.
76. Walker, H. M.; Mattson, R. H.; and Buckley, N. K. "Special Class

Placement as a Treatment Alternative for Deviant Behavior in Children." In Monograph 1, Department of Special Education. University of Oregon, Eugene, Oreg., 1969.

77. Ward, M. H., and Baker, B. L. "Reinforcement Therapy in the Classroom." *Journal of Applied Behavior Analysis* 1 (1968): 323-28.

78. Weber, L. *The English Infant School and Informal Education.* Englewood Cliffs, N.J.: Prentice-Hall, 1971.

79. Winett, R. A.; Richards, C. S.; Krasner, L.; and Krasner, M. "Child Monitored Token Reading Program." *Psychology in the Schools,* 8 (1971): 259-62.

80. Winett, R. A., and Winkler, R. C. "Current Behavior Modification in the Classroom: Be Still, Be Quiet, Be Docile." *Journal of Applied Behavior Analysis,* 1972, in press.

81. Winkler, R. C. "Management of Chronic Psychiatric Patients by a Token Reinforcement System." *Journal of Applied Behavior Analysis* 3 (1970): 47-55.

82. Winkler, R. C., and Krasner, L. "The Contribution of Economics to Token Economies." Paper presented at annual meeting, Eastern Psychological Association, New York City, April, 1971.

83. Wolf, M. M.; Giles, D. K.; and Hall, R. V. "Experiments with Token Reinforcement in a Remedial Classroom." *Behaviour Research and Therapy* 6 (1968): 51-64.

84. Wolpe, J. *Psychotherapy by Reciprocal Inhibition.* Stanford: Stanford University Press, 1958.

85. Zimmerman, E. H.; Zimmerman, J.; and Russell, C. D. "Differential Effects of Token Reinforcement on Instruction-Following Behavior in Retarded Students Instructed as a Group." *Journal of Applied Behavior Analyses* 2 (1969): 101-12.

PROBLEMS AND PROSPECTS

CHAPTER XII

Behavioral Humanism

CARL E. THORESEN

Educators and behavioral scientists can act to help individuals experience life in more positive ways. There are many possible ways to take such actions. One offers considerable promise: the synthesizing of social learning–behavioral principles and techniques with the goals and concerns of humanistic psychology. This synthesis is termed behavioral humanism. We can benefit from the work of behaviorists and humanists if we act to reduce the confusion and ambiguity about contemporary behaviorism and humanism and if we develop and use new scientific methods tailored to the study of human phenomena. In this chapter an effort is made to reduce some of the misunderstanding about contemporary humanism and behaviorism. The intensive experimental study of individuals ($N=1$ design) is discussed as an "intimate" research design well suited to the study of humanistic concerns. A behavioral approach to self-control is briefly presented as one way of helping the individual gain power for self-direction. A translation of humanistic concepts into human action (response) terms is suggested.

On Humanism

A variety of humanisms have existed since the time of Hellenic civilization. Today there are classical, ethical, scientific, religious, Christian, and rational humanists. Many individuals are essentially humanists, although they do not label themselves as such. Those

The work described herein was conducted at the Stanford Center for Research and Development in Teaching, which is supported in part as a Research and Development Center under Contract No. OEC-6-10-078 with the United States Office of Education, Department of Health, Education, and Welfare. The opinions expressed in this publication do not necessarily reflect the position or policy of the Office of Education, and no official endorsement by the Office of Education should be inferred.

who identify with humanistic psychology can be seen as representing a blending of psychology as a discipline with ethical forms of humanism (118).

Humanism was and is primarily a philosophical and literary movement. It emerged in the early Renaissance as a reaction against the revealed truth of the Church and the dominance of Aristotelian thinking (1). The early humanists argued that man, through his own intellect, had the power (and the responsibility) to determine his own destiny. It was the Renaissance humanists who made the definitive break that opened the way for the rise of Western science. Interestingly, many contemporary humanists now oppose the scientific world view initiated by earlier humanists.

Kurtz (53) suggests that two basic principles characterize humanism: a rejection of any supernatural world view as established fact and a rejection of any metaphysical divinity as the source of human values. Some people may believe in supernatural powers but, since there is no known empirical means to prove or refute these views, the existence of such powers is a matter not of fact but of personal belief. For the humanist, man must be responsible for himself, especially in deciding what is good, desirable, and worthwhile. Man is the maker of values and man's actions represent, in effect, his values.

Not all humanists, however, accept two other basic principles offered by Kurtz (53): that ethical principles and value judgments should be open to empirical, rational scrutiny and that the methods of science can be applied in solving man's problems. The humanist is generally concerned with what people do in this life—with human actions in life's present circumstances. Many humanists further believe that the use of reason and methods of science provides the best single means of solving human problems and improving the quality of human life. For example, Eysenck (30:25) states that "the use of reason in human affairs applied in the service of compassion" reflects a basic spirit of many humanists.

Definitions of what constitutes humanism are as diverse as the individuals offering the definitions. Interestingly, many contemporary "behaviorists," i.e., behavior therapists, behavioral counselors, and operant psychologists or social learning psychologists consider themselves humanists (see 21, 43, 48, 58, 64, 97, 103, 110,

111). Several reasons explain why behavior-oriented professionals see themselves this way. First of all, they focus on what the individual person *does* in the present life and not on who he *is* in terms of vague social labels or obscure descriptions. Secondly, they emphasize human problems as primarily learning situations where the person is seen as capable of changing. Thirdly, they examine how environments can be altered to reduce and prevent human problems, and, finally, they use scientific procedures to improve techniques for helping individuals.

Differences or distinctions between contemporary behaviorists and humanists do exist. For example, many contemporary humanists have rejected methods of science as a means of problem-solving, whereas behaviorists are strongly committed to the need for rigorous empirical inquiry. As many differences exist, however, within heterogeneous groupings called behaviorist or humanist as between such groupings. The issue is not behaviorism versus humanism; that is a pseudoissue that has been promoted by crude caricatures of these positions. Instead, the issue is how best to utilize the concepts and methodologies of both behavioral and humanistic psychology. An examination of the literature of humanistic psychology should help us clarify the concerns of humanists.

Humanistic Psychology and Education

Many people have written about the concerns of humanistic psychology and education (e.g., see 2, 13, 15, 28, 31, 41, 45, 46, 57, 70, 71, 72, 80, 85, 89, 117). Humanistic psychology and education have been influenced by a host of Eastern and Western schools of philosophy, psychology, and religious thought. Abraham Maslow, Carl Rogers, Rollo May, and Viktor Frankl have in particular extended this influence. The tolerance for diversity and pluralism that characterizes humanistic psychology brings about a confluence of theoretical orientations such as neopsychoanalytic, phenomenological, gestalt, existential, and Rogerian. As a result, the field at present lacks a coherent, integrated, theoretical rationale. This theoretical looseness, though cherished by some, has discouraged empirical research. Buhler (15), in presenting the basic theoretical concepts of humanistic psychology, has distinguished it from the philosophy of humanism in that different concepts, methods, and goals are involved. For Buhler, humanistic psychology must use scientific methods to discover ways of helping the person "experience his existence as real." The humanistic psychologist is seen as more action-oriented than the traditional literary humanist who is seen as one engaged in philosophical disputes and antireligious quarrels.

Jourard (46) has emphasized transcendent behaviors, where the individual learns by committing himself fully in thinking, perceiving, and achieving, by going beyond the typical, by acting divergently, by taking risks, and by using fantasy. Transcendent behavior is made possible by an openness to experience, the ability to focus selectively, skill in using symbols and metaphors, and self-confidence. For Landsman (57) the key unit of behavior is "positive experiencing." He suggests that efforts should be directed toward the "experimental creation of positive experiences." Maslow (69, 70) sees the major task of humanistic psychology as collaborating with the behavioral sciences in the study of how to create physical and social environments that will nurture self-actualization. In discussing humanistic education, Brown (13) has stressed the need for a confluence of the cognitive and the affective aspects of learning. With this integration the curriculum could provide planned educational experiences for all kinds of human learning.

Maslow (70:732) offered what can be viewed as the basic theme of humanistic psychology and education: "The first and overarching Big Problem is to make the Good Person." This concept of creating the good person permeates the writings of humanistic psychology. The task of psychology is to develop methods to help the individual person act in more positive, meaningful ways with himself and with others. An examination of the literature of humanistic psychologists and educators reveals the following concerns:

1. The person as the unit of focus rather than the average performance of large groups and populations
2. The search for unity in human experience; the recognition that the person must exist in harmony with himself and nature
3. Awareness and awakening; attempts to increase the conscious range of the person's behavior, especially in his own internal behavior, such as thoughts, images, and physiological responses
4. The need for compassionate persons, individuals who can communi-

cate personally and intimately with others in a variety of ways and
who can also help others experience life more positively

5. Self-determination and responsibility; the ability to identify alternatives, clarify values, make decisions, and accept the responsibility for
   one's actions

6. Diversity and pluralism; a reverence for the idiosyncratic and the
   unique in individuals

7. The need for new research techniques and methodologies tailored to
   the intensive study of the individual person—techniques that avoid
   the detachment and impersonality of traditional physical science
   methods

8. The need for educational experiences that engage the individual in a
   comprehensive sense, involving social, emotional, and sensual actions
   as well as the so-called academic or cognitive

The focus of action-oriented humanists is on what the individual
person does internally and externally. These concerns highlight the
interdependence of action in stressing the need for unity and
harmony in experience. The self-actualizing person is someone who
knows what is happening, someone who is aware of a variety of
responses taking place both within himself and with others in the
external environment. Further, such a person is seen as one who
has the skills to "make things happen."

Contemporary Behaviorism

The term *behaviorist* represents a variety of theoretical positions
and technical practices. There is diversity and disagreement among
those who consider themselves to be behaviorists (22, 88). While
all aspects of what constitutes behaviorism cannot be discussed here,
a brief discussion may clarify the situation enough to eliminate some
stereotypes.

Clearly, the behaviorism lamented by its critics (50, 51, 71) is a
dated and inaccurate representation. Behaviorism is not, for example,
the simple (minded) application of reinforcement schedules to
persons as if they were no different than rats or pigeons. Nor is all
behaviorism a physicalistic, empty (headed) black-box psychology.
Behaviorism or behavior therapy does not deny thoughts and complex emotions nor does it treat individuals as "simple mechanical
entities" (86). At present there is no one type of behaviorism. Behaviorists today range from experimental psychologists who meticu-

lously study specific animal responses in highly controlled labora- tories to counselors and therapists who work with the immediate complex problems of individuals. Contemporary behaviorism is, in fact, a rich conglomeration of principles, assumptions, and tech- niques.

Perhaps what characterizes all behaviorists is their use of experi- mental methods, their reliance on empirical data based on careful observation, their concern for objectivity and replication of results, their focus on the environment and what the organism is doing currently, and their rejection of inner causes or entities as the sole or most important determinant of human action. To the behaviorist, the "here and now" contemporary environment is a prime focus of concern because much of what a person does is a function of environmental events.

Popular conceptions of behaviorism often fail to acknowledge differences between behaviorists. Some *conventional* behaviorists have emphasized internal processes such as drive reduction or habit strength to explain behavior (23, 44). Others have suggested curios- ity and exploratory drives that are elicited by external stimuli (8, 40) while still others have conceptualized internal sensory feedback processes to explain behavior (79). In addition, conventional be- haviorism has emphasized operational definitions and the direct observation of physical responses. Some conventional behaviorists are also dualistic in the Cartesian mind-body sense. To them the events of the mind are not to be understood in the same fashion as physical behavior, i.e., sensory motor (88). Conventional behav- iorists have also relied heavily on extensive deductive theories and have typically employed experimental group designs in their re- search (e.g., 44).

In contrast, the *radical* behaviorist rejected this mind-body dual- ism, the reliance on operational definitions and mentalistic explana- tions such as drive states and drive reduction (101).[1] Private events, that is, what goes on within the person, are viewed as influenced by the same learning principles as is external behavior. The radical be-

[1] A distinction is sometimes made between the early radical behaviorism of John Watson and B. F. Skinner's contemporary radical behaviorism (Day, 22; Terrace, 107). Both are labeled radical in rejecting mentalistic inner explanations such as drives. However, Watson's highly physicalistic S-R rationale, coupled with a dualistic perspective, differs markedly from Skinner's operant theory (99).

haviorist also rejects elaborate experimental group designs and reliance on inferential statistics of the conventionalists based on the average performance of groups of subjects. Instead, he considers that the individual organism serves as the focus of research and that observations are to be made continuously before, during, and after planned interventions with an emphasis on careful description.

Besides conventional and radical behaviorists there are social learning or cognitive behaviorists (e.g., 6), who emphasize internal processes such as thoughts and imagery in explaining how learning occurs. At the present, the term *behaviorist* may therefore refer to conventional, radical, or cognitive-oriented behaviorism.

The early behaviorism of Watson (115) sought to reduce all human action to physical terms and to explain it in those terms. Figuratively, the early S-R advocates believed that if the phenomenon could not be reduced to units that comfortably fitted in their scientific test tube, then the phenomenon was metaphysical and meaningless. Watson denied the existence of consciousness and awareness, rejected introspection (self-report) as a valid scientific method, and saw all of man's actions as determined by forces outside the person. The spirit of Watson's viewpoint is represented in a recent article (61) in which it is argued that much of what is called behavior therapy today is not behavioristic since these therapies, e.g., the systematic desensitization of Wolpe (122), use covert processes, rely on self-reports from clients, and are not restricted to behavior directly observable by others. For the early Watsonian behaviorist and some conventional behaviorists today, the focus is on physically based operational definitions and direct physical assessment. If the phenomenon in question cannot be measured directly with some type of physical device—ruler, scale, calipers, polygraph—then the phenomenon is beyond scientific interest. Except for physiological responses such as heart rate, which can be measured directly and independent of the individual, covert events are deemed beyond controlled inquiry.

The radical behaviorism of Skinner differs from the conventional S-R framework in several ways. Skinner rejected the positivistic operationalism and the limited physicalistic rationale of the earlier behaviorists and functionalists (101). He argued that in an adequate

science of behavior nothing that determines conduct can be overlooked, no matter how difficult of access it may be. Skinner acknowledged the role of private events in explaining behavior and the
person's internal environment. He observed, "It would be a mistake
to refuse to consider them (private events) as data just because a
second observer cannot feel or see them . . ." (99:242). He remained skeptical, however, concerning how central a role internal
responses play in determining what the individual does. Covert responses such as thoughts or internal sentences are not autonomous
but, rather, owe their existence to a public history of learning.

Skinner also rejected the animistic and mentalistic explanations
of behavior, such as ego, positive growth force, drive reduction or
sensory drive mechanism, as explanatory fictions created to explain
what is not yet understood. Skinner contended that the individual
behaves internally and these covert responses are explainable by the
same principles as are observable external responses (100, 102). Since
the individual may be the only person with access to a private event
such as a self-verbalization, self-reports of private events are justified.
Skinner (97, 100, 102) has consistently acknowledged the difficulties
in dealing scientifically with internal phenomena. While his own
work has avoided inquiry into the area, his theoretical rationale
clearly recognizes the import of the individual's internal behavior.

Skinner's basic unit of analysis, the three-term contingency, is
very significant for its relevance in understanding the causes of individual action. Human behavior (internal or external) is influenced
by preceding events (stimulus control) *and* by events that follow
certain actions (outcome control). These antecedent and consequent events may be internal, within the person, as well as external
to the person. To understand why the individual does certain things,
one must carefully observe the conditions and circumstances surrounding his actions.[2]

---

[2] Interestingly, the "radical" position of Skinner is shared considerably by
the radical phenomenology of Sartre and Merleau-Ponty (74) who reject
what they consider the introspective, dualistic, idealistic views of American
phenomenologists such as Rogers and May. These radical phenomenologists
stress the primacy of observing and describing human behavior. Mentalistic
causes and notions of inner man are rejected. Instead, human behavior is to
be understood by examining the interaction between the person and his environment. See Kvale and Grenners (54).

SOCIAL LEARNING

The most recent development in contemporary behaviorism can be called the social behavior or social learning approach (6, 78). This type of behaviorism does not conceptualize behavior in Skinner's operant response terms (e.g., the three-term contingency). Further, it does not utilize the traits, motives, and drive explanations of conventional behaviorists (23, 29), nor does it reject the relevance of internal processes and events. Indeed, to social learning behaviorists the often-cited empty "black box" is considered quite full.

In the social behavior view, individual actions are seen as regulated by three basic processes: stimulus control, internal symbolic control, and outcome control (6). A major focus of the social behavior theory is on the person's covert symbolic responses. Mediation, what goes on with the person, is viewed as important data, as is the "meaning" or significance of a particular situation to the person. Bandura (6) has emphasized the importance of vicarious or observational learning which takes place by means of symbolic processes within the individual. Observational learning is not explained in an external stimulus cue and reinforcement paradigm. Rather, observational learning is presented as a dynamic sequence of complex processes involving attentional, retentional, reproductive, and motivational factors.

In the social learning perspective a distinction is made between acquisition of behavior (learning) and its performance. Internal symbolic and sensory process play the major part in learning new behavior while the external contingencies of reinforcement (outcomes) determine if the behavior is then performed. Reinforcement is seen as primarily of informational and incentive value. The individual can learn without overtly performing and without any direct reinforcement. Social behaviorists view the individual person as a dynamically changing organism rather than as a passive receptacle of enduring responses. The internal and external actions of each person are primarily influenced by the specific "here and now" experiences.

Social behaviorism and Skinner's radical behaviorism are highly similar in stressing current environmental situations as prime determinants of human action. While Skinner's theoretical work has clearly recognized private events and the individual's internal environment, the research and practice of radical behaviorists has generally avoided this area. Social behaviorists, however, have pursued the more complex area of symbolic behavior, seeking to understand how covert events as responses interact with external responses to regulate what the person does.

Behaviorism today is far more than the psychology of Watson with its physicalistic concerns or the drive reduction–oriented animal experiments of the conventionalists. *Behaviorism* as a term denotes an emphasis on the comprehensive and systematic study of the individual, which uses empirical methods to examine how current environments may be influencing the individual's action. What goes on within the individual—covert responses—represents important data.

Some basic characteristics of contemporary radical behaviorism and social learning approaches are as follows:

1. A monistic view of the individual and a rejection of a dualistic mind-body theory
2. A belief that public or observable events are functionally similar to private or covert events and that both kinds of events are influenced by the same learning processes and principles
3. A rejection of inner "mentalistic" explanations of behavior
4. A belief that behavior is determined primarily by the immediate environment, including the person's internal environment
5. A use of scientific methods that stress careful, systematic observation and control of behavior, including self-observation and self-control
6. A rejection of using trait-state labels (e.g., introvert) to describe the person, based on the belief that the individual is best described and understood by examining what he does in particular situations

Intensive Study of the Individual

Traditional research designs and techniques have been grossly inadequate for the scientific study of the individual person. Prevailing research methodologies have been criticized for their irrelevance in understanding the actions of individuals (19, 69, 105, 109, 123). Controlled psychological research has relied almost exclusively on a particular type of research design that requires the use of large groups of subjects and the concomitant need for elaborate statistical procedures. This type of design has been often exalted as the only true and legitimate strategy for scientific inquiry (19).

A cursory review of research textbooks used in psychology testifies to the dominance of comparative group designs. These extensive designs with their focus on the mean performance of groups of individuals have yielded limited information about the whats and whys of individual performance. A major reason for this has to do with the underlying assumptions of extensive designs, such as the concept of "intrinsic" variability of individuals within groups and the role of the central limit theorem (94). In effect, most psychological research has sought generalizations that apply to the performance of populations. Such generalizations have required the need for random sampling from populations—an assumption almost always violated by psychological researchers (27)—and the use of statistical techniques to handle troublesome individual variability. Such variability is sometimes referred to as error or nuisance variance or unexplained individual fluctuations. Extensive designs using group comparisons represent a powerful strategy to verify hypotheses about hypothetical populations. However, such designs are concerned with only one facet of the cycle of scientific inquiry, which includes discovery, description, observation, induction, deduction, and verification (55, 84). Scientific inquiry requires a variety of designs and techniques; there is no one best method.

Fortunately, an alternative design, one with a long and honorable history in science (25), is available. The intensive empirical study of the single case, N=1, is an experimental design ideally suited for the kind of "intimate" inquiry required for the concerns of humanists. The intensive design avoids many of the problems of large-group studies deriving from the use of statistical techniques to control for individual variation rather than precise experimental control, from random sampling from hypothetical populations, from the failure to pinpoint specific cause-and-effect relationships for individual behavior, and from not providing continuous data on changes of every subject throughout all phases of the investigation. The intensive design, sometimes referred to as the experimental study of the individual, is based on different assumptions than the group designs. Further, it seeks to answer different questions, such as how specific conditions influence certain individual actions over time. The concern is not with what Kurt Lewin (59) once called "on the average thinking," but with understanding how each individual is influenced by specific interventions.

Comprehensive discussions of the intensive experimental study of individual behavior are available (14, 19, 94, 108, 120). These discussions provide detailed information on different types of intensive designs such as multiple time series, the base-line treatment reversals, and multiple base-line procedures. The discussion here is (a) to introduce the relevance of intensive designs for examining the kind of overt and covert human behavior of concern to humanists, (b) to suggest that criticism of behavioral or scientific research has been misdirected because of stereotyped conceptions, and (c) to summarize the merits of intensive designs in studying individual behavior.

Maslow (69), one of the founders of humanistic psychology, deplored the rigid conventionalism of psychological researchers. He believed it was possible and desirable to develop new methods and designs for studying the individual scientifically. Allport (3) long ago urged that idiographic rather than nomothetic strategies should be used if we are to understand individuals. Allport developed a variety of what he called morphogenic methods, such as personal letters, questionnaires, structured interviews, and biographies, along with self-anchoring rating scales, to study the structure of each individual. Similarly, Lewin (59) argued that the individual should be studied in relation to his current environment, which he described as "concrete whole situations." Lewin criticized the Aristotelian logic underlying extensive designs and classical statistics, which required the individual to be viewed as a random or capricious event. Instead, Lewin believed that the actions of each individual were lawful and understandable through scientific investigation if appropriate designs were developed. Skinner (98), somewhat in the tradition of the early $N = 1$ experimental psychologists of the late nineteenth century (e.g., Ebbinghaus), challenged the orthodoxy of statistical group research methodologies. Skinner argued that the prevalent use of inferential statistical operations kept investigators away from working directly with data, an argument also raised by others (5, 104). To Skinner, functional or causal relationships could best be discovered and confirmed by exercising tight experimental control of the situation. Elaborate group statistics were too often used as an excuse for failing to use experimental control.

Skinner's early work with animal subjects was based on a continuous observing and recording of data over long periods of time. Various interventions were tried and the results directly observed. On the basis of these observations, interventions were often altered. In this way the investigator learned from the data; his actions were determined by what the individual subject was observed to do. It is the potential for this rich interplay between the researcher and the individual subject that makes the intensive design a powerful research strategy—a design similar to the Taoist approach to inquiry advanced by Maslow (69).

Some critics of behavioral psychology have used the "subjective" revolution in physics with its concepts of indeterminacy, complementarity, and uncertainty as a basis of rejecting the methods of scientific psychology (71). Since the performance of individual atoms and electrons can neither be predicted nor controlled, man, it is argued, is also beyond prediction and control. Man is seen as just as complex as an atom or an electron. Therefore, behavioral psychology with its deterministic rationale of classical science derived from Newton and Hume is viewed as inappropriate for the study of man.

The problem of this kind of analogous thinking is that it assumes that *all* human action functions in the same way as subatomic particles. All human activity, from the movement of blood cells to verbal responses, cannot be explained by any single rationale. Physics did not reject classical determinism totally in the twentieth century but, instead, expanded its rationales to fit various phenomena. The question is what types of human behavior are best understood by what explanatory rationales. The determinism versus indeterminism argument is a pseudoissue that fails to capture the complexities involved. We do not know enough at present about how different types of human behavior are influenced. Undoubtedly the rigid, mechanistic determinism of classical Western science with its notions of absolute prediction is invalid for much of the human activity of concern to humanists. Clearly there is a need for a variety of causal models and research strategies (9). Our task is to find out which human actions are best explained by what principles and which kinds of research designs are most appropriate to facilitate such inquiry.

Given the limited status of our understanding about individual human behavior, the intensive experimental study of individuals seems very promising. Every design of course has its limitations. Bandura (6:243-44) presents shortcomings of intensive designs, such as the problem of not being able to return to the base line after treatment and the confounding of sequential treatment effects. However, much is to be learned from focusing carefully on the individual through controlled observation and description. An intensive approach to research promises to create inquiry that is more personal and intimate in dealing with the individual. If we are to learn, the individual person cannot be treated as an inanimate object to be manipulated, but must be viewed as a dynamic, active organism. The individual has much to teach us. When it comes to understanding man, perhaps the person himself can be one of the best scientific tools in existence.

The intensive experimental study of the individual offers the following advantages:

1. The unit of focus is the specific actions of the individual subjects rather than average performance of groups.
2. The frequency, magnitude and/or variability of the individual's actions can be examined continuously during and between each phase of the investigation.
3. The individual subject serves as his own control in that the magnitude and duration of change is compared to his own base line of actions. In this way, past experience and individual differences are fully controlled.
4. Experimental control of variables is greatly facilitated, thereby reducing the need for statistical control through complex inferential statistics.
5. The effects of treatment administered simultaneously or sequentially on one or more individual behaviors can be examined over time for a particular individual.
6. Causal or functional relationships are established by replication (reproducibility) of specific results for the same individual and across individuals. In this way, evidence of generalization is systematically gathered without recourse to the often untenable assumption of random sampling.

7. The clinician as researcher can determine the extent of specific changes in individual actions continuously before, during, and after treatment; changes in treatment can be made and evaluated promptly.
8. Scientific inquiry into both external and internal behavior is possible.

Freedom and Self-Control

A growing area of behavioral research concerns self-control. What are the internal and external controlling responses that influence internal and external actions? Behavioral researchers are particularly interested in developing techniques to teach individuals how to manage their own actions. Some humanistic writers (10, 72) have criticized behaviorists for their failure to consider freedom and self-direction. Believing that the person is and should be free to decide what he shall do in a given situation, that human action is not predetermined and is not predictable, they see the behaviorist as someone who would deprive man of this freedom to determine his own actions. They equate the prediction and control of human behavior by others with the demise of freedom and dignity. But they view the individual's ability to predict and control his *own* actions as freedom.

The problem with this view of the individual's freedom is that past and present experiences with other persons do subtly influence what an individual may decide to do in the present. Common sense would suggest that the person can decide to do something completely independent of anything else. And a venerable literary tradition supports the view that self-direction operates entirely within the person. The person who thus charts his own course and makes his own choices is a free and dignified individual (56).

Freedom and dignity, however, are measured in individual actions. The free person has the power to take certain actions. The power, and therefore the freedom, depends on awareness, that is, the conscious processing of all kinds of information. Recall the premium placed on awareness by humanistic psychologists. Awareness is crucial, since information (stimuli, to use a technical term) influences the individual's behavior. The person who has information and who can control it is free. Terrace (107) argues that awareness is actually a learned behavior. The person learns to distinguish certain internal responses which he then labels "angry," "happy," "upset," and so forth. Awareness therefore consists of discriminating items of information or stimuli and describing them in some way. How a person "labels" information about his own behavior has been studied recently in attribution research (91). Inaccurate labeling and faulty stimulus discrimination by a person may be one type of maladaptive behavior pattern. The person, unable to explain adequately to himself the high arousal he is experiencing, concludes he is irrational and mentally disturbed (124).

In many ways the difference between individual freedom and control by others lies in "who is manipulating what stimuli" (62:214) or who is using and controlling information that influences human action. Awareness is the basis of freedom and self-control because it provides the individual with the information he needs to change his own sources of stimulation, both internal and external. Freedom versus determinism is therefore a pseudoissue. The freedom to act depends on the person's being aware of, or knowing, what kinds of information (stimuli) influence his own behavior. This awareness must include internal or covert stimuli as well as external data for both internal and external behavior.

Staats (103) has suggested that the very young child learns self-control by observing others. The young child talks aloud to himself at first, then gradually replaces these overt verbalizations with covert talk or self-verbalization in the form of self-instructions. After the first few years of life, the person engages in a great deal of covert speech (63, 113). However, his awareness of this internal behavior quickly diminishes. Thus, over time it *seems* to the person as if what he does is spontaneous and totally determined from within. Once behavior such as covert speech is learned from environmental experiences, however, that behavior can determine, in part, what the person will do. In this way it may be said that the person causes his own current and future behavior through what he has learned in the past. The person therefore acquires covert responses such as self-verbalization from others in his verbal community. The availability of these learned covert responses to the person determines whether that person is "free to act."

A series of experiments by Meichenbaum (75) and his colleagues illustrates how persons can be taught through social learning techniques "to talk to themselves differently" as a way of gaining greater freedom and self-control. In one study, children who had difficulty attending to a task were first provided concrete examples (social models) of others instructing themselves by speaking aloud. The children then practiced self-verbalizations with fewer external cues until they could direct their own actions without external support. In another study, adults labeled as schizophrenics were taught how to use covert self-instructions along with how to become aware of certain information that usually preceded their "crazy behavior." This training in using covert responses helped these individuals to gain greater self-control.

Viktor Frankl's modern classic, *Man's Search for Meaning* (34), exemplifies how the verbal community in most Western cultures teaches the person to conceptualize self-control as a vague inner force. Throughout Frankl's moving description of life in a concentration camp, he describes circumstances in which he used self-verbalization or vivid imagery. For long periods of time Frankl managed his inner environment by carrying on covert conversations with his wife or with friends, coupled with "mental pictures" of persons and situations. In this way aversive external stimuli—the sight of dead bodies, the verbal abuse by guards, and physiological cues such as hunger—were controlled. Frankl did not conceptualize his covert actions as influencing other behaviors, however. Instead, he explained them in terms of inner life and freedom. Frankl survived, he states, not because he was able to use a variety of effective covert responses in an extremely aversive external environment, but because he possessed an inner strength, a sense of meaning, and dignity. It might also be said that he survived because he had learned to use vivid images and to carry on covert dialogues with himself.

Techniques for self-control have had a long, though somewhat obscure, history. Varieties of Yoga and Zen procedures for self-managing thoughts and physiological responses have existed for over two thousand years. There is evidence that certain individuals have achieved astonishing levels of self-control. Green (37), for example, has reported laboratory studies with a yoga master who radically altered his heart rate, body temperature, and brain wave patterns repeatedly on demand. The yogi was engaging in a complex pattern of covert behavior that altered these responses. The unanswered questions are, What were these controlling behaviors? How did they function to effect such changes?

Research by behavior-oriented investigators has been expanding recently into physiological feedback (biofeedback) training, cognitive focusing, and the instrumental (operant) conditioning of glandular and visceral responses (26, 38, 77, 83, 116). DuPraw (26), for example, utilizing the work of Schultz and Luthe (93) in autogenic training, demonstrated that some individuals could significantly reduce their heart rate by using self-instructions (covert verbalizations) and selected imagery responses. Miller (77) and his colleagues have provided data in a series of animal studies which show that a great variety of internal physiological responses can be "voluntarily" controlled by the organism if reinforcing stimuli are provided. The well-publicized biofeedback studies (e.g., 20) involving EEG alpha waves have suggested that the person can learn to alter his "state of consciousness" if information or awareness of his current performance is provided.

These developments merit acknowledgement for their relevance in understanding self-control. A comprehensive discussion of these developments is beyond the scope of this paper. (For a comprehensive collection of research studies on biofeedback and self-control techniques, see Barber et al. [7].) Only a brief discussion of one framework for research and practice in self-control is presented here. A more complete account of this approach is available in Thoresen and Mahoney (110).

Behavioral Self-Control

The behavioral approach to self-control presented here examines both the internal and external events that precede and follow the behavior in question. Some specific action of the person is taken as the focus of self-control, such as smoking fewer cigarettes, making more positive statements, eating less, or having fewer fearful fantasies. Self-control is not conceptualized as a basic personality trait of the person, nor is it viewed as a force wholly within the person, such as "willpower." Self-control viewed as individual action is best understood as a complex interaction of internal and external responses. Consistent with a basic humanistic premise, this behavioral view sees the ability to manage or control oneself as a valued human act. Every person is capable of learning self-control. Every person is also responsible or accountable for his actions. The concerns of humanistic psychologists for the individual as summarized earlier are well served by this behavioral perspective.

The person in this behavioral perspective is conceptualized as a "personal scientist," much in the same way as some existential-phenomenological psychologists have suggested (e.g., 49). The person is helped to be a critical and careful observer of his own actions and those of others. The person is also helped to generate hypotheses about what kind of intervention may bring about the desired change. Giving the person the power to change is the prime focus.

CONTROLLING AND CONTROLLED ACTIONS

Self-control is not viewed as a discrete category separate from external control or other methods of influencing behavior. Instead, self-control is conceptualized as a broad continuum in which internal control and external control interact to bring about change, Thus, the chronic smoker and the angry father may use different self-control techniques to quit smoking or to respond more positively to a child, but either one will also be influenced by external factors such as his health or the actions of other members of the family.

The distinction between self-controlled and self-controlling responses is important. The person's self-controlling responses (SCR) are subject to the same environmental influences as the responses to be controlled (RC). For example, the self-controlling behaviors (SCR) of relaxation practice and rehearsing "small talk" used by a shy teenager to improve her personal conversations with boys (RC) are both behaviors. The person uses one set of responses (SCR) to control other responses (RC). One of the practical problems for persons trying to change their own actions is how to *maintain* their self-controlling actions (SCR). The person's self-controlling behavior (SCR) is inevitably influenced by the external environment (e.g., social praise, changes in family activities, improved medical report). A major task of the person is to arrange the external environment to support rather than discourage his self-controlling behavior. A mother who cooks large, high-calorie meals and insists that everyone have seconds makes it more difficult for her obese son to maintain SCRs designed to reduce eating behavior. It therefore makes sense to consider self-control as a continuum of various activities rather than as a category or entity that is opposed to external control.

Various behavioral definitions of self-control (16, 32, 36, 48) have contained elements such as physical restraint, deprivation, resistance to deviation, aversive techniques, abstaining from available reinforcers, delay of gratification, stimulus manipulation, action despite known aversive consequences, and alteration of behavior-environment relations. The following definition draws on some of these elements:

> A person displays self-control when, given two or more response options and facing no immediate external constraints, he engages in a behavior whose previous likelihood has been relatively less than that of alternatively available behavior.

This tentative definition highlights three important features of self-control phenomena: (a) two or more behaviors are possible, hence a choice or decision must be made, (b) the consequences of these behaviors are usually conflicting, and (c) the self-controlling behavior is usually prompted and/or maintained by external factors. For example, the person who chooses to quit smoking has the option to smoke or not to smoke. The consequences of smoking are immediately pleasant but ultimately aversive; however, the consequences of not smoking are just the opposite. The person's effort to control his smoking does not, of course, take place in an environmental vacuum; he is influenced by such external events as doctor's orders, friends' remarks, and medical research reports.

SELF-CONTROLLING RESPONSES

Self-controlling responses (SCR) may be exercised through three strategies: self-observation, environmental planning, and behavioral programming. These strategies are not completely independent of each other. For example, self-observation can be viewed as a type of individual programming in which the person is using his own behavior to change. For discussion purposes, however, the three strategies are presented separately.

Self-observation. In order to observe and record the behavior to be controlled (RC), the person must be aware of what he is doing. Skills of self-observation—sometimes referred to as self-monitoring or self-recording—represent one way of developing awareness. Earlier, the concept of awareness was presented as knowledge of stimuli or information that might influence one's actions. Here, the person gathers data on his own actions. Consistent with a behavioral perspective, data should be gathered on the behavior of concern, i.e., the response to be controlled (RC) *before* any type of change is tried. Data might also be gathered on other concurrent events. But the gathering always takes place first.

Most persons are generally unaware of their actions in daily life situations. While some persons may attend sporadically to a particular behavior, seldom is such attention carried out systematically over a period of time. Herein lies the potential power of self-observation as a self-controlling strategy. The systematic observing, recording, and analyzing of one's own behavior provides the person with an ongoing record of his actions. Provision of this kind of information feedback usually influences the behavior being observed. A psychological Heisenberg principle can be suggested: the act of self-observing, along with recording and analyzing behavior, invariably influences the behavior being observed. The person who records his own behavior not only becomes more aware of his actions but also receives immediate and cumulative feedback on what he is doing. It is therefore not surprising that self-observation influences the behavior being observed.

How does a person systematically self-observe? Many methods are available. The instruments for self-observation remain primitive; many types of devices used have not yet been carefully studied. Wall charts, wrist counters, wrist alarms, behavioral diaries, and small pocket-sized cards are some devices used to facilitate the monitoring of certain actions so that a record can be made and studied. For example, a weight chart in the bathroom or a wrist counter to record positive self-thoughts might reflect trends in day-to-day changes, e.g., weekend responses compared to workday responses. The recorded tabulation might provide feedback on gradual changes which would otherwise go unnoticed. Self-recorded data might also provide significant information on the rate of a behavior, what events tend to elicit the behavior, and what consequences may be maintaining it. Recording devices also provide a more objective basis for self-evaluation. If the data gathered indicates that the person is changing in a desired direction, then he has good reason to have positive feelings about himself.

The research evidence on self-observation suggests that behaviors desired by the person can often be increased simply by being recorded (65). The effects of self-observation on undesired behaviors, while less clear, also suggest that observing reduces the undesired behavior. The processes involved in self-observation are confounded by the possibility that covert self-reinforcement and punishment may take place when the person engages in observing and recording his behavior. Several smoking studies have shown, for example, that self-monitoring in itself generally has been as effective as various types of treatments (68). The smoker in the self-observation treatment may covertly be rewarding himself with "good feelings" or positive comments about reducing his smoking when he self-monitors his smoking.

A recent study by Bolstad and Johnson (11) with disruptive elementary school children suggests that self-observation and recording by young children of their own disruptive behavior in the classroom may function in a self-punishing way. In this study, when each child recorded a disruptive response, the child knew that this reduced the number of points he would receive for not being disruptive. In part, the problem lies in how to assess the separate effects of self-observation per se from some kind of self-change procedure. Broden, Hall, and Mitts (12) found that an adolescent girl, concerned with doing better schoolwork, especially during class time, increased her studying time in class from about 30 percent to almost 80 percent in one week. The girl used a recording slip on which she marked an X after she had studied for a few minutes. After about three weeks of self-observation, the procedure was discontinued; studying promptly declined to an average of 27 percent for the week. When self-observation was reinstated, studying again increased to about 80 percent. When the self-observation procedure was finally discontinued, the rate of studying remained at the 80 percent level.

The many methodological issues in self-observation highlight some of the major problems in using scientific methods. The traditional objective/subjective dichotomy in conventional science—the usual notions of reliability, the matter of demand characteristics and expectancy effects, and the importance of unobtrusive, nonreactive measures—is brought into question (81, 95). At present, very little is known about how to resolve these problems. For this reason, studies concerning the processes of self-observation phenomena represent a high priority area for research. Some of the problems were reflected in an observation made by Maslow (69) concerning the fatal weakness of conventional research—"its inability to deal impersonally with the personal." Clearly, if we are to fully understand the intricacies of complex processes such as self-observation and develop ways to teach it to persons, we need to expand research methodologies and design new "personal" instrumentations. We need to tailor a new philosophy of science that is appropriate to the kind of human phenomena of concern such as self-observation.

Environmental planning. The second self-controlling strategy involves changing one's environment so that either the stimulus cues which precede the behavior or its immediate consequences are changed. This restructuring of the environment often involves the elimination or avoidance of daily life situations where a choice or decision is necessary. Several studies have demonstrated that self-control is very effective through "stimulus control" in which a person alters the environment so that the problem behavior is associated with progressively fewer stimulus cues (33, 36, 106). The overeater or drug user, for example, may avoid those situations associated with the behavior that "stimulates" the problem behavior, or he may gradually narrow the situations in which he engages in the RC. Smoking cigarettes only in the basement by oneself after 10:00 P.M. represents a restricted stimulus situation. The drug user may gradually reduce the types of social situations in which drugs are usually taken. Similarly, the obese eater may control eating by removing environmental cues, such as the television set, the cookie jar, and close friends, when eating. The physical environment such as the kitchen often elicits excessive eating. Eating meals in another room without all the cues to eat can reduce eating.

In a study to reduce smoking, Upper and Meredith (112) trained heavy smokers to reduce long-standing smoking patterns by changing the physical cues to smoke. Smokers recorded their daily smoking rate. Using small portable timers, smokers set the timer for their average intercigarette time interval (e.g., seventeen minutes). Smokers were then instructed to smoke *only* after the timer's buzz. By establishing this new environmental cue to smoke—one completely under the person's control—the previous cueing situations, such as a beer, or completing a meal, or conversation with a friend, were displaced. Gradually the smokers increased the time interval until smoking was either eliminated or considerably reduced.

A second type of environmental programming, besides altering the stimulus environment, involves altering the external consequences of behavior. The person can make arrangements, for example, to have someone such as a close friend, wife, or sister, provide certain positive or negative consequences when the RC occurs. If a father is trying to reduce his negative episodes with the children and his wife invariably consoles him shortly after these experiences, the father might ask his wife to avoid paying attention to him following these situations. A college student might control evening studying in the room by asking his roommate to respond positively at certain time intervals contingent on studying and to respond critically if studying has not occurred during the time interval. The use of a contingency-based point or token system is one type of environmental programming for self-control. A person can arrange to receive a certain number of points contingent upon the occurrence or nonoccurrence of a behavior. Advantages of a point system are that a variety of behaviors to be controlled can be included and that all types of self-control strategies are possible.

Environmental planning as a self-controlling strategy generally takes place prior to the RC, i.e., the person makes the arrangement in advance. Avoiding certain stimulus situations or asking a friend to make a certain kind of response when the RC occurs represents prior arrangements. Many of the changes in behavior that have been attributed to the inner self or willpower are actually the result of subtle environmental events. Environmental planning allows the person to take advantage of the powerful effects of the immediate environment.

Behavioral programming. The third strategy is called behavioral programming because the person himself uses some antecedents or consequences relative to the RC. The individual may use overt or covert processes to change stimulus cues or to reinforce consequences. For example, the person can set a wrist alarm to sound every hour to cue him to engage in a positive self-thought. Or a person can reinforce himself with a positive image, such as skiing in powder snow or lying in the sun at the beach, contingent upon a certain action taking place. Individual techniques of self-control represent the strategy that most individuals commonly associate with something the person does all by himself. The self-control techniques of Yoga and Zen are types of behavioral programming in that various overt and covert actions are taken by the person to control certain responses. However, self-control is *not* restricted to actions carried out solely by the person. This kind of exclusive perspective has prevented the development of a broadly based strategy of self-control.

Behavioral programming is composed of several kinds of specific techniques, such as self-reinforcement, self-punishment, and stimulus control. A partial list of these follows:

1. Positive self-reinforcement: providing oneself with a freely available reinforcing event only after performing a certain response
2. Negative self-reinforcement: avoiding or escaping from a freely avoidable aversive stimulus only after performing a certain response
3. Positive self-punishment: removing a freely available reinforcer only after a certain response is performed.
4. Negative self-punishment: presenting oneself with a freely avoidable aversive stimulus after performing a specific response
5. Self-regulated stimulus control: presenting, altering or eliminating stimulus cues that are considered relevant to changing the RC. These might include self-instruction, internal control of autonomic responses, covert rehearsal, physical relaxation exercises, and vivid imagery.

Several covert techniques have been used in behavior therapy and counseling to help individuals control their own covert or overt behaviors (6, 17). Vivid imagery responses have been coupled with physical relaxation to reduce covert stress responses of anxiety (35). Pleasant or extremely unpleasant images have been systematically associated by the person with problem behaviors (also imagined) to change specific overt behaviors. A procedure called covert sensitization has been used in which a very nauseating or aversive image is associated with the RC. These noxious images have helped smokers, homosexuals, overeaters, and alcoholics control their own overt and covert behaviors (16, 17, 18, 114).

Covert responses have also been employed as symbolic positive or negative consequences with promising results. Homme (42) illustrates how the individual can use covert responses. In Homme's procedure the person seeking to control a behavior such as smoking immediately follows the stimulus cue or urge to smoke with a strong antismoking thought, e.g., "smoking will reduce my life span," or an image of pouring a full ashtray of cigarette butts into his mouth. Following this covert response, the person then engages in a positive thought or image that is incompatible with smoking, e.g., swimming skillfully in a beautiful pool. Finally, drawing on Premack's high-probability principle (87), the person then reinforces himself by engaging in a high-probability behavior, such as having a cup of coffee, looking at one's watch, or talking with a secretary.

A recent illustration of self-administered programming is provided by a case history of a young man diagnosed schizophrenic whose problem behavior involved frequent obsessive thoughts about being physically unattractive, stupid, and brain-damaged (66). After assessing the initial frequency of these maladaptive thoughts through self-observation, the individual was instructed to punish himself by snapping a heavy-gauge rubber band against his wrist whenever he engaged in obsessional thoughts. This procedure is an example of negative self-punishment. When these thoughts had been drastically reduced, positive self-thoughts were established and gradually increased by using a cueing procedure paired with self-reinforcement.

In the case described above, self-observation had shown that positive self-thoughts seldom occurred. Therefore, the first task was to help this individual identify something positive about himself, e.g., "I'm proud of being in good physical shape." To prime these positive self-thoughts, a high-probability behavior was used as positive self-reinforcement. Cards were attached to his cigarette pack. Whenever he reached for a cigarette, he first read (self-verbalization) a positive self-statement and then reinforced himself with a cigarette. A "wild card" alternated with the other three and required a spontaneous, original, positive self-thought.

The individual soon began to generate positive self-thoughts without prior cueing and without smoking as a self-reinforcing event. This treatment enabled the person to resume a normal and adaptive life without lengthy hospitalization or extended therapy. A six-month follow-up indicated that he had been accepted at a college, had obtained a job, and was still using self-control techniques to further his progress. This individual also reported that he had greatly increased his liking of himself and that he looked forward to each day much more positively.

The possible applications of self-programming are as endless as they are exciting. The humanistic implication of this strategy and others is that the individual can learn the skills to direct and control his own life in ways that can increase his personal meaning and satisfaction.

Humanistic Behaviors

Earlier a summary of humanistic concerns was presented. These concerns were stated in rather abstract terms. It seems possible, however, to reconceptualize or translate these important ideas directly into statements of human action. Such a translation will encourage empirical research that examines how the frequency and magnitude of these human actions can be changed. In addition, it is reasonable to consider these humanistic concepts in terms of internal (covert) and external (overt) behavior (60). Because the human organism is a complex system which responds within and without *simultaneously*, the use of an internal-external classification is arbitrary. Such a classification may be helpful at this point, however, in facilitating understanding and in fostering controlled research.

Some humanists may argue that translating these concerns into human response terms is oversimplistic and reductionistic and that it is merely another thinly disguised effort at resurrecting the same old behaviorist mentality of only dealing with simple, readily observed behavior (72). Admittedly, the approach is simple and may fail to capture *all* aspects of the phenomena involved. However, proceeding from the simple to the more complex has been one of the most successful strategies of modern science (69). In an area where relatively little empirical data are available, moving from the simple to the complex on the basis of empirically derived data is crucial. The major question concerns the development of methods to help persons act in more humanistic ways. If a translation is indeed too simple, then the methods will not work. The answer is to be found empirically, not in logical argument.

Internal response. An examination of the humanistic literature suggests a variety of statements that can be translated into response terms. First let us consider internal actions. The following is a sample of internal response categories in which the importance of the increase/decrease factor is evident. The humanistic phrases are in parentheses.

1. Increase the frequency, variety, and accuracy of internal self-observation responses (self-knowledge; *knows* what is going on within; is really aware of self).
2. Increase the frequency of perceptually accurate responses (can see things for what they really are; knows what others are experiencing).
3. Increase the frequency and variety of low-probability responses (has new and unusual thoughts, physical sensations, images).
4. Decrease the frequency of stress and tension responses within the body (experience tranquility; calmness in everyday life).
5. Increase the frequency of highly consistent psychophysiological responses (experiences sense of unity within; the body is in agreement with the head).
6. Increase the frequency and variety of imagery responses (engages in rich fantasy; has a well-developed imagination).
7. Increase the frequency of using psychophysiological responses in specific situations as criteria (trusts his own experiences; reads himself and uses personal reactions to decide).
8. Decrease the frequency and variety of self-critical, negative responses (accepts oneself as worthy; experiences oneself as positive; thinks positively about self and others).

Let us explore a few of these translations. The first item on self-observation of internal responses (thoughts, images, and physiological responses) is one example of translating humanistic statements into response terms. One way of conceptualizing self-observation is the systematic recording of a particular internal response such as positive self-thoughts. Here the individual makes discriminations about whether certain covert verbalizations constitute positive self-thoughts. The individual can record these positive self-thoughts by tallying each occurrence on a card or using a wrist counter. At the end of a particular time period, such as a day, the person notes the total frequency of positive self-thoughts. This represents one way that self-knowledge of internal events can be examined.

Item 4, concerning stress and tension responses, might be dealt with by teaching the person how to use deep muscle relaxation techniques, or how to stop stressful thoughts when they occur. Once instructed, the person may experience more tranquility and calmness in his everyday life.

Self-critical, negative responses constitute a major factor in self-esteem and self-acceptance (39). Thus, helping a person reduce the frequency and variety of self-critical thoughts represents one way of encouraging self-esteem. The individual, of course, should also be engaging in external actions that encourage positive thoughts about himself. Since some persons manifest high frequencies of negative self-thoughts that lack any external basis, reducing these negative internal responses may be prerequisite to promoting more positive responses about oneself.

External responses. Here are a few tentative translations of other humanistic phrases into external response categories. Examples of external response categories are as follows:

1. Increase the frequency, variety, and accuracy of external observation responses, both of the self and of others (knows what is happening with others around him; knows what is happening with himself).
2. Increase the frequency and variety of positive verbal responses (can self-disclose; can be assertive when necessary; can empathize with others).
3. Increase the frequency and variety of positive nonverbal responses (can relate to others in many ways; seems to really care and be concerned).
4. Increase the frequency of using environmental stimulus cues by altering physical environments (makes things happen for himself and for others).
5. Decrease the frequency and variety of socially aversive, negative verbal and nonverbal responses (positive, accepting person; deals with disagreement and disapproval in constructive ways).
6. Increase the frequency and variety of positive verbal and nonverbal responses to animate and inanimate natural situations (good relationships with nature; feels close to nature).

Positive verbal responses (item 2) is obviously a very broad response category. The notion of what constitutes a positive verbal response is relative to the consequences of such behavior in particular situations. However, specific verbal responses such as self-disclosing behavior can be defined, and planned learning situations can be used to increase such behaviors (107). Similarly, aversive talk and gestures (item 5) can be specified and then altered through structured learning situations. One way of "making things happen" (item 4) is by changing certain features of the physical environment. For example, the person can rearrange room furnishings to prompt certain behaviors and to discourage others.

Since the concerns of humanists have to do with what the individual does, a translation of these concerns into more specific action or response terms will help in promoting humanistic behavior. Well-controlled empirical studies of how individuals change will reveal if the suggested translation into terms of specific actions has missed the humanistic mark.

In Summary

Contemporary environments, in their complexities and subtle manipulations, have reduced the individual person's power to manage his own life (76). Modern humanists and contemporary behaviorists are both concerned with helping the person experience life more positively. The translation of humanistic concerns into human response terms represents one way of encouraging meaningful scientific inquiry. Literary, nonempirical, and antiscientific orientations cannot provide the data needed to develop techniques for giving power to the individual. Polemics and stereotyping by humanists have accomplished little, except to retard scientific progress. Furthermore, the myopic perspective of conventional behaviorists and other scientists preoccupied with "hard" data have also impeded research.

We need a synthesizing perspective that draws from a variety of sources and avoids invidious dichotomies—humanist versus behaviorist. The beginnings of one such perspective has been suggested. Humanistic psychologists and educators share much with contemporary behaviorists. All are concerned with increasing our understanding of overt and covert processes that influence the actions of individuals. The intensive, empirical study of the individual offers a methodology highly relevant to the intimate study of the individual.

One way of conceptualizing self-control that stresses the continuity of behavior has been suggested. Self-controlling actions are possible through self-observation as well as through individual and environmental planning. Some promising self-control techniques are already available.

Misunderstanding and misinformation among behavioral scientists, educators, and humanistic scholars has prevented much needed scientific inquiry. Well-controlled empirical research can provide valuable data. With such data we can learn how to help the individual engage in self-actualizing behavior.

REFERENCES

1. Abbagnano, N. *The Encyclopedia of Philosophy*, vol. 4. New York: Macmillan Co. and the Free Press, 1967.
2. Allport, G. W. *Pattern and Growth in Personality*. New York: Holt, Rinehart & Winston, 1963.
3. Allport, G. W. *Personality: A Psychological Interpretation*. New York: Holt, Rinehart, & Winston, 1937.
4. Ashem, B., and Donner, L. "Covert Sensitization with Alcoholics: A Controlled Replication." *Behaviour Research and Therapy* 6 (1968): 7-12.
5. Bakan, D. *On Method: Toward a Reconstruction of Psychological Investigation*. San Francisco: Jossey-Bass, 1967.
6. Bandura, A. *Principles of Behavior Modification*. New York: Holt, Rinehart & Winston, 1969.
7. Barber, T.; Di Cara, L. V.; Kamiya, J.; Miller, N. E.; Shapiro, D.; and Stoyva, J.; eds. *Biofeedback and Self-Control*. Chicago: Aldine Publishing Co., 1971.
8. Berlyne, D. E. *Conflict, Arousal, and Curiosity*. New York: McGraw-Hill Book Co., 1960.
9. Blackburn, J. R. "Sensuous-Intellectual Complementarity in Science." *Science* 172 (1971): 1003-7.
10. Blanshard, B. "The Limits of Naturalism." *Mind Science and History*, vol. 2 of Contemporary Philosophic Thought: The International Philosophy Year Conferences at Brockport. Albany: State University of New York Press, 1970.
11. Bolstad, O. D., and Johnson, S. M. "Self-Regulation in the Modification of Disruptive Classroom Behavior." Unpublished manuscript, University of Oregon, 1971.
12. Broden, M.; Hall, R. V.; and Mitts, B. "The Effect of Self-Recording on the Classroom Behavior of Two Eighth-Grade Students." *Journal of Applied Behavior Analysis* 4 (1971): 191-99.

13. Brown, G. *Human Teaching for Human Learning.* New York: Viking Press, 1970.
14. Browning, R. M.; and Stover, D. D. *Behavior Modification in Child Treatment.* Chicago: Aldine-Atherton, 1971.
15. Buhler, C. "Basic Theoretical Concepts of Humanistic Psychology." *American Psychologist* 26 (1971): 378-86.
16. Cautela, J. R. "Behavior Therapy and Self-Control." In *Behavior Therapy Appraisal and Status,* edited by C. Franks, pp. 323-40. New York: McGraw-Hill Book Co., 1969.
17. ———. "Covert Conditioning." *The Psychology of Private Events: Perspectives on Covert Response Systems,* edited by A. Jacobs and L. Sachs, pp. 112-30. New York: Academic Press, 1971.
18. ———. "Covert Sensitization." *Psychological Record* 20 (1967): 459-68.
19. Chassan, J. B. *Research Design in Clinical Psychology and Psychiatry.* New York: Appleton-Centry-Crofts, 1967.
20. Collier, B. L. "Brain Power—the Case for Bio-Feedback Training." *Saturday Review,* April 10, 1971, 10-13ff.
21. Day, W. F. "Humanistic Psychology and Contemporary Humanism." *Humanist* 31 (1971): 13-16.
22. ———. "Radical Behaviorism in Reconciliation with Phenomenology." *Journal of the Experimental Analysis of Behavior* 12 (1969): 315-28.
23. Dollard, J., and Miller, N. E. *Personality and Psychotherapy: An Analysis in Terms of Learning, Thinking, and Culture.* New York: McGraw-Hill Book Co., 1950.
24. Dubos, R. *So Human an Animal.* New York: Charles Scribner's Sons, 1968.
25. Dukes, W. F. "N=1." *Psychological Bulletin* 64 (1965): 74-79.
26. DuPraw, V. "Self-Management of Internal Responses: Heart Rate Control." Doctoral dissertation. Stanford University, 1972.
27. Edgington, E. S. "Statistical Inference and Nonrandom Samples." *Psychological Bulletin* 66 (1966): 485-87.
28. Edwards, I. *A Humanistic View.* Sydney: Angus & Robertson, 1969.
29. Eysenck, H. J. *Behaviour Therapy and the Neuroses.* London: Pergammon Press, 1960.
30. ———. "Behavior Therapy as a Scientific Discipline." *Journal of Consulting and Clinical Psychology* 36 (1971): 314-19.
31. Fairfield, R. P., ed. *Humanistic Frontiers in American Education.* Englewood Cliffs, N.J.: Prentice-Hall, 1971.
32. Ferster, C. B. "Classification of Behavioral Pathology." In *Research in Behavior Modification,* edited by L. Krasner and L. Ullmann, pp. 6-26. New York: Holt, Rinehart & Winston, 1965.
33. Ferster, C. B.; Nurnberger, J. I.; and Levitt, E. B. "The Control of Eating." *Journal of Mathetics* 1 (1962): 87-109.

34. Frankl, V. E. *Man's Search for Meaning: An Introduction to Logotherapy.* New York: Washington Square Press, 1959.
35. Goldfried, M. R. "Systematic Desensitization As Training in Self-Control." *Journal of Consulting and Clinical Psychology* 37 (1971): 228-34.
36. Goldiamond, I. "Self-Control Procedures in Personal Behavior Problems." *Psychological Reports* 17 (1965): 851-68.
37. Green, E. "Varieties of Healing Experiences." Invited address, De Anza College, October 30, 1971.
38. Green, E.; Green A.; and Walters, E. "Self-Regulation of Internal States", *Progress of Cybernics: Proceedings of the International Congress of Cybernics, London, 1969,* edited by J. Rose, et al. London, 1970.
38a. Hannum, J. W. "The Modification of Evaluative Self-Thoughts and Their Effects on Overt Behavior." Doctoral dissertation, Stanford University, 1972.
39. Harris, M. B. "Self-directed Program for Weight Control: A Pilot Study." *Journal of Abnormal Psychology* 74 (1969): 263-70.
40. Harlow, H. F. "Motivation as a Factor in the Acquisition of New Responses." In *Current Theory and Research in Motivation: A Symposium,* pp. 24-49. Lincoln: University of Nebraska Press, 1953.
41. Heath, R. S. *The Reasonable Adventurer.* Pittsburgh: University of Pittsburgh Press, 1969.
42. Homme, L. E. "Perspective in Psychology: XXIV. Control of Coverants, the Operants of the Mind." *Psychological Record* 15 (1965): 501-11.
43. Hosford, R. E., and Zimmer, J. "Humanism through Behaviorism." *Counseling and Values* 16 (1972): 1-7.
44. Hull, C. L. *Principles of Behavior.* New York: Appleton-Century-Crofts, 1943.
45. Huxley, A. "Education on the Non-Verbal Level." In *Contemporary Educational Psychology,* edited by R. M. Jones, pp. 44-60. New York: Harper Torchbooks, 1966.
46. Jourard, S. M. *Disclosing Man to Himself.* Princeton, N.J.: D. Van Nostrand Co., 1968.
47. Kanfer, F. H. "The Maintenance of Behavior by Self-generated Stimuli and Reinforcement." In *The Psychology of Private Events,* edited by A. Jacobs and L. Sachs, pp. 39-59. New York: Academic Press, 1971.
48. Kanfer, F. H., and Phillips, J. S. *Learning Foundations of Behavior Therapy.* New York: John Wiley & Sons, 1970.
49. Kelly, G. *The Psychology of Personal Constructs,* vol. 1. New York: W. W. Norton & Co., 1955.
50. Koch, S. "Psychology and Emerging Conceptions of Knowledge as Unitary." In *Behaviorism and Phenomenology: Contrasting*

Bases for Modern Psychology, edited by T. W. Wann. Chicago: University of Chicago Press, 1964.

51. Koestler, A. *The Ghost in the Machine*. New York: Macmillan Co., 1967.

52. Krasner, L. "Behavior Therapy." In *Annual Review of Psychology* 22 (1971): 483-532.

53. Kurtz, P. "What Is Humanism?" In *Moral Problems in Contemporary Society*, edited by P. Kurtz. New York: Prentice-Hall, 1969.

54. Kvale, S., and Grenness, C. E. "Skinner and Sartre: Towards a Radical Phenomenology of Behavior?" *Review of Existential Psychology and Psychiatry* 7 (1967): 128-48.

55. Lackenmeyer, C. W. "Experimentation—A Misunderstood Methodology in Psychological and Social-Psychological Research." *American Psychologist* 25 (1970): 617-24.

56. Lamont, C. *Freedom of Choice Affirmed*. New York: Horizon Press, 1967.

57. Landsman, T. "Positive Experience and the Beautiful Person." Presidential address, Southeastern Psychological Association, April 5, 1968.

58. Lazarus, A. *Behavior Therapy and Beyond*. New York: McGraw-Hill Book Co., 1971.

59. Lewin, K. *A Dynamic Theory of Personality—Selected Papers*. New York: McGraw-Hill Book Co., 1935.

60. Lichtenstein, P. E. "A Behavioral Approach to 'Phenomenological Data'." *Psychological Record* 21 (1971): 1-16.

61. Locke, E. A. "Is 'Behavior Therapy' Behavioristic? (An Analysis of Wolpe's Psychotherapeutic Methods)." *Psychological Bulletin* 76 (1971): 318-27.

62. London, P. *Behavior Control*, New York: Harper & Row, 1969.

63. Luria, A. R. *The Role of Speech in the Regulation of Normal and Abnormal Behavior*. New York: Liveright, 1961.

64. MacCorquodale, K. "Behaviorism Is a Humanism." *Humanist* 31 (April-May 1971): 12-13.

65. Mahoney, M. J. "Research Issues in Self-Management." *Behavior Therapy* 3 (1972): 45-63.

66. ———. "The Self-Management of Covert Behaviors: A Case Study." *Behavior Therapy* 2 (1971): 575-78.

67. ———. "Toward an Experimental Analysis of Coverant Control." *Behavior Therapy* 1 (1970): 510-21.

68. Marston, A., and McFall, R. M. "Comparison of Behavior Modification Approaches to Smoking Reduction." *Journal of Consulting and Clinical Psychology* 36 (1971): 153-62.

69. Maslow, A. H. *The Psychology of Science*. New York: Harper & Row, 1966.

70. ———. "Towards a Humanistic Biology." *American Psychologist* 24 (1965): 724-35.

71. Matsen, F. *The Broken Image.* New York: George Braziller, 1964.

72. Matsen, F. W. "Counterrebuttal." *Humanist* 31 (April-May 1971): 18-19.

73. McFall, R. "Effects of Self-Monitoring on Normal Smoking Behavior." *Journal of Consulting and Clinical Psychology* 35 (1970): 135-42.

74. Merleau-Ponty, M. *The Structure of Behaviour.* London: Methusen, 1965.

75. Meichenbaum, D. H. "Cognitive Factors in Behavior Modification: Modifying What Clients Say to Themselves." Paper presented at annual meeting of Association for Advancement of Behavior Therapy, Washington, D.C., September, 1970.

76. Michael, D. N. *The Unprepared Society: Planning for a Precarious Future.* New York: Basic Books, 1968.

77. Miller, N. E. "Learning of Visceral and Glandular Responses." *Science* 163 (1969): 434-53.

78. Mischel, W. *Introduction to Personality.* New York: Holt, Rinehart & Winston, 1971.

79. Mowrer, O. H. *Learning Theory and Behavior.* New York: John Wiley & Sons, 1960.

80. Murphy, G. "Psychology in the Year 2000." *American Psychologist* 24 (1969): 523-30.

81. Nelson, C. M., and McReynolds, W. T. "Self-Recording and Control of Behavior: A Reply to Simkins." *Behavior Therapy* 2 (1971): 594-97.

82. Nolan, J. D. "Self-Control Procedures in the Modification of Smoking Behavior." *Journal of Consulting and Clinical Psychology* 32 (1968): 92-93.

83. Nowlis, D., and Kamiya, J. "The Control of Electroencephalographic Alpha Rhythms through Auditory Feedback and the Associated Mental Activity." *Psychophysiology*, in press.

84. Paul, G. L. "Behavior Modification Research: Design and Tactics." In *Behavior Therapy: Appraisal and Status*, edited by C. Frank, pp. 29-62. New York: McGraw-Hill Book Co., 1969.

85. Platt, J. R. *The Step to Man.* New York: John Wiley & Sons, 1966.

86. Portes, A. "On the Emergence of Behavior Therapy in Modern Society." *Journal of Consulting and Clinical Psychology* 36 (1971): 303-16.

87. Premack, D. "Reinforcement Theory." In *Nebraska Symposium on Motivation: 1965*, edited by D. Levine, pp. 123-80. Lincoln: University of Nebraska Press, 1965.

88. Rachlin, H. *Introduction to Modern Behaviorism.* San Francisco: Freeman, 1970.

89. Rogers, C. *Freedom to Learn.* Columbus, Ohio: Charles Merrill Books, 1969.

90. ———. "The Person of Tomorrow." Commencement address, Sonoma State College, June, 1968.

91. Ross, L.; Rodin, J.; and Zimbardo, P. "Toward an Attribution Therapy: The Reduction of Fear through Induced Cognitive Misattribution." *Journal of Personality and Social Psychology* 12 (1969): 279-88.

92. Rutner, I. T., and Bugle, C. "An Experimental Procedure for the Modification of Psychotic Behavior." *Journal of Consulting and Clinical Psychology* 33 (1969): 651-53.

93. Schultz, H. H., and Luthe, W. *Autogenic Methods,* vol. 1. New York: Grune & Stratton, 1969.

94. Sidman, M. *The Tactics of Scientific Research: Evaluating Experimental Data in Psychology.* New York: Basic Books, 1960.

95. Simkins, L. "The Reliability of Self-recorded Behavior." *Behavior Therapy* 2 (1971): 83-87.

96. Skinner, B. F. "Behaviorism at Fifty." *Science* 140 (1963): 951-58.

97. ———. *Beyond Freedom and Dignity.* New York: A. Knopf, 1971.

98. ———. "A Case History in Scientific Method." In *Psychology: A Study of a Science,* vol. 2, edited by S. Koch. New York: McGraw-Hill Book Co., 1959.

99. ———. *The Contingencies of Reinforcement.* New York: Appleton-Century-Crofts, 1969.

100. ———. "Discussion of Behaviorism at Fifty." In *Behaviorism and Phenomenology,* edited by T. W. Wann. Chicago: University of Chicago Press, 1964.

101. ———. "The Operational Analysis of Psychological Terms." *Psychological Review* 52 (1945): 270-73.

102. ———. *Science and Human Behavior.* New York: Macmillan Co., 1953.

103. Staats, A. W. *Child Learning, Intelligence and Personality.* New York: Harper & Row, 1971.

104. Stevens, S. S. "Measurement, Statistics, and the Schemapiric View." *Science* 171 (1972): 849-56.

105. Strupp, H. H., and Bergin, A. W. "Some Empirical and Conceptual Bases for Coordinated Research in Psychotherapy: A Critical Review of Issues, Trends, and Evidence." *International Journal of Psychiatry* 72 (1969): 1-90.

106. Stuart, R. B. "Behavioral Control of Overeating." *Behaviour Research and Therapy* 5 (1967): 357-65.

106a. Stuhr, D. E. "The Effects of Social Model Characteristics in Eliciting Personal Feeling Questions." Doctoral dissertation, Stanford University, 1972.

107. Terrace, H. S. "Awareness As Viewed by Conventional and Radical

Behaviorism." Paper presented at annual meeting of American Psychological Association, Washington, D.C., September, 1971.

108. Thoresen, C. E. "The Intensive Design: An Intimate Approach to Counseling Research." Paper presented at the American Educational Research Association, Chicago, 1972.

109. ———. "Relevance and Research in Counseling." *Review of Educational Research* 39 (1969): 264-82.

110. Thoresen, S. E., and Mahoney, M. J. *Behavioral Self-Control.* New York: Holt, Rinehart & Winston, forthcoming.

111. Ullmann, L. P., and Krasner, L. *A Psychological Approach to Abnormal Behavior.* Englewood Cliffs, N.J.: Prentice-Hall, 1969.

112. Upper, D., and Meredith, L. "A Stimulus Control Approach to the Modification of Smoking Behavior." *Proceedings of the 78th Annual Convention,* American Psychological Association, 1970.

113. Vygotsky, L. S. *Thought and Language.* New York: John Wiley & Sons, 1962.

114. Wagner, M. K., and Bragg, R. A. "Comparing Behavior Modification Approaches to Habit Decrement—Smoking." *Journal of Consulting and Clinical Psychology* 34 (1970): 258-63.

115. Watson, J. B. *Psychology from the Standpoint of a Behaviorist.* Philadelphia: J. B. Lippincott Co., 1924.

116. Wegner, M. A.; Bagchi, B. U.; and Anand, G. "Voluntary Heart and Pulse Control by Yoga Methods." *International Journal of Parapsychology* 5 (1963): 25-40.

117. Weinstein, G., and Fanbini, M., eds. *Toward Humanistic Education: A Curriculum of Affect.* New York: Frederick A. Praeger, 1970.

118. Wilson, E. H. "Humanism's Many Dimensions." *Humanist* 30 (1970): 35-36.

119. Wisocki, P. "Treatment of Obsessive-Compulsive Behavior by Covert Sensitization and Covert Reinforcement: A Case Report." *Journal of Behaviour Therapy and Experimental Psychiatry* 1 (1970): 223-39.

120. Wolf, M., and Risley, T. "Reinforcement: Applied Research." In *The Nature of Reinforcement,* edited by R. Glaser, pp. 310-25. New York: Academic Press, 1971.

121. Wolman, B. B. "Does Psychology Need Its Own Philosophy of Science?" *American Psychologist* 26 (1971): 877-86.

122. Wolpe, J. *Psychotherapy by Reciprocal Exhibition.* Stanford: Stanford University Press, 1958.

123. Yates, A. *Behavior Therapy.* New York: John Wiley & Sons, 1970.

124. Zimbardo, P.; Maslach, C.; and Marshall, G. "Unexplained Arousal." In *Current Trends in Hypnosis Research,* edited by E. Fromm and R. Shor, forthcoming.

CHAPTER XIII

The Philosophy of Behavioral Modification

MICHAEL SCRIVEN

Introduction

Behavioral modification is perhaps the nearest approach to an atheoretical slice of psychology that we have seen. Pavlov and Skinner are not noted as theoreticians, Skinner denying vehemently that he is one at all. Yet the whole movement is redolent of ideology, and that is usually the smoke from a small theoretical fire, or at least from the embers of immolated theory. In any case, whether behavioral modification has more of a theory than it admits, or a worse one, or is an ideology, it is of great interest to a philosopher to explore these more general issues that arise from it since the behavioral engineering approach has nearly always been the practical arm of a crusade in the name of empiricism or materialism or mechanism. The philosophical foundations (or consequences) of a scientific movement interact with its successes and failures in a complex way. Without suggesting that the philosophy *is* primary, I would argue that philosophical errors in behavior modification often have an important effect on the direction and quality of scientific research.

In this paper I shall first try to show the extent to which Skinner, the prophet of the present revival, is profoundly wrong in his philosophical conclusions as exemplified in *Beyond Freedom and Dignity* (3); and, second, I shall argue that many of those who apply his approach, as exemplified by contributions to this volume, are in dire need of a better philosophical position, without which they are severely handicapped both scientifically and humanistically.

None of these criticisms imply that behavior modification is either philosophically worse than any other contemporary movement in psychology or education, or that its achievements should be regarded as surpassed by those of any other twentieth-century movement concerned with psychology or education. In point of fact, the concept of "being philosophically more confused than 'humanistic psychology', " for example, not only lacks instances but is probably beyond the reach of human comprehension.

In my view, Skinner's practice has long stood as a powerful paradigm of what psychology should do. Yet, his philosophy of psychology has long been a mere monument to the seductive power of ancient fallacies and fantasies. One might reasonably conclude that this shows how irrelevant philosophy of science is to good scientific practice. But I also happen to believe that philosophy of science is the principal intellectual influence on the shape of science, and that improved philosophy of science is almost always productive of improved science. Strictly speaking, this *is* compatible with the recognition that a sound philosophy is not a *necessary* condition for sound science. Nevertheless, there is a certain tension between valuing philosophy of science for *its* contribution to science, valuing Skinner for *his* contribution to science, and believing that his philosophy of science is almost totally wrong.

In the works of the Catholic novelists G. K. Chesterton and Graham Greene, as in those of the humanist Camus, who often wrote about priests, one frequently finds that the man of God exhibits a strange fascination for an atheist who seems strikingly good, and strong, and honest. Does the priest see in him a threat or a hope? The risk of losing faith, or the hope of gaining a great convert? Whichever it is, he spends more time with the atheist than with any of the more obvious sinners, whose salvation—or even amelioration—would seem likely to improve the world far more. Perhaps that is because those novelists are intellectuals writing for intellectuals.

At any rate, as a man of no God but with some theology nonetheless, I have found myself closely engaged with Skinner and Skinner's work over the years. Nearly twenty years ago I wrote what may still retain the dubious but quantitative distinction of being the longest study of his work in print (2). In the years since, I have worked for and advised a number of the programmed text publishers (and written my own), discussed *Walden Two* with would-be community founders, evaluated behavior modification projects in the schools, and from time to time amiably exchanged views with Fred Skinner. We come now to his latest and best known work.

The Philosopher Skinner

I think everyone should have a hobby or two for his days of retirement, and I am delighted that Skinner should have chosen philosophy as one of his. Moreover, as an amateur (in some sense) he does as well as many professionals in what is indeed a pretty sloppy field. No more sloppy than pyschology, in reality, or education, but the sloppiness is perhaps more pervasive since in philosophy there are essentially *no* givens and no unarguable data. The solipsist is just as much a member of the club as the realist. But this is as much the strength of philosophy as its weakness, for it is just this property which ensures that *all* the really fundamental disputes remain within philosophy. There is nowhere else for them to go. Physics has that special position in the natural sciences—as does psychology in the behavioral sciences—but philosophy has it in the whole structure of knowledge including physics and psychology.

Philosophy thus has a monopoly on the ultimate issues: they cannot be swept under the well-knit rug of a nearby science. They are remarkably well adapted for survival after several millenia of raids by carnivores from the neighboring jungles. And their principal adaptive mutation has been slipperiness. Just when the marauder is certain he has them in his jaws, he finds them smiling serenely from beneath a neighboring banyan tree, or vanishing like the Chesire Cat in that anti-Walden fantasy written by another rather good part-time philosopher, Lewis Carroll (who taught mathematics and the philosophy of mathematics at Oxford).

Philosophy is very hard to do well, easy to do spectacularly, and impossible to avoid. As a scientist or a citizen you are always making philosophical assumptions, whether you've heard of the subject or not. You take your stand on a moral issue, showing your rejection of moral relativism; you pray, showing your theistic views; you try to give up smoking, showing your acceptance of responsibility. And if, like Skinner, you are skeptical about accepting assumptions, you soon find your way into the field of philosophy to begin your own trophy hunt. Skinner got there before me, and is probably less of an amateur than I am if we look at certification, since I have only taken one course in the subject, and I think he took two. So we shall have to settle this one by looking at some arguments rather than diplomas or number of allies, since we have too few of the first and too many of the second. Now the uneasy thing about philosophical arguments is that they are almost never completely conclusive, no doubt contaminated by the slipperiness of the problems with which they have been associated so long. Nevertheless, it is my aim to convey to you the power of an alternative position, the hazards of his, and where to go if you wish to look into the matter further. I shall argue for or comment briefly on the following propositions.

1. Skinner's philosophical position is untenable.
2. Skinner's practical-social contributions are valuable.
3. Skinner's philosophical errors may well be responsible for some of his valuable contributions in the practical-social area; but they are neither logically sound bases nor generalizable incentives for such research and applications.
4. Nevertheless, correction of his philosophical errors make possible, and perhaps probable—even if it does not make certain—considerable progress beyond Skinner's practical-social contributions.

Skinner's Philosophy

There is no short way to deal conclusively with all the issues in *Beyond Freedom and Dignity* (3). But there is a kind of shock therapy which can break its spell on some of the bewitched, and I shall attempt that here. The book is an attack on the conception of "autonomous man" as defined by Skinner and identified by him with a tradition of naive antiscientific humanism, in contrast with what he calls the scientific or experimental approach. No matter how telling Skinner's arguments are against some naive antiscientific humanists when they were being philosophical, nothing that he says affects anything that they ever said *at the practical or social level.* And that is the level with which they were principally concerned. (*Serious* philosophers, on the other hand, are immune to his criti-

cisms.) For example, such humanists have said that man is characterized by freedom and dignity and should therefore be respected.
Much of *BFD* is devoted to attacking this thesis. In discussions and
reviews most readers will have heard the matter discussed at considerable length. I will try to approach it in a fresh and, I believe,
fundamental way.

What Skinner never realizes, in his overweening commitment
to the natural-sciences model for psychology, is the extreme epistem-
ological significance of the self-referent nature of psychology. Although thinking that *p* is true never makes it true when *p* is a
proposition about planets, the opposite is often the case when *p*
is about people. It is obvious to those not blinded by bad philosophy
that there is an important range of antecedent conditions—though
by no means the whole and perhaps not even a tenth of those conditions—over which propositions about performance are true or
false accordingly as they are believed or not believed by those to
whom they refer. For example, *sometimes some* people are so situ-
ated that it's correct to say of one of them, "If you will *believe*
that you can give up smoking for a few days, you *will* give up
smoking, at least for a few days." And some of those people are
such that saying this to them will lead them (a) to consider it, (b)
to accept it, (c) to give up smoking *because* they accepted it,
thereby (d) proving that it was true. It is then appropriate to describe such a person, in advance of making any such statement to
him, as *capable* of giving up smoking, as *not* being "hopelessly
addicted," and hence possessing a degree of freedom, of autonomy,
which he thought he had lost. (There are many others who are
also capable of the same thing, of course.) "Capable" means that
under certain circumstances of a kind which appear to be possible,
e.g., by deliberate arrangement, the performance of which someone
is said to be capable would eventuate. If one locates an ideology
which can persuade people of its truth and thereby become true,
one has demonstrated peoples' capacity for whatever achievement
the ideology refers to. "Believe and ye shall be saved" is an apolitical
example.

Much of the "literature of freedom," which Skinner attacks as
philosophically unsound, is a generalization of this same point.
"Workers of the world, unite; you have nothing to lose but your

chains," is a proposition whose truth emerges *only* if it is widely believed, as the unions at first argued and then accepted. It is not irrelevant to note that eminent college professors find it very difficult to join unions. I think one reason for this is their dislike of the "subjective" element in situations where "one's thinking makes it so," especially when the thinking in question has to be group thinking. They are only comfortable with *distance*; their ego-ideal incorporates the idea of *objectivity as separation*, an error *only* in the social sciences. Such separation is not seen as error, however, if one accepts Skinner's philosophy of science which subsumes those subjects under the paradigm of natural science.

Man's control over his destiny has often sprung from a blind faith that he could do something when in fact there was no good evidence that he could. In the absence of that belief, it is highly probable that in many of these cases he would *not* have succeeded. Nor is the paradigm here the Slaves' Revolt or the Russian Revolution. The most pressing message of the view of *science* found in Koyré-Butterfield-Feyerabend-Conant-Kuhn is that the irrational commitment succeeds—sporadically, but crucially—where no measured opposition to the prevailing paradigms would have overthrown them. Indeed, if I am right about the poor logical basis for his philosophy of science, Skinner himself is an excellent example of someone who got things done by transcending the apparently reasonable. (And what drove him was a vision of how things should be, an inner state if there ever was one.) The inescapable fact is that this belief-controllability makes man most unlike planets and atoms.[1] In part, it means that some of man's internal states which are involved in his information-processing and information-acquiring activities and of which he is aware by his own perceptions of his own brain states (i.e., introspection) often dominate his overt behavior, explain it, and even control the truth of predictions about his later behavior. That is what sticks in Skinner's craw.

Let me give you some quotes to support the claim that he denies this, and then go on to the question of why he slips at this

---

1. However, it does not make man different from a supercomputer. Naive mechanists and naive humanists alike have great difficulty in dividing the realm of physical structures. They want to treat them all alike, whether as the same or as different from man.

point. The whole error can be summed up in a favorite slogan of his: "no theory changes what it is a theory about; man remains what he has always been" (3:215). False—and reactionary, naive, and unscientific to boot. In fact, this statement is incompatible, not only with evidence about self-fulfilling beliefs, revolutions, etc., but with his own discussions of self-management and the evolution of culture. But let us look at the microstructure of his argument.

He says, "Man's struggle for freedom is not due to a will to be free" (3:42). But *sometimes* it is, and in leaders and in those we wish to inspire to leadership, this is qiute often and importantly so. The literature of freedom is right: it did not make what Skinner calls "the mistake of defining freedom in terms of states of mind or feelings." In the first place it is not simply a mistake; *sometimes* a free state of mind is exactly what guarantees and constitutes freedom.

Skinner means more by these quotes than I have so far discussed. He is involved in another point—a good one—and two other errors. The good point is that a happy slave is still a slave, that objective bonds may not be perceived. We may be unconscious of these bonds because of ignorance or brainwashing. But it is an error to suggest that the "literature of freedom" failed to see this point, i.e., that "the literature" has defined freedom purely subjectively. Where Mill and Leibnitz and Voltaire, the authors he does quote, make this claim, they are doing so as a clarifying first step, to focus first on *freedom from perceived bonds*, the ones that hurt now. Plenty of other writers have been aware of the "happy slave" problems. In fact, it is the principal argument of the Marxists against free elections in a recently liberated country or in favor of revolution in this society with its biased media (Marcuse). It is also one of the best arguments against the press censorship typical of most communist countries. This apparent contradiction in practice is related to another one in much Marxist literature, which both denies freedom in the name of determinism and also exhorts the proletariat to strike for freedom. There certainly are conflicting *tendencies* in our concept of freedom, in Skinner's notions as well as those of the U.S. Supreme Court, among others; but one cannot represent this as a situation where "the literature of freedom" is subjectivist and the facts of psychology show it to be wrong.

The actual contradictions in Skinner become clear when we examine his alternative to defining freedom in terms of inner states. He recommends that we should instead define it in terms of arrangements that avoid long-term "exploitative and hence aversive" consequences such as misery (3:40). The authors of the introspectionist definitions of freedom might well sink back with a smile at this point. Skinner has done what he calls rescuing the happy slave, who was abandoned by those authors, by arguing that *eventually* the slave will not be happy. So eventually *their* "definition" applies. Since Mill was a utilitarian, wholly consequence-oriented, that gives him the best of reasons for changing the exploitative system now, since it will have bad consequences that will be phenomenologically apparent as bad, i.e., misery. So he is in no difficulty at all.

I will not tackle Skinner's claim to define "aversive" without reference to sensations in any detail here, because I'm not making an issue of it. But it is noticeable that Skinner slides from behavioristic to mentalistic language so often that I'm not misrepresenting him when I do likewise. He would of course justify his slides by saying that a "feeling" like "misery" implies or means overt aversive responses. But it is interesting to note that this kind of translation will work only if the organism is *free to respond*, so that the definition of "aversive" involves a notion of freedom, which makes it a little awkward to proclaim the reverse (his definition of freedom in terms of aversive responses) as an illuminating analysis.

Behind the scenes of all this discussion of freedom, Skinner is fighting another battle, one for the semantic prize of rescuing the word *control* from its generally negative connotations. And in this battle he fights dirty. The scenario goes like this: "The literature of freedom has been forced to brand all control as wrong . . . it is unprepared for the next step which is not to free men from control but to analyze and change the kinds of control to which they are exposed" (3:42-43). The dirty play is a barefaced semantic sneak with the word *control*. Skinner does not pull off a deep reanalysis of the concept. He simply *misses* the distinction that is built into its normal use. What he thinks of as an insight is that "the problem is to free men, not from control, but from certain kinds of control" (3:41); Skinner thinks it's acceptable to use "control which does not have aversive consequences at any time."

What he did not see was that in the literature of freedom the term *control* already incorporates this qualification. Political control is normally taken to mean what is *imposed* to *restrict* freedom, i.e., to restrict the range of available reinforcing responses. Hence his "insight," expressed as a distinction between two kinds of control, is a precise translation of the usual distinction between control and freedom—into a confusing language because it is nonstandard and evocative of misleading implications. (One thinks of the hard words of Chomsky's review in the *New York Review*. But the reasons Chomsky offers are quite different from those I have given and would be unacceptable to almost any behavioral researcher today. I shall return to them later.)

It is impossible not to speculate that this error in analyzing freedom may spring from a desire to control the world by semantic fiat, coming as it does from the author of *Walden Two*. Philosophers are often accused of winning points by redefining terms, and by this criterion Skinner is indeed a philosopher many times over. I have focused on a few crucial pages—there are a dozen such nodes in *BFD* where one can turn on the highspeed camera, run it back slowly and see exactly how the rabbit is being brought out of the hat. In each of these cases the usual language does indeed need to have a little semantic tidying up, and it can be done by local repair or—absurdly—by insisting on perfection and thus rejecting the whole concept, or giving it a new definition, be it "freedom," "dignity," "control," or "moral value." With "control" Skinner redefines it to cover all nonaversive goal-directed social interaction, which makes one feel delightfully imperial, as when one passes someone the salt, knowing that he will probably take it.

In the concept of "freedom," on the other hand, he smells a theological rat and, with an equally cavalier gesture, banishes it forever. For no one is free from control-as-redefined, and that, he says, is what freedom means. No! What it means is freedom from control-as-*originally*-defined, i.e., freedom from *aversive* control; that kind of freedom is not only real, but a major goal of his own planned societies.

What about the brainwashed individual who is really controlled, but not aware of it—the happy slave? This presents a serious problem but one that is just as serious for Skinner, in translation. His improbable answer is that the *long-term* consequences of such a system would be aversive. If Skinner were right, such an individual would over the long run have suffered from control in the usual sense, and hence would not in fact have been free, again in the usual sense of the term. So the usual way of talking identifies such an individual as not free. To be realistic, however, one would have to face the problem of the slave who is happy *all his life*. With Skinner's definition he is free and this is absurd. The poor victims of Skinner's attack, the writers of the literature of freedom, saw deeper than he. They suggested that such slaves have been deprived of greater happiness, a better life, dignity and justice. These suggestions look better than his.

Behind Skinner's rejection of freedom as involving lack of control there lies a subplot whose theme is that determinism eliminates freedom, a somewhat stronger claim. This comes out most clearly in the totally illicit contrasts he constantly offers the reader. For example, he says, in a passage of which we have so far considered only the first part: "Man's struggle for freedom is not due to a will to be free, but to certain behavioral processes characteristic of the human organism, the chief effect of which is the avoidance of or escape from so-called aversive features of the environment" (3:42).

Taken in its standard sense, as we have previously discussed it, the categorical denial that freedom is ever due to the will to be free is simply an empirically false generalization. We realize, however, that he intends "will to be free" (used as a cause of behavior) to be *incompatible* with behavioral processes involving "the avoidance of . . . aversive stimuli." Since we are (mostly) inclined favorably towards the idea that most molar behavior is explicable in terms of contingencies of reinforcement and since it is now clear that he means the first explanation, the reference to free will, to be *excluded* by the second, we also feel the need to reject the will-to-be-free notion. This is simply a con job. There is absolutely no good reason to take the first alternative to be incompatible with the second; Skinner is simply wrong to think there is. Certainly he gives no plausible reasons to suppose it incompatible. Hence the proper response is not to accept his implicit redefinition of free will and to junk the explanatory status of volitions; the proper response is to reject the incompatibility and retain both types of explanation. One can explain the fact that a slot machine ejects a bar of chocolate by reference to someone's insertion of a coin *or* by reference to the inner machinery. Neither excludes the other.

This same line of argument demolishes many other false dilemmas in the book and gives some credence to my major point: Skinner's main argument is completely fallacious and is misleadingly represented.

There is another side to the matter. Skinner initially states that "The text will often seem inconsistent" (p. 23). An external world explanation of this phenomenological event of seeming is that it *is* inconsistent. Time and again Skinner slips in a way that cannot be patched up. The man that denies the explanatory significance of the will (p. 10 and passim.) ends his book with the ringing paeans of the planner: man, he says, "is indeed controlled by his environment, but we must remember that it is an environment largely of his own making. The evaluation of a culture is a gigantic exercise in self-control" (3:215 and cf. 207-8. Precisely what was there in the literature of freedom or of naive humanists that was different from this? Really nothing at all. It is for this reason that I began my critique by saying I would try to show that Skinner's arguments do not count at all against the social and practical content of those against whom he rails. The book is a philosophical shambles —but still, as intriguing as astrology is to the untrained mind. (And just as far from philosophy or science.)

The Revolutionary Skinner

My third thesis is that much of Skinner's practical contribution may well spring from his philosophical position. To understand how good from errors sometimes comes, it may help to recount an anecdote. I once gave a talk to the graduate colloquium at the University of Minnesota, attended by many psychology graduate students. In the talk I explained how quantum theory and certain classical paradoxes have destroyed the thesis of physical determinism. A professor of psychology came up to me afterwards and attacked me bitterly on the grounds that such talk will undermine the researcher's drive to search for causes. Now, he may have been right. It may be true that one will do better as a scientist in a particular field if one believes what is in fact scientifically false about the whole nature of science. And I think Skinner's passionate methodological commitment to the emptiness of the human organism may be a major factor in his success in developing devices and management systems that have, in my view, substantially benefited education and educational research. That he does not *actually* believe in the emptiness of the organism is clear enough in this book. ("It would be foolish to deny the existence of that private world . . . There is an exclusive intimacy about a headache, or heartache . . ." p. 191). Yet his *research activities*, if analyzed by a "cognitive functionalist," would certainly be described as evidencing a commitment to radical behaviorism. And his theoretical works, including this one, have always shown at least some strands of argument which make clear that he hankers after and wishes desperately for the truth of radical behaviorism. If he had come any closer, especially earlier in his career, to believing in the functionality of the conscious mind for psychological explanation and even manipulation, he might well have been caught in a swamp from which he would never have struggled ashore to do good things. The defensible residue of the Kuhn thesis (1958) applies: revolutions require irrational commitment.

Nevertheless, there is no general moral here. That the error leads to good in one man is no grounds for worshipping it in general. In fact, it is no reason for becoming even slightly more casual about it. It is only a reason for avoiding fanatical oversimplification about its evil consequences, for treating it like parents treat their children's involvement with sex or drugs—by grotesque exaggerations that eventually contribute to the undesired outcome rather than preventing it.

There may possibly have been a budding psychologist or two in that audience in Minneapolis who slackened off a little. But it is a better bet (though still a poor one) that there were some who avoided butting their heads against a wall over some problem in social psychology or psephology where self-reference destroys determinism. It is now almost certain that Einstein's uncharacteristic rigidity about determinism led to the waste of his later years' research. But that rigidity might have made him a hero once again. Indeed, our philosophy of science controls our science. And the best bet is the best philosophy of science; Skinner is an exception who only proves the rule that rules about behavior have exceptions.

Let me now turn towards a version of psychology and its philosophy and of education and society that goes beyond Skinner.

Beyond Skinner

I have read about ten major reviews of *BFD* and a few score of letters or papers concerning it. Virtually all were unfavorable. But I do not think they represent the modal judgment of leading psychologists and educational researchers today. The long hand of behaviorism retains a very firm grip on a very large number of professorial positions. And in reading the critics it seems unlikely that they will much affect the hardheaded behaviorist. There is too much petulance, too many careless misreadings in the reviews. Sennet's review in *The New York Times Book Review* is the worst example of this, since he persisted in his misreading after Skinner's exposure of it and offered too much simple dogmatism on the other side. I am sure that some will feel my own comments have these faults. But perhaps it will be a *different* group that feels this, and then I will have reached some new ones.

Chomsky's review, in particular, by a man whose intellect, courage, and friendship I value beyond almost all others, is committed to a degree of skepticism about behavioral science that few of us would share. He says, "At the moment, we have virtually no scientific evidence and not even the germs of an interesting hypothesis about how human behavior is determined." I cannot accept that as a fair description of the social sciences, though I am hard to beat in a race for the skeptic's cup. His own views on determinism are so hard to extract from that review that I hesitate to comment on them, yet enough is plain so that I suspect there would not be five hands in his support in a room full of psychologists or educational researchers. Parts of his comments, however, are better than any of the others, from *Die Welt* to *New Society*.

What are the bright pennants with which we should replace the tattered banners of behaviorism? Let me sketch out the coats of arms on three such pennants. The detail will be slight but perhaps just enough to convince us that they are more than fantasy.

The task is easier with freedom, for much of what I would say is implicit in the criticisms I have already made. When Skinner says that the problem is not whether there will be control, but simply whether there will be good or bad control, he adds nothing to our understanding, because he simply translates the received view into his own terminology. He is concerned only with *external* control, the control of the environment. Later he comes to talk somewhat of self-control, as in the concluding paragraph of the book, already quoted. Now I propose a similar but I hope less trivial treatment of freedom. I would say that freedom—in the sense of importance to man—dwells within and at harmony with the constraints of natural and psychological laws.

The crucial question is not whether our actions are probabilistically determined, but whether they are *wholly* determined by external factors which *override* any variation in mental state—in which case we are not free—or whether one of the *intervening* determinants is a mental state or event such as preferring or choosing. Notice that I do not suggest for one moment that the subject's belief that he is free is decisive. What is decisive is the properties of the actual causal chain. He may think he is free, though he is not (the alcoholic, for example); he may think he is not free, though he is (the man waking from a successful operation to remedy a locked joint). The philosophical lure of determinism will tempt us to say that if his decision or preference is itself determined, then it is absurd to call him free. But I call him free because he is in fact *capable* and *able* to do something besides what he does. It may be asked how he can be "capable" of doing what is physically guaranteed not to happen? Look at what "capacity," "ability," "potentiality" really mean and turn your eyes away from the dazzling glare of the Mad Determinist's magic. Instead, cast them back to earth again. You will find in your everyday use the basic sense of those terms, and, if you cling firmly to that sense, you will find the spell has no power over you. For example, it is probably true that everyone who reads this is *capable*, has the *ability* or *capacity* to multiply 17 by 13 in his head. Supposing that the universe is so set up that a reader dies as he reads these words. Does that refute my claim? Not for one moment. It is true that he had that power at the time I claimed it, and the proof is not that he ever did it but evidence that tells us about his education and check-balancing skills, or more direct evidence of the present state of his brain. You are able to do many things that you never do or did, just as a table is able to support weights that it never will support. Determinism does not destroy or even bear on your capacity to do things which you do not in fact do. Throw off its thrall! And if you succeed, as a special bonus I will award you a small medal on which is engraved the words "Determinism is false, anyway." [2]

The immediate effect of the revised doctrine on educational research is far more than you might suppose at first sight. It immediately becomes appropriate to talk forbidden talk once more, to talk, for example, about "the will" and "strength of will" in terms of the *amount* of aversive reinforcement that it can withstand; and we can begin to discuss again without embarrassment the question of training the will, of strengthening it. Notice that I talk of reinforcement, the language of behaviorism. In fact, most recent works on education for self-control have come from the behavior modification people, Skinnerians mostly. What I am trying to do is free them from a verbal taboo which simply confuses their whole perception of what *they* are trying to do. There is no reason for them not to talk of "building character." They are now grown-up enough to be able to discard the politics of their father, though not his good advice. His good advice was not to rely on talking about character improvement to effect real behavior change. They must go out and find the educational *procedures* and *experiences* that will bring about a *demonstrable* change in *behavior*, of the kind that produces *demonstrable benefits*. The old man's advice was good in substance, but they do not have to say this is *control* and they don't have to deny that the subject is now able to do things of his *own free will* that he couldn't manage before. Further, they do not have to deny that the person does them because he chooses to. In short, we can respect, admire, and benefit from B. F. Skinner but we do not have to buy the ideological absurdities. Like those graduate students, we ought to be mature enough to face up to the false-

2. For more details see my chapter "Responsibility" in *Primary Philosophy* (New York: McGraw-Hill Book Co., 1966).

hood of the philosophical doctrine of determinism without becoming lousy scientists.

Look at the word "autonomy." *BFD* is a polemic against "autonomous man," whose most obvious property is being constituted entirely of straw. I have spent little time on him so far, mainly for that reason. But let me try to show you that the mistaken philosophical objections to autonomy have prevented the Skinnerians from proceeding in directions of the utmost value to us all. One begins with the suspicion that those many writers who have taken the autonomy of the student to be a principal or *the* principal goal of education have not been making a simple logical or scientific mistake, as one would suppose from reading Skinner. Take the following practical problem.

Suppose we discover that the use of a token economy in some classrooms that were previously notorious for rowdiness and lack of learning produces a good learning environment and good learning achievement—along with great gains in teacher satisfaction. However, there are two objections to or shortcomings of the project. First, we find that when a substitute teacher comes in, the students revert completely to their previous behavior. (And the same thing happens when they go on to the next grade.) That is, there is no transfer of this behavior to the classroom, the teacher, or training in general. The improved behavior is simply tied to the token system. Second, there is a feeling that something immoral is going on in tying rewards to learning and in commercializing the classroom. (The second objection would be much weakened but not eliminated if it were not for the first point.) The above situation happens to be one that I have been involved with, and a reading of the surveys of experimental work in this volume makes clear that it is fairly typical. Many of the studies reported, however, do not inform us about or investigate transfer or generalization effects.

Clearly the crucial task, in order to meet these objections, is to develop in the students what we would normally call an *autonomous* drive for learning or—at the worst—for "law and order." There was very little thinking about this with the project I know about. Why? If one is mostly interested in behavior and its external conditioners, one runs the risk of not focusing on the inner man. But only the inner man goes home after school, with the student. Only the inner man goes up to the next grade; the reinforcers do not. You do not control the ones that will be there, and they are not set up to elicit the desired behavior. "Not our business," some are inclined to say. When I have asked behaviorally oriented trainers to *focus* on the real problem, they come up with a dozen ingenious and promising suggestions for transfer schedules, reentry conditioning, and so on. The failure of these procedures to have become the great focus in the literature that they are in terms of educational problems is not explicable without reference to the doctrinaire allergy about autonomy. The spirit of Skinner demands environmental manipulation at each point where you want an effect; but the practice need not be so limited. It has been shackled by the philosophy. Behavioral methods can focus on getting residual changes *after* the environmental manipulation ceases to be possible. This, in fact, is almost what the teaching machine–programmed text is set up to do, but behavior modification in general has not gone after maintaining performance without external reinforcers.

MORALITY

Consider moral education. Look up the topic in the *Handbook of Research on Teaching* or the *Encyclopedia of Educational Research*. What explains the lack of entries? The lack of social importance of the subject? Scarcely. The impossibility of success, established by Hartshorne and May forty-four years ago? Similar results can be shown for inquiry teaching or problem-solving and a dozen other popular entries. No—it was the positivist legacy of moral skepticism that the behaviorist brought to educational research which principally destroyed moral education. And that moral skepticism is as poorly founded as the rejection of autonomy. In fact, there is a very close connection, and it is particularly in this area that one can benefit immensely from throwing off the blinkers of bad philosophy.

One reason for optimism is the extent to which Skinner himself has come to understand the provable value of morality for the society as a whole. These parts of *BFD* are far ahead of anything which has come from the positivist-behaviorist camp of morality in its entire history. And yet he does not see where behaviorism can contribute most. He sees the crucial importance of "doing good for its own sake," of "aiding the society for the sake of the common good." He describes ways in which societies have reinforced such behavior. But he cannot make the break with existing contingencies. Time after time, he backs away from the obvious necessity, the necessity to *train* ourselves and our children towards an *autonomous* moral drive, one that will work in the absence of any possible reinforcement. It is selfless commitment, not the prudence which he confusedly calls "natural morality," which epitomizes moral behavior as such—and for which the evolutionary advantages are greatest.

It is not easy to bring students to the point where they find unselfish acts rewarding. It is a challenge for a master trainer, an inventive teacher, a behavioral scientist, but Skinner blocks on it, because he cannot quite bring himself to the task of modifying the *interior* of the organism in such a way that it will continue to follow a certain behavior pattern in the *absence* of the contingencies that are presently reinforcing for it. To do so is to recognize a further dimension of autonomy in man—his capacity to develop new valences, new sets, new values.

The most recent book on behavior modification applied to children, an excellent and practical work, *Changing Children's Behavior* (1) is a further example of this point. I think it's fair to say that there is nothing in this book on developing the autonomous drive to respect or help others. And yet there is everything else—and the Krumboltzes themselves, kind enough to attend a seminar of mine, were quickly able to suggest a dozen ploys that might work for us. We must find out whether they will.

Am I now sounding like the worst bogey of the anti-Skinnerians? Brainwashing the kids, out-skinning Skinner? That is a matter of the gravest concern, not a mere propaganda war, and we must spend careful professional time on it. Moral education is a moral matter, and if it is indoctrination, it may be immoral. Let us legitimate such questions. The forces against value-free social sciences are now overwhelming. Before dying for the cause of empiricism, make sure you read Skinner's argument for the objective validity of morality. Skinner's instincts are right, the instincts which have so often led him in the right direction in these practical matters. Perhaps the philosophical war cries had to be wrong, shockingly wrong, to attract attention. Moderation has always had a bad press. Perhaps the survival value of shocking falsehoods even in science today is greater than that of truth. As Skinner would say, if that is true and as undesirable as it appears, then we ought to change the contingencies.

Comments on Yearbook Collaborators

It may be of interest to give further instances of the points made above in some of my coauthors' contributions to this volume. I say nothing about the most philosophical of these papers, Carl Thoresen's, despite the strong temptation to do so, because discussing a long philosophical paper usually requires at least the same length. It is clear that Thoresen speaks to (and often for) many of the points I have made. I also say nothing about Kanfer's valuable review because it raises no issues not raised in more specific contexts in the other papers. It is more feasible to pick up more limited points from the other papers and even then to restrict myself to illustrating the claims of methodological and philosophical deficiency and educational-ethical intentions.

When one gets down to empirical case studies ($N \neq 1$) with students instead of pigeons or rats, one begins to encounter special problems for Skinner's philosophy-of-natural-science paradigm. For example, Skinner has always spurned control-group methodology, partly no doubt because of its essential absence from the usual natural sciences. And he is quite right—it is only one way, not the only way, to demonstrate causality. Indeed, it is not even a very reliable way to do that; however, *sometimes* it is the best way. The use of subjects as their own controls or time-series analysis in general is quite appropriate under certain circumstances. For example, a schedule change for a pigeon responding every few seconds will often show up as a sharp break in the response curve. But it is not so easy to eyeball causality in larger groups of idiosyncratic human subjects, where responses are relatively rare. And so the

Skinner model too often leads to careless work and more careless conclusions when used in education. We see hints of this in some of the reports in this volume. The systematic skills of educational evaluation are not obtained by osmosis from work with laboratory animals.

HAROLD COHEN

The general prologue raises interesting questions and makes important points, but the real interest emerges in the experiments. The CASE study shows that paying some imprisoned students to learn, with cash or privileges, was quite effective with respect to academic performance and possibly significant with respect to short-term improvement in recidivism. But any favorable conclusion, let alone any generalization, is dependent on whether the group was randomly chosen; no comment is made on that score. Whatever the story in the full report, it is significant that an account of it by one of the experimenters would omit reference to this. To talk of "demonstrating" something without covering such an obvious threat as a higher motivation towards socially acceptable forms of self-improvement in the experimental group is sad indeed.

The second project described by Cohen, the PICA project, is covered in more detail. The sophistication of the research design is unfortunately negligible. The study uses subjects as their own controls without consideration of regression to the mean or other statistical/measurement problems (e.g., contamination of judgments). The N was small and there is not the slightest attempt at justifying the conclusion that the behavior modification arrangements were the causative factor. Intensive small-group tutoring, programmed texts, and payment of students for achievement, along with an extravagant support system for interviewing, liaison with family, scheduling, etc., which exacerbates the Hawthorne effect, provide plenty of alternative examples of possible causes. In short, the work is naive but still well worth trying on a larger scale and hopefully with some external evaluation of the results.

The PICA study also raises some of the ethical issues mentioned. It is very difficult for someone who thinks he has a neat new way to change behavior not to fire at any target someone suggests, like a kid with a new pistol. We find the use of drugs by students entered on the admission profile as "inappropriate behavior towards self." Why is it inappropriate? Because it's disapproved of and punished? Such a view is strongly suggested by the discussion earlier in the paper, but this is a total cop out. The response by the authorities may be the inappropriate one, and Skinnerians who accept the present social norms as defining appropriateness should reread *Walden Two*.

As we look ahead with Cohen to the community effort of BPLAY, we can see some of these difficulties recurring and still applaud the effort. But we also might ask ourselves whether this kind of intensive intervention will be necessary in each community. In so doing, it should occur to us to ask why the schools fail to convey a value system that would prevent the need for delinquency control. Is it because they lack something like PICA? There is not much in PICA on ethics and attitudes, by contrast with law and behavior, as far as one can tell from this paper. (It's significant enough that eight topics should be mentioned without mentioning either of these.) Just talking about ethics and attitudes of course will not make saints. But not talking about them may make manipulators. And why should one just talk about them? Why not experiment with them, role-play them, and study them in other cultures? This may not be easy for a positivist-behaviorist but, I submit, it is necessary for education.

Notice that the support system of PICA is extended into the home; the parents are trained to run a token economy there, too. But the question immediately arises: what is going to happen when the student finds himself or herself away from this support system? Where is the element in the experimental design that will test this, the real measure of success? We want *autonomous* good citizens, not paid models or well-behaved wage-slaves. I suggest that the aversion to autonomy has again shown its influence in these omissions. Of course, a short report cannot cover everything; but is it more important to show that intensive personal care and reward can effect temporary improvement or that they can change long-term dispositions? No one ever doubted the first. A behavior modification approach helps to do it more systematically and *possibly* more effectively. But that may be more than offset if it diverts attention from the long-term goal.

KRASNER AND KRASNER

This paper is considerably more concerned with philosophical and ethical issues, and valuably so. But some comments may still be useful. It is interesting to note the early ideological assertion, in the discussion of the British infant schools, that the concept of the "free" school is incompatible with the behavior modification approach "to the extent that it is based upon the hypothesis that behavior is determined by the inner forces of autonomous individuals." Not at all. They are incompatible only if one holds that such inner forces are not in turn determined by external conditions. The evidence suggests that genetic "control" of behavior *is* substantial, so there is still some incompatibility, but not as much as the superficial Skinnerian dichotomy suggests. And once one begins to focus on creating and changing an individual who is to go on autonomously, one starts to take more account of the *durability* of these changes, not just their size.

As the Krasners turn to token economies in the classroom, we find a welcome mention of fading the token reinforcers and generalization to other situations in the discussion of the O'Leary and Becker study. But the concern with this is minimal since there is only "anecdotal" evidence of its success, and no mention at all of its durability. Further, the list of defining elements of token programs in the classroom does not even mention this. Similar comments apply to the Hewett study, which was on a larger scale and somewhat less effective.

Incidentally, one must note that the management costs of token economies are rather high. There is usually an aide working full time, there are trips to be arranged, redemption "stores" to be run, and so on. With those resources, several other options become potentially competitive, a fact not usually noticed by the investigators surveyed here. There is also the interesting problem of counter-strategies to the "speed-up" of performance requirements for a reinforcer. Students, like union members, will begin to react to this if the approach becomes general.

The Krasners report favorably on the Winett and Winkler critique of target behaviors as conformist, but they do not go on to propose ways to resist, avoid, handle, or replace this tendency. They see the problem about generalization and quote the useful suggestions by O'Leary and Drabman, but we must remember that we lack experimental evidence as to the success of these suggestions.

Overall, the Krasners are not aware of the extreme weakness of most studies. They say: "A hardheaded reviewer could conclude from the research evidence that the traditional token economy . . . is indeed an effective technique for modifying behaviors labeled by somebody as deviant or undesirable." A hardheaded reviewer could not draw this conclusion. It is a very general conclusion, involving far too little qualification of population, situation, duration, treatment, or behaviors, given the research data reviewed. Behavior modification is only a promising entry in those stakes; and it is a much weaker entry in the stakes of a desirable or optimal treatment, but still a very significant one. Its contribution stems not from any theory, but from a systematic rational approach to a complex problem, the mark of the engineer or manager. The "theory," really just an ideology, may have given the movement its original impetus, but now it is holding it back.

BECKER

The opening section of this paper is most valuable—a direct attack on the slogans of the opposition. Notice how low the level of the "theory" is; but it is just at this level that it has the most effect, and we *should* treat it there. We should not attempt some grandiose, over-inflated, jargon-ridden, pseudoquantitative performance that is supposed to look like classical physics. One "Hull" is enough.

Becker's review of individual case studies raises one's anxiety level sharply about the justification for choice of goal behavior, which appears (on these brief accounts) capricious and/or conformist. Individual studies may mislead because of the natural tendency to report only successes; they demonstrate a possible but (probably) not a universal treatment. (And the residual level of undesirable behavior may still be above the threshold of acceptability.)

But there can be no doubt that a teacher training (or parent training) program which does not involve careful training in behavior-management techniques is simply not justified. One may have reservations and criticisms but, in the present state of darkness, a candle, even if described as a lighthouse, is something no one can pass up. Nor is this kind of candle going to be replaced by something entirely different. For the *systematic self-study* and *analytic* elements that are a prerequisite for these behavioral management exercises are *never* going to be superseded. They are to teaching what the clock, the thermometer, and the measuring cup are to cooking—it may remain an art, but you need these to keep it from being a disaster.

Another attractive feature of Becker's position is that he has transcended Skinner's metaphysics of punishment, reiterated in the two papers previously considered. Punishment may or may not work, just like (conventional) rewards; and it may or may not be legitimate. It was an insight for Skinner to see that punishment is *often* ill-planned; unfortunately, it got converted into a rule, which lacked not only empirical support but even operational content (since withholding rewards is—in context—often equivalent to punishment). Becker gives us the beginnings of the needed taxonomy and practice of punishment, previously totally obscured by the sweeping coverage of positive versus negative reinforcement. This alone is a giant step beyond Skinner's philosophy, towards more effective practice.

REFERENCES

1. Krumboltz, J. D., and Krumboltz, H. B. *Changing Children's Behavior.* Englewood Cliffs, N.J.: Prentice-Hall, 1972.
2. Scriven, Michael. "A Critique of Radical Behaviorism." *Minnesota Studies in the Philosophy of Science* 1 (1956): 88-130.
3. Skinner, B. F. *Beyond Freedom and Dignity.* New York: Alfred A. Knopf, 1971.

CHAPTER XIV

Some Implications of Making Education More Efficient

B. F. SKINNER

There is little doubt that education is in trouble. It faces many different kinds of problems, for which many different kinds of solutions will have to be found. One of them is economic. The educational assignment grows steadily greater. For example, children are to start school at an earlier age, special classes are to be arranged for exceptional children, students are to be admitted to college with fewer qualifications, and new fields are to be covered to improve the relevance of education. These changes come at a time when costs are rising sharply. Tuition and taxes continue to rise, teachers are asked to take on more work and cut down on outside activities, and many schools, particularly parochial schools, are closing.

One solution to the economic problem is simply to make instruction more efficient. If we could teach, say, twice as much in the same time and with the same effort, our present staff and facilities would suffice to teach more students, teach each one more, allow for a wider range of abilities, and cover more fields, while at the same time holding smaller classes, giving teachers a more reasonable work day and more pay, and getting more support from the public by giving more in return for its money. Almost any other enterprise would try to solve an economic problem in that way. It would see whether its practices could not be made more efficient. But teachers and school administrators seldom look in that direction. Why?

Some Reasons for Inefficiency

Past experience with research in the field of learning may be at fault. The learning curves obtained with mazes and the forgetting curves obtained with memory drums have never given the teacher any real help. Educational psychologists soon turned from basic research on the processes underlying teaching to the measurement of their effects—a change exemplified in the personal history of Edward L. Thorndike.

Part of the explanation may be a distaste for pedagogy or educational method. Can teaching really be taught? Does not any reasonably intelligent person already know what is needed? A teacher must attract the students' attention and keep them interested, but he will have learned how to do this in his daily life. The neglect of pedagogy is seen in current books which tell us how to improve our schools. One needs no special vocabulary or any scientific knowledge to read the contributions of men like John Holt, Jonathan Kozol, Paul Goodman, and Charles Silberman. Even the teaching aids which are most commonly mentioned (audiovisual devices and television, for example) simply do what people do and make no use of a more technical analysis of basic processes. Teaching, in other words, is regarded not as a special skill but as an art in dealing with people. The only problem is to find those who practice it well.

Many educators have gone a step further. They show no interest in making teaching more efficient because they do not believe in teaching. In the classical expression, the teacher cannot teach, he can only help the student learn, and he cannot help much. Carl Rogers has recently said that in his opinion teaching is a "vastly overrated function" (4). "Free schools" (for example, Summerhill) and many experimental colleges boast of how little teaching actually goes on, and Ivan Illich (1) has completed the reductio ad absurdum by calling for the deschooling of society. It will be enough simply to make the world a "livable learning environment." There is often a note of despair in these proposals. We have tried so hard and failed so miserably; there must be a better way.

The way that is most often suggested goes back to Jean Jacques Rousseau. We are to let the child learn in school as he learns in the world at large—through a natural love of learning, a natural curiosity. Let him know the joy of discovery. The proposal is especially appealing in contrast with what goes on in the joyless punitive schools which have so long characterized education. It is also attractive because it seems to raise no problems. The real world is conveniently at hand and it does not need to be made to work. But Rousseau's proposal has been tried, episodically at least, for two hundred years and that is presumably time enough to demonstrate its feasibility. Why, then, are we still at the stage of making proposals? Why is it that the average life of an experimental free school is said to be something on the order of eighteen months? It is true that new proposals in education, as elsewhere, are not likely to be well supported, and that the great changes which need to be made in established practices can be made only slowly. Nevertheless, more progress should have been made.

A more likely explanation is that the real world is not an effective teacher. Children do not learn much from the natural environment. The feral child, the child said to have been raised by wolves, or, one said to have matured alone in a benevolent environment, is about all we have to show for unaided natural curiosity or a love of learning. A physical environment breeds awkward, dangerous, and superstitious behavior, and a social environment breeds hostile as well as friendly behavior, selfish as well as generous behavior. What seem like successful demonstrations of "free" classrooms must be attributed to unanalyzed skills in dealing with people, and the difficulty is that because they have not been analyzed, they cannot be transmitted. There has been no accumulation of better ways of teaching within Rousseau's program. On the contrary, apparent successes have usually meant a contraction in the educational assignment. Less and less is taught, by definition, as learning is left to the natural environment, but to that we must add that less and less is learned. The extent to which we have accepted this consequence is suggested by current proposals to reduce if not abolish "compulsory education."

Education is an important function of a culture—possibly in the long run its most important or only function. A culture, as a social environment, must transmit itself to its new members. Some transmission occurs when new members learn from those with whom they are in contact, with or without informal instruction; but transmission on a scale needed to make people maximally effective needs a carefully designed system.

A lack of confidence in any effort to improve teaching is especially crucial because there are many other reasons why new practices are not likely to be adopted. So far as most administrators and teachers are concerned, an improvement in teaching will demand troublesome changes, in which much is to be lost and not much to be gained. No penalty is imposed if an administrator or teacher overlooks a better way of teaching, and current inefficiencies can be justified by arguing that the task is too difficult, that there are too many students, that facilities are inadequate, and that social and racial problems are insurmountable. If this is not enough, it is possible to fall back upon that argument which has always been used to exonerate bad teaching: it is the student who fails the course, not the teacher or school.

It is a hopeful sign that administrators and teachers are beginning to be held accountable for their work. This has always been true in other professions. A doctor may not cure every patient, but if he cures few or none, he fails as a doctor. A lawyer may not win every case, but if he wins few or none, he will not last long as a lawyer. The salesman may not make every sale, but if he makes few or none, he fails as a salesman. And of course artisans have always been judged in terms of the quality of their work. Why should the teacher not also be held accountable for the results of his teaching?

The commonest answer is that the results cannot be evaluated. They are not as obvious as a cure, a favorable verdict, a sale, or a job well done. Some specialists in educational measurement, in a surprising reversal of an earlier position, have been quick to agree. For more than half a century we have been told that measures of ability and achievement are reliable and valid. But suddenly they have become socially relevant: intelligence has taken on racial overtones, and achievement has been tied to the accountability of teachers. Some authorities are therefore beating a retreat. Henry S. Dyer, vice-president of the Educational Testing Service, has characterized tests of intelligence and of grade equivalency as "monstrosities" and has said that the development of tests which could be used to hold teachers accountable for their work would be an enterprise of the order of magnitude of the atomic bomb (3). But *students* have been held accountable with the same kinds of tests for decades; they have been admitted to college according to measured abilities and promoted and graduated according to measured achievements. (That we should not hold students accountable, that we should admit them to college regardless of measured abilities and give no examinations to measure their achievement is, of course, part of the philosophy of a natural learning environment.)

It is no doubt easier to measure some effects of teaching than others. How well a student has learned to read is more obvious than what he has learned in, say, social studies. But education would be in serious trouble if we could not tell whether a student has learned anything in social studies. Both the teacher and the student need evidence of progress. One source of trouble is the traditional practice of defining the goals of education in terms of mental processes. If the teacher is to "transmit knowledge," "cultivate skills," "evoke ideas," or "change attitudes," neither he nor the student is likely to have any clear evidence that a change has occurred. Another source of trouble is that the very large repertoire acquired in a course cannot be reliably sampled in a brief examination. We shall see how these problems can be solved in other ways.

Teachers and administrators are likely to reject any proposal that they be held accountable, mainly for economic reasons. There is always the danger that a teacher who is not very efficient will be fired or paid less than one who is conspicuously successful. But only when the administrator or teacher is held accountable will he search most actively for better ways of teaching.

It would be unfair to say that teachers and administrators do little to make teaching more effective only because they lack economic incentives. A better explanation is that they do not know what to do. It has always been supposed that the principal source of technical knowledge in education is classroom experience. The young teacher learns how to teach either by teaching or by emulating someone who has learned how to teach by teaching. The possibility that technical help may come from outside the profession is seldom recognized. There was a comparable stage in the history of medicine. Medical practices were once entirely the product of the experience of physicians, but most physicians accept the fact that advances in medicine will now come from the scientific laboratory. A change in provenance is inevitable as soon as a relevant science appears, and that stage has now been reached in education.

Experimental Analysis of Behavior

TASK OF THE TEACHER

What has come to be called the "experimental analysis of behavior" has already given rise to an effective technology of teaching, although it is not yet widely known or used. Three contributions may be noted. One has to do with the teacher's assignment. It has long been supposed that the task of the teacher is to impart *information*, train the *mind*, help the student *grasp relations*, teach him to *appreciate* literature, art and music, encourage *creativity*, and change his *attitudes* (for example, toward racial problems). But the teacher does not act upon the mind or its faculties, or upon traits of character or personality. He acts upon the behavior of the student, and he does so by changing the verbal or nonverbal environment in which the student lives.

It is not always easy to redefine the goals of teaching. In particular, an analysis of the so-called higher mental processes may be quite complex. But progress has already been made, and it has given the teacher a clearer conception of his assignment and better evidence of the extent to which it has been fulfilled. It has also made it less likely that he will seek exoneration for failure by inventing mental objectives which he can claim to have achieved. He is less likely to discount the fact that a child cannot read by arguing that he is acquiring reading readiness or an interest in reading, or that a student who cannot solve problems in arithmetic is nevertheless learning to understand mathematics or acquiring a love for it.

CLASSROOM MANAGEMENT

A second contribution of the experimental analysis of behavior has to do with classroom management. Why does a student come to school, behave well in class, pay attention, apply himself to his assignments, answer questions, and so forth? So far as traditional practice is concerned, the answer is simple: to avoid the consequences of not doing so. It is now clear that many of the disciplinary problems faced by teachers (truancy, vandalism, and apathy) are the by-products of a long history of aversive control, which has not yet come to an end. The experimental analysis of behavior has suggested powerful alternatives through the use of positively reinforc-

ing consequences. To put it roughly, the student can be given positive reasons for doing the kinds of things which will advance his
education. The layman speaks of these as rewards and may object
to new classroom practices as bribery, but to do so is to misunder-
stand the whole science of contingency management. What is important is not only the rewarding things a student gets but the
ways in which they are contingent upon his behavior. The power
of contingency management in the classroom is well established—
though, again, it is not yet widely used.

INSTRUCTIONAL MATERIALS AND DESIGN

The experimental analysis of behavior has made a third contribution to education in the design of instructional materials—both
in the material itself and in modes of presentation. Techniques of
shaping complex behavior through a program of progressive approximation emerged from the operant laboratory, particularly in
the extension of basic principles to the analysis of verbal behavior.
The main features of a good program are well known: the student is
asked to proceed in small steps and to master each step before moving on to the next. Material is so designed that correct responses are
highly probable, and progress through a program may be all that
is needed to keep the student at work. A good program imparts
an extensive repertoire in a very efficient way.

The personalized system of instruction (PSI) designed by F. S.
Keller (2) brings these contributions together in the redesign of
courses in colleges and graduate schools. The basic elements have
been described by Keller as follows:

(1) the go-at-your-own-pace feature which permits a student to move
through a course of study at a speed commensurate with his ability and
other demands upon his time; (2) the unit-perfection requirement for
advance, which lets the student go ahead to any material only after
demonstrating mastery of that which precedes it; (3) the use of lectures
and demonstrations as vehicles of motivation rather than sources of
critical information; (4) the related stress upon the written word in
teacher communication; and, finally, (5) the use of [a] proctor (student), which permits repeated testing, immediate scoring, almost unavoidable tutoring, and a marked enhancement of his personal social
aspect of the educational process (p. 13).

The PSI system is spreading rapidly throughout colleges and universities, and there is no reason why it cannot be adapted to high school and the lower grades.

The definition of objectives in behavioral terms, the design of effective classroom contingencies, and the programming of instructional materials may be all that is needed to solve many current problems in education. Operant conditioning is a matter of both "acquisition" and "motivation," and signs of progress through a program are for most students a highly reinforcing consequence. Individualized treatment removes the greatest source of inefficiency in traditional instruction—the requirement that large numbers of students advance at the same speed, which is almost necessarily the wrong speed for most of them. But perhaps the most important result is that there is no need for final examinations. In a well-designed course of instruction, the behavior a student is acquiring is obvious because he uses it in pursuing the course. A glance ahead shows him what he does not yet know; a glance backward shows him what he has learned. Both student and teacher can see what has been done without trying to sample large repertoires. Such instruction is rather like teaching a manual skill or a sport. The golf instructor does not give his student a final examination, measuring the length of ten drives from a tee, the distances from the pin in ten approaches from a sand trap, and scoring the number of successes in ten long putts and ten short putts, and then assign a grade showing how well his student has learned to play. Each step in a program may be considered an examination because the student responds and his response is evaluated. In the Keller system brief tests are taken to determine mastery at each level, but this is very different from trying to measure all that a student has learned at the end of a course.

Impending examinations have well-known emotional effects due, in part, to the feared risk of inaccurate sampling. Administrators and teachers also, faced with accountability, are now beginning to show these effects and for the same reasons. But a well-designed course of instruction solves the problem for both students and teachers. The course itself is the examination. If the student is to receive a grade, it will indicate only how far he has advanced. It is not necessary to determine the degree to which the materials of the whole course are retained, since most of them must have been retained in order to finish the course. The critic may complain that retention is not being measured, but a final examination does not measure it successfully, and it encourages practices, such as last-minute cramming, which actually interfere with the retention the examination is designed to guarantee.

How much improvement is to be expected? Is it fair to say that what is now taught could be taught in half the time and with half the effort on the part of student and teacher? Anyone who has worked through a well-designed program of instruction (in a subject with which he was not until then familiar), anyone who has seen a high school class under good contingency management, or anyone who has talked with or read the reports of students in a personalized system of instruction will be inclined to say yes. Comparisons with so-called control groups in set experiments are not very helpful. The comparison should be with what now prevails in our schools and colleges. There are no doubt other ways in which teaching can be made more effective, but the practices derived from an experimental analysis of behavior already have shown great promise.

Other Problems

We shall not be in the clear, however, until other problems have been solved. Simply to change from a system in which large numbers of students progress at the same rate to a truly individualized mode of instruction may mean drastic changes in the architecture of schools, in the roles of supervisors and teachers, and in daily routines. "More efficient instruction" should mean, if it means anything, that students will learn more rapidly, but if the first-grade teacher also teaches what has been reserved for the second grade, what is the second-grade teacher to teach? The recent history of education in America has been marked by a postponement of instruction—for example, until students are "ready"—but the trend may now be reversed. A classical example is the course in logic designed by Professor Layman Allen of Yale University Law School. The course worked so well with law students that it was tried in college, and it worked so well there that it was tried in high school. At last report it was being taught in the sixth grade. What happens to a standard curriculum when changes of that magnitude become possible?

A reasonable answer might be that students will be taught a great deal more during the same period of instruction. But it may be tempting, instead, to terminate education at an earlier age and this raises other problems. What happens to employment figures if large numbers of young people are turned loose on the job market at an earlier age? (The terminal age in Britain has recently been raised one year, in part, it is said, to solve such a problem.)

Improved instruction will also affect the employment of teachers. Individualized instruction could mean a return to the tutorial practices which existed before there were schools in the present sense, and that may mean that more teachers would be needed. But tutorial instruction was not feasible for large numbers and is clearly out of the reach of present educational systems. Hence the search for new types of materials suitable for self-instruction and for devices which evaluate students' responses to such materials. The Keller system takes advantage of the fact that one learns most effectively when teaching, that individualized instruction may be furthered by letting students teach each other. These solutions seem to suggest that it will eventually be possible to dispense with teachers. But any increase in efficiency brings added educational objectives within reach, many of which demand personal attention.

A loss in personal contact between student and teacher is not necessarily a disadvantage in some fields of learning. The student does not need a person to tell him whether he has correctly translated a particular sentence or solved a problem. The "approval" offered by a teacher differs from the confirmation to be found in programmed materials, but it is not a "natural" consequence of behaving correctly and may, in fact, cause trouble. And before regretting a loss in personal contact, we should look at the kinds which now prevail in classrooms. When large numbers of students are taught at the same time, few of them acquire effective verbal behavior, oral or written. In multiple-choice examinations and in some kinds of programmed materials, students merely check sentences which have been composed by others. They have no chance to learn to compose sentences themselves. Programmed materials can teach effective composition, but the flexibility characteristic of social discourse calls for a teacher as an essential figure because verbal exchange is almost necessarily individualized. We may see a revival of the art of speaking and writing, and it will be important because it involves much of the art of thinking.

Improved efficiency in education makes time available for a greater emphasis on personal exchange between teacher and student. In addition, the teacher remains an essential figure in following the progress of a student and advising him on different courses of action. These new demands will require new kinds of training, and some direct contact with the experimental analysis of behavior may be needed if the teacher is to take advantage of available behavioral technology. The important thing is that more efficient practices will give the teacher far greater power in fulfilling a far more explicit assignment, and that should mean a vast improvement in the status of the teaching profession.

REFERENCES

1. Illich, Ivan. *Deschooling Society*. New York: Harper & Row, 1971.
2. Keller, F. S. "Neglected Rewards in the Educational Process." *Proceedings of the Twenty-third Annual Meeting of the American Conference of Academic Deans*, pp. 9-22. Los Angeles, January 16, 1967.
3. *New York Times*, March 23, 1971.
4. Rogers, Carl R. *Freedom to Learn*. Columbus, Ohio: Charles Merrill Books, 1969.

Index

Accelerating cognitive learning, principle of, illustrated (chart), 212

Achievement Place (Kans.), token reinforcement system in, 308

Accountability: attitude of teachers towards, 456; concept of, 449; reversal of opinions of some educators on, 449-50

Acquired reinforcers, nature of, 266

Activity reinforcers, 92-93

Affect isolation, autistic child characterized by, 231

Aggressive behavior: evaluative criteria for determination of, 171-73; errors of parents in rating of, 172-73; means of acquiring data on, 154-55; physical setting in relation to, 157-58; see also Deviant child behavior

Alexis, definition of, 211

Allen, Layman, 454

American Medical Association, factors in psychological category of, 263

Analytic field studies, place of, in research, 225

ANOVA, results of, for repeated measures, 181, 182

Antisocial acts, means of deterrence of, 300-1; see also Aggressive behavior, Deviant child behavior

Aristotle, 396

Autism and behavior theory, 237-54

Autism: contemporary research on, 251-54; developmental theories of, 236; meanings of, 232-37– from behavioral viewpoint, 233-34, from traditional viewpoints, 234-35, in psychodynamic theories, 236, in developmental theories, 236, in arousal theories, 237

Austistic behaviors: discussion of, 230-32; measures on treatment of (chart), 250

Austistic children: behaviors of, 230-32; early use of behavior modification methods with, 240-43; generalization and follow-up results of work with, 249-51; recent approaches to behavior modification of, 243-49; reports of attempts to build language in, 248-49; studies of Wolf, Risley, and Mees on, 240-43; treatment of, in classroom, 254-55; see also Autism

Autonomy, critique of Skinner's views on, 417-18

Aversive consequences, sources of, 156-57

Aversive counterconditioning: use of chemicals in, 133-36; use of electric shock in, 132-33; see also Punishment

Aversive techniques, 129-37; limitations on use of, 129-30

Aversive therapy: concept of, 130; discussion of, 132-36; symbolically induced aversion in, 134-35

Awareness, behaviorists' premium on, 399-400

Baer, D. M., quoted (with others), 364

Bandura, Albert, influence of, on behavioral approaches to counseling, 109-10

Bandura's social learning theory, research undergirding, 65-66

Banghart, F., quoted, 37, 317-18

Becker, Wesley C., critique of work of, 444-45; quoted (with K. D. O'Leary), 358

Behavior: change of, through behavior modification techniques, 4; contributions of school to shaping of, 298-99; control of, by contingencies, 164; criticisms of techniques for change of, 12-13; distinction between performance and acquisition of, 393-94; experimental analysis of, 451-54; focus of learning-based models on, 9-10; influence of religious groups on, 297-98

Behavioral analysis procedural flow chart, 329

Behavioral approach: basis of, in real life, 139; contribution of, to coun-

INFORMATION CONCERNING THE NATIONAL SOCIETY FOR THE STUDY OF EDUCATION

1. PURPOSE. The purpose of the National Society is to promote the investigation and discussion of educational questions. To this end it holds an annual meeting and publishes a series of yearbooks.

2. ELIGIBILITY TO MEMBERSHIP. Any person who is interested in receiving its publications may become a member by sending to the Secretary-Treasurer information concerning name, title, and address, and a check for $11.00 (includes entrance fee), (see Item 5), except that graduate students, on the recommendation of a faculty member, may become members by paying $9.00 for the first year of their membership. Dues for all subsequent years are the same as for other members (see Item 4).

Membership is not transferable; it is limited to individuals, and may not be held by libraries, schools, or other institutions, either directly or indirectly.

3. PERIOD OF MEMBERSHIP. Applicants for membership may not date their entrance back of the current calendar year, and all memberships terminate automatically on December 31, unless the dues for the ensuing year are paid as indicated in Item 6.

4. DUTIES AND PRIVILEGES OF MEMBERS. Members pay dues of $10.00 annually, receive a clothbound copy of each publication, are entitled to vote, to participate in discussion, and (under certain conditions) to hold office. The names of members are printed in the yearbooks.

Persons who are sixty years of age or above may become life members on payment of fee based on average life-expectancy of their age group. For information, apply to Secretary-Treasurer.

5. ENTRANCE FEE. New members are required the first year to pay, in addition to the dues, an entrance fee of one dollar.

6. PAYMENT OF DUES. Statements of dues are rendered in October for the following calendar year. Any member so notified whose dues remain unpaid on January 1 thereby loses his membership and can be reinstated only by paying a reinstatement fee of fifty cents.

School warrants and vouchers from institutions must be accompanied by definite information concerning the name and address of the person for whom membership fee is being paid. Statements of dues are rendered on our own form only. The Secretary's office cannot undertake to fill out special invoice forms of any sort or to affix notary's affidavit to statements or receipts.

Cancelled checks serve as receipts. Members desiring an additional receipt must enclose a stamped and addressed envelope therefor.

7. DISTRIBUTION OF YEARBOOKS TO MEMBERS. The yearbooks, ready prior to each February meeting, will be mailed from the office of the distributor only to members whose dues for that year have been paid. Members who desire yearbooks prior to the current year must purchase them directly from the distributor (see Item 8).

8. COMMERCIAL SALES. The distribution of all yearbooks prior to the current year, and also of those of the current year not regularly mailed to members in exchange for their dues, is in the hands of the distributor, not of the Secretary. For such commercial sales, communicate directly with the University of Chicago Press, Chicago, Illinois 60637, which will gladly send a price list covering all the publications of this Society. This list is also printed in the yearbook.

9. YEARBOOKS. The yearbooks are issued about one month before the February meeting. They comprise from 600 to 800 pages annually. Unusual effort has been made to make them, on the one hand, of immediate practical value and, on the other hand, representative of sound scholarship and scientific investigation.

10. MEETINGS. The annual meeting, at which the yearbooks are discussed, is held, as a rule, in February at the same time and place as the meeting of the American Association of School Administrators. Members will be notified of other meetings.

Applications for membership will be handled promptly at any time on receipt of name and address, together with check for $11.00 (or $10.50 for reinstatement). Applications entitle the new members to the yearbook slated for discussion during the calendar year the application is made.

KENNETH J. REHAGE, Secretary-Treasurer

5835 Kimbark Ave.
Chicago, Illinois 60637

PUBLICATIONS OF THE NATIONAL SOCIETY FOR THE STUDY OF EDUCATION

NOTICE: Many of the early Yearbooks of this series are now out of print. In the following list, those titles to which an asterisk is prefixed are not available for purchase.

POSTPAID
PRICE

*Fifteenth Yearbook, 1916, Part III—*The Junior High School.* Aubrey A. Douglas..

*Sixteenth Yearbook, 1917, Part I—*Second Report of the Committee on Minimum Essentials in Elementary-School Subjects.* W. C. Bagley, W. W. Charters, F. N. Freeman, W. S. Gray, Ernest Horn, J. H. Hoskinson, W. S. Monroe, C. F. Munson, H. C. Pryor, L. W. Rapeer, G. M. Wilson, and H. B. Wilson...........

*Sixteenth Yearbook, 1917, Part II—*The Efficiency of College Students as Conditioned by Age at Entrance and Size of High School.* B. F. Pittenger.................

*Seventeenth Yearbook, 1918, Part I—*Third Report of the Committee on Economy of Time in Education.* W. C. Bagley, B. B. Bassett, M. E. Branom, Alice Camerer, J. E. Dealey, C. A. Ellwood, E. B. Greene, A. B. Hart, J. F. Hosic, E. T. Housh, W. H. Mace, L. R. Marston, H. C. McKown, H. E. Mitchell, W. C. Reavis, D. Snedden, and H. B. Wilson.........................

*Seventeenth Yearbook, 1918, Part II—*The Measurement of Educational Products.* E. J. Ashbaugh, W. A. Averill, L. P. Ayers, F. W. Ballou, Edna Bryner, B. R. Buckingham, S. A. Courtis, M. E. Haggerty, C. H. Judd, George Melcher, W. S. Monroe, E. A. Nifenecker, and E. L. Thorndike.......................

*Eighteenth Yearbook, 1919, Part I—*The Professional Preparation of High-School Teachers.* G. N. Cade, S. S. Colvin, Charles Fordyce, H. H. Foster, T. S. Gosling, W. S. Gray, L. V. Koos, A. R. Mead, H. L. Miller, F. C. Whitcomb, and Clifford Woody . . . .

*Eighteenth Yearbook, 1919, Part II—*Fourth Report of Committee on Economy of Time in Education.* F. C. Ayer, F. N. Freeman, W. S. Gray, Ernest Horn, W. S. Monroe, and C. E. Seashore......................

*Nineteenth Yearbook, 1920, Part I—*New Materials of Instruction.* Prepared by the Society's Committee on Materials of Instruction......................

*Nineteenth Yearbook, 1920, Part II—*Classroom Problems in the Education of Gifted Children.* T. S. Henry...........................

*Twentieth Yearbook, 1921, Part I—*New Materials of Instruction.* Second Report by Society's Committee . . .

*Twentieth Yearbook, 1921, Part II—*Report of the Society's Committee on Silent Reading.* M. A. Burgess, S. A. Courtis, C. E. Germane, W. S. Gray, H. A. Greene, Regina R. Heller, J. H. Hoover, J. A. O'Brien, J. L. Packer, Daniel Starch, W. W. Theisen, G. A. Yoakam, and representatives of other school systems........

*Twenty-first Yearbook, 1922, Parts I and II—*Intelligence Tests and Their Use,* Part I—*The Nature, History, and General Principles of Intelligence Testing.* E. L. Thorndike, S. S. Colvin, Harold Rugg, G. M. Whipple, Part II—*The Administrative Use of Intelligence Tests.* H. W. Holmes, W. K. Layton, Helen Davis, Agnes L. Rogers, Rudolf Pintner, M. R. Trabue, W. S. Miller, Bessie L. Gambrill, and others. The two parts are bound together................

*Twenty-second Yearbook, 1923, Part I—*English Composition: Its Aims, Methods and Measurements.* Earl Hudelson.......................

*Twenty-second Yearbook, 1923, Part II—*The Social Studies in the Elementary and Secondary School.* A. S. Barr, J. J. Coss, Henry Harap, R. W. Hatch, H. C. Hill, Ernest Horn, C. H. Judd, L. C. Marshall, F. M. McMurry, Earle Rugg, H. O. Rugg, Emma Schweppe, Mabel Snedaker, and C. W. Washburne.

*Twenty-third Yearbook, 1924, Part I—*The Education of Gifted Children.* Report of the Society's Committee. Guy M. Whipple, Chairman...................

*Twenty-third Yearbook, 1924, Part II—*Vocational Guidance and Vocational Education for Industries.* A. H. Edgerton and Others.......................

*Twenty-fourth Yearbook, 1925, Part I—*Report of the National Committee on Reading.* W. S. Gray, Chairman, F. W. Ballou, Rose L. Hardy, Ernest Horn, Francis Jenkins, S. A. Leonard, Estaline Wilson, and Laura Zirbes.................

*Twenty-fourth Yearbook, 1925, Part II—*Adapting the Schools to Individual Differences.* Report of the Society's Committee. Carleton W. Washburn, Chairman....

*Twenty-fifth Yearbook, 1926, Part I—*The Present Status of Safety Education.* Report of the Society's Committee. Guy M. Whipple, Chairman...................

*Twenty-fifth Yearbook, 1926, Part II—*Extra-Curricular Activities.* Report of the Society's Committee. Leonard V. Koos, Chairman.......................

*Twenty-sixth Yearbook, 1927, Part I—*Curriculum-making: Past and Present.* Report of the Society's Committee. Harold O. Rugg, Chairman...................

*Twenty-sixth Yearbook, 1927, Part II—*The Foundations of Curriculum-making.* Prepared by individual members of the Society's Committee. Harold O. Rugg, Chairman

*Twenty-seventh Yearbook, 1928, Part I—*Nature and Nurture: Their Influence upon Intelligence.* Prepared by the Society's Committee. Lewis M. Terman, Chairman..

*Twenty-seventh Yearbook, 1928, Part II—*Nature and Nurture: Their Influence upon Achievement.* Prepared by the Society's Committee. Lewis M. Terman, Chairman.

Twenty-eighth Yearbook, 1929, Parts I and II—*Preschool and Parental Education.* Part I—*Organization and Development.* Part II—*Research and Method.* Prepared by the Society's Committee. Lois H. Meek, Chairman. Bound in one volume. Cloth $5.00

*Twenty-ninth Yearbook, 1930, Parts I and II—*Report of the Society's Committee on Arithmetic.* Part I—*Some Aspects of Modern Thought on Arithmetic.* Part II— *Research in Arithmetic.* Prepared by the Society's Committee. F. B. Knight, Chairman. Bound in one volume. Cloth ....

Thirtieth Yearbook, 1931, Part I—*The Status of Rural Education.* First Report of the Society's Committee on Rural Education. Orville G. Brim, Chairman. Cloth ... **$2.50**

Thirtieth Yearbook, 1931, Part II—*The Textbook in American Education.* Report of the Society's Committee on the Textbook. J. B. Edmonson, Chairman. Cloth 2.50
Paper 1.75

*Thirty-first Yearbook, 1932, Part I—*A Program for Teaching Science.* Prepared by the Society's Committee on the Teaching of Science. S. Ralph Powers, Chairman. Paper . . . .

Thirty-first Yearbook, 1932, Part II—*Changes and Experiments in Liberal-Arts Education.* Prepared by Kathryn McHale, with numerous collaborators. Cloth 3.00

*Thirty-second Yearbook, 1933—*The Teaching of Geography.* Prepared by the Society's Committee on the Teaching of Geography. A. E. Parkins, Chairman. Cloth ......
Paper 3.75

Thirty-third Yearbook, 1934, Part I—*The Planning and Construction of School Buildings.* Prepared by the Society's Committee on School Buildings. N. L. Engelhardt, Chairman. Cloth 2.50

Thirty-third Yearbook, 1934, Part II—*The Activity Movement.* Prepared by the Society's Committee on the Activity Movement. Lois Coffey Mossman, Chairman. Cloth 3.00
Paper 2.25

Thirty-fourth Yearbook, 1935—*Educational Diagnosis.* Prepared by the Society's Committee on Educational Diagnosis. L. J. Brueckner, Chairman. Cloth 5.00
Paper 3.75

*Thirty-fifth Yearbook, 1936, Part I—*The Grouping of Pupils.* Prepared by the Society's Committee. W. W. Coxe, Chairman. Cloth ....

*Thirty-fifth Yearbook, 1936, Part II—*Music Education.* Prepared by the Society's Committee. W. L. Uhl, Chairman. Cloth ....

*Thirty-sixth Yearbook, 1937, Part I—*The Teaching of Reading.* Prepared by the Society's Committee. W. S. Gray, Chairman. Cloth ....

*Thirty-sixth Yearbook, 1937, Part II—*International Understanding through the Public-School Curriculum.* Prepared by the Society's Committee. I. L. Kandel, Chairman. Paper . . . .

*Thirty-seventh Yearbook, 1938, Part I—*Guidance in Educational Institutions.* Prepared by the Society's Committee. G. N. Kefauver, Chairman. Cloth ....

*Thirty-seventh Yearbook, 1938, Part II—*The Scientific Movement in Education.* Prepared by the Society's Committee. F. N. Freeman, Chairman. Paper ....

*Thirty-eighth Yearbook, 1939, Part I—*Child Development and the Curriculum.* Prepared by the Society's Committee. Carleton Washburne, Chairman. Paper ....

Thirty-eighth Yearbook, 1939 Part II—*General Education in the American College.* Prepared by the Society's Committee. Alvin Eurich, Chairman. Cloth 2.75

*Thirty-ninth Yearbook, 1940, Part I—*Intelligence: Its Nature and Nurture. Comparative and Critical Exposition.* Prepared by the Society's Committee. G. D. Stoddard, Chairman. Cloth ....

*Thirty-ninth Yearbook, 1940, Part II—*Intelligence: Its Nature and Nurture. Original Studies and Experiments.* Prepared by the Society's Committee. G. D. Stoddard, Chairman. Cloth ....

*Fortieth Yearbook, 1941—*Art in American Life and Education.* Prepared by the Society's Committee. Thomas Munro, Chairman. Paper ....

Forty-first Yearbook, 1942, Part I—*Philosophies of Education.* Prepared by the Society's Committee. John S. Brubacher, Chairman. Cloth 4.00
Paper 3.25

Forty-first Yearbook, 1942, Part II—*The Psychology of Learning.* Prepared by the Society's Committee. T. R. McConnell, Chairman. Cloth 4.50
Paper 3.75

Forty-second Yearbook, 1943, Part I—*Vocational Education.* Prepared by the Society's Committee. F. J. Keller, Chairman. Cloth 3.25
Paper 2.50

Forty-second Yearbook, 1943, Part II—*The Library in General Education.* Prepared by the Society's Committee. L. R. Wilson, Chairman. Cloth 4.00

*Forty-third Yearbook, 1944, Part I—*Adolescence.* Prepared by the Society's Committee. Harold E. Jones, Chairman. Cloth ....
Paper **3.25**

POSTPAID
PRICE

Fifty-fifth Yearbook, 1956, Part II—*Adult Reading*. Prepared by the Society's Committee. David H. Clift, Chairman. Cloth....................................
Paper...

Fifty-sixth Yearbook, 1957, Part I—*In-service Education of Teachers, Supervisors, and Administrators*. Prepared by the Society's Committee. Stephen M. Corey, Chairman. Cloth... 4.50
Paper... 3.75

Fifty-sixth Yearbook, 1957, Part II—*Social Studies in the Elementary School*. Prepared by the Society's Committee. Ralph C. Preston, Chairman. Cloth........ 4.50
Paper... 3.75

Fifty-seventh Yearbook, 1958, Part I—*Basic Concepts in Music Education*. Prepared by the Society's Committee. Thurber H. Madison, Chairman. Cloth........... 4.50

Fifty-seventh Yearbook, 1958, Part II—*Education for the Gifted*. Prepared by the Society's Committee. Robert J. Havighurst, Chairman. Cloth................... 4.50
Paper... 3.75

Fifty-seventh Yearbook, 1958, Part III—*The Integration of Educational Experiences*. Prepared by the Society's Committee. Paul L. Dressel, Chairman. Cloth....... 4.50

Fifty-eighth Yearbook, 1959, Part I—*Community Education: Principles and Practices from World-wide Experience*. Prepared by the Society's Committee. C. O. Arndt, Chairman. Cloth.. 4.50
Paper... 3.75

Fifty-eighth Yearbook, 1959, Part II—*Personnel Services in Education*. Prepared by the Society's Committee. Melvene D. Hardee, Chairman. Cloth................ 4.50
Paper... 3.75

Fifty-ninth Yearbook, 1960, Part I—*Rethinking Science Education*. Prepared by the Society's Committee. J. Darrell Barnard, Chairman. Cloth...................

Fifty-ninth Yearbook, 1960, Part II—*The Dynamics of Instructional Groups*. Prepared by the Society's Committee. Gale E. Jensen, Chairman. Cloth................. 4.50
Paper... 3.75

Sixtieth Yearbook, 1961, Part I—*Development in and through Reading*. Prepared by the Society's Committee. Paul A. Witty, Chairman, Cloth................... 5.00
Paper... 4.25

Sixtieth Yearbook, 1961, Part II—*Social Forces Influencing American Education*. Prepared by the Society's Committee. Ralph W. Tyler, Chairman. Cloth........ 4.50

Sixty-first Yearbook, 1962, Part I—*Individualizing Instruction*. Prepared by the Society's Committee. Fred T. Tyler, Chairman. Cloth...................... 4.50

Sixty-first Yearbook, 1962, Part II—*Education for the Professions*. Prepared by the Society's Committee. G. Lester Anderson, Chairman. Cloth................. 4.50

Sixty-second Yearbook, 1963, Part I—*Child Psychology*. Prepared by the Society's Committee. Harold W. Stevenson, Editor. Cloth............................. 6.50

Sixty-second Yearbook, 1963, Part II—*The Impact and Improvement of School Testing Programs*. Prepared by the Society's Committee. Warren G. Findley, Editor. Cloth... 4.50

Sixty-third Yearbook, 1964, Part I—*Theories of Learning and Instruction*. Prepared by the Society's Committee. Ernest R. Hilgard, Editor. Cloth............... 5.50

Sixty-third Yearbook, 1964, Part II—*Behavioral Science and Educational Administration*. Prepared by the Society's Committee. Daniel E. Griffiths, Editor. Cloth.. 5.50

Sixty-fourth Yearbook, 1965, Part I—*Vocational Education*. Prepared by the Society's Committee. Melvin L. Barlow, Editor. Cloth........................... 5.00

Sixty-fourth Yearbook, 1965, Part II—*Art Education*. Prepared by the Society's Committee. W. Reid Hastie, Editor. Cloth.................................... 5.00

Sixty-fifth Yearbook, 1966, Part I—*Social Deviancy among Youth*. Prepared by the Society's Committee. William W. Wattenberg, Editor. Cloth................. 5.50

Sixty-fifth Yearbook, 1966, Part II—*The Changing American School*. Prepared by the Society's Committee. John I. Goodlad, Editor. Cloth..................... 5.00

Sixty-sixth Yearbook, 1967, Part I—*The Educationally Retarded and Disadvantaged*. Prepared by the Society's Committee. Paul A. Witty, Editor. Cloth............. 5.50

Sixty-sixth Yearbook, 1967, Part II—*Programed Instruction*. Prepared by the Society's Committee. Phil C. Lange, Editor. Cloth................................ 5.00

Sixty-seventh Yearbook, 1968, Part I—*Metropolitanism: Its Challenge to Education*. Prepared by the Society's Committee. Robert J. Havighurst, Editor. Cloth....... 5.50

Sixty-seventh Yearbook, 1968, Part II—*Innovation and Change in Reading Instruction*. Prepared by the Society's Committee. Helen M. Robinson, Editor. Cloth.... 5.50

Sixty-eighth Yearbook, 1969, Part I—*The United States and International Education*. Prepared by the Society's Committee. Harold G. Shane, Editor. Cloth......... 5.50

Distributed by

THE UNIVERSITY OF CHICAGO PRESS, CHICAGO, ILLINOIS 60637

1972

Please direct all orders for books to the University of Chicago Press.